Intergenerational Continuity of Criminal and Antisocial Behaviour

The relationship between a parent and a child is without any doubt one of the most influential and intimate relationships over the life course of an individual. Children resemble their parents in a variety of life outcomes such as socioeconomic status, family formation characteristics, and political views. There is growing evidence that some families – despite interventions by child protection services, judicial sanctions, and social mobility – are stuck in patterns of criminal behaviour, poverty, substance abuse, teenage parenthood, and other negative life events. This is a growing global problem for which currently no solution is available.

This book brings together the most important and unique findings of intergenerational studies of criminal behaviour from around the world, and from a variety of disciplines, from criminology to sociology to anthropology. Each chapter explores the historical background of a specific study, its most important objectives, and the unique conclusions and implications that can be drawn from the data.

Essential reading for all those interested in criminal behaviour, psychological criminology, and intergenerational psychology, this book provides an extensive overview of intergenerational studies on patterns of continuity and discontinuity of criminal, antisocial, or delinquent behaviour, as well as related behaviours or risk factors such as the intergenerational continuities in (harsh) parenting and family relationship quality.

Veroni I. Eichelsheim is a senior researcher at the Netherlands Institute for the Study of Crime and Law Enforcement (NSCR), Amsterdam, the Netherlands. Her research focuses on (intergenerational continuity in) the quality of family relationships, parenting, and delinquent behaviour – and the role of family interventions.

Steve G. A. van de Weijer is a postdoctoral researcher at the Netherlands Institute for the Study of Crime and Law Enforcement (NSCR), Amsterdam, the Netherlands. His research focuses on life-course criminology, intergenerational transmission of crime, and genetic influences on criminal behaviour.

Routledge Studies in Criminal Behaviour

Criminal Behaviour from School to the Workplace: Untangling the Complex Relations
Between employment, education and crime
Edited by Frank Weerman and Catrien Bijleveld

Pathways to Sexual Aggression
Edited by Jean Proulx, Eric Beauregard, Patrick Lussier, and Benoit Leclerc

The Psychology of Crime, Policing and Courts
Edited by Andreas Kapardis and David P. Farrington

The Sexual Murderer
Offender behaviour and implications for practice
Eric Beauregard and Melissa Martineau

Psychological Violence in the Workplace
New perspectives and shifting frameworks
Emily Schindeler, Janet Ransley and Danielle Reynald

Domestic Homicide
Patterns and dynamics
Marieke Liem and Frans Koenraadt

Intergenerational Continuity of Criminal and Antisocial Behaviour
An international overview of studies
Edited by Veroni I. Eichelsheim and Steve G.A. van de Weijer

For more information about this series, please visit: www.routledge.com/Routledge-Studies-in-Criminal-Behaviour/book-series/RSCB

Intergenerational Continuity of Criminal and Antisocial Behaviour

An international overview of studies

Edited by Veroni I. Eichelsheim
and Steve G. A. van de Weijer

Routledge
Taylor & Francis Group
LONDON AND NEW YORK

First published 2018
by Routledge
2 Park Square, Milton Park, Abingdon, Oxon OX14 4RN

and by Routledge
711 Third Avenue, New York, NY 10017

Routledge is an imprint of the Taylor & Francis Group, an informa business

First issued in paperback 2020

British Library Cataloguing-in-Publication Data
A catalogue record for this book is available from the British Library

Library of Congress Cataloging-in-Publication Data
A catalog record for this book has been requested

ISBN: 978-1-138-10337-5 (hbk)

ISBN: 978-0-367-48339-5 (pbk)

ISBN: 978-1-315-10278-8 (ebk)

Typeset in Bembo
by Apex CoVantage, LLC

Contents

Figures

Tables

Appendices/textboxes

Chapter-specific

Appendices to full book

Contributors

Biographies of all contributors (per chapter)

Editors

Veroni I. Eichelsheim is a senior researcher at the Netherlands Institute for the Study of Crime and Law Enforcement (NSCR), Amsterdam, the Netherlands. Her research focuses on (intergenerational continuity in) the quality of family relationships, parenting, and delinquent behaviour – and the role of family interventions.

Steve G.A. van de Weijer is a postdoctoral researcher at the Netherlands Institute for the Study of Crime and Law Enforcement (NSCR), Amsterdam, the Netherlands. His research focuses on life-course criminology, intergenerational transmission of crime, and genetic influences on criminal behaviour.

Chapter 1

Mikko Aaltonen is a senior researcher at the Institute of Criminology and Legal Policy, University of Helsinki. His research focuses on life-course criminology, especially on the socioeconomic causes and consequences of crime.

Janne Mikkonen is a social demographer at the Population Research Unit, University of Helsinki. His research focuses on the social consequences of childhood illness and the intergenerational transmission of adversity.

Chapter 2

Lars Højsgaard Andersen is a senior researcher at the Rockwool Foundation in Copenhagen, Denmark. His main research interests include the consequences of criminal justice contact, not only for people experiencing it, but also for their families, and he uses Danish register data to describe these consequences and exploit policy reforms for causal inference.

Chapter 3

Ruben van Gaalen is a researcher at Statistics Netherlands and a professor by special appointment of register analyses of life-course dynamics at the sociology department, Faculty of Social and Behavioural Sciences, University of Amsterdam. He is interested in life-course dynamics, parent–child relationships, and social inequality and has published widely in the area of family studies.

Gregory Besjes is a researcher at Statistics Netherlands in the field of social security. He has a background in sociology and chemistry. His main expertise is working with and doing research on very large datasets.

Chapter 4

Barry Godfrey is the principal investigator for the AHRC-funded Digital Panopticon project. Based at the University of Liverpool, he writes on crime history, life-course offending, and sentencing.

Kris Inwood is professor of economics and history at the University of Guelph. He has published widely on economic history, colonial history, imprisonment, and the experiences of indigenous peoples.

Hamish Maxwell-Stewart has authored several books and is an internationally renowned expert on convicts. He is based at the University of Tasmania., and was prominent in the development of the Founders and Survivors database.

Chapter 5

Stacy Tzoumakis is a lecturer in criminology at UNSW Sydney. Her research takes a developmental life-course perspective to understanding antisocial behaviour and offending. She works on the New South Wales Child Development Study, a large population-based, multi-agency, intergenerational data linkage study of 87,000 children and their parents.

Melissa J. Green is an associate professor in psychiatry at UNSW Sydney and an Australian National Health and Medical Research Council Career Development fellow. Her research uses epidemiology, genetics, and cognitive neuroscience methods to study the developmental pathways from early life stressors to psychotic and related mental disorders. She is the co-leader of the New South Wales Child Development Study.

Kristin R. Laurens is an associate professor in psychology at Australian Catholic University and an adjunct associate professor in the School of Psychiatry at UNSW Sydney. She uses cognitive neuroscience and epidemiological methods to characterize healthy and pathological trajectories of emotional, behavioural, social, and cognitive development from childhood to young adulthood, drawing data from multiple longitudinal developmental cohorts, including the New South Wales Child Development Study.

Kimberlie Dean is Chair of Forensic Mental Health in the School of Psychiatry at UNSW Sydney and a clinical academic forensic psychiatrist with the Justice Health and Forensic Mental Health Network. She is a psychiatric epidemiologist with a research focus on improving the health and offending outcomes of mentally ill offenders.

Vaughan J. Carr is a professor of psychiatry at UNSW Sydney, an adjunct professor of psychiatry at Monash University, and a senior consultant psychiatrist in Monash Health. He is the lead investigator of the New South Wales Child Development Study.

Chapter 6

Steve van de Weijer is a postdoctoral researcher at the Netherlands Institute for the Study of Crime and Law Enforcement (NSCR). His research focuses on life-course criminology, intergenerational transmission of crime, and genetic influences on criminal behaviour.

Catrien Bijleveld studied psychology and criminal law, and is professor of research methods in criminology at Vrije Universiteit Amsterdam, as well as director of the Netherlands Institute for the Study of Crime and Law Enforcement (NSCR). Her research interests are criminal careers, female offenders, the intergenerational transmission of crime, genocide, and sex offending. She is the author of several textbooks, as well as of edited books, on crime and justice in the Netherlands, and on the association between employment and offending.

Chapter 7

David P. Farrington is the Emeritus Professor of Psychological Criminology at Cambridge University, UK. His research focusses on the development and prevention of offending and antisocial behaviour.

Maria M. Ttofi is the University Lecturer in Psychological Criminology at Cambridge University, UK. Her research focusses on the development and prevention of offending and bullying, and she is particularly interested in the influence of grandparents on grandchildren.

Rebecca V. Crago was a research assistant in the Institute of Criminology, Cambridge University, UK, and is now a Ph.D. student in psychology at the

University of East Anglia, UK. Her Ph.D. research is investigating the neural correlates of cognitive biases in aggressive populations.

Chapter 8

Deborah M. Capaldi is a senior scientist at the Oregon Social Learning Center. Her research interests include the study of individual, social and contextual influences on the development of psychopathology and substance use from childhood through adulthood, as well as in intergenerational perspective.

David C. R. Kerr is a clinical psychologist with research interests in developmental psychopathology and the prevention of substance abuse and suicide. He completed his doctoral and post-doctoral studies at the University of Michigan and is currently a Research Scientist at the Oregon Social Learning Center and an Associate Professor at the School of Psychological Science at Oregon State University. His current work focuses on intergenerational transmission of risks for substance abuse and other problem behaviors and the effects of marijuana legalization on adolescents and young adults.

Stacey S. Tiberio is a research scientist at the Oregon Social Learning Center. Methodologically, her primary research interests include longitudinal data analysis, the modeling of how processes change over time. Her substantive research interests are broad but predominantly focus on gaining a better understanding of how individuals' physical and mental health may be influenced by their own behaviours, the behaviours of those around them, and their social contexts.

Chapter 9

Eric F. Dubow is research professor at the University of Michigan's Institute for Social Research and a Distinguished Research Professor of Psychology at Bowling Green State University. His research interests include: the development of risk and protective factors in children's adjustment, the development of aggression over time and across generations, and effects of exposure to ethnic-political violence and potential protective factors. He is a co-investigator of the Columbia County Longitudinal Study.

L. Rowell Huesmann is the Amos N. Tversky Collegiate Professor of Psychology and Communication Studies at the University of Michigan and director of the Aggression Research Program at Michigan's Institute for Social Research. His research has focused on the psychological foundations of aggressive and antisocial behavior and in particular on how exposure to violence (political violence, family violence, community violence, media violence) in childhood changes children's thinking and perceptions and increases the risk of interpersonal aggressive behavior later in life. He is the principal investigator of the Columbia County Longitudinal Study.

Paul Boxer is a professor of psychology at Rutgers University-Newark, a senior fellow in the Rutgers School of Criminal Justice, and an adjunct research scientist at the Institute for Social Research at the University of Michigan. He studies the development, prevention, and treatment of violent and nonviolent antisocial behavior, particularly among youths involved in the juvenile justice system and other high-risk settings. He is a co-investigator of the Columbia County Longitudinal Study.

Cathy Smith is a research tech associate in the Aggression Research Group at the University of Michigan's Institute for Social Research and a graduate student in the biostatistics program at the University of Michigan. She assists research investigators conducting longitudinal studies of human aggression in data processing and conducting statistical data analyses. She conducts data analyses for the Columbia County Longitudinal Study.

Aaron E. Sedlar is a Ph.D. student at Bowling Green State University working under Eric Dubow. His main research interests are the effects of violence on family functioning as well as the role caregivers play in socializing children to cope with traumatic experiences. He has helped to analyse data from the Columbia County Longitudinal Study.

Chapter 10

Jennifer A. Bailey is a senior research scientist at the Social Development Research Group at the University of Washington in Seattle, and is the current principal investigator of the TIP and SSDP projects. Her background is in developmental psychology, and her research interests include intergenerational transmission of substance use and problem behavior, cross-national drug policy differences, marijuana policy, and analysis of longitudinal data.

Karl G. Hill is professor and director of the Problem Behavior and Positive Youth Development Program at the Institute of Behavioral Science, University of Colorado, Boulder, and was the founding principal investigator of the TIP study, as well as the principal investigator of the SSDP study. His background is in developmental psychology, and his research has focused on understanding the development and intergenerational transmission of substance use and antisocial behaviour in order to develop and test preventive interventions.

Marina Epstein is a research scientist at the Social Development Research group at the University of Washington in Seattle, and is the current project director of the TIP study. Her training is in developmental psychology, and her research interests include intergenerational transmission of substance use, e-cigarette use, marijuana policy, and the development of sexual behaviour.

Christine Steeger is a research associate at the Institute of Behavioral Science, University of Colorado, Boulder, and has worked on both the TIP and SSDP studies. Her training is in developmental psychology, and her research interests include marijuana policy, reciprocal parent–child processes, development of child behaviour problems, and family-based intervention and prevention.

J. David Hawkins is Endowed Professor of Prevention Emeritus in the School of Social Work, University of Washington, the founding director of the Social Development Research Group, and the founding principal investigator of the SSDP study. His background is in sociology, and his research is focused on understanding risk and protective factors predictive of antisocial behaviour and on developing and testing preventive interventions and positive youth development programs.

Chapter 11

Terence P. Thornberry is Distinguished Professor Emeritus in the School of Criminal Justice at the University at Albany and a research professor in the Department of Criminology and Criminal Justice at the University of Maryland. He is the founding principal investigator of the Rochester Youth Development Study.

Kimberly L. Henry is an associate professor in the Department of Psychology and the Colorado School of Public Health at Colorado State University. She is the current principal investigator of the Rochester Intergenerational Study.

Marvin D. Krohn is a professor in the Department of Sociology and Criminology and Law at the University of Florida. He was a co-principal investigator of the Rochester Youth Development Study, a three-generation panel study begun in 1986.

Alan J. Lizotte is the former dean and distinguished professor in the School of Criminal Justice at the University at Albany. Since the beginning he has been a co-principal investigator on the Rochester Youth Development Study.

Emily L. Nadel is a doctoral student in the Department of Criminology and Criminal Justice at the University of Maryland.

Chapter 12

Christina Bentrup is sociologist and the project coordinator of the CrimoC team at the Department of Criminology, University of Münster, Germany. Her criminological research interests are social learning, biosocial criminological approaches, intergenerational transmission processes, and data analyses with latent variables.

Chapter 13

Brandon C. Welsh is a professor of criminology and director of the Cambridge–Somerville Youth Study in the School of Criminology and Criminal Justice at Northeastern University and a senior research fellow at the NSCR.

Steven N. Zane is a doctoral candidate and the Joan McCord Research Fellow in the School of Criminology and Criminal Justice at Northeastern University.

Andrea B. Wexler is a doctoral student in the School of Criminology and Criminal Justice at Northeastern University.

Chapter 14

Monica J. Martin is an assistant professor at Texas Tech University and studies the influence of economic, racial, and ethnic disparities on families and individual development, with a primary focus on behavioural and mental health problems such as delinquency, substance involvement, and criminal behaviours. She has been working with the Family Transitions Project for over a decade.

Katherine J. Conger is a professor emerita at the University of California Davis. She studies the quality and course of sibling relationships, sibling influences on competence and maladjustment, interpersonal processes in families with an emphasis on the linkages between family stress and adolescent adjustment, effects of economic hardship on families and individuals, and observational research methods.

Chapter 15

Peggy C. Giordano is a distinguished research professor of sociology at Bowling Green State University. Her research interests include the role of social network processes in the etiology of delinquency, men's and women's desistance from crime, and mechanisms underlying intergenerational transmission.

Chapter 16

Lidewyde Berckmoes works as a researcher at the Netherlands Institute for the Study of Crime and Law Enforcement in Amsterdam. She has a background in cultural anthropology and has worked extensively with conflict-affected children and youth, especially in and from the Great Lakes region of Africa. She is currently developing further research on intergenerational processes by combining anthropological and criminological perspectives.

Ria Reis is a professor of medical anthropology at the Department of Public Health and Primary Care at Leiden University Medical Center, an associate professor at the Department of Anthropology of the University in Amsterdam, and an honorary professor at the Children's Institute, School of Child and Adolescent Health, University of Cape Town. She investigates young people's health perceptions and strategies, mostly in collaborative projects with partners in policy and practice and with a focus on intergenerational transmission of vulnerabilities in contexts of inequality and (post)conflict.

Introduction

Crime over the course of generations: Interdependent lives and risks

An introduction to "intergenerational continuity of crime and antisocial behaviour: An international overview of studies"

Veroni Eichelsheim and Steve van de Weijer

The relationship between a parent and a child is without any doubt one of the most influential and intimate relationships over the life course of an individual. Children resemble their parents in a wide variety of characteristics such as physical appearance, socioeconomic status, family formation characteristics, personality, and political views (e.g., Langenhof et al. 2016). In addition, similarities in antisocial, criminal, and violent behaviour between parents, children, and other family members exist and have been the topic of scientific studies since the late nineteenth century.

One of the first examples of a multigenerational study on criminal behaviour in families goes back to 1877, when Richard Dugdale published the first scientific study on a criminal family: *The Jukes*. Dugdale started this study when he visited the Ulster County jail, as an inspector for the New York Prison Association. During this visit, he discovered that six people being held in this jail were from the same family. In an attempt to discover the roots of these criminal relatives, Dugdale traced their ancestors seven generations back and collected data on 709 Jukes, related by blood or by marriage or cohabitation. Among them a strong concentration of criminals, habitual thieves, and prostitutes was found (Dugdale 1877).

Some decades later Henry Goddard (1912) published his study on the Kallikak family (a pseudonym composed of the Greek words καλός and κακός, meaning 'beautiful' and 'bad', respectively). As the director of research at the New Jersey Home for the Education and Care of Feebleminded Children, Goddard traced back the roots of one of the children in this institution, Deborah Kallikak. Her great-great-great-grandfather was Martin Kallikak Sr., a respectable citizen who married a reputable girl from a good family. The children and descendants born from this marriage were described as upright citizens, prominent in every phase of social life, including lawyers, judges, doctors, traders, and landholders. However, prior to this marriage, Martin Kallikak Sr. fought in the American

Revolutionary War and had a short-term romance with a 'feeble-minded' girl[1] whom he met in one of the taverns frequented by the soldiers. A child was born from this relationship, who was considered to have "been handed down to posterity the father's name and the mother's mental capacity" (Goddard 1912: 18). Martin Kallikak Sr. never paid attention to this son, but "society has had to pay the heavy price of all the evil he engendered" (Goddard 1912: 29) since the descendants from this relationship included "paupers, criminals, prostitutes, drunkards, and examples of all forms of social pest with which modern society is burdened" (Goddard 1912: 116).

In the subsequent decades, studies specifically focusing on the intergenerational transmission of crime were scarce. For a long time, many scholars were reluctant to study the potential biosocial aetiology of crime as such research has been linked to sexism, racism, and immoral eugenic policies (Wright and Miller 1998). However, several examples of multigenerational studies between the 1930s and 1980s underline the growing interest in intergenerational processes in general and sometimes also incorporate intergenerational data of criminal, delinquent, or 'problem' behaviour more generally. From the 1930s, a growing research interest can be observed in how or why intergenerational continuities in behaviour may occur. In a five-generation sample, Gilmore (1932: 774) investigated potential mechanisms that underlied the intergenerational transmission of begging and concluded that "In short, when the child reached adulthood, he had the philosophy of life, the technical knowledge, and the status which tended to make it easier for him to secure a livelihood through begging than through any other profession." Elder, who followed up on children during the times of the Great Depression, investigated the role of poverty on parenting styles and subsequent deviant behaviour in children (Elder 1998; Elder et al. 1984). Other studies have focused on intergenerational transmission of social mobility (Aldous 1965) or welfare dependency and its association with deviant behaviour over multiple generations (Morrison 1958). Moreover, many studies in the earlier days of intergenerational research also focused on the (mediating) role of parenting in intergenerational continuity of behaviour or on the intergenerational transmission of harsh or abusive parenting or parental attachment styles (e.g., Belsky et al. 1989; Itkin 1952).

Conducting an adequate intergenerational study is an expensive and long-winded endeavour, because longitudinal and prospective data measured over an extended period is necessary for at least two consecutive generations. Despite that, over the last decades, intergenerational transmission of crime as a research topic has increased in popularity, and several intergenerational studies have been initiated across Europe and the United States. This is illustrated by the meta-analysis of Besemer and colleagues (2017) showing that since 2000, 17 papers have been published about different intergenerational samples, while only 7 different intergenerational samples were used in papers prior to that year. This meta-analysis also showed that the degree of intergenerational transmission increases over time; among children born before 1981 the intergenerational transmission of criminal offending was considerably less strong than among those born after 1981.

The studies we describe in this volume clearly show that studying intergenerational continuities in criminal and antisocial behaviour remains of great importance for society. It shows that, despite child protection services, judicial interventions, or social mobility, there are some families that – despite youth care or judicial interventions or social mobility – are stuck in patterns of criminal behaviour over the course of multiple generations. Therefore, there is a need for research to address *why, how*, and *under which circumstances* children continue their parents' criminal behaviour. Similarities between parents and their children can be explained from several theoretical perspectives and numerous possible mechanisms. Some of these explanations can be considered as *direct* mechanisms. For example, biological and genetic factors may play a role in the intergenerational transmission of crime and other relevant behaviours; for example, when a genetic predisposition for criminal behaviour is transmitted from one generation to the next. Moreover, social learning theories suggest that children imitate and learn the criminal behaviour from their parents. On the other hand, several *indirect* mechanisms have also been forwarded in the literature. Parents and children, for example, may share psychosocial, cultural, and historical contextual factors that may shape intergenerational continuities in criminal behaviour. This is what Farrington (2010: 205) refers to as "intergenerational continuity of risk factors" or "the cycle of deprivation". Farrington (2010) furthermore describes the role relationships with others may play in intergenerational continuities in antisocial behaviour. The constellation of antisocial family features may be reinforced through *assortative mating* (i.e., selecting a partner with similar antisocial tendencies, attitudes, and behaviour) or through social contagion among, for example, siblings. The possibility of an official record bias against children of known criminal offenders should not be ignored either. Children of offenders have been shown to have a larger chance of getting convicted than others with similar degrees of antisocial behaviour (Besemer et al. 2013). However, all of these and other mechanisms that explain intergenerational continuity in criminal behaviour are not mutually exclusive and may operate in complex and interacting ways, as is described in several chapters of this book.

In addition to studying intergenerational continuity in criminal behaviour, studies on intergenerational discontinuity also are important. Such studies are well suited to define mechanisms through which criminal behaviour, potentially against expectations, is not being transferred from one generation to the next (e.g., Thornberry 2016), and are therefore of key importance to guide policy and interventions. Factors that might be important in buffering the intergenerational continuity of crime, for example, include a prosocial partner, changing socioeconomic circumstances, and interventions in high-risk families (e.g., Belsky et al. 2005). Moreover, based on the literature on intergenerational continuities in health, psychosocial functioning, and problematic behaviour, parenting behaviour (although highly continuous across generations itself) also seems to be an important mediator (e.g., Serbin and Karp 2004). Patterns of intergenerational transmission might also differ depending on culture, context, and types of offending. In sum, both research on intergenerational continuity and discontinuity of criminal behaviour is important to form a proper understanding of these intergenerational patterns, their underlying mechanisms, and potential interventions in high-risk families.

This volume

Despite the fact that the study of criminal and antisocial behaviour from an intergenerational perspective is receiving increased attention (Besemer et al. 2017), intergenerational datasets are still scarce; all over the world, only a handful of datasets are available that have at least some information about offending, delinquency, or antisocial behaviour over the course of multiple generations. With this book, we aim to bring together, and give an overview of, the most important intergenerational datasets from all over the world. In doing so, this book also summarizes the available evidence concerning the intergenerational continuity and discontinuity of criminal and antisocial behaviour that emerges from these studies, and will give inspiration and directions for future intergenerational studies.

In total, 15 different datasets are described in this book. Initially, the aim was to include all datasets with prospectively collected measures of criminal or antisocial behaviour of at least two consecutive generations. We contacted principal investigators of, or researchers working with, all datasets meeting these criteria that were known to us. Unfortunately, it was not possible for all contacted researchers to write a chapter for this book within the given time frame. Therefore, some intergenerational datasets, which do meet the criteria, are not included in this book. Moreover, some studies that do not yet meet the criteria are included in the book as they have concrete plans to extend their current dataset into a study with prospective data on two consecutive generations.

Among the intergenerational studies that are included in this book, a couple are specifically designed to capture criminal or delinquent behaviour over the course of multiple generations. However, nowadays many studies known as intergenerational studies are actually long-term follow-ups of children from respondents of research projects that initially started out as longitudinal panel studies or experimentally designed intervention studies. Moreover, some of these studies have always had a specific focus on criminal behaviour, whereas others had a different focus, for example, on health, but also gathered additional information about criminal offending, aggression, substance use, or other deviant behaviours over the life course. There are also differences between studies with regard to data sources, research designs, sampling methods, and measurements used. Although this may make results hard to compare between studies, the advantage of these between-study differences is that data have been gathered among respondents of different socioeconomical and cultural backgrounds, among different offender groups, during different historical periods with different judicial climates, and with a huge variety of measured individual and family characteristics.

The authors of each chapter were asked to describe the historical context of the onset of the study; to provide information about the most important general study characteristics, operationalisations used, and measurements; and to describe the most striking results from each intergenerational dataset. In some cases, the authors chose to describe their dataset by doing new research and presenting new results. This book therefore not only summarizes results from previous studies, but also presents some new findings on the intergenerational transmission of criminal behaviour. Finally, we gathered authors' own expert views on possible explanations for intergenerational continuity or discontinuity, and to describe future plans for their own intergenerational dataset and topics that future intergenerational studies should cover.

Outline of the volume

Part I of this volume includes chapters that describe **population-based registration data**. Although these data are not collected for the purpose of studying the intergenerational transmission of criminal behaviour, they are well suited to conduct such studies (see, e.g., Besjes and van Gaalen 2008; Frisell et al. 2011). In this book, population-based registration datasets from three different countries are described. In Chapter 1, Aaltonen and Mikkonen describe the Finnish register-linkage data and discuss how the dataset provides opportunities to study intergenerational continuity of criminal offending. In Chapter 2, Andersen discusses the use of register data from Denmark, while van Gaalen and Besjes do the same for the Dutch register data in Chapter 3.

In **Part II** of this volume, we include studies that created a multigenerational dataset by combining other types of **official record or registration data**. In Chapter 4, Godfrey, Inwood, and Maxwell-Stewart describe how they build an intergenerational dataset by linking register data on 160,000 British convicts who were transported to Australian penal colonies with birth, death, and marriage registers. In Chapter 5, Tzoumakis, Green, Laurens, Dean, and Carr discuss the New South Wales Child Development Study, which utilizes administrative record linkage of data from multiple sources in Australia, such as criminal justice, health, welfare, and education. Finally, van de Weijer and Bijleveld used official records and register data to trace back the parents and all descendants of 198 boys who were placed in a Catholic reform school at the beginning of the twentieth century. This resulted in a dataset with five consecutive generations, the Transfive Study, which is described in Chapter 6.

In **Part III** of this volume, we include studies that utilize **survey data**. Survey studies allow researchers to study family processes such as parenting and social learning or contagion in more detail. Most survey studies rely on self-reported data, although linkages between survey data (e.g., about behaviours, attitudes, family interactions, and relationship quality) and more or less registered data (e.g., arrests or conviction data) are also possible. In Chapter 7, Farrington, Ttofi, and Crago, describe the Cambridge Study in Delinquent Development and present new results on the intergenerational transmission of self-reported offending. Next, in Chapter 8, Capaldi, Kerr, and Tiberio discuss an extension of the Oregon Youth Study: the Three Generational Study. The Columbia County Longitudinal Study and its main findings on the intergenerational transmission of aggression, violence, and criminality are described by Dubow, Huesmann, Boxer, Smith, and Sedla in Chapter 9. In Chapter 10, Bailey, Hill, Epstein, Steeger, and Hawkins discuss two prospective, longitudinal studies that link three generations: the Seattle Social Development Project and The Intergenerational Project. Next, Thornberry, Henry, Krohn, Lizotte, and Nadel discuss the key findings from the Rochester Intergenerational Study, an extension of the Rochester Youth Development Study, in Chapter 11. Bentrup, in Chapter 12, describes the intergenerational transmission of violent parenting in the Crime in the Modern City dataset, which started as a German panel study among seventh-grade pupils in Duisburg. Welsh, Zane, and Wexler discuss the Cambridge-Somerville Youth Study in Chapter 13, and describe the main findings on intergenerational transmission of criminal offending as well as their plans to extend this dataset with an extra generation. Finally, in Chapter 14, Martin and Conger present information on the Family Transitions Project (FTP), a longitudinal, intergenerational study of families originally from rural areas of Iowa.

Although **qualitative and mixed method approaches** are well suited to provide answers to how and why phenomena may or may not occur, the use of these methods in intergenerational studies on crime and delinquency is still scarce. In **Part IV** of this volume, Giordano (Chapter 15) presents the Ohio Life Course Study, a thorough **mixed methods study** that clearly shows how interview data may guide interpretation of survey data results, or vice versa. In the final chapter of this volume (Chapter 16), rather than focusing on one specific dataset, Berckmoes and Reis provide insight into how purely qualitative methods in certain contexts are extremely suited to address intergenerational continuity of (societal) violence in post-conflict settings, such as in Burundi and Rwanda.

In closing, we would like to thank all those who helped us with the realization of this book. We want to thank the staff of Routledge, and Thomas Sutton and Hannah Catterall in particular, for giving us the opportunity to publish this project and for their help throughout the process. We furthermore want to thank the management of the Netherlands Institute for the Study of Crime and Law Enforcement (NSCR), and especially director Catrien Bijleveld, for providing us with the opportunity and time to initiate this book. We thank the Royal Netherlands Academy of Arts and Sciences (KNAW) for co-funding the international conference that eventually led to this initiative. Moreover, we thank all external reviewers (please see Appendix B) for their time and effort in reviewing the chapters in this volume, and Holly Smallbone for her help in editing the book. Of course, we would also like to thank the authors of each chapter for their advice in shaping this book, their efforts in writing their chapters, and for reviewing each other's work. We are happy that so many of you enthusiastically participated in this project, and we hope that this book will be an inspiration for many others to study criminal behaviour from an intergenerational perspective, and that this book may form the basis for, or continuation of, widespread international cooperation.

Note

1 At the end of the nineteenth century, mental deficiency was believed to consist out of distinct groups of ability, ranging from idiocy (i.e., the most severe deficiency) through imbecility to feeble-mindedness. 'Feeble-mindedness' was referred to as "the borderland of imbecility" (Jackson 1998: 364).

References

Aldous, J. (1965) The consequences of intergenerational continuity. *Journal of Marriage and Family* 27: 462–468.

Belsky, J., Jaffee, S.R., Sligo, J., et al. (2005) Intergenerational transmission of warm-sensitive-stimulating parenting: A prospective study of mothers and fathers of 3-year-olds. *Child Development* 76: 384–396.

Belsky, J., Youngblade, L. and Pensky, E. (1989) Childrearing history, marital quality, and maternal affect: Intergenerational transmission in a low-risk sample. *Development and Psychopathology* 1: 291–304.

Besemer, S., Ahmad, S.I., Hinshaw, S.P., et al. (2017) A systematic review and meta-analysis of the intergenerational transmission of criminal behavior. *Aggression and Violent Behavior* 37: 161–178.

Besemer, S., Farrington, D.P. and Bijleveld, C. (2013) Official bias in intergenerational transmission of criminal behaviour. *British Journal of Criminology* 53: 438–455.

Besjes, G. and Van Gaalen, R. (2008) *Jong geleerd, fout gedaan. Bevolkingstrends* (2e kwartaal), 23–31. Statistics Netherlands.

Dugdale, R.L. (1877) *"The Jukes": A study in crime, pauperism, disease and heredity: Also further studies of criminals.* GP Putnam's Sons.

Elder, G.H. (1998) *Children of the great depression.* Boulder: Westview Press.

Elder, G.H., Liker, J.K. and Cross, C.E. (1984) Parent-child behavior in the Great Depression: Life course and intergenerational influences. *Life-Span Development and Behavior* 6: 109–158.

Farrington, D.P. (2010) Family influences on delinquency. *Juvenile Justice and Delinquency* 10: 203–222.

Frisell, T., Lichtenstein, P. and Långström, N. (2011) Violent crime runs in families: A total population study of 12.5 million individuals. *Psychological Medicine* 41(1): 97–105.

Gilmore, H.W. (1932) Five generations of a begging family. *American Journal of Sociology* 37: 768–774.

Goddard, H.H. (1912) *The Kallikak family: A study in the heredity of feeble-mindedness.* Macmillan Company.

Itkin, W. (1952) Some relationships between intra-family attitudes and pre-parental attitudes toward children. *The Pedagogical Seminary and Journal of Genetic Psychology* 80: 221–252.

Jackson, M. (1998) 'It begins with the goose and ends with the goose': Medical, legal, and lay understandings of imbecility in Ingram v Wyatt, 1824–1832. *Social History of Medicine* 11(3), 361–380.

Langenhof, M.R., Komdeur, J. and Oldehinkel, A.J. (2016) Effects of parenting quality on adolescents' personality resemblance to their parents: The TRAILS study. *Journal of Adolescence* 51: 163–175.

Morrison, A.O. (1958) *Some patterns of dependency: An examination of ninety family units who were in receipt of social allowance in the Social Welfare Department of the District of Coquitlam.* University of British Columbia.

Serbin, L.A. and Karp, J. (2004) The intergenerational transfer of psychosocial risk: Mediators of vulnerability and resilience. *Annual Review of Psychology* 55: 333–363.

Thornberry, T.P. (2016) Three generation studies: Methodological challenges and promise. *Handbook of the Life Course* Springer: 571–596.

Wright, R.A. and Miller, J.M. (1998) Taboo until today? The coverage of biological arguments in criminology textbooks, 1961 to 1970 and 1987 to 1996. *Journal of Criminal Justice* 26: 1–19.

Part I

Studies using general population register data

Chapter 1

Using register-linkage data to study intergenerational continuity of criminal offending

Finland as a case example

Mikko Aaltonen and Janne Mikkonen

Many of the datasets described in this volume are based on various kinds of prospective longitudinal surveys that have tracked family members for long periods. Another possibility in the study of intergenerational continuity of crime is to build datasets purely on administrative data. Such *register-linkage datasets* derive information from various governmental or administrative sources, and use personal identification numbers or other unique identifiers to link data across different databases. Identification of familial relationships is based on national population records. In Finland, the key source for such data is the Population Information System maintained by the Population Register Centre, which also forms the basis for the national statistics on population structure compiled by Statistics Finland (see also Lyngstad and Skardhamar 2011 for a description of the highly similar Norwegian system). Using such data, kinship networks can be determined.

In recent years, we have seen an increasing number of criminological studies relying on register-linkage data from the Netherlands or from the Nordic countries of Denmark, Norway, Sweden and Finland. Typically such datasets include at least demographic (marriages, divorces, births, residential mobility) and socioeconomic (employment, education, income) measures, but they can also include other kinds of variables such as IQ (Schwartz et al. 2015; Frisell, Pawitan and Långström 2012), medicine purchases (Lichtenstein et al. 2012) and hospital care after violent victimization (Aaltonen, Martikainen, et al. 2016). Crime measures can be based on police-reported crimes, charges or convictions, and sometimes data on incarceration periods is also available. Some key strengths of register-linkage datasets are the possibility of retrospective data collection, lack of non-response and attrition, flexibility in sampling and large sample sizes.

Despite the potential, thorough register-based studies of intergenerational transmission of crime have not yet been conducted in Finland. Until recently, access to register-based data on crime has been somewhat limited, whereas another difficulty has been the short temporal coverage of relevant crime outcomes. The aim of this chapter is to provide an illustrative example of how register-based data can be used to study intergenerational continuity in crime in the current Finnish context. We use a dataset called EKSY014, a 20 per cent sample of all Finnish households with children aged 0–14 in 2000, to provide a concrete example of such data at work.

This chapter is structured as follows. We start by briefly reviewing the existing Finnish criminological research that has utilized register-linkage data. Next, we present the two research questions that we use to illustrate the data: (1) to what extent does parental crime and its frequency predict children's offending? and (2) does the timing or accumulation of parental crime matter for children's crime? We then describe the EKSY014 sample and measures. We end the chapter by discussing the possibilities and limitations that the current availability of register-linkage data entails for the study of intergenerational continuity of crime in Finland, and offer our take on the "optimal" data design for the study of this phenomenon with the currently available data.

Brief history of register-based research in Finland

Register-linkage research became possible in Finland with the introduction of the contemporary personal identification number in 1971 after the 1970 census. Tapani Valkonen, a demographer and a sociologist, was the first to present the idea that the 1970 census data could be linked with death certificate records that contained the same identification numbers. The first Living Conditions and Causes of Death data file, "EKSY70", was collated in 1978, and it was specifically used for studying socioeconomic differentials in mortality and causes of death – a tradition that could be called the driving force of Finnish register-based research. By and by, the study focus widened to other kinds of social determinants, but mortality remained the main outcome of interest throughout the 1980s and 1990s.

Since then, the gradual expansion of available data resources has enabled researchers to approach increasingly diverse topics with register-linkage data. On top of demographic studies on mortality, the fields of medical research, epidemiology and population health have extensively utilized records on hospital discharges, specific illnesses and drug reimbursements that already cover several decades (Furu et al. 2010; Gissler and Haukka 2004; Miettunen et al. 2011). Within register-based social and economic research, prominent topics have included marriage and divorce patterns (Jalovaara 2003), voting behavior (Martikainen et al. 2005), educational fertility patterns (Nisén et al. 2014), social mobility (Erola and Moisio 2007), determinants of debt problems (Oksanen et al. 2015), IQ and stock market participation (Grinblatt et al. 2011), determinants of disability retirement (Leinonen et al. 2012) and intergenerational income transmission (Sirniö et al. 2013), of which many would have been difficult or even impossible to approach reliably without the complete linkages of different data sources and the longitudinal, attrition- and non-response-free follow-ups allowed by the use of administrative data.

Within criminological research, Finnish register-based data has most commonly been used to examine socioeconomic differences in criminal offending and victimization (Aaltonen et al. 2011; Aaltonen et al. 2012; Aaltonen, Martikainen, et al. 2016). Other recent topics have included gender differences in sentencing (Kruttschnitt and Savolainen 2009), the role of social institutions in criminal desistance (Savolainen 2009), debt problems and crime (Aaltonen, Oksanen and Kivivuori 2016), antidepressant use and violent crime (Hemminki et al. 2016), unemployment–crime association (Aaltonen et al. 2013) and post-release employment trajectories of prison inmates (Aaltonen 2015). On top of these, Finnish register data on crime has been utilized in some Nordic comparisons (Aaltonen, Skardhamar, et al. 2016; Skardhamar et al. 2014) and comparisons of survey and administrative data sources (Kuoppamäki et al. 2011). A general description of register-linkage data in criminological context is provided in Lyngstad and Skardhamar (2011).

Within intergenerational research, a handful of studies on homicide offenders have analysed the intergenerational continuity of crime in Finland. One study examined whether psychopathy in homicide offenders is associated with offspring criminal offending (Repo-Tiihonen et al. 2010). Another study shows that about 10 per cent of young homicide offenders have a close relative who has also committed a homicide, whereas about 24 per cent of their fathers have convictions for violent crime and 59 per cent have a criminal record (Lehti 2007).

Before 2013, register data was usually provided for researchers in the form of completely anonymized samples on a CD-ROM. Datasets including sensitive information such as crime were not typically provided outside Statistics Finland, and datasets containing such variables had to be analysed at the premises of the Statistics Finland Research Lab. After the passage of the Amendment of Statistical Act in 2013, it has been possible to provide researchers access to data where individual persons can be indirectly identified and where only the direct identifiers (e.g., PIN and name) have been removed. Consequently, researchers now more commonly receive access to whole population data if the data is used through the remote access system of Statistics Finland (Cabrera 2016). Even when the data does not include the whole population, remote access usually enables access to more delicate information, such as crime records, as has been the case with the present data. To use remote access data, researchers must sign the terms and conditions of the user license, and they are not able to transfer data into the system or out from it without contacting Statistics Finland personnel (Statistics Finland 2017).

Current study

The main aim of the current study is to illustrate some of the possibilities that register-linkage data holds for the study of intergenerational continuity of crime in the current Finnish context. While the data we use has many applications for criminological research as well, it needs to be stressed that the sample was not initially designed to maximize the possibilities to specifically study the intergenerational transmission of crime. The next section describes the data in more detail.

We approach this theme through two different analyses. First, we provide a basic analysis of intergenerational continuity of crime in modern-day Finland, as such estimates have not been available. Given that the data includes several children from the same families, we use a multilevel logistic regression model that separates the variance of children's crime into within- and between-family components. We do this to the association between parents' crime and children's crime, while also providing estimates for within-family intraclass correlations (Rabe-Hesketh and Skrondal 2012) for crimes committed by siblings in the same family.

Second, as another illustration, we examine the significance of the timing and accumulation of parental offending. Some prior studies (van de Rakt et al. 2010; Besemer 2014; van de Weijer et al. 2014) have sought to establish whether the timing of parental offending matters for later offspring crime, and we analyse this question by comparing children exposed to parental crime at different ages. In addition to between-family comparisons, we also run sibling fixed-effects models (e.g., Sariaslan et al. 2014) to see whether siblings exposed to parental crime at different ages are impacted differently.

The sibling fixed-effect model focuses on siblings discordant on the outcome (Frisell, Öberg et al. 2012), and thus discards those families with no variation in the outcome. The positive trade-off is that the model simultaneously controls for unmeasured familial confounding factors, including all shared environmental influences and varying degrees of genetic influences (100 per cent for monozygotic twins and around 50 per cent for full siblings). If an association between the covariates and the outcome persists in such a model, it supports the claim that the associations between the timing or the accumulation of parental crime and children's crime are causal rather than spurious (Kendler 2017). However, although these models remove some key sources of confounding, their parameters cannot be given a causal interpretation (for caveats of the method, see Frisell, Öberg et al. 2012).

All models were estimated using Stata 14.2 software.

Data

The dataset, EKSY014, is a 20 per cent nationally representative random sample of Finnish households with children aged 0–14 in 2000 (N = 414,931). It was partly designed to provide a point of reference for the earlier census-based datasets from years 1950 and 1975. It includes identical, mostly annual measures for all household members and identifiers that associate household and family members with each other. On top of coresident parents, the dataset includes all biological parents who lived in Finland in 2000 but did not dwell in the same household with the sampled children (N = 27,809), as well as a separate sample of children not living in private households in 2000 (N = 1,599).

All children in the data have an identification code for their biological mother and father with which it is possible to derive information about the parents and identify biological siblings. This dataset has been previously used in a study that examined the intergenerational transmission of depressive symptoms (Mikkonen et al. 2016).

Statistics Finland drew the original sample and conducted the individual-level linkage of the data delivered by different register authorities. Statistics Finland also provided the sociodemographic and socioeconomic data (e.g., income, education, occupational status, family type and mortality), that is currently available for years 1987–2012 annually and for individual census years 1970, 1975, 1980 and 1985. The National Institute for Health and Welfare provided records on visits to inpatient care (1996–2011) and outpatient specialized services (1998–2011), information on the use of child welfare (1991–2012) and social welfare (1995–2012) and the medical birth register (1987–2012). The Finnish Social Insurance institution delivered records on prescription medicine purchases (1995–2012) and special reimbursement rights for long-term medication (1997–2012). The remote access data also includes country of birth for immigrants and grade point average at the end of compulsory education.

Sample selection criteria

For the current illustration, we excluded observations from the full sample to focus on a more specific group of parents and children. First of all, given that the crime data is available from 1996 onwards, we selected a group of children for whom we could measure both parental offending and their own offending from as long a period as possible. Simply put, the oldest children in the data have limited information on parental crime due to missing crime data before 1996, whereas the youngest children do not reach ages where a reliable measure of their own crime would be available. As a compromise, from the initial sample of children born between 1986 and 2000, we selected those born between 1989 and 1995 (N = 90,761). In addition to these criteria, we only selected children who were living with both biological parents at age 7 and only included children whose parents did not die before their children reached the age of 15 and children who did not die or emigrate before the age of 18. This leaves us with a final sample of 69,139 children from 47,631 families. The number of children per family varies from 1 to 7, the average number being 1.5. This relatively low mean count is explained by the fact that we only chose children born between 1989 and 1995, not the total count of children born into these families

Police-reported crime

The crime outcomes used in the current analysis are based on police-reported crimes between 1996 and 2012. We exclude minor traffic offences because they are coded inconsistently during the follow-up, but otherwise we include

year of birth	96	97	98	99	00	01	02	03	04	05	06	07	08	09	10	11	12
1989	7	8	9	10	11	12	13	14	15	16	17						
1990		7	8	9	10	11	12	13	14	15	16	17					
1991			7	8	9	10	11	12	13	14	15	16	17				
1992				7	8	9	10	11	12	13	14	15	16	17			
1993					7	8	9	10	11	12	13	14	15	16	17		
1994						7	8	9	10	11	12	13	14	15	16	17	
1995							7	8	9	10	11	12	13	14	15	16	17

(calendar year across the top)

Figure 1.1 Timing of measurements for parental crime (grey) and children's crime (outline), by year of birth of the child (row), calendar year (column) and age of the child (cells)

all offences. In legal terms, these crimes amount to suspected crimes rather than solved crimes or convictions, but are naturally such where at least one suspect was identified.

In an optimal scenario, we would like to measure all crimes committed during a criminal career for both the children and their parents. This way we could create measures for crimes committed within the same age periods for both generations. Because the crime data starts from 1996, this kind of measure is unachievable in the current data. This is the most important current limitation for studying intergenerational continuity of crime in Finland, to which we will return in the discussion. For this reason, we use different measures for parents and children. In the first analysis, children's crimes are measured at ages 15–17 as a binary variable, whereas for their parents we measure crimes when the child was 7–15. Figure 1.1 presents the measurement years of parental and offspring crime for the birth cohorts included.

In the first part of the analysis, we measure paternal and maternal crimes separately and create a combined variable indicating whether father, mother or both committed crimes when their child was 7–15 years old. As another specification tapping into the frequency of parental offending, we include similar variables differentiating between 0, 1, 2 and 3 or more crimes committed by the father and the mother. In the second part of the analysis, the measure of parental crime is divided into three categories by children's age at parental offending: 7–9, 10–12 and 13–15. The other measure we use in this analysis is a cumulative measure of those age periods that ranges from 0 (no parental offending) to 3 (parental offending during all three age periods).

In addition to the variables measuring parental crime, we control for both maternal and paternal age and both maternal and paternal education. The age of parents should have an impact on measures of parental crime, whereas parental education is an established correlate of children's crime in Finland. Finally, we also control for the birth year and sex of the child.

Results

Table 1.1 shows descriptive statistics on the distributions of the independent variables. Experiencing parental crime at ages 7–15 is rather common in the data: 14 per cent of children have at least one parent suspected of a police-reported crime. Expectedly, paternal crime (11 per cent) is much more common

Table 1.1 Descriptive statistics (*N* = 69,139)

Variable	*%/mean*	*N/(SD)*
Year of birth	1992	(1.99)
Sex		
Boy	51.1	35,301
Girl	48.9	33,383
Parental crime when 7–15		
None	86.2	59,587
Father only	10.6	7,346
Mother only	1.8	1,211
Both	1.4	995
Paternal crime when 7–15		
0 offence	87.9	60,798
1 offence	6.7	4,648
2 offences	2.6	1,767
3+ offences	2.8	1,926
Maternal crime when 7–15		
0 offence	96.8	66,933
1 offence	2.2	1,493
2 offences	0.6	392
3+ offences	0.5	321
Paternal education		
Secondary+	81.5	56,345
Basic or missing	18.5	12,794
Maternal education		
Secondary+	87.2	60,259
Basic or missing	12.8	8,880
Paternal age when 7	38.9	(5.5)
Maternal age when 7	36.7	(4.9)
Children's crime 15–17		
No	91.1	62,977
Yes	8.9	6,162
		69,139

than maternal crime (2 per cent); 1.4 per cent of children have both father and mother suspected of a crime. Fathers are two years older than mothers on average, and they are more likely to have a low level of education. Nine percent of children were suspected of crime at ages 15–17.

Table 1.2 shows results from two multilevel logistic regression models examining the association between parental crime and children's crime. Both models

Table 1.2 The associations between parental crime and children's crime. Odds ratios and confidence intervals from multilevel (random intercept) logistic regression models (N = 69,139).

Variable	*Model 1*		*Model 2*	
	OR	*CI 95%*	*OR*	*CI 95%*
Parental crime when 7–15				
None	1			
Father only	1.89***	1.73–2.06		
Mother only	2.19***	1.81–2.64		
Both	3.26***	2.69–3.94		
Paternal crime when 7–15				
0 offence			1	
1 offence			1.58***	
2 offences			1.93***	
3+ offences			2.47***	
Maternal crime when 7–15				
0 offence			1	
1 offence			1.82***	
2 offences			1.64**	
3+ offences			2.42***	
Sex				
Girl	1		1	
Boy	2.31***	2.17–2.46	2.32***	2.17–2.47
Paternal education				
Secondary+	1		1	
Basic or missing	1.37***	1.27–1.48	1.36***	1.26–1.46
Maternal education				
Secondary+	1		1	
Basic or missing	1.62***	1.49–1.76	1.61***	1.48–1.75
Paternal age	.99	.98–1.00	.99	.98–1.00
Maternal age	.98***	.97–.98	.98***	.97–.99
ρ (intraclass correlation)	.26***	.22–.29	.26***	.22–.30
σ (between-family variance)	1.07	.97–1.17	1.07	.97–1.17
Log likelihood	−19,851		−19,838	

Coefficients for birth year omitted from the table; *p < .05, **p <.01, ***p < .001.

include the same control variables, but the variable measuring parental crime differs. In model 1, the variable denoting whether father, mother or both parents committed crimes when the child was 7–15 has a clear association with children's crime. The odds ratio (OR) for a child with a father committing at least one offence is 1.9, whereas the corresponding OR for a mother's offending is 2.2. If both parents committed crimes, the odds of committing a crime is roughly three times higher than in the reference group of children whose parents have not committed crimes. Residual intraclass correlation on the latent scale (Rabe-Hesketh and Skrondal 2012) is estimated to be .26, indicating that there is substantial between-family variance (or sibling similarity) not explained by the included parental covariates.[1]

Model 2 examines the frequency of parental crime, with findings suggestive of a dose-response association with children's crime. The risk of children's crime grows in a roughly linear manner with the frequency of paternal offending, whereas the association between maternal offending and children's offending is not quite as consistent, although children of mothers with three or more offences are the most crime-prone. Given that the measures of fathers' and mothers' offending are correlated ($r = .23$), it is no surprise that the dose-response pattern for maternal offending also appears somewhat clearer if we exclude paternal offending from the model (results not shown). Taken together, these results indicate clear intergenerational continuity in criminal offending in Finland.

Table 1.3 presents the results on the second illustration, the timing and frequency of parental crime. Our prior results suggest that the frequency of parental offending has a positive association with children's crime, but they do not distinguish the timing of exposure. Starting with a random effects model similar to the one used in Table 1.2, the first estimates suggest that later exposure to

Table 1.3 The associations between timing of parental crime and children's crime. Odds ratios and confidence intervals from multilevel (random intercept) logistic regression models ($N = 69{,}139$) and sibling fixed-effects models ($n = 6{,}357$).

Variable	*Random effects*		*Fixed effects*	
	OR	*CI95%*	*OR*	*CI95%*
Timing of parental crime				
Parental crime 7–9	1.67***	1.48–1.88	.97	.73–1.27
Parental crime 10–12	1.72***	1.55–1.93	.98	.74–1.30
Parental crime 13–15	1.98***	1.79–2.18	1.16	.91–1.47
Number of exposure periods	1		1	
1 age period	1.95***	1.79–2.13	1.08	.84–1.39
2 age periods	3.25***	2.81–3.76	1.06	.69–1.62
3 age periods	4.61***	3.55–5.99	1.32	.56–3.10
N	69,139		6,357	

*$p < .05$, **$p < .01$, ***$p < .001$.

parental crime might be more detrimental, although the confidence intervals are overlapping. What is more, the number of periods of exposure seems to matter as well: children who were exposed to parental crime during all three age periods (7–9, 10–12, 13–15) have an OR of 4.6 when compared to unexposed children.

Interestingly, these associations cannot be detected in sibling comparisons. When we restrict the analysis to siblings who are discordant in terms of the outcome (e.g., one committing crimes and the other not), exposure to parental offending does not seem to explain differences in offending. This applies to both the period-specific dummy variables and the cumulative variable. There are some indications of later/greater exposure being more criminogenic, but none of these estimates reaches the conventional levels of statistical significance.

Discussion

In this study, we have provided a simple illustration of how Finnish register-linkage data can be used to study the intergenerational continuity of crime, and what the basic associations between parental crime and children's crime are. Like elsewhere, we observe clear intergenerational continuities in criminal offending. These associations are similarly strong for children with either offending father or offending mother, but the strongest for children with both parents offending. The number of parental crimes seems to increase the risk in a dose-response manner, while there is also some evidence that the risk of offspring offending is particularly large in close proximity to parental offending. We were, however, unable confirm this result in the sibling fixed-effects analysis that utilized a smaller subsample. It is thus possible that some of our results reflect familial confounding (differences between families where parents commit crimes at different ages of the children) rather than an actual causal effect of timing. Furthermore, as we were unable to measure offending before 1996, we could not examine or account for the effects of earlier incidents of parental offending when the children were 0–6 years old. Next, we will first discuss the strengths and limitations of administrative data and our present study design and finish by envisioning the future prospects of the register-based research on the intergenerational continuity of crime in Finland.

Strengths and limitations

Finnish register-linkage data provides excellent opportunities for the study of intergenerational transmission of crime and other outcomes. For a large, nationally representative sample, we were able to comprehensively observe police-reported offending at ages 15–17 and parental police-reported offending at ages 7–15 while avoiding the common problems of longitudinal survey studies, such as attrition, preferential reporting, recall bias and non-response. The benefits of a large sample size were especially demonstrated by the fact that we were able to provide precise estimates for children with mother only or both parents offending despite the rarity of such cases (<2 per cent). Another strength of the current data is its inclusion of several potentially relevant annually measured confounders, such as parental employment, education and health outcomes. Moreover, owing to the inclusion of all household members of the sampled children, we were able to take advantage of sibling variation in exposures and outcomes to control for unobserved heterogeneity.

It should be noted that we specified our study design in a rather strict manner given the possibilities of the data. We restricted our analysis to children who dwelled with both their biological mother and their biological father at age 7, which rules out around 22 per cent of children born in 1989–1995. Because the dataset also includes similar measurements on all non-coresident biological parents, it would allow for analyses comparing the strength of intergenerational continuity between children who do and do not dwell with their offending parents. However, this would already form its own separate question that would go beyond the scope of the present study. Considering this strict specification, our results may not generalize to all family types and intergenerational associations between parental and offspring crime in Finland.

The use of administrative data also sets some limitations for the study of intergenerational crime. Although we are able to identify whether the children dwelled with their biological parents at the given age, we are unable to measure the quality of the parent–child relationship; for instance, the amount of time spent together. Overall, the number of variables that would enable us to observe the direct mechanisms of intergenerational transmission or provide tests for constructs based on criminological theory (i.e., social control, self-control, exposure to delinquent peers) is limited in administrative data. All the potential issues with official data on crime apply in this case, as well.

Our illustrative analysis also tangibly demonstrates the huge data requirements related to the study of intergenerational transmission of crime. Despite the large sample size and the relatively long 17-year follow-up of police-reported crime, we were obliged to make compromises when selecting the measurement periods for parental and offspring crime, while our sibling fixed-effects analysis was clearly underpowered to detect the potentially increased risks related to later and longer-term exposures to parental crime. Recent studies that have used family-based quasi-experimental designs (D'Onofrio et al. 2013) have relied on much larger samples (e.g., Sariaslan et al. 2016, 1.8 million Swedish twins/siblings), and despite the impressive sample size of our data, it is evident that the study of relatively rare outcomes on the population level – especially when using methods that focus on discordant siblings and often exclude most observations – could yet benefit from access to even larger samples. Although family-based approaches have often been used to estimate the heritability of different behaviors, they also provide study designs in the study of environmental causation (D'Onofrio et al. 2013).

Conclusion: optimal Finnish register-based data for the study of intergenerational continuity of crime?

As mentioned, the key limitation with the current data is the unavailability of crime data before the year 1996. EKSY014 data provides several interesting opportunities to examine associations between familial factors and children's offending, but this temporal limitation makes it suboptimal for the study of intergenerational continuity of crime at the time of writing. However, Statistics Finland also has a database on convictions that starts from the year 1977, and includes all convictions from district courts for all individuals. Although less serious crimes are excluded from this data source, at present this data seems the most promising alternative for the study of intergenerational continuity of crime. Given the long follow-up, it is evident that the Finnish criminal code, policing practices and the society as a whole have changed, and especially the changes in the penal code need to be accounted for before using the data. In any case, such changes pose a difficulty to all studies that seek to use comparable measures from different historical periods.

At present, the longest follow-up for both generations could be achieved by focusing on parental cohorts born in 1962 or soon after, given that the age of criminal responsibility in Finland is 15. For these cohorts, it is currently possible to construct up to 40-year-long conviction careers. The majority of the children of these parents were born in the 1980s and the 1990s, which would in turn enable the measurement of children's conviction careers for relatively long periods. As a general rule, the readily available annual measures for socioeconomic variables start from the year 1987, which would in turn mean that such data could also include rich time-varying information about parental factors in childhood and adolescence.

To sum up, the Finnish register-linkage dataset holds much potential for the study of intergenerational continuity of crime. We have illustrated some of the possibilities with a couple of simple examples that only scratch the surface. Large datasets enable the study of rare types of crimes, crime-type specific continuities, effects of timing and the potentially confounding/mediating role of adverse life events. Designs focusing on sibling comparisons are very promising, and they are being increasingly used to rigorously study environmental causation as well (Sariaslan et al. 2014; Kendler et al. 2014).

Note

1 In the model without covariates (variance components model), intraclass correlation is .29. Higher intraclass correlation indicates greater sibling similarity in crime, and thus a greater proportion of variance explained by between-family differences.

References

Aaltonen, M. (2015). 'Post-release employment of desisting inmates', *British Journal of Criminology*, *56*: 350–369.

Aaltonen, M., Kivivuori, J., and Martikainen, P. (2011). 'Social determinants of crime in a welfare state: Do they still matter?', *Acta Sociologica*, *54*: 161–181.

Aaltonen, M., Kivivuori, J., Martikainen, P., and Sirén, R. (2012). 'Socioeconomic differences in violent victimization: Exploring the impact of data source and the inclusivity of the violence concept', *European Journal of Criminology, 9*: 567–583.

Aaltonen, M., MacDonald, J. M., Martikainen, P., and Kivivuori, J. (2013). 'Examining the generality of the unemployment – crime association', *Criminology, 51*: 561–594.

Aaltonen, M., Martikainen, P., Moustgaard, H., Peltonen, R., and Remes, H. (2016). 'Childhood family income and violent victimization during youth and young adulthood: Trends in hospital care during 1988–2007 in Finland', *Journal of Interpersonal Violence, 31*: 2338–2359.

Aaltonen, M., Oksanen, A., and Kivivuori, J. (2016). 'Debt problems and crime', *Criminology, 54*: 307–331.

Aaltonen, M., Skardhamar, T., Nilsson, A., Andersen, L. H., Bäckman, O., Estrada, F., and Danielsson, P. (2016). 'Comparing employment trajectories before and after first imprisonment in four Nordic countries', *British Journal of Criminology, 57*: 828–847.

Besemer, S. (2014). 'The impact of timing and frequency of parental criminal behaviour and risk factors on offspring offending', *Psychology, Crime & Law, 20*: 78–99.

Cabrera, A. (2016, September). 'Towards a national remote access system for register-based research', In *International Conference on Privacy in Statistical Databases*, 181–189. Springer International Publishing.

D'Onofrio, B., Lahey, B., Turkheimer, E., and Lichtenstein, P. (2013). 'Critical need for family-based, quasi-experimental designs in integrating genetic and social science research', *American Journal of Public Health, 103*: 46–55.

Erola, J., and Moisio, P. (2007). 'Social mobility over three generations in Finland, 1950–2000', *European Sociological Review, 23*: 169–183.

Frisell, T., Öberg, S., Kuja-Halkola, R., and Sjölander, A. (2012). 'Sibling comparison designs: Bias from non-shared confounders and measurement error', *Epidemiology, 23*: 713–720.

Frisell, T., Pawitan, Y., and Långström, N. (2012). 'Is the association between general cognitive ability and violent crime caused by family-level confounders?', *PLoS ONE*, 7: 1–7.

Furu, K., Wettermark, B., Andersen, M., Martikainen, J. E., Almarsdottir, A. B., and Sørensen, H. T. (2010). 'The Nordic countries as a cohort for pharmacoepidemiological research', *Basic & Clinical Pharmacology & Toxicology, 106*: 86–94.

Gissler, M., and Haukka, J. (2004). 'Finnish health and social welfare registers in epidemiological research', *Norsk Epidemiologi, 14*: 113–120.

Grinblatt, M., Keloharju, M., and Linnainmaa, J. (2011). 'IQ and stock market participation', *The Journal of Finance, 66*: 2121–2164.

Hemminki, E., Merikukka, M., Gissler, M., Wahlbeck, K., Savolainen, J., Ristikari, T., and Aaltonen, M. (2016). 'Antidepressant use and violent crimes among young people: A longitudinal examination of the Finnish 1987 birth cohort', *Journal of Epidemiology and Community Health, 71*: 12–18.

Hovde Lyngstad, T., and Skardhamar, T. (2011). 'Nordic register data and their untapped potential for criminological knowledge', *Crime and Justice, 40*: 613–645.

Jalovaara, M. (2003). 'The joint effects of marriage partners' socioeconomic positions on the risk of divorce', *Demography, 40*: 67–81.

Kendler, K. (2017). 'Causal inference in psychiatric epidemiology', *JAMA Psychiatry, 74*: 561–562.

Kendler, K., Morris, N., Lönn, S., Sundquist, J., and Sundquist, K. (2014). 'Environmental transmission of violent criminal behavior in siblings: A Swedish national study', *Psychological Medicine, 44*: 3181–3187.

Kruttschnitt, C., and Savolainen, J. (2009). 'Ages of chivalry, places of paternalism: Gender and criminal sentencing in Finland', *European Journal of Criminology, 6*: 225–247.

Kuoppamäki, S. M., Kääriäinen, J., and Ellonen, N. (2011). 'Physical violence against children reported to the police: Discrepancies between register-based data and child victim survey', *Violence and Victims, 26*: 257–268.

Lehti, M. (2007). *Nuoret ja henkirikollisuus 1980–2004' (Young Homicide Offenders 1980–2004)*. Helsinki: National Research Institute of Legal Policy.

Leinonen, T., Martikainen, P., and Lahelma, E. (2012). 'Interrelationships between education, occupational social class, and income as determinants of disability retirement', *Scandinavian Journal of Social Medicine, 40*: 157–166.

Lichtenstein, P., Halldner, L., Zetterqvist, J., Sjölander, A., Serlachius, E., Fazel, S., Långström, N., and Larsson, H. (2012). 'Medication for attention deficit-hyperactivity disorder and criminality', *New England Journal of Medicine, 367*: 2006–2014.

Lyngstad, T., and Skardhamar, T. (2011). 'Nordic register data and their untapped potential for criminological knowledge', In M. Tonry and T. Lappi-Seppälä (eds.): *Crime & Justice: A Review of Research*, vol. 40, 613–645. Chicago: Chicago University Press.

Martikainen, P., Martikainen, T., and Wass, H. (2005). 'The effect of socioeconomic factors on voter turnout in Finland: A register-based study of 2.9 million voters', *European Journal of Political Research, 44*: 645–669.

Miettunen, J., Suvisaari, J., Haukka, J., and Isohanni, M. (2011). 'Use of register data for psychiatric epidemiology in the Nordic countries', *Textbook of Psychiatric Epidemiology, Third Edition*: 117–131.

Mikkonen, J., Moustgaard, H., Remes, H., and Martikainen, P. (2016). 'Intergenerational transmission of depressive symptoms: The role of gender, socioeconomic circumstances, and the accumulation of parental symptoms', *Journal of Affective Disorders, 204*: 74–82.

Nisén, J., Martikainen, P., Silventoinen, K., and Myrskylä, M. (2014). 'Age-specific fertility by educational level in the Finnish male cohort born 1940–50', *Demographic Research, 31*(1): 119–136.

Oksanen, A., Aaltonen, M., and Rantala, K. (2015). 'Social determinants of debt problems in a Nordic welfare state: A Finnish register-based study', *Journal of Consumer Policy, 38*: 229–246.

Rabe-Hesketh, S., and Skrondal, A. (2012). *Multilevel and Longitudinal Modeling Using Stata, Volume II: Categorical Responses, Counts, and Survival.* College Station, TX: StataCorp.

Repo-Tiihonen, E., Tiihonen, J., Lindberg, N., Weizmann-Henelius, G., Putkonen, H., and Häkkänen, H. (2010). 'The intergenerational cycle of criminality: Association with psychopathy', *Journal of Forensic Sciences, 55*: 116–120.

Sariaslan, A., Larsson, H., and Fazel, S. (2016). 'Genetic and environmental determinants of violence risk in psychotic disorders: A multivariate quantitative genetic study of 1.8 million Swedish twins and siblings', *Molecular Psychiatry, 21*: 1251–1256.

Sariaslan, A., Larsson, H., D'Onofrio, B., Långström, N., and Lichtenstein, P. (2014). 'Childhood family income, adolescent violent criminality and substance misuse: Quasi-experimental total population study', *British Journal of Psychiatry, 205*: 286–290.

Savolainen, J. (2009). 'Work, family and criminal desistance adult social bonds in a Nordic welfare state', *British Journal of Criminology, 49*: 285–304.

Schwartz, J., Savolainen, J., Aaltonen, M., Merikukka, M., Paananen, R., and Gissler, M. (2015). Intelligence and criminal behavior in a total birth cohort: An examination of functional form, dimensions of intelligence, and the nature of offending', *Intelligence, 51*: 109–118.

Sirniö, O., Martikainen, P., and Kauppinen, T. M. (2013). 'Intergenerational determinants of income level in Finland', *Social Forces, 92*: 463–490.

Skardhamar, T., Aaltonen, M., and Lehti, M. (2014). 'Immigrant crime in Norway and Finland', *Journal of Scandinavian Studies in Criminology and Crime Prevention, 15*: 107–127.
Statistics Finland (2017). *Remote access use.* <http://tilastokeskus.fi/tup/mikroaineistot/etakaytto_en.html> (accessed 4 April, 2017).
Van de Rakt, M., Ruiter, S., De Graaf, N., and Nieuwbeerta, P. (2010). 'When does the Apple Fall from the tree? Static versus dynamic theories predicting intergenerational transmission of convictions', *Journal of Quantitative Criminology, 26*: 371–389.
Van de Weijer, S., Bijleveld, C., and Blokland, A. (2014). 'The intergenerational transmission of violent offending', *Journal of Family Violence, 29*: 109–118.

Chapter 2

Danish register data

Flexible administrative data and their relevance for studies of intergenerational transmission

Lars Højsgaard Andersen

Few data that are available to researchers can match the richness and flexibility of register data from Denmark, and the potential of this data source for studies of intergenerational transmission is large (although, as will be clear, largely untapped). A short description of Danish register data could go along these lines: Danish register data comprise a full population panel of all residents in Denmark, effectively covering all people who were legally in the country on January 1, 1980, or who were born later or immigrated legally to Denmark since then, and variables include various administrative records of contact between the residents and the welfare state and its agencies. The data, which are generally accurate, are growing at a fast rate, and information is either discontinued or introduced into the registries over time in accordance with societal developments.

In this chapter, I describe the context and practicalities of this intriguing data source, and I outline the data's potential for the study of intergenerational transmission of crime and punishment. In doing so, I present my views on how the richness and flexibility of Danish register data should be exploited to advance knowledge on the intergenerational continuity in offending and contact with the criminal justice system.

Danish register data: it's not a dataset

The most important thing to recognize when working with Danish register data is that they are not a dataset and are not part of any particular study. No one set out to establish a dataset suitable for answering a specific research question and ended up with the data organism which Danish register data are. Danish register data is a broad term which refers to the fact that in Denmark numerous types of contact between residents and welfare state agencies, such as the tax authorities, physical and mental health services, employment offices, and, importantly for the topic covered in this book, the criminal justice system, are recorded. All these types of information are reported to Statistics Denmark, the national statistical agency, which then documents each register (including pointing out discontinuities in variables across years and the like) and makes the registers available to researchers, provided that the researcher and the research project are formally approved for access (approval is required both from Statistics Denmark and the Danish Data Protection Agency). Researchers do not get access to personally identifiable information but to de-identified versions of those. Information on how to obtain access to the registers may be found at the Division of Research Services at Statistics Denmark online at www.dst.dk/en.

We talk about Danish register data as a full population panel because we can construct individual-level panels from the registers and because we can combine individual-level information across the many registers. In Denmark, all residents have a unique personal identification number which is used to identify them in transactions with the welfare state. Residents need the identification number to pay their taxes, for medical services to find their medical record, and so on. The richness and flexibility of Danish register data then comes from the fact that it is the same identification number which identifies a resident across the many registers, allowing researchers to merge individual level information across registers and across years.

Importantly, Statistics Denmark documents all registers and variables to ensure transparency and make it easier for researchers to use the data. The documentation (which is available online, although only in Danish, at http://dst.dk/da/TilSalg/Forskningsservice/Dokumentation/hoejkvalitetsvariable) describes where any given register comes from, such as which agency delivered the data. And it describes the content of, and lists the values and labels of, each variable. Importantly, and conveniently for researchers, the documentation also contains information on the comparability of each variable over time, highlighting potential discontinuities in the variable definition over time.

Data on intergenerational transmission in offending

Studies of intergenerational continuity in offending and contact with the criminal justice system require information on (1) family relations to identify intergenerational links and (2) criminal offending and contact with the criminal justice system.

The population register provides detailed information on family relations. First, this register records a person's date of birth and gender; it also includes the personal identification numbers of a person's parents. This makes it straightforward to match biological relatives both across (parent–child) and within (siblings) generations. Second, a unique family identifier matches people to households, effectively allowing researchers to observe whether a child lives with his or her biological parents, any stepparents, or in a single-headed household. This information is essential when one wishes to analyse the consequences of, for example, the incarceration of a resident or non-resident parent. Third, the register also records information on family type, including marriage and divorce dates, which is important information if one wishes to analyse, for example, how intergenerational transmission differs across children born in and out of wedlock. In short, the population register records family relations, which is the key to studies of intergenerational transmission. Spouses, children, siblings, cousins, and parents can be identified, as can people with whom a person resides (stepfathers and cohabiting partners, for example), providing researchers with entire family trees rather than "just" parent–child relations.

The criminal justice registers provide detailed information on contacts between the criminal justice system in Denmark and residents (and, for example, also on tourists charged of crimes in Denmark, but tourists cannot be merged to other registries). Table 2.1 summarizes the information which is available in the criminal justice registers. In addition to relying on personal identification numbers to identify persons across registers, the criminal justice registers also rely on case-specific identification numbers. This has the advantage that researchers may observe how cases progress, such as which charges a person faces on a particular case and which charges that person is convicted of (and what the punishment is) on the same case. It also allows researchers to observe whether,

Table 2.1 Summary of criminal justice registers available from Statistics Denmark

Register	*Availability*	*Variables*
Reported crimes register	1990–	Unique case identifier, date of crime, crime type
Charges register	1980–	Unique individual identifier, unique case identifier, charge date, offense date, crime type
Convictions register	1980–	Unique individual identifier, unique case identifier, conviction date, decision type (court ruling, confession, etc.), name of court, crime type (acc. to conviction), sanction (sentence length, imprisonment/probation/community service/fine, amount fined)
Incarcerations register	1991–[a]	Unique individual identifier, unique case identifier, admission date, release date, facility identifier, transfer dates, sentence served at home under electronic monitoring
Juvenile charges register[b]	2005–	Unique individual identifier, unique case identifier, below age of criminal responsibility, juveniles are not prosecuted/sanctioned but offenders are registered here
Victims register[c]	2001–	Unique individual identifier, unique case identifier

a From 1980 to 1991 the Incarcerations register only holds information on admission dates for people serving prison sentences (as well as personal and case identifiers). Arrest and pretrial detention is not recorded during this period, nor are release dates recorded during this period.

b The age of criminal responsibility in Denmark is 15 years, except for a period from mid-2010 to early 2012 during which it was 14 years.

c The Victims register only holds information on victims of violent crimes.

for example, an arrest or a period of pretrial detention precedes imprisonment on the same case, or whether these periods of incarceration stem from different criminal cases.

Importantly, the criminal justice registers hold information on crime type and offense date (charges and convictions registers) and on the exact timing of incarcerations (incarcerations register), including transfers across prisons. The level of detail is high, and "offense type", for example, consists of more than 1,000 offense categories which are hierarchically coded to make it easier to bundle them into broader crime-type categories, such as violent crimes, property crimes, and so on. Such information is crucial when researchers wish to analyse the consequences of the severity of crimes and of the timing of parental conviction or incarceration for children, for example. Also, because of the accuracy of the offense data in the charges register, researchers may analyse the timing of children's criminal responses to their parents' contact with the criminal justice system, in many cases down to the time of day which the offense occurred.

Not all offenses are recorded in the criminal justice registers, however. A specific act, the Act on Processing Personal Information in the Central Criminal Justice Register (latest version at the time of writing this chapter is Act no. 881 of July 4, 2014), regulates which offenses are recorded. Offenses against the penal code, the weapons' law, the law on illicit drugs, and DUI offenses (and traffic offenses which could incur the confiscation of a driver's license or punishment exceeding a fine) are always recorded. Other charges are only recorded provided that the offense may offset a fine of at least DKK 2,500 (approximately EUR 330). Before 2012, the fine had to exceed DKK 1,500 (approximately EUR 200). In earlier years, the amount was even lower yet has always been set to exclude only minor non-criminal offenses. These limits for which charges enter the criminal justice registers imply that sometimes a new minor offense type enters the registers, while others might leave them. It is therefore advisable, and also common practice among criminological researchers in Denmark, to focus analyses on more serious crimes, such as violations of the penal code (which are always recorded, no matter the level of the fine they could offset).

Table 2.2 provides an overview of the number of children born in birth cohorts 1980–2000 in Denmark, and thus shows the potential sample size one may obtain from working with Danish register data on these birth cohorts. Data are available for later birth cohorts, too, yet because the age of criminal responsibility in Denmark is 15 years, and the last available data year in the criminal justice registers (at the time of writing) is 2015, this birth cohort selection makes sense. Between 50,000 and 70,000 children are born each year. Bundling these children into one sample would then produce a total sample of 1.3 million children who can be followed up to between age 15 (2000 cohort) and 35 (1980 cohort). These children have a total of almost 2.5 million registered parents who can be tracked in the registers both back in time and up to today (or until they died or emigrated).

Table 2.2 Data description, birth cohorts 1980–2000

Child cohort	*Children born in cohort*	*Parents registered at childbirth*	*Parental conviction by age 15*	*Parental incarceration > 24 hours by age 15*[a]	*Parental incarceration < 24 hours between 1991 and age 15*[b]	*Conviction by 2015*	*Incarceration > 24 hours by 2015*	*Incarceration < 24 hours between 1991 and 2015*[b]
1980	57,166	108,933	7,486	4,610	6,445	6,983	1,912	5,879
1981	52,980	100,787	6,898	4,406	6,114	6,371	1,788	5,478
1982	52,642	99,548	6,902	4,295	6,152	6,559	1,795	5,506
1983	50,844	96,510	6,617	4,442	6,196	6,340	1,714	5,339
1984	51,801	98,354	6,623	4,599	6,400	6,394	1,653	5,491
1985	53,831	101,997	6,585	4,874	6,811	6,374	1,711	5,326
1986	55,385	104,734	7,007	5,000	7,123	6,244	1,642	5,320
1987	56,190	106,153	7,103	5,191	7,447	6,340	1,630	5,426
1988	58,797	111,032	7,301	5,434	7,900	6,460	1,638	5,626
1989	61,198	115,570	7,588	5,710	8,454	6,377	1,524	5,515
1990	63,428	119,845	7,649	5,892	8,824	6,234	1,435	5,369
1991	64,323	121,386	7,610	5,787	8,910	5,618	1,279	4,909
1992	67,651	127,930	7,814	6,033	9,446	5,257	1,106	4,544
1993	67,360	127,205	7,470	5,962	9,465	4,428	884	3,858
1994	69,705	131,695	7,520	6,138	10,160	3,573	639	3,171
1995	70,105	132,674	7,488	6,259	10,291	2,832	419	2,318
1996	67,791	128,072	7,018	5,936	10,429	2,245	252	1,628
1997	67,642	128,259	7,006	5,793	10,445	1,111	146	988
1998	66,204	125,614	6,501	5,347	10,001	496	46	444
1999	66,299	125,195	6,134	5,288	10,205	214	11	152
2000	67,090	126,700	5,987	5,179	10,400	39	< 5	< 5

Note: Own calculations on data from Statistics Denmark. Data are also available for later birth cohorts.

a Before 1991 only incarceration reflecting a prison sentence was recorded, and arrests and pretrial detentions were thus not recorded.

b Information on incarcerations for less than 24 hours was unavailable before 1991.

On average, 11.5 per cent of the children experienced parental conviction before age 15, a proportion that ranges between 13.1 per cent in the 1980 and 1982 cohorts and 8.9 per cent in the 2000 birth cohort. Parental incarceration is split into the number of children who experienced parental incarceration for more or less than 24 hours before their 15th birthday. This cutoff makes sense, as the police can hold people in custody for up to 24 hours without bringing them before a court, and such brief stints of incarceration are thus likely to reflect public disorder or drunkenness, whereas incarceration for more than 24 hours implies a more serious offense. On average, almost 9 per cent of the children experienced parental incarceration for more than 24 hours during their childhood, whereas almost 14 per cent (on average) experienced it for less than 24 hours. Before 1991, however, only incarceration spells referring to a sentence being served were recorded (see table note), and the number of children from earlier birth cohorts who experienced parental incarceration is thus likely to be understated.

The last three columns of Table 2.2 report the number of children from each birth cohort who experienced conviction and/or incarceration by 2015. Because the children from earlier birth cohorts are older in 2015 than children from later cohorts, there is a natural decrease in these types of contact with the criminal justice system over the birth cohorts. The columns show that 12 per cent of birth cohort 1980 (7,000 out of 57,000) were convicted by 2015, 10 per cent were detained by the police for less than 24 hours (almost 6,000), and 3 per cent (1,900) were incarcerated for longer periods. Among children from the 2000 birth cohort, who only were older than the age of criminal responsibility for less than a year in 2015, only a few had contact with the criminal justice system, as one would expect.

Other data

Danish register data consist of a host of individual registries, as mentioned. This implies that researchers may add various other register variables to their sample on intergenerational continuity in offending and criminal justice contact. These other data may be used as control variables, as alternative outcome variables, or they may be used to craft any specific dataset with which researchers seek to answer their research questions. The number of registers and variables outgrows what could reasonably be described in detail in this chapter, and Table 2.3 therefore simply summarizes a selection of the most relevant registers. To obtain information on any specific register, or to get an overview of the full availability of registers, researchers should contact Statistics Denmark.

To provide an example of the quality of an important socioeconomic indicator variable, consider the example of labour market status. All information on labour market status relies on administrative records obtained from third-party reports (which means that employers or unemployment offices, for example, are required to inform authorities about their employees/clients – the information

Table 2.3 Summary of a selection of other available registers from Statistics Denmark

Register	*Availability*	*Variables*
Demographic register	1980–	Unique individual identifier, date of birth, gender, ethnicity, parental identifiers, marital status, date of marriage (divorce), household identifier, municipality of residence, parish of residence
Housing register	1981–	Unique individual identifier, unique address identifier, size of home, type of ownership, municipality, city/town identifiers
Educational register	1981–	Unique individual identifier, completed educations, years of completed schooling, education enrollment, education drop out, unique school identifier
Labour force register	1980–	Unique individual identifier, labour market status (employment, unemployment, out of labour force, details about status)
Birth register	1973–	Unique individual identifier, birth weight, gestational length, various birth statistics. Also includes parental identifiers
Death register	1970–	Unique individual identifier, date of death, cause of death
Day care register	1995–	Unique individual identifier, identifier of day care or not (and during schooling ages: after-school care or not), unique institution identifier
Reception of transfers	1991–	Unique individual identifier, weekly information on main reception of public transfer for all Danes receiving public benefits
Income register (annual)	1980–	Unique individual identifier, detailed information of income (+assets/wealth) reported from tax authorities
E-income register (monthly)	2008–	Unique individual identifier, detailed information of income+ employment (from 2006) reported from tax authorities
Occupation register	1980–	Unique individual identifier, detailed information of type of occupation
Hospital admission register*	1991–	Unique individual identifier, information of hospital contacts/admissions (date), diagnosis, hospital identifier, type of treatment, number of contacts to other specialists, contact with GPs
Grades, final exam 9th grade	2002–	Unique individual identifier, grades from final year of compulsory schooling (by subject, test type, etc.)
Grades, high school	1997–	Unique individual identifier, all grades from high school
Test scores grade 2–8	2008–	Unique individual identifier, Danish (grades 2, 4, 6, 8), math (grades 3, 6), English (grade 7), natural sciences (grade 8), self-rated wellbeing, absenteeism
Psychiatric hospital register*	1991–	Unique individual identifier, information of hospital contacts/admissions (date), diagnosis, type of treatment, hospital identifier
Foster care register*	1980–	Unique individual identifier, type of foster care, date of care start/end

* Access to register restricted such that it is not straightforward to merge to all of the other data.

does not come from individuals themselves). Labour market status can be obtained from at least three different sources. First, the labour force register measures each citizen's primary labour market status on the last day of November each year. The level of measurement follows the International Classification of Status in Employment, which is proposed by the International Labour Organisation (ILO) to secure comparability across countries. Values include employed, unemployed (but employable), and people outside the labour force (who are not expected to be able to take up employment). The group of employed people can be subdivided by level of skills required to take up the employment which they hold, again following the definitions from ILO: the International Standard Classification of Occupations. Second, since 2008 the Danish Customs and Tax Administration has measured monthly employment information in the e-income register, including the amount earned during the month in each job a person holds and the number of hours worked during the month in each job a person holds (before 2008, only yearly income measures were available). Third, labour market status may also be obtained from the DREAM register (reception of transfers) which is compiled from information from the Danish Ministry of Employment, the Danish Ministry of Education, and the Danish Customs and Tax Administration. This register measures the primary type of public benefit a person receives each week and allows researchers to distinguish between people on (different types of) social assistance, on education benefits, in job training, on early retirement, on sickness leave, on parental leave, and so on. This register only covers people who receive public benefits, and it is thus important to note that people who are not in this register either hold employment or are self-employed (meaning that they do not have a job yet do not receive any public benefits; a group that is likely to be small in Denmark).

Context: Denmark

Danish register data are, as mentioned, not a dataset or part of any specific study. They are simply the totality of the information which various agencies in Denmark collect on residents and make available for research. The context from which the data come is thus, broadly speaking, Denmark since the 1980s. Denmark is a geographically small and socially homogenous country with strong welfare institutions and one of the lowest levels of social inequality in the world (with the third lowest Gini coefficient among OECD countries in 2013, 0.254, which may be compared to the OECD average of 0.318 and 0.394 for the United States, OECD 2016).

Like so many other countries, family formation, which is particularly important when we focus on intergenerational transmission, has changed in Denmark over the past decades in accordance with the second demographic transition (Sobotka 2008). In the 1980s, for example, 48 per cent of children were born in marriage. In 2015, the number was 36 per cent (Table FAM44B from Statistics Denmark, available on www.statistikbanken.dk). Also, people's age when they first become parents increased over the same period, from 24.6 years in the early 1980s to 29.1 years in 2015 for mothers (Table FOD11 from Statistics Denmark, available on www.statistikbanken.dk). Age at first birth has been shown to matter for children's risk of criminal conviction (Coyne, Långström, Rickert, and Lichtenstein 2013), and is also likely to matter for children's risk of experiencing parental offending and contact with the criminal justice system, simply because more children are now born after their parents' criminality has peaked in the early 20s (Lizotte, Phillips, Krohn, Thornberry, Bushway, and Schmidt 2015).

The criminal landscape in Denmark has changed since the early 1980s, too. Not only have crime and incarceration rates fluctuated according to societal developments, as they have in all countries, but a number of important policy reforms have changed the character of contact with the criminal justice system which parents may experience. Changes have been particularly impactful and rapid since the turn of the century, and reforms have gradually replaced the use of imprisonment with noncustodial alternatives for sentences up to six months (see Andersen, Andersen, Fitzpatrick, and Wildeman, forthcoming, for descriptions of the main policy changes). Many offenders in Denmark may thus be eligible for serving their prison sentence in non-custodial alternatives, as sentences are generally short. The shortest prison sentence is seven days, around two out of three sentences are three months or shorter, and as little as one in four sentences exceed six months (Danish Prison and Probation Service 2016). In international comparison, the Danish incarceration rate is among the lowest, at 61 per 100,000 (including pretrial detention and arrestees), which may be compared to 698 per 100,000 in the United States and 84 per 100,000 in Europe, all numbers from 2015 (Walmsley 2016).

Figure 2.1 shows trends in sanction rates in Denmark during 1980–2016, and depicts, per 10,000 in the population, the number of people sentenced to imprisonment, probation, and to other sanctions (excluding fines, see figure note; the "other sanctions" category entails, for example, special youth sanctions under the social services but also the treatment of mentally ill offenders). Cases are categorized by the most serious sanction, and cases in the "Prison" category could thus also include a period of probation or the like. Although there is some fluctuation in the rates over the period, the general impression from the figure is that the rates are quite stable. Rates of imprisonment and probation did increase during the 1980s and early 1990s, as has also been seen in other countries, yet from that point the rates have slowly declined. In 2016, 23 per 10,000 were sentenced to imprisonment and 12 per 10,000 were sentenced to no more than probation.

Around one out of three of incarcerated people in Denmark is detained pretrial (Smith and Jakobsen 2017; note that this type of incarceration is not counted in Figure 2.1). In this area of criminal justice policy, Denmark – like the other Scandinavian countries – differs from other countries, too, although in the opposite direction of what one might expect considering the comparatively

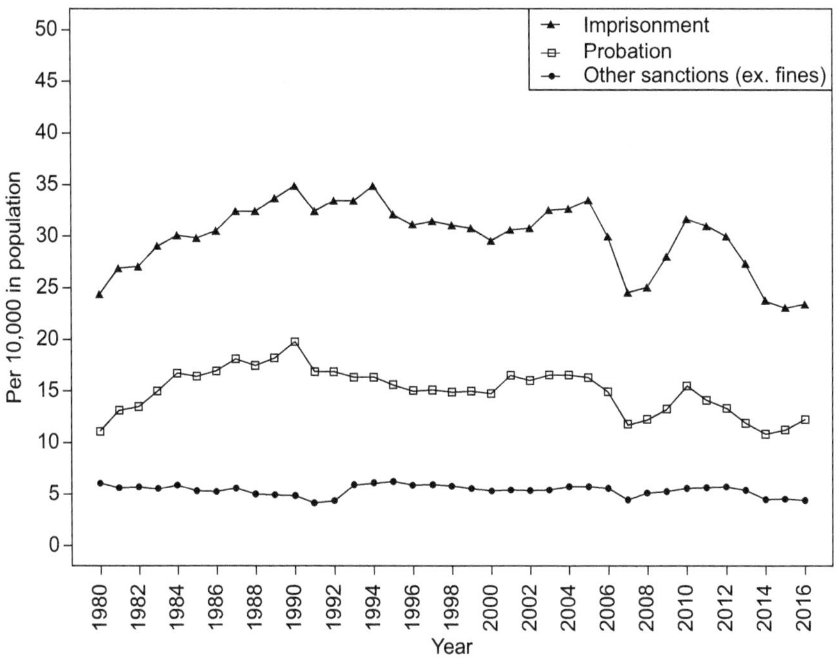

Figure 2.1 Trends in sanction rates (by 10,000 in population), Denmark 1980–2016

Note: Own calculations on data from Statistics Denmark (Tables STRAF40 and FOLK2 available online at http://statistikbanken.dk). Categories refer to the most serious sanction on a case, and cases in the "Prison" category may for example also include periods of probation. Fines are excluded because the amount of registered fines varies over time due to the registration practices described in the Act on Processing Personal Information in the Central Criminal Justice Register, see section "Data on Intergenerational Transmission in Offending" in this chapter.

short prison sentences. Pretrial detention in Denmark rests on a tradition of separating suspected offenders from others to avoid collusion (i.e., to avoid that suspects interfere with police investigations). This implies that most pretrial detainees in Denmark are placed in solitary confinement–like cells for most hours of the day; they can only take up employment which can be carried out in the cell; and many are not allowed family contact without strict surveillance (Smith 2012; Smith and Jakobsen 2017). Pretrial incarceration in Denmark has to be validated by a judge every four weeks but suspects are often detained pretrial for substantial periods, and more than one in four pretrial detention spells exceeds three months and are on average half a year (Smith and Jakobsen 2017).

Denmark thus represents an extreme country for the study of the intergenerational transmission of offending and contact with the criminal justice system, in the sense that Denmark is small, homogenous, with changing family dynamics, and with low levels of incarceration and social inequality – but with harsh conditions of pretrial incarceration. It is important to keep these contextual factors in mind when one wants to extrapolate results from Denmark to other contexts. Even though Danish register data are a unique source of data, they describe life and social processes within the somewhat extreme context that was just described, which could well have implications for the generalizability of results.

Showcasing the flexibility of Danish register data

Even though Danish register data are a great data source, these data have only recently been used to study the intergenerational transmission of offending and contact with the criminal justice system. The studies which do exist provide important advancements to research on the consequences of parental (paternal) incarceration in particular.

One set of studies exploits the fact that so much information may be combined at the individual level and provides detailed descriptive evidence on how children respond to parental incarceration and contact with the criminal justice system. One example is Andersen (2016), a study which analyses the association between the frequency and duration of paternal incarceration and children's educational outcomes and criminality. The study follows the 1991 birth cohort up to age 20, and adds information on these children's exposure to paternal incarceration as well as whether the children were convicted of violating the Penal Code, whether they were convicted of violent crimes, whether they experienced any incarceration (including jail stays shorter than 24 hours), whether they were sentenced to imprisonment, the share of elementary school exams that the children failed, and whether they dropped out of high school, all cumulated at age 20. Two main results emerge from the study. First, paternal incarceration is not something children either experience or not. In fact, around half of the children in the Andersen (2016) sample who did experience paternal incarceration did so more than once, and around 13 per cent of them experienced it five times or more. A similar result was found for duration of paternal incarceration, and children thus differ in the total duration of paternal incarceration experiences. Second, the associations between frequency and duration of paternal incarceration and the mentioned educational outcomes and criminality of the children are strong – suggesting worse outcomes for children who experience more or longer paternal incarceration spells – and persist even after controlling for the confounding role of a wide array of individual, parental, and family characteristics. Another example is Olsen (2014) who uses data on nine birth cohorts (1982–1990) in 2008 to analyze the development in parental incarceration in Denmark and its link to social inequality. She finds a strong correlation between family income and parental incarceration, something which adds to existing social disadvantage for these families. Wildeman, Andersen, Lee, and Karlson (2014) use register data on the full 1991 birth cohort to analyze the link between parental incarceration and child mortality up to age 20. Controlling for a range of sociodemographic characteristics, they find no association for girls but higher mortality rates among boys who experienced parental incarceration. Also, Wildeman and Andersen (2015) use Danish register data and information from published studies from the United States to display the gap in children's cumulative risk of experiencing paternal and maternal incarceration in Denmark and the United States. They find that rates of parental incarceration differ drastically between these two countries, which was expected since the United States and Denmark represent the most punitive and one of the least punitive countries.

Another set of studies exploit the flexibility of Danish register data and the policy changes that have characterized the penal landscape in Denmark since the year 2000. Because of the nature of the register data, researchers may select relevant samples of offenders just before and after a policy reform, which is a very powerful tool for policy analysis. Policy analyses of this and similar designs have recently become common in criminological research in Denmark (e.g., Andersen 2015; Andersen and Andersen 2014; Fallesen and Andersen 2017; Landersø 2015; Larsen 2017). But turning to intergenerational transmission, the amount of existing research that relies on policy changes is not impressive. Two studies are notable exceptions, both relying on data around the timing of a policy reform which expanded the use of community service as a noncustodial alternative to imprisonment in 2000. Andersen and Wildeman (2014) exploit the policy reform to identify a causal effect of paternal incarceration on children's risk of being placed in foster care, using an instrumental variable approach. And Wildeman and Andersen (2017) prove that the link between paternal incarceration and sons' risk of being charged with crimes in young adulthood is indeed causal. This study uses a difference-in-differences framework to compare charge rates at age 22–28 among children (age 12–18 years) whose fathers were sentenced before the penal reform (and who were all imprisoned) and after it (of whom some were eligible for the non-custodial sentence instead of imprisonment because of the reform). Charge rates among boys with fathers in the latter group were lower than among boys with fathers in the former group. No effect was found for girls. Importantly, the empirical setup and the applied statistical model ensure that results are not driven by time trends or by unobserved differences between the two groups of children. Because of their rigorous research designs and their access to flexible and accurate data around policy reforms, these studies thus add significant empirical evidence to some of the most important debates in research on intergenerational transmission of contact with the criminal justice system: debates over correlation versus causation.

The future of research on intergenerational transmission

The current state of criminological research on intergenerational transmission using Danish register data may best be described as emerging. Despite the uniquely good data source which Danish register data are, criminological research, and research on the intergenerational transmission of offending and contact with the criminal justice system in particular, that uses these data is still very new. But as a growing number of researchers now devote themselves to using these register data in the study of criminological issues, there is reason for optimism.

And, in my opinion, there are ample reasons for devoting research attention to the intergenerational transmission of offending and contact with the criminal justice system using Danish register data. At a point when research has established many key aspects of the parent–child correlation in offending and risk of ending up in contact with the criminal justice system, it seems about time to begin broadening our research scope and take influences from the broader family and demographic context into account. Punishment and criminal offending matter for families, and families matter for how and why punishment and criminal offending transmit through generations. Therefore, it is essential that we analyse the social distribution not only of criminal behaviour and punishment but also of family formation processes which may or may not matter for (1) children's risk of experiencing parental offending and contact with the criminal justice system and (2) children's chances of coping with or risk of suffering from these experiences.

A few very recent studies advance research along these lines using Danish register data. First, Fallesen and Andersen (2017) establish that incarceration indeed has a causal effect on men's singlehood and relationship dissolution rates. This study relies on a sample of comparable men from before and after a penal policy reform in 2008 which expanded the use of home confinement under electronic monitoring as a noncustodial alternative to imprisonment. Men sentenced before the reform, and who were all imprisoned for their crimes, had higher singlehood rates following their sentence than men who were sentenced after the reform (and of whom some served their sentence at home under electronic monitoring). The same result was found for men who were in a relationship at the time of the sentence. Importantly, during the years before the sentence, rates of singlehood were identical for men sentenced before and after the reform – yet the authors still apply a difference-in-differences setup to ensure that general time trends do not affect results. The Fallesen and Andersen (2017) study thus shows that incarceration has a profound impact on dynamics within families, and indeed increases relationship dissolution rates; something which could matter for children's wellbeing (e.g., Lee and McLanahan 2015). The findings in Fallesen and Andersen (2017) promote the fear that effects of incarceration could accumulate disadvantage and criminality in families – which again could have severe consequences for social inequality.

Second, another way in which criminality tends to concentrate in family networks is through the social processes which family dynamics spur. A recent study (Andersen 2017) uses Danish register data to show that influences from the wider social network one is exposed to through marriage may matter for criminal desistance. Not only does assortative mating (non-random partner selection) tend to pair spouses from families in which crime runs (thus concentrating criminality in families), but the influence of spousal criminality or criminality in the wider family network matters for men's criminal desistance, too (thus promoting criminality even more in those families; Andersen, Andersen, and Skov 2015; Andersen 2017).

The wider social context and family networks which parents and their children are part of may thus matter for the intergenerational transmission of offending and contact with the criminal justice system. We should analyse these mechanisms in more depth. And, as mentioned, this is where a major advantage of Danish register data presents itself: the possibility to gather information on family trees rather than just parent–child relationships. The recent studies that were just mentioned tend to focus on one specific attribute of family trees, criminality. Yet the social stratification literature (e.g., Jæger 2012) urges us to include prosocial attributes of family members into our analyses, too. Prosocial attributes in family networks, such as having a well-educated aunt or uncle, could help explain why it is far from all children who grow up in families with contact with the criminal justice system who end up experiencing such contact themselves. Again, families are not closed social units, and positive as well as negative influences from the wider family network could matter for children's wellbeing.

Despite the advantages, Danish register data come with the disadvantage that all information in the data is administrative and all variables essentially contain administrative definitions. This implies that all measures are administratively defined, expressing system contact and measuring objective statuses such as labour market status, years of education, and criminal conviction. Such information is important for measuring of how people fare in important domains of life. But Danish register data lack theoretically derived measures, such as measures of self-control, delinquency, and attitudes, which are very important to antisocial processes, and which are often obtained from surveys. The data thus include information on whether people hold employment or not, yet they do not provide information on attitudes or people's feelings.

Statistics Denmark does allow researchers, however, to merge surveys onto the register data, which opens a potentially fruitful avenue of research (Statistics Denmark even offers to sample and survey specific subpopulations, in addition to their ongoing general survey of the population, ensuring high levels of sampling accuracy and data which are directly combinable with the registers, see http://dst.dk/en/TilSalg/interview). This possibility could, for example, allow researchers to answer fundamentally important research questions related to qualitative aspects of how contact with the criminal justice systems concentrates in family networks, and how different extended and/or immediate family members might mitigate some of the consequences of contact with the criminal justice system for other family members, such as children.

As a first step, however, and in my opinion, we should exploit the richness of the data which are already at hand. No matter whether researchers focus on intergenerational associations or aim to provide causal estimates of these associations, Danish register data offer unique possibilities for unfolding analyses to include not only bi-generational relations within immediate families, as has often been done in the existing literature. Advances in the field of intergenerational transmission of offending and contact with the criminal justice system should include the analysis of mechanisms which extend to several generations and mechanisms which extend beyond the immediate family, something Danish register data may be used for. Research in these issues using these data is new, but growing, and there is reason to continue our efforts to advance knowledge using this approach (simply because there are still so many unanswered questions in this area of research). The data have been lying around for years – but the time has come to put them to use.

References

Andersen, L.H. (2016) 'How Children's Educational Outcomes and Criminality Vary by Duration and Frequency of Paternal Incarceration', *The ANNALS of the American Academy of Political and Social Science*, 665(1): 149–170. Doi 10.1177/0002716216632782.

Andersen, L.H. (2017) 'Marriage, in-Laws, and Crime: The Case of Delinquent Brothers-in-Law', *Criminology*, online first: 1–27. Doi 10.1111/1745-9125.12137.

Andersen, L.H. and Andersen, S.H. (2014) 'Effect of Electronic Monitoring on Social Welfare Dependence', *Criminology & Public Policy*, 13(3): 349–379. Doi 10.1111/1745-9133.12087.

Andersen, S.H. (2015) 'Serving Time or Serving the Community? Exploiting a Policy Reform to Assess the Causal Effects of Community Service on Income, Social Benefit Dependency and Recidivism', *Journal of Quantitative Criminology*, 31(4): 537–563. Doi 10.1007/s10940-014-9237-2.

Andersen, S.H., Andersen, L.H., Fitzpatrick, M.D. and Wildeman, C. (forthcoming) 'How Alternatives to Imprisonment Could Affect Child Well-Being', in Wildeman, C., Haskins, A.R. and Poehlmann-Tynan, J. (eds.) *When Parents Are Incarcerated: Interdisciplinary Research and Interventions to Support Children*, Washington, DC: American Psychological Association Press.

Andersen, S.H., Andersen, L.H. and Skov, P.E. (2015) 'Effect of Marriage and Spousal Criminality on Recidivism', *Journal of Marriage and Family*, 77(2): 496–509. Doi 10.1111/jomf.12176.

Andersen, S.H. and Wildeman, C. (2014) 'The Effect of Paternal Incarceration on Children's Risk of Foster Care Placement', *Social Forces*, 93(1): 269–298. Doi 10.1093/sf/sou027.

Coyne, C.A., Långström, N., Rickert, M.E. and Lichtenstein, P. (2013) 'Maternal Age at First Birth and Offspring Criminality: Using the Children of Twins Design to Test Causal Hypotheses', *Development and Psychology*, 25(1): 17–35. Doi 10.1017/S0954579412000879.

Danish Prison and Probation Service. (2016) *Statistik 2015*, Report, Copenhagen: Danish Prison and Probation Service: 1–64.

Fallesen, P. and Andersen, L.H. (2017) 'Explaining the Consequences of Imprisonment for Union Formation and Dissolution in Denmark', *Journal of Policy Analysis and Management*, 36(1): 154–177. Doi 10.1002/pam.21933.

Jæger, M.M. (2012) 'The Extended Family and Children's Educational Success', *American Sociological Review*, 77(6): 903–922. Doi 10.1177/0003122412464040.

Landersø, R. (2015) 'Does Incarceration Length Affect Labor Market Outcomes?', *The Journal of Law and Economics*, 58(1): 205–234. Doi 10.1086/682911.

Larsen, B.Ø. (2017) 'Educational Outcomes after Serving with Electronic Monitoring: Results from a Natural Experiment', *Journal of Quantitative Criminology*, 33(1): 157–178. Doi 10.1007/s10940-016-9287-8.

Lee, D. and McLanahan, S. (2015) 'Family Structure Transitions and Child Development: Instability, Selection, and Population Heterogeneity', *American Sociological Review*, 80(4): 738–763. Doi 10.1177/0003122415592129.

Lizotte, A.J., Phillips, M.D., Krohn, M.D., Thornberry, T.P., Bushway, S.D. and Schmidt, N.M. (2015) 'Like Parent Like Child? The Role of Delayed Childrearing in Breaking the Link Between Parent's Offending and Their Children's Antisocial Behavior', *Justice Quarterly*, 32(3): 410–444. Doi 10.1080/07418825.2013.771206.

OECD. (2016) 'Income Inequality Remains High in the Face of Weak Recovery', *Income Inequality Update*, Centre for Opportunity and Equality, OECD: 1–6.

Olsen, R.F. (2014) 'Forældres fængsling – en stratificerende livsbegivenhed?', *Dansk Sociologi*, 25(1): 57–80.

Smith, P.S. (2012) 'A Critical Look at Scandinavian Exceptionalism: Welfare State Theories, Penal Populism and Prison Conditions in Denmark and Scandinavia', in Ugelvik, T. and Dullum, J. (eds.) *Penal Exceptionalism? Nordic Prison Policy and Practice*, London: Routledge.

Smith, P.S. and Jakobsen, J. (2017) *Varetægtsfængsling. Danmarks hårdeste straf?*, Copenhagen: Jurist-og økonomforbundets forlag.

Sobotka, T. (2008) 'The Diverse Faces of the Second Demographic Transition in Europe', *Demographic Research*, 19: 171–224. Doi 10.4054/DemRes.2008.19.8.

Walmsley, R. (2016) 'World Prison Population List: Eleventh Edition', *Institute for Criminal Policy Research*: 1–15.

Wildeman, C. and Andersen, L.H. (2015) 'Cumulative Risks of Paternal and Maternal Incarceration in Denmark and the United States', *Demographic Research*, 32: 1567–1580. Doi 10.4054/DemRes.2015.32.57.

Wildeman, C. and Andersen, S.H. (2017) 'Paternal Incarceration and Children's Risk of Being Charged by Early Adulthood: Evidence from a Danish Policy Shock', *Criminology*, 55(1): 32–58. Doi 10.1111/1745-9125.12124.

Wildeman, C., Andersen, S.H., Lee, H. and Karlson, K.B. (2014) 'Parental Incarceration and Child Mortality in Denmark', *American Journal of Public Health*, 104(3): 428–433. Doi 10.2105/AJPH.2013.301590.

Chapter 3

Studying the intergenerational transmission of crime with population data

The System of Social statistical Datasets (SSD) of Statistics Netherlands

Ruben van Gaalen and Gregory Besjes

The need for population-based data

The consequences of deviant behaviour of relatively small groups of parents can be great for their children. Social scientists face more and more difficulties in measuring all relevant sentiments and behaviours across the social spectrum of the Dutch population with conventional methods. Despite excellent nationwide cohort studies, Dutch survey research has suffered from decreasing participation rates for decades (Stoop 2005). In particular, the socially more deprived – those with low education levels, migrants and the unemployed – are of growing interest for policy makers, but are among those least likely to participate in surveys. It seems almost impossible to turn current trends of low response rates, especially among groups currently underrepresented in most survey studies. It is also difficult to study crime using surveys (only), as victims and offenders are often reluctant to report about deviant behaviours.

In order to advance our knowledge on the sources and intergenerational transmission of crime, population-based datasets can be very valuable, especially those that cover multiple birth cohorts over a long period of historical time, are intergenerational and contain detailed information about offending, as well as information on families of origin, labour market participation, income and educational attainment. In addition, policy makers are in need of population-based and detailed information on very specific subgroups within Dutch society. Most social problems (e.g., poverty, unemployment, divorce, health problems, crime) cumulate within persons, households, and families or particular regions, and most policy efforts and monetary means flow in the direction of these relatively small groups. Relying solely on conventional survey research, which is very expensive and has low participation rates among these groups, does not give the best information.

In this chapter, we provide a general picture of the extent to which offending is transmitted over generations, controlled for demographic and socioeconomic confounders of criminal behaviours of parents, using population-based data on both parents and children in the Netherlands. First, we will give an introduction of the Dutch System of Social statistical Datasets (SSD) hosted by Statistics Netherlands. Second, we will give an overview of the data on crime and the possible determinants of criminal behaviours that are in the SSD. Third, we will present an example of a study on the intergenerational transmission of crime conducted with the SSD. Last, we will discuss limitations and pitfalls as well as promising possibilities for future scientific research using these data.

The Dutch System of Social statistical Datasets (SSD)

Statistics Netherlands is one of the frontrunners among statistical institutes internationally in terms of both the access and use of its microdata for scientific research. Statistics Netherlands has become a global leader, together with the Scandinavian countries, in using register or administrative data for national statistics, as well as for scientific and social policy–driven research. The SSD is an integrated, longitudinal system of registers and surveys, containing important socioeconomic, demographic, health, crime, income and wealth variables of the complete population of the Netherlands, including day-by-day information on co-residence, marriage and parenthood and detailed information on parents, children, siblings, partners, colleagues, companies, communities and neighbours (Bakker, Van Rooijen and Van Toor 2014; see Box 3.1 and also Appendix 3.A).

Although the SSD has information on all 17 million people who currently live in the Netherlands, with records that stretch back over decades, the SSD is still relatively 'young', as the backbone, the electronic population register, started in October 1994. Statistics Netherlands has the ambition to further develop the SSD and provide greater integration with the Dutch community of large data collections (both surveys and registers). The development of the SSD has had a great impact on the way information is gathered and statistics are produced within Statistics Netherlands. The SSD consists of a library of standardized and linked statistical registers, as well as an organization which has been put in place to control various aspects of the system. It has made an invaluable set of registers readily accessible to researchers and has resulted in many valuable publications (Bakker, Van Rooijen and Van Toor 2014: 422).

Currently, administrative data originating from public institutions such as the tax office, banks, municipalities, educational institutes, the Employee Insurance Agency, and hospitals can be accessed on-site within Statistics Netherlands by external researchers, but there is also a possibility to access the data at the

Box 3.1 SSD information at a glance

Demographic (daily)

Examples: Nationality, country of birth, year and month of birth, gender, marital status, position in household, partner (no partner, cohabitation, marriage), cause of death, household type, household composition, number of children in household

Socioeconomic (monthly/yearly)

Examples: Being enrolled in education, receiving scholarship, Standard Classification of Education, year/stage of education, educational attainment, personal income, having a job, wages, hours worked, temporary or permanent labour contract, employee type, collective labour agreement, company car, discharge reason, being self-employed, operating profit, industrial classification (NACE), receiving social security benefit, type of benefit (income support, unemployment, disablement, survivor, benefits from abroad, other), amount received, receiving pension, type of pension (state or employer pension), household disposable income, household wealth and debts, registered at employment agency, desired working hours

Other (yearly)

Examples: Building taxation value, rented or owner-occupied home, type of home, energy label, regional classifications, geographic coordinates, crime reports (police/courts; see next section), registered as medical practitioner, medical profession, hospitalizations, number of hospitalizations, number of days in hospital, owning a vehicle

Entities and levels

Individuals, relationships (parent–child, siblings, partners, colleagues, neighbours), households, families, schools, universities, penitentiaries, firms, neighbourhoods, municipalities, NUTS3, provinces

institute of the researcher through a remote access option. This university or institute can also be located outside of the Netherlands. Strict protection of privacy and confidentiality is guaranteed by a number of administrative procedures and technical measures, such as a special secured remote access environment that can be accessed via one's own computer.

Register data on crime suspects, convicted and incarcerated

Police registers of crime suspects

The *HKS registration of crime suspects (1996–2014)* contains a selection of police detection systems variables that detect all suspects against whom a criminal record has been made. The *GIDS registration of crime-related incidents (2005–present)* is a more recent database that contains a selection of variables from the Police (Integrated Interactive Database for Strategic Business Information) Registration System, which records all persons who are reasonably suspected of being guilty of a crime. All persons have recorded how often and what crime they were suspected of. Each record represents a registered crime suspect. The GIDS contains more detailed information on the types of offences. The HKS is older and therefore more suitable for studies on the intergenerational transmission of crime. Whether both sources can be integrated is unclear. They seem similar but are quite different sources. The HKS was a suspect registration system, whereas the GIDS is an incident registration system. In the HKS, only arrested persons were registered. In the GIDS, any person who has been identified as a suspect in an incident has been registered – even if there are no sufficient grounds for arrest. For now, Statistics Netherlands focusses on the latest and more complete register (GIDS), but future research on the parent–child transmission of crime could profit from the extended time frame of a combined file (1996–present).

Court registers on convicted

The *court registers (1982–present)* contain information on the manner of handling of criminal cases by the district attorney (OM) and the judge. In the past, the flow of information to Statistics Netherlands merely served statistical purposes (descriptive publications). From the early 1990s, the data on crime and criminal justice from the Communications System Public Prosecutor's Office Administration, shortly referred to as COMPAS, have been delivered to Statistics Netherlands. The Public Prosecution Service has developed the Integrated Processing System (GPS) in recent years to replace COMPAS (2008). Since 2015, data from the GPS on inflow and decisions of the OM has been delivered to the CBS from the OM data warehouse system Phoenix. Especially the microdata of the recent years can be analysed. Although data on convictions and settlements might be better than data on crime suspects, the content and quality of these registers changed over time and the time window is much too short for the study of the transmission of crime over generations. In the near future, microdata on convictions will be transferred to the CBS and probably will go back to 2003.

Registers on incarcerated

A special group within the convicted population is formed by those who are sentenced to go to prison. The *DJI incarcerated register (2005–present)* provides the CBS with three types of registers: all persons entering a particular year in detention, all persons leaving detention in a particular year and all persons in prison on December 31 of a particular year. For every person the most serious offense for which that person was detained in the year in question is determined. The crimes are classified according to the Standard Classification Crimes 2010. In most cases, the most severe offense is determined correctly. However, a person may be punished within one detention for several offenses. In some cases, the heaviest crime cannot be registered in the source files and a person receives a lighter crime as the heaviest crime. These data can be very suitable if one is interested in the determinants and consequences of being in prison, but not for the general study on the intergenerational transmission of crime.

Registers on youth offenders

The *Halt (The ALTernative) register (2005–present)* contains information on young offenders (12–18 years old), who have been sentenced to follow a special trajectory or intervention. How often youngsters were referred to Halt and for what type of crime they first came into contact with Halt are registered. Halt offers young people the opportunity to correct their criminal behaviour without having long-term consequences. If a young person completes the Halt penalty properly, he or she avoids a legal note. That does not mean that a Halt penalty is free of charge: if a youngster does not participate in his Halt punishment, he or she will still be in contact with Justice. Of the Halt cases registered annually, about 10 per cent of young people have previously had a Halt intervention and around 2 per cent twice.

Example using crime suspects

In our example study, we investigate the association between criminal behaviour of parents and their children as young adults. This study is a slightly different version of an earlier published paper in Dutch (Besjes and Van Gaalen 2008). Our data allow us to take all registered criminal activities of the parents into account when their children are small and the household composition and the socioeconomic circumstances of the family. Our data enable us to distinguish between fathers and mothers.

Intergenerational transmission

Studies on the intergenerational transmission of criminal behaviour show clear relationships: Children of criminal parents are far more likely to become offenders themselves (see Van de Rakt, Nieuwbeerta and De Graaf 2008; Murray, Janson and Farrington 2007; Hirschi and Laub 2002; Van de Weijer 2014). But how does intergenerational transmission of criminal behaviour work? We focus on two potential mechanisms: status transmission and socialisation (Liefbroer and Dykstra 2007).

Status transmission is the transfer of certain characteristics of parents on children that will influence their future limitations and possibilities in life. The reproduction of genetic, social, cultural and financial resources enables children to develop themselves (De Graaf and Kalmijn 2001; Nagel and Ganzeboom 2002; Boomsma et al. 2005). Crime is more prevalent in the lower classes than in the middle or upper classes (Jennissen and Blom 2007). An unemployed parent and a low household income are not only associated with a higher risk of the parents committing a crime, but also with a decreasing level of social control over the behaviours of children (closure) (Salmi and Kiviuori 2006; Hirschi and Laub 2002).

Socialization theory assumes that children conform their behaviour to their parents' because of learning processes (Bandura 1977). This partly explains the finding that children and parents often choose the same studies and profession (Van de Werfhorst, De Graaf and Kraaykamp 2001). The association between parental divorce and behavioural problems of children has been found in many studies (e.g., Amato and Cheadle 2008). The availability of both parents in the household increases the probability that children stay on the right track.

Mothers play an important role in families (Rosenthal 1985). The negative consequences of criminal behaviour of mothers on children may be stronger than in the case of criminal fathers. Furthermore, criminal mothers form a very select group, since far more fathers get arrested than mothers (Van Gaalen 2016). In addition, we expect that the effect of first-offending parents will be small compared to that of parents who are frequent offenders.

Data

We use the HKS register in this study, because these data go back until 1996. When we use terms like 'committed a crime', 'crime suspect' or 'contact with the police' etc., we always mean that someone has a police record. Our dataset contains information on 939,600 young adults and their parents; these are all 18- to 22-year-olds (born 1983–1987) living in the Netherlands in 2005. The main question is whether parental criminal activities before the child turned 17 can be associated with criminal behaviour of the child between the ages of 18 and 22. This means that for the parents register information is used from 1996 onwards, until the child turned 17 (in 1999–2003). We take into account the characteristics of the household in which the child lived at the age of 16.

Analysis

The influence of parental criminal behaviour is operationalized in three ways. First, we consider whether the parent was ever suspected of a crime (1) or not (0). Second, we consider the number of times a parent was suspected of a crime before the child turned 17 in four categories: never (0), once (1), between 2 and 9 times (3), and more than 10 times (4). Third, we consider the type of crime the parent committed. In the analyses we concentrated on young adults aged between 18 and 22 in 2005. In 2005, there were almost 940,000 young adults in the Netherlands. This age group was chosen for several reasons. First, this age group forms the top of the age–crime curve: the percentage of offences is the highest between 18 and 22. The intergenerational transfer of crime should be most visible in this age group. Moreover, everyone over 18 is considered and treated as an adult in the criminal law system.

Results

It turned out that 6.0 per cent of the children had a father and 1.6 per cent had a mother who had been in contact with the police (Table 3.1). Over 50 per cent of these fathers and 60 per cent of these mothers had only been a crime suspect once, while almost 12 per cent of these fathers committed more than 10 crimes. Over 80 per cent of the suspected fathers and almost 90 per cent of the suspected mothers were suspected of property offences without violence, traffic offences, or public safety violations. In our sample, 0.7 per cent of the children had both a father and a mother who came into contact with the police. We present no percentages on the number or the nature of the offences for this group, because the categories used cannot be assigned to the parents.

In 2005, 12.4 per cent of the young adults aged between 18 and 22 in the period from 1996 had been suspected of an offence. Fathers and sons were considerably more often suspected of an offence than mothers and daughters. Almost 20 per cent of the sons between 18 and 22 were ever recorded in police registrations, against about 5 per cent of the daughters.

Table 3.1 reveals a clear association between criminal activities of parents and children. First, about 11 per cent of the children of whom the parents never were suspected of an offence could be found in HKS registrations. Most of these children had been registered only once as a suspect when they were aged 18 and 22 (60.7 per cent). If the mother was the only parent with a criminal record, the percentage of children ever suspected of a crime is 32.2 per cent. About 15 per cent of them have 10 offences or more. The association with the father's criminal activities is weaker: almost a quarter (23.5 per cent) of the children comes into contact with the police if only the father was suspect of an offence. More than 11 per cent have 10 offences or more, and 40.9 per cent of the 18–22 age group of whom both parents have been crime suspects committed an offence. Almost 18 per cent fall in the category with more than 10 offences.

Table 3.1 Police registrations (suspects) of parents and their children (aged 18–22)*

	N	*Ever*	*Number of offences (%)*		
		(%)	*Once*	*2–9 times*	*> 9 times*
Parents (from 1996 until child turned 17)					
Only father	890,200	6,0	50,6	37,8	11,6
Only mother	931,800	1,6	60,3	35,1	4,6
Both	882,500	0,7	–	–	–
Children					
Child	939,600	12.4	58.4	34.2	7.4
Son	479,900	19.8	55.0	36.4	8.6
Daughter	459,600	4.8	73.0	24.8	2.2
Child without suspect parents	865,700	11.2	60.7	32.9	6.4
Child with only suspect father	53,300	23.5	47.9	40.4	11.7
Child with only suspect mother	14,700	32.2	42.7	41.7	15.6
Child with suspect father and mother	5,900	40.9	38.8	43.6	17.6

Source: System of social Statistical Datasets (SSD)

* The percentages do not add up to 100 because someone may have committed several offences.

Multivariate analyses

Using logistic regression analysis we estimate the relative probability that a young adult has ever been suspected of an offence, taking into account several background variables. These are sex and year of birth of the child and whether the child lived in the father's or mother's household (1) or not (0), the year of birth of the parent, the total household income, the number of children in the household and whether the parents lived on social security benefits (1) or not (0). The results of the analyses are transformed into odds ratios and 95 per cent confidence intervals. Within population data, any difference could be argued to be relevant. However, because one could also state that population data represent a sample within time, we do report whether an effect is statistically significant ($p < .001$).

Table 3.2 reflects the results of multivariate analyses. The intergenerational transmission of crime is clear, and strongest from mothers to children. If both parents were crime suspects while bringing up the child, then the probability of the child committing a crime as a young adult is five times higher than for other children.

After correction for background characteristics, the correlation between criminal activities in two successive generations decreased, but did not disappear. The Nagelkerke R^2, which represents the explained variance by the

Table 3.2 The likelihood of an offence of young adults (18–22 years) in 2005

Intergenerational transmission	*Only father*	*95% C.I.*			*95% C.I.*		*Only mother*	*95% C.I.*			*95% C.I.*	
	OR	*Lower*	*Upper*	*OR*	*Lower*	*Upper*	*OR*	*Lower*	*Upper*	*OR*	*Lower*	*Upper*
Parent never suspect from 1996 until child turned 17 (reference category)	1.00			1.00			1.00			1.00		
Parent suspect from 1996 until child turned 17	2.47*	2.41	2.52	1.55*	1.49	1.61	3.36*	3.24	3.48	1.65*	1.48	1.84
Household situation (child 16 years old)												
Child lived with father and mother (ref.)				1.00						1.00		
Child lived without parents				2.24*	2.09	2.41				2.18*	2.04	2.33
Child lived with father (not with mother)				1.75*	1.69	1.81				1.72*	1.66	1.78
Child lived with mother (not with father)				1.58*	1.55	1.61				1.55*	1.52	1.59
Parent suspect* lived with parent				1.32*	1.26	1.39				1.44*	1.28	1.61
Socio-economic situation household (child 16 years old)												
Household income less than 1,250 Euro				1.26*	1.23	1.30				1.35*	1.32	1.38
1,251–2,000 Euro				1.32*	1.29	1.35				1.35*	1.32	1.38
2,001–3,000 Euro (ref.)				1.00						1.00		
3,001–4,000 Euro				0.73*	0.89	0.93				0.91*	0.89	0.92
More than 4,000 Euro				0.73*	0.71	0.74				0.74*	0.72	0.75
Both parents no social security benefits (ref.)				1.00						1.00		
Unknown				1.18	0.91	1.52				1.38*	1.15	1.67
One parent social security benefits				1.46*	1.44	1.49				1.49*	1.46	1.51
Both parents social security benefits				2.30*	2.24	2.36				2.36*	2.30	2.42
Data one parent known: social security benefits				1.20*	1.13	1.28				1.55*	1.49	1.60
Data one parent known: no social security benefits				1.17*	1.12	1.23				1.60*	1.55	1.65
Gender												
Daughter (ref.)				1.00						1.00		
Son				5.74*	5.64	5.84				5.50*	5.39	5.56
Nagelkerke R^2	0.01			0.17			0.01			0.18		
N	939600						939600					

Source: System of social Statistical Datasets (SSD)

Controlled for birth year parents and children, number of children in household.

* $p < .001$

added variables, increases substantially: from 2 to 18 per cent. The transmission remains strongest if both parents were suspected of an offence. The transmission of crime from mother to child also is larger after controlling for the background variables than the transmission from father to child. Living with both parents (intact family) is negatively associated with the probability that the child becomes a suspect of an offence. If the child lived with the suspected parent at the age of 16, this increases the probability that the child will become a crime suspect. This association is also stronger for mothers than for fathers. The odds for a young adult sanctioned by the police are greatest if he or she did not live with the parents during childhood (OR = 2.24), greater than for all other living arrangements. The child is more likely to becoming a suspect of a crime if the parents have a low household income and/or the parents live on social security benefits. We can also confirm that young adult sons are much more likely to commit a crime then daughters. The interaction effects depict the combined effects of crime of the parent and the different parental structures during childhood. The highest odds for young adults to develop criminal activities are when the child lives with the criminal parent (and not with the other parent). The impact of parental crime seems to be stronger, measured by the transmission probability, if the child lives with that criminal parent.

Conclusion

The transmission of crime is found in more than 25 per cent of all father–child and almost 35 per cent of all mother–child dyads in which parents were ever suspected of a crime. If both parents were crime suspects, this percentage exceeds 40 per cent. We find a significant transmission of crime from parents to their children, even after controlling for important predictors of criminal behaviour such as divorce and the socioeconomic situation during childhood. The direct transfer of mothers on children is larger than those of fathers on children. The socioeconomic position of the family in which the children grew up (approached by the situation when the child was 16 years old) seems to reduce this impact to some extent, but it certainly does not disappear. A family where the father is absent during childhood increases the probability of criminal behaviour as a young adult. The transmission is stronger if the child lived with the parent who committed a crime. This confirms the importance of socialization and role modelling, besides genetic resemblance over generations. The intensity of criminal behaviour is important, too: the probability that children of parents who committed more than nine offences will commit a crime is much higher than for children of other parents.

A possible shortcoming of our study is that we do not take account clustering within families, although we have information on all parent–child relationships. The data enable to conduct multilevel analyses, so one could distinguish family-level and personal-level effects; for example, use the fact that the behavioural exposure varies among siblings. Second, other determinants of criminal behaviour are the influence of peer groups and personal characteristics such as reduced levels of self-control. And because the mechanisms behind social learning and social class are not fully independent of each other, interactions between class and criminal activities of parents may provide more insight into whether the transmission works differently in the lower and higher classes. We want to know why some children start a criminal career, whereas their siblings do not. We also want to include characteristics of the young adult (partner, educational level, income) in our analysis. It would also be interesting to investigate the association between the types of offences of the parents and the children. Finally, it would be interesting to distinguish biological from step ties. In general, what parts of the association we find are based on social learning, social class, and genetic resemblance?

Discussion

The register of crime suspects is of high quality but does not provide a complete picture of crime in the Netherlands. Data of the special investigation services (FIOD-ECD, Customs) often are not included so that various types of crimes, such as economic crimes, environmental offences or benefit fraud, are underrepresented in the data. Also, the data are on crime suspects and not on convicted criminals, although about 75 per cent of all suspects received a settlement from the district attorney (OM) or were found guilty by a judge. These records are then removed from the suspect file by the register holder (police). More than 95 per cent of all registered suspects can be linked to the SSD. Suspects are sometimes not found in the SSD when their personal data are incomplete or incorrectly recorded or if the suspects are not registered in the Municipal Administration (e.g., foreign residents). In addition, much criminal behaviour is not registered simply because criminals do not get caught by the police or because victims do not report crimes to the police. We probably underestimate the percentage of fathers and mothers on the registers of the Dutch police. And importantly, police data suffer from the 'dark number'.

From safety surveys we know that only 35 per cent of the incidents are reported to the police (Akkermans 2016). This seems alarming, but 60 per cent of the people who do not report say that the 'problem was solved', that it is 'not important' or that it is 'not a case for the police'. Another problem might be that, on average, only 25 per cent of the reported cases are solved. This percentage is higher with more severe incidents (e.g., violence, 60 per cent; thefts, 12 per cent). This means that crime registers on suspects are skewed towards more severe cases regarding the number (more) and type (violence) of offences. With regard to the study of parents and children, one could assume that the police might over-monitor criminal families, which would mean that the registered offences of parents and children are not entirely independent. However, we assume that the mechanisms under study are not systematically affected by these issues, although we cannot be too certain about that.

Recently, Van Ham, Bervoets and Ferwerda (2015) gave a general reflection on the usefulness of crime data retrieved form administrative sources. In general, societal developments in social standards can transfer normal behaviour into deviant behaviour and even into a criminal offence or, the other way around, normalize past offences. This should somehow be accounted for if we want to understand developments in the transmission probability across generations. Furthermore, the police are the first to register crime. This can be based on reports of victims or third parties or because police forces detect crimes themselves. However, not all reported and detected crimes are registered. Several factors could affect the completeness and reliability ('registration effect') of the police registration. There is a probability that a criminal offence is reported to the police (reporting probability), that the police detect crime (detection probability) and that the police will recognize and report it as a criminal offence (registration probability). The findings from the scientific overview in Van Ham, Bervoets and Ferwerda (2015) show that the characteristics of a person, crime and perpetrator affect the willingness to report. Female victims are more likely to go to the police than male victims, whereas adults are more likely to report than young adults and minors. There is also a higher probability of reporting if it has been committed by a group and results in an injury or damage of properties. The location of the crime also may play a role. Victims are more likely to report when a crime is committed in their own house or direct surroundings. Moreover, the reporting probability decreases when a minor is involved or the perpetrator is from within the inner circle of the victim. Additionally, the police work may also affect the willingness to report. When a victim is advised to report or if there are many ways to report (going to the police station, via internet), she or he is more willing to do so. Besides, if reporting takes too much time, the victim's willingness to report decreases. More police on the streets will result in a higher detection probability, although not all scientific literature is certain about this (Van Ham, Bervoets and Ferwerda 2015).

In sum, survey research is under pressure (response rates and costs), and it is hard to gather information on topics like crime or deviance in general. Despite the drawbacks and known problems with registers, we need population-based datasets that contain information about offending, family structure, labour market behaviour, income and educational attainment. We think that the data source we used in this study is very suitable for the study of the transmission of crime across generations. Further research is necessary though, possibly on the basis of a combination of registers and survey data to examine to what extent unobserved factors explain the found association between the criminal activities of parents and children. And regarding the quality of the data, in the future, all available register information on crime (suspects, convicted, incarcerated, victim and survey data) should be combined and micro-integrated, resulting in one longitudinal SSD crime database for the Netherlands.

References

Akkermans, M. (2016) 'Melding en aangifte van veelvoorkomende criminaliteit. Stand van zaken, trends en kenmerken', *Sociaaleconomische Trends*, 10, CBS Den Haag/Heerlen.

Amato, P.R. and Cheadle, J.E. (2008) 'Parental divorce, marital conflict and children's behavioral problems: A comparison of adopted and biological children', *Social Forces*, 86: 1139–1161.

Bakker, B.F.M., Van Rooijen, J., and Van Toor, L. (2014) 'The system of social statistical datasets of Statistics Netherlands: An integral approach to the production of register-based social statistics', *Statistical Journal of the IAOS*, 30: 411–424.

Bandura, A. (1977) *Social learning theory*, Upper Saddle River, NJ: Prentice Hall.

Besjes, G. and Van Gaalen, R. (2008) 'Jong geleerd, fout gedaan?', *Bevolkingstrends*, 56: 23–31, CBS Den Haag/Heerlen.

Boomsma, D.I., Willemsen, G., Dolan, C.V., Hawkley, L.C., and Cacioppo, J.T. (2005) 'Genetic and environmental contributions to loneliness in adults: The Netherlands twin register study', *Behavior Genetics*, 35: 745–752.

De Graaf, P.M. and Kalmijn, M. (2001) 'Trends in the intergenerational transmission of cultural and economic status', *Acta Sociologica*, 44: 51–66.

Hirschi, T. and Laub, J.H. (2002) *The craft of criminology: Selected papers*, Transaction Publishers.

Jennissen, R.P.W and Blom, M. (2007) *Allochtone en autochtone verdachten van verschillende delicttypen nader bekeken. Cahier 2007–4*. Voorburg/Den Haag: CBS/WODC.

Liefbroer, A.C. and Dykstra, P.A. (Eds.) (2007) 'Van generatie op generatie: Gelijkenis tussen ouders en kinderen', *Special Issue of Mens & Maatschappij*, 82.

Murray, J., Janson, C.-G., and Farrington, D.P. (2007) 'Crime in adult offspring of prisoners a cross-national comparison of two longitudinal Samples', *Criminal Justice and Behavior*, 34: 133–149.

Nagel, I. and Ganzeboom, H.B.G. (2002) 'Participation in legitimate culture: Family and school effects from adolescence to adulthood', *The Netherlands Journal of Social Sciences*, 38: 102–120.

Rosenthal, C.J. (1985) 'Kinkeeping in the familial division of labor', *Journal of Marriage and the Family*, 47: 965–974.

Salmi, V. and Kiviuori, J. (2006) 'The association between social capital and juvenile crime', *European Journal of Criminology*, 3: 123–148.

Stoop, I.A.L. (2005) *The hunt for the last respondent*, The Hague: Social and Cultural Planning Office.

Van de Rakt, M., Nieuwbeerta, P., and De Graaf, N.D. (2008) 'Like father, like son? The relationships between conviction trajectories of father and their sons and their daughters', *British Journal of Criminology*, 48: 538–556.

Van de Weijer, S.G.M. (2014) *The intergenerational transmission of violent crime*. PhD diss., VU University Amsterdam, the Netherlands.

Van de Werfhorst, H.G., De Graaf, N.D., and Kraaykamp, G. (2001) 'Intergenerational resemblance in field of study in the Netherlands', *European Sociological Review*, 17: 275–293.

Van Gaalen, R. (2016) 'Parental crime and the safety and survival of small children', *Advances in Life Course Research*, 28: 100–107.

Van Ham, T., Bervoets, E., and Ferwerda, H. (2015) *Een hypothesevormend onderzoek naar de invloed van registratie-effecten op de omvang van de geregistreerde jeugdcriminaliteit*, WODC, Ministerie van Veiligheid en Justitie.

Appendix 3.A

Description of independent variables used in the multivariate analysis

Household situation (child 16 years old)	*Percent (%)*
Child lived with father and mother	76.1
Child lived without parents	2.8
Child only lived with father	3.4
Child only lived with mother	17.7
Number of children in household (mean)	2.4
Socioeconomic situation household (child 16 years old)	
Household income less than 1,250 Euro	11.6
1,251–2,000 Euro	11.9
2,001–3,000 Euro	21.2
3,001–4,000 Euro	21.4
More than 4,000 Euro	33.9
Both parents no social security benefits	70.6
Unknown	0.7
One parent social security benefits	15.4
Both parents social security benefits	4.9
Data one parent known: social security benefits	4.8
Data one parent known: no social security benefits	3.6
Gender	
Daughter	48.9
Son	51.1

Part II

Studies using register data

Chapter 4

Exploring the life-course and intergenerational impact of convict transportation

Barry Godfrey, Kris Inwood and Hamish Maxwell-Stewart

In recent years, historians interested in the mechanisms by which outcomes for one generation might influence the life-courses of children and grandchildren have started to employ data sourced from criminal justice records. One reason for this is that they include data for women as well as men (Godfrey et al., 2007; Inwood and Maxwell-Stewart, 2016; Meredith and Oxley, 2015). Police, court and prison recording systems also have the advantage of noting socio-economic variables such as occupation, literacy and height, as well as criminal offending.

In this chapter, we describe early results stemming from analysis of data from two databases: Founders and Survivors and the Digital Panopticon. Between 1803 and 1853 over 72,000 convicts were transported to the British penal colony of Van Diemen's Land, later renamed Tasmania. Using the rich resources of the Tasmanian Archive and Heritage Office, volunteers have collected, collated, digitised and transcribed much of the information about these unwilling migrants. The Founders and Survivors project which created this database was a partnership among historians, volunteer genealogists, demographers and population health researchers recording the most complete descriptions of convicts when they arrived in Van Diemen's Land, whilst they served their sentence, when they were released under conditions and their lives when they were finally freed. As the Founders and Survivors website states:

> The records created of our convict founders are the most detailed descriptions of the bodies and lives of men, women and children created anywhere in the world in the 19th century. No other settler society has such a record of their founders' heights, eye colour, literacy, skills, family history, problems and temperament.
>
> (www.foundersandsurvivors.org/project)

These data have now been combined with additional record sets to form the Digital Panopticon. This very large database of millions of records reveals the pre-transportation offending and civil data (births, marriages, residence, occupation, family structure) of convicts, and also produces the same data for convicted felons who were never sent to Australia, but who served out their time in British convict prisons. Like Founders and Survivors, the Digital Panopticon recreates the life-courses of convicts. It follows approximately 90,000 men and women who were convicted at London's Central Criminal Court (the Old Bailey) between 1750 and 1925 through various record sets (over 60 in number) to record their lives before, during and after periods of offending (www.digitalpanopticon.org).

The individuals whose lives are reconstructed from these data are of particular interest to life-course and intergenerational researchers for three reasons. First, as a result of their interactions with metropolitan and colonial criminal justice systems, their lives were recorded in extraordinary detail. Second, they were sent to a place characterised by low population levels and excellent civil registration systems – circumstances that lend themselves to intergenerational familial reconstitution. Third, their colonially born children were raised in neighbourhoods radically different from those they had themselves experienced in infancy.

Both the Founders and Survivors and Digital Panopticon projects focus on a number of discrete research questions about re-offending, the impact of confinement on behaviour and the impact on bodies. Founders and Survivors aims to study the impact of convict transportation to Tasmania on health and well-being, including intergenerational outcomes. While it is primarily concerned with the physical and socio-economic impacts of British and Irish penal policy, the data collected includes a wealth of conviction data for both transported convicts and other colonial populations (Bradley et al., 2010). By contrast, Digital Panopticon is an endeavour squarely focussed on comparative life-course conviction outcomes. It seeks to answer a question first posed by the Utilitarian philosopher Jeremy Bentham (although also with a significant focus on health). Bentham argued that penal transportation was an ill-conceived and expensive judicial system of punishment that would prove an inefficient means of curbing offending compared to incarceration in a purpose-built system of metropolitan penitentiaries (Gascoigne, 2002: 126–127). The Digital Panopticon project seeks to follow the estimated 29,600 prisoners sentenced in the Old Bailey to transportation to Australia in the period 1787–1868, and a larger cohort of London offenders who were convicted but subsequently not transported, in order to put these claims to the test (Ward and Williams, 2016).

When investigating the intergenerational transmission of health outcomes and life-course offending, the record-keeping systems used to regulate convict and assisted migration from Britain and Ireland provide an excellent opportunity to reconstitute life-course outcomes for birth cohorts raised under radically different circumstances. Intergenerational datasets composed of many linked life-course events, including records of interaction with criminal justice systems, are a necessary prerequisite for any exploration of the underlying causes of both persistent familial offending and inequality. Given the time and expense involved in piecing together large complex historical datasets that follow multiple individuals in successive linked generations from cradle to grave, it makes sense for researchers to join forces. This allows us to draw on a wider range of sources and methods than is common in discipline-specific research.

The transported prisoners may be compared to two reference groups. One group consists of prisoners convicted in British courts for similar offences to those that attracted a sentence to transportation – but who for one reason or another were never sent into colonial exile. The 1853 Penal Servitude Act substituted terms of transportation for terms of penal servitude at home in the UK. Those undergoing penal servitude were granted licences which gave them conditional freedom before the expiration of their sentence. This in effect mirrored the Australian 'ticket-of-leave' system. The licence or ticket-of-leave system remained in place well into the twentieth century in the UK, enabling researchers to follow convicted prisoners after they had left prison. As well as providing information on height and weight, the prison licences give details of next of kin, providing an opportunity to reconstitute families in order to piece together a record of intergenerational conviction.

Because convicts were asked to provide information on next of kin on arrival in Australia, it is possible to identify their brothers and sisters who remained in Britain and Ireland. We therefore have details of the family of transported convicts (who, of course, remained in the UK). We can now compare the experiences of transported and non-transported subjects. By tracking their lives and those of their children, comparative data can be assembled on intergenerational conviction patterns for the children of transported convicts and those born to siblings who remained behind.

Individually each of these undertakings would constitute a large project in its own right. Before the recent explosion in digital data it would have been prohibitively expensive to contemplate trans-global family reconstitution on anything like this scale. For example, sampling suggests that a four-generation study of life-course outcomes for convicts and assisted migrants who arrived in Tasmania before 1860 and their siblings and parents who remained behind would involve reconstituting the lives of an estimated 220,000 individuals (see Figure 4.1).

Advances in archival finding aids, collaborations between archives, data provision services such as Ancestry and Find My Past, family historians and academic researchers make it possible to contemplate such an undertaking. The Founders and Survivors and Digital Panopticon databases have been formed as a result of such collaborations, providing the necessary framework to enable detailed intergenerational record linkage on a large scale. The rest of this chapter will discuss some of the preliminary results of analysis of Founders and Survivors

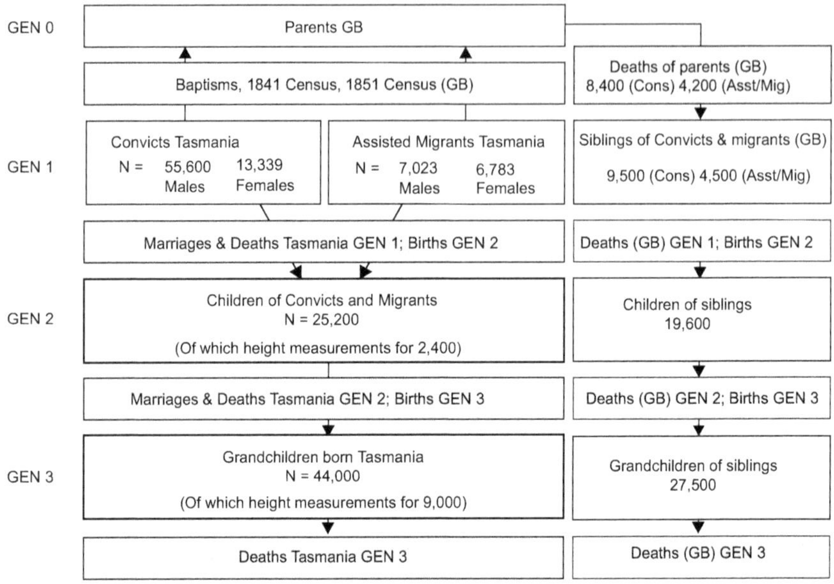

Figure 4.1 Estimated linkage rates for an intergenerational model centred on pre-1860 migrants to Tasmania (GEN 1)

and Digital Panopticon data to show how intergenerational effects on health and criminality (and the relationship between the two) are evident in the lives of transported convicts and their children in the nineteenth century.

Intergenerational health effects

We already know from existing research that colonially born children grew up tall in Australia. This was the case for children of convicts and for the children of people who had freely emigrated to Australia rather than being sent there as a punishment. The colonial auditor, G.T.W.B. Boyes was certainly not alone in describing the offspring of convicts as being 'a different race from the old stock' who 'shoot up as fast as mushrooms to a very considerable stature' (Chapman, 1985: 191–192). The height advantage enjoyed by the colonially born vividly illustrates the variation in conditions experienced by British and Australian working populations in the late eighteenth and early nineteenth centuries (Maxwell-Stewart, Inwood and Stankovich, 2015). This difference in growth patterns could reflect increased availability of food (protein was comparatively abundant and affordable in the Australian colonies), and/or comparatively benign environmental conditions resulting from factors such as lower population densities and access to clean drinking water. Increased foetal and infant calorie consumption and/or a reduction in environmental insults associated with the stunting of the British population enabled the colonially born to realize a greater proportion of their biologically programmed height than had been the case for their parents' generation.

The Founders and Survivors and Digital Panopticon data do not suggest that children born to convict parents were disadvantaged in health outcomes. Prisoners with a transported father were not short compared to others born in the colony after controlling for year of birth, place of birth (those born in towns were shorter) and parental occupation. Astoundingly, those born to convict mothers were taller than average – a result significant at the 1 per cent level (Maxwell-Stewart, Inwood and Stankovich, 2015). Family size may account for this unexpected result. The number of colonial births registered to convict women was surprisingly low – an average of just over one per marriage. Low female convict fertility may reflect a high incidence of sexually transmitted disease (Brunham and Embree, 1992). Alternatively, small family size might have resulted from the manner in which female convict sexuality was policed (Reid, 2007: 123–155). As convicts were generally not permitted to marry until the bulk of their sentence had been served, they tended to start families later in life than most couples. Whatever the reason for small families, the result may have been greater resource availability per child in convict-headed families. The importance of family size for the adult height of children in this period is documented elsewhere (Bailey, Hatton and Inwood, 2016).

Intergenerational transmission of criminality

Our preliminary analysis indicates that the children of convicts had better health outcomes than did their parents, and also that the children of Australian convicts had better health outcomes than the children of convicts punished in British prisons. But did Australian convicts and their children also offend less than their British counterparts? Analysis of reoffending rates amongst transported convicts (and the criminal careers their children) are other sites of analysis for the Digital Panopticon team. Historical research confirms that the children of convicted criminals had a significantly elevated risk of conviction (Williams and Godfrey, 2015). While the analysis of offending across generations offers the possibility of being able to better understand and control for criminogenic factors, the pathways through which intergenerational transmission might occur are complex and confounded (van de Weijer et al. 2014). This chapter will begin to describe some of the thinking around these questions, beginning with the mechanisms that might have encouraged or inhibited social transmission of criminality.

Methods

Much of the data for analysis comes from the Conduct Records of 48,878 males and 12,376 females who were sent to Van Diemen's Land. The records contain their confessions of past offending, details of the crime and date of hearing for the offence for which they were transported, details of their behaviour whilst under sentence and where they were sent on employment assignment. Occasionally it records post-release offending and date of death (Tasmanian Archives and Heritage Office, Con 31, 33, 40 and 41).

The 73,500 convicts landed in Van Diemen's Land between 1803 and 1853 were interrogated, stripped and described at multiple points over the course of their arrest, trial and shipment to the Australian penal colonies. Information garnered from prisoners as a result of these exercises was supplemented with data drawn from other institutional sources, including British and Irish gaolers' reports. In fact, these two exercises informed one another at the time. Before they were disembarked from the convict vessel that had brought them to Van Diemen's Land, each prisoner was told that much of their previous history, including interactions with the courts, was already known to their penal masters. Cognizant of the fact that any attempt to pull the wool over the eyes of the colonial administration was likely to result in punishment, convicts appear to have largely told the truth about the number of previous convictions, albeit with some understatement of the severity of past indiscretions (Rogers, 2015). In all, 61 per cent of male convicts and 70 per cent of female convicts admitted that they had previously been in court on at least one previous occasion before the conviction for which they were transported. It is of particular note that 20 per cent of those with gaol reports describing them as 'unknown' admitted to having been convicted at least once before (Maxwell-Stewart, 2016: 419). The evidence suggest that transported prisoners were effectively tricked into coughing up details of far more encounters with the courts than their gaolers had knowledge of.

There are other indications that this confessional data is broadly trustworthy. The rate at which convicts admitted to former convictions varied according to sentence length and a variety of measures of social capital. Those sentenced to transportation for periods of 15 years or longer were less likely to have a confessed record of prior conviction, a result consistent with other findings for historical populations (Godfrey, Cox and Farrell, 2010: 271). Literate convicts and those who were landed in Australia with financial assets were also less likely to admit to a prior conviction, as were those who were taller than the average for their age or who were convicted at a distance from the place of their recorded birth (Godfrey and Maxwell-Stewart, 2018).

The number of prior convictions divided by the convict's age on arrival is a good predictor of the extent of subsequent encounters with the colonial court system. Courts played an important role in the day-to-day running of the Australian penal colonies. Following an increase in convict numbers that accompanied the ending of the Napoleonic Wars, the colonial state sought to farm prison labour out to the private sector with the aim of stimulating the economy while slashing the costs of maintaining its penal charges. While colonial masters benefited from the services of cheap convict labour, they had to cover the costs of clothing, feeding and accommodating their unfree charges, thereby saving the government from considerable expense. By the early 1820s, the bulk of convicts worked for landed proprietors or were employed in colonial businesses. Although masters did not have the right to punish their convict servants, they could bring charges against them via a magistrates' bench.

Each bench was empowered to administer sanctions that varied from fines through to other physical punishments such as floggings and sentences to a treadwheel. After 1830 sentences to solitary confinement became particularly common (Edmonds and Maxwell-Stewart, 2016). Offences that were regarded as severe could result in the convict being forcibly relocated to a government-run punishment gang. For male convicts this usually meant hard labour in a road party, although sentences to chain gangs and remote penal stations such as Macquarie Harbour and Port Arthur were not uncommon. Female convicts were sent to one of a number of houses of correction where they were ordered to perform washing and other menial tasks, such as picking oakum. Masters who lost convict labour as a result of court-imposed sanctions were entitled to a replacement.

A system of registers designed to keep track of the number of charges brought against each convict while under sentence in the colony was set up in 1817 (TNA [UK], HO/10/43 Muster or List of Convicts 1817–1821; Tasmanian Archive and Heritage Office, Con 31, 32, 33, 40, 41, 35, 36 and 37). These contain summaries of all colonial court encounters for convicts under sentence and many incurred after the transported prisoner had attained freedom. The colonial administration used these conduct registers, or 'black books' as they were euphemistically known, to set appropriate levels of punishment as well as to evaluate convict claims for indulgences and other boons. The latter included the awarding of ticket-of-leaves (a certificate that gave the convict the right to work for a wage) and permission to marry. Convicts still under sentence could not marry without permission of the state. While the level at which these registers were maintained deteriorates with the winding-up of the convict system in the 1850s, other records can be used to fill the gap in conviction histories.

From the 1850s on every Australian colony published a version of the British publication the *Hue and Cry*. These police gazettes differed from their British model in that they routinely printed descriptions of discharged prisoners. Amongst the identifying details contained in these notices are information on place and year of birth, height, ship that brought an individual to the colony and details of the offence for which the prisoner had been convicted. This information allows us to track recidivism rates for former convicts arrested long after they had served out their sentence to transportation. While not every convicted prisoner had their details circulated in the *Police Gazette*, most court encounters that resulted in a custodial sentence were recorded. This was even the case for sentences of less than a week's duration. Thus, as well as providing information about cases brought in the colony's supreme court or courts of quarter session, much information about sentences handed down in the police courts and local magistrates' bench is also captured in this remarkable record series.

There are multiple mechanisms that might explain the perpetuation of offending patterns within particular families. These include poor parenting, poverty of expectation and poverty of opportunity, and possibly even the genetic transmission of traits likely to heighten the risk of arrest – such as schizophrenia (Morgan et al., 2008). While most researchers emphasise the importance of socio-economic pathways over genetic, the former can be driven by dynamics that are both internal and external to the family. That conviction histories cluster in families suffering from sustained intergenerational financial and or socio-cultural deprivation is in itself not surprising (Bijleveld and Wijkman, 2009). While poverty is not a crime, an impoverished upbringing is likely to increase life-course risk of conviction. That risk may be heightened by policing strategies – rather than the transmission of a propensity to offend from parent to child. The children of those who are 'known to the police' are likely to be subject to greater surveillance than others. When offences are detected, formal prosecution might also be a more likely in families with a known prosecution history (Besemer, Farrington and Bijleveld, 2017). There is some disagreement over the extent to which former convicts managed to steer clear of the courts. Braithwaite, in particular, contrasts penal transportation with other systems of institutional correction. He argues that transportation was an inclusionary system that was relatively successful at integrating convicts into the workplace, and hence curbing rates of offending after release and, by implication, intergenerationally (Braithwaite, 2001). Using quarter session and supreme court data he points out that Tasmania, the colony most impacted upon by transportation, had the lowest conviction rate of all Australian colonies by the end of the nineteenth century. Analysis of post-transportation outcomes in Western Australia reveals a more complex picture. It is true that by and large the convicts transported to that colony did not go on to commit offences of the magnitude of those for which they had been transported, but this did not necessarily mean that they stayed clear of the courts. Former convicts featured disproportionately amongst lower court convictions, especially those for minor larcenies, vagrancies and public order offences (Godfrey and Cox, 2008).

Results

Analysis of the data for Tasmania reveals a similar picture to that found by Godfrey and Cox (2008). Between 1865 and 1924 over 50,000 individual descriptions of prisoners were circulated in the pages of the *Tasmanian Police Gazette*. These included details for 6,549 male and 2,205 female former convicts (Maxwell-Stewart, Cracknell and Inwood, 2015: 31). About one in five former male convicts who were still alive and present in Tasmania in 1865 appear at least once in the pages of the *Tasmania Police Gazette* as a convicted and discharged prisoner. Given the aging nature of the convict population, this is a significant number. As in Western Australia, many of these convictions were for comparatively minor offences – a quarter, for example, were for vagrancy, begging or being idle and disorderly (Maxwell-Stewart and Kippen, 2015).

By linking information contained in the *Tasmanian Police Gazette* to conduct records it is possible to assemble a remarkably complete record of court interactions for the 59,000 male and 13,500 female convicts transported to Van Diemen's Land. While colonial conviction rates were influenced by a number of factors, including the operation of colonial labour markets, they are strongly correlated with levels of confessed prior conviction. As recorded in the Conduct Records, prisoners who confessed to high rates of incarceration (adjusted for age on arrival in the colony) were significantly more likely to accumulate a colonial conviction record (Tasmanian Archives and Heritage Office, Con 31, 33, 40 and 41). This applied to both convictions acquired while under sentence and post-sentence encounters with the colonial courts.

Some other patterns are apparent. Higher levels of punishment exposure while under sentence, especially solitary confinement and stints of hard labour on the roads, were positively associated with reconviction after release from transportation. Individuals convicted in London were more likely to escape the courts after their release from the clutches of the convict department, while those convicted in Ireland were at much greater risk of post-release conviction than their pre-transportation record of offending would suggest. Finally, marriage appeared to have little impact on later life conviction rates (Maxwell-Stewart and Kippen, 2015; Godfrey and Maxwell-Stewart, 2018).

In summary, analysis of life-course conviction histories for convicts reveals a statistically significant relationship between confessed levels of conviction prior to transportation and the level of subsequent encounters with colonial courts. This is a consistent relationship – the higher the number of pre-transportation incarcerations admitted to, the greater the probability that a convict would go on to accumulate a higher than average number of convictions in the colony. The bulk of convictions that occurred after a convict was released from a sentence to transportation, however, were for offences that might be described as petty. Murder, robbery, housebreaking and burglary, animal theft and indecent assault combined accounted for less than 9 per cent of all convictions (Maxwell-Stewart and Kippen, 2015: 177).

Intergenerational offending

The extent to which the legacies of transportation helped to shape lives in settler Australia has also been a subject for discussion. Many in the Australian colonies in the second half of the nineteenth century thought that the progeny of those who had 'left their country for their country's good' made poor citizens. As one prominent settler argued, if a free colonist married, 'his family produces wealth to the state', but, by contrast, convict families produced 'an equal degree of evil' (Henderson, 1832: 33). By mid-century, it was common to see convicts as a source of contamination who could spread criminal vice to others – especially their offspring. Transportation, it was said, led to the 'transmission from parents to progeny of depraved habits and felonious proclivities' (*Bathurst Free Press and Mining Journal*, 28 September 1889). Thus, even before the works of the Italian criminologist Cesar Lombroso appeared in 1878 – translated into English in the early twentieth century – it was common for both colonial and metropolitan observers of crime to claim that deviant traits could be passed from one generation to another (Hahn Rafter, 1998).

The eugenics movement, which argued for improvement of the human 'race' by selective breeding (and even more frighteningly, selective 'culling'), was influential in Australia. Its Antipodean popularity reflects the cultural and political sensitivity towards convicts and their children in the first half of the twentieth century (Roberts, 2011). There was a sense of relief that Australian troops had not been found wanting in overseas conflicts – an outcome that for many proved that convict genes had either been effectively washed out by subsequent migration or that transportation had not resulted in permanent ill-effects. In more recent years others have argued that there is little evidence that transportation led to increases in crime rates or other long-term societal disadvantage (Smith, 2008).

The colonial police gazettes provide an opportunity to test this claim. Between 1864 and 1924 discharge notices for over 23,000 Tasmanian-born offenders were circulated in the Tasmanian and Victorian versions of these weekly periodicals. In all, around 8 per cent of those born in the colony in the years to 1912 had their descriptions circulated. By linking these records to birth registration data, it is possible to place colonially born offenders within the household of their birth. For those born after 1870, a direct comparison can be made between birth households for children who went on to accumulate at least one conviction and those who volunteered for service in Australian Imperial Force (AIF) over the course of the First World War. This reveals that while the occupations of the fathers of soldiers closely matched the distribution of occupations in Tasmania as a whole, this was not true for those children who subsequently accumulated a record of incarceration. The prisoners were less likely to be born into a household headed by a higher or lower manager or a small holder, and more likely to be raised by a father who was a manual worker (see Table 4.1).

Some prisoners born in the colony (largely before 1870) can be linked to parents who arrived as convicts. Although this process reveals little about the overall risk of conviction and imprisonment for the children of convicts, it does provide an indication of the extent to which offenders born into households where at least one parent had been transported were likely to accumulate multiple life-course convictions. The linked *Police Gazette* data provide no evidence that this was the case. Prisoners who had at least one parent who was a convict were, in fact, at lower risk of multiple convictions than the other colonially born inmates they rubbed shoulders with in the colony's lock-ups, police stations

Table 4.1 Occupations of fathers recorded on birth certificates for all registered births, colonially born prisoners and First World War volunteers by percentage

	Birth registers (%)	*Prisoners (%)*	*AIF (%)*
Higher managers	3.22	1.85	3.38
Lower managers	10.92	7.56	10.91
Foremen and skilled workers	31.52	32.46	28.23
Small holders and fishermen	25.35	17.36	26.57
Lower skilled workers	3.63	4.90	3.14
Unskilled workers	22.21	32.26	24.61
Farm workers	3.16	3.60	3.14
	100.00	100.00	100.00

Sources: *Tasmanian Police Gazette*; Tasmanian Archive and Heritage Office: Registers of Births in Hobart, Launceston and Country Districts, RGD33. Australian National Archive, First Australian Imperial Force Personnel Dossiers, 1914–1920, B2455.

Note: Registered births: *n* = 189,342; prisoners: *n* = 3,483; AIF: *n* = 1,686.

and gaols. Further work is needed to establish if the children of former convicts were responsible for a disproportionate number of colonial convictions. Already we know from *Police Gazette* data that the children of convicts were no more likely to be serially convicted compared to those born to non-transported parents. This is an interesting finding if for no other reason than that it can be assumed that knowledge about parental origins was widely shared in colonial Tasmania. There is little to suggest that the children of former convicts were as heavily policed as their parents, or, indeed, that they were policed more than the children of free-migrants. Despite colonial middle-class fears, the early evidence does not suggest that transportation exposed Australian society to an intergenerationally transmitted delinquency problem.

The relationship between health inequality and criminality

There are good reasons to suspect that some mechanisms responsible for intergenerational transmission of health inequalities are also associated with increased risk of conviction. For example, we know nineteenth-century male prisoners with a record of multiple conviction were relatively short for all prisoners of their age (Bodenhorn, Moehling and Price, 2012; Maxwell-Stewart, Cracknell and Inwood, 2015). Undoubtedly, this reflects conditions encountered in utero and early childhood that inhibited the realization of biologically programmed height (Steckel, 2009). It is distinctly possible that early childhood insults severe enough to retard or stunt growth might also prove criminogenic. Admittedly, the number of generations affected by such transmission mechanisms and the extent to which these factors (and their various interactions) may compound from one generation to another are difficult to determine. One particular problem, for example, is the identification of pathways responsible for intergenerational transmission and the extent to which parent and child were raised in similar neighbourhoods. This makes it difficult to determine the extent to which a record of conviction (or, for that matter, poor health) can be attributed to parenting or other inherited characteristics – as distinct from those stemming from a shared record of disadvantage.

As with crime, there are multiple mechanisms that may, or may not, be responsible for shaping the health outcomes of both parents and their children (Kuzawa and Eisenberg, 2014). Maternal literacy is powerfully associated with improved intergenerational outcomes for example, while elevated levels of alcohol consumption during pregnancy can stunt offspring growth and retard cognitive development (Riley, 2001; Rose and Cherpitel, 2011). The thrifty phenotype hypothesis posits that a history of maternal undernutrition may trigger foetal responses that favour the development of critical organs at the expense of others, leading to increased risk of chronic illness later in life (especially cardiovascular disease and type 2 diabetes – Hales and Barker, 2001). Recent work also links thriftier metabolism mechanisms in early life to poorer cognitive, immune system and reproductive development (Pike, 2016: 16). Genetic factors play a role in the determinants of intergenerational health, although the difficulty of distinguishing genetic and environmental pathways is further complicated by interactions between the two. There is some evidence that effects associated with trauma exposure, for example, can be transmitted from one generation to another through the chemical coating of chromosomes (Kellerman, 2013).

Our preliminary analysis shows, then, that an understanding of intergenerational transmission relies not just on an examination of health and criminality, but on the interrelationship between the two effects, and also the mechanisms of transmission for both health and for criminality.

Future research on intergenerational effects

While most of those who arrived in Van Diemen's Land before 1860 were transported convicts, there were also substantial numbers of assisted migrants. This was especially so in the years immediately following the ending of transportation to the colony in 1853 (Haines and Shlomowitz, 1991). While these men and women were not sent to the Antipodes as a result of a sentence passed by a court, they were described in similar detail to convicts. It is possible to use this information to reconstitute their life-courses. Such an approach enables a comparison of the history of incarceration following arrival in the colony for settlers who arrived free and those who were transported. It is also possible to reconstitute and compare the conviction records of the children of assisted migrants and convicts.

Given time, and with greater use of the rich record sets provided by the Digital Panopticon, it would be possible to stretch the intergenerational chains still further. We will have access to census data from 1841 to 1911, as well as the British 1939 Register (Williams and Godfrey, 2016). We will have access to trial records of both higher and lower courts in Britain and the UK from 1850 – and in time these will be digitised in order to link them into current datasets – and we already have access to online British and Australian newspapers which give details of crimes and trials. We can connect data to the Prosecution Project which will tell us whether convicts and their children appeared in the higher Australian courts from 1850 to 1950 (Finnane and Piper, 2016). Lastly, we have the possibility of linking our data to employment and military records so that we can explore the progress of peoples' lives in non-offending contexts. We will therefore be able to deepen our research with evidence from longer generational chains, and with both criminal and non-criminal data sources. This should reveal a much clearer picture of the extent to which penal transportation left a legacy in the form of elevated intergenerational offending and employment/military careers.

It should also be possible to explore the relationship between offending transmission rates and other inequalities. Such work might even extend Bentham's notion that incarceration in a penitentiary and transportation would produce divergent outcomes – enabling comparative assessment of conviction rates for both prisoners and their children. Such work might also make an important contribution to understandings of intergenerational transmission pathways by exploring outcomes for offspring born in both similar and contrasting environments to those that characterised the formative years of their parents.

References

Bailey, R.; Hatton, T. and Inwood, K. (2016), 'Health, Height and the Household at the Turn of the 20th Century', *Economic History Review*, 69: 35–53.

Besemer, S.; Farrington, D. and Bijleveld, C. (2017), 'Labelling and Intergenerational Transmission of Crime: The Interaction between Criminal Justice Intervention and a Convicted Parent', *PLoS ONE*, 12, 3: e0172419.

Bijleveld, C.C.J.H. and Wijkman, M.D.S. (2009), 'Intergenerational Continuity in Convictions: A Five-Generation Study', *Criminal Behaviour and Mental Health*, 19: 142–155.

Bodenhorn, H.; Moehling, C. and Price, G.N. (2012), 'Short Criminals: Stature and Crime in Early America', *Journal of Law and Economics*, 55, 2: 393–418.

Bradley, J.; Kippen, R.; Maxwell-Stewart, H.; McCalman, J. and Silcot, S. (2010), 'Research Note: The Founders and Survivors Project', *The History of the Family*, 15, 4: 467–477.

Braithwaite, J. (2001), 'Crime in the Convict Republic', *Modern Law Review*, 64, 1: 11–50.

Brunham, R.C. and Embree, J.E. (1992), 'Sexually Transmitted Diseases: Current and Future Dimensions of the Problem in the Third World', in Germain, A.; Holmes, H.; Piot, P. and Wasserheit, J. (eds.) *Reproductive Tract Infections: Global Impact and Priorities for Women's Global Health* (New York, Springer): 35–58.

Chapman, P. (1985), *The Diaries and Letters of G.T.W.B. Boyes* (Melbourne, Oxford University Press).

Edmonds, P. and Maxwell-Stewart, H. (2016), '"The Whip Is a Very Contagious Kind of Thing": Flogging and Humanitarian Reform in Penal Australia', *Journal of Colonialism and Colonial History*, 17, 1.

Finnane, M. and Piper, A. (2016), 'The Prosecution Project: Understanding the Changing Criminal Trial through Digital Tools', *Law and History Review*, 34, 4: 873–891.

Gascoigne, P. (2002), *The Enlightenment and the Origins of European Australia* (Cambridge, Cambridge University Press).

Godfrey, B. and Cox, D. (2008), '"The Last Fleet": Crime, Reformation, and Punishment in Western Australia after 1868', *The Australian and New Zealand Journal of Criminology*, 41, 2: 236–258.

Godfrey, B.; Cox, D. and Farrall, S. (2007), *Criminal Lives: Family, Employment and Offending* (Clarendon Series in Criminology, Oxford, Oxford University Press).

Godfrey, B.; Cox, D. and Farrall, S. (2010), *Serious Offenders: A Historical Study of Habitual Offenders* (Clarendon Series in Criminology, Oxford, Oxford University Press).

Godfrey, B. and Maxwell-Stewart, H. (2018 forthcoming), 'Transportation, Life-Course Offending and London Convicts', in Finnane, M. (ed.) *Bloomsbury Global History of Crime and Punishment* Vol. 5 (London, Bloomsbury).

Hahn Rafter, N. (1998), *Creating Born Criminals* (Chicago, University of Illinois Press).

Haines, R. and Shlomowitz, R. (1991), 'Nineteenth Century Government-Assisted and Total Immigration from the United Kingdom to Australia: Quinquennial Estimates by Colony', *Journal of the Australian Population Association*, 8, 1: 50–61.

Hales, C.N. and Barker, D.J. (2001), 'The Thrifty Phenotype Hypothesis', *British Medical Journal*, 60: 5–20.

Henderson, J. (1832), *Observations on the Colonies of New South Wales and Van Diemen's Land* (Calcutta, Baptist Mission Press): 33.

Inwood, K. and Maxwell-Stewart, H. (2016), 'Demography and the Prison', in Kok, J.; Matthijs, K.; Matsuo, H. and Hin, S. (eds.) *The Future of Historical Demography* (Leuven, Acco): 41–44.

Kellermann, N.P. (2013), 'Epigenetic Transmission of Holocaust Trauma: Can Nightmares be Inherited?', *The Israel Journal of Psychiatry and Related Sciences*, 50, 1: 33–39.

Kuzawa, C. and Eisenberg, D. (2014), *The Long Reach of History: Intergenerational and Transgenerational Pathways to Plasticity in Human Longevity* (Washington, National Academies Press).

Maxwell-Stewart, H. (2016), 'The State, Convicts and Longitudinal Analysis', *Australian Historical Studies*, 47, 3: 414–429.

Maxwell-Stewart, H.; Cracknell, M. and Inwood, K. (2015), 'Height, Crime and Colonial History', *Law, Crime and History*, 5, 1: 25–42.

Maxwell-Stewart, H.; Inwood, K. and Stankovich, J. (2015), 'The Prison and the Colonial Family', *History of the Family*, 20, 2: 231–248.

Maxwell-Stewart, H. and Kippen, R. (2015), '"What Is a Man That Is a Bolter to Do? I Would Steal the Governor's Axe Rather Than Starve": Old Lags and Recidivism in the Tasmanian Penal Colony', in Campbell, J. and Miller, V. (eds.) *Transnational Penal Cultures* (London, Routledge): 165–183.

Meredith, D. and Oxley, D. (2015), 'Blood and Bone: Body Mass, Gender and Health Inequality in Nineteenth-Century British Families', *The History of the Family*, 20, 2: 204–230.

Morgan, F.; Morgan, V.; Clare, J.; Valuri, G.; Woodman, R.; Ferrante, A.; Castle, D. and Jablensky, A. (2008), 'Schizophrenia and Offending: Area of Residence and the Impact of Social Disorganisation and Urbanicity', *Trends & Issues in Crime and Criminal Justice*, 365.

Pike, I. (2016), 'Calibrating the Next Generation: Mothers, Early Life Experiences, and Reproductive Development', in Sievert, L.L. and Brown, D.E. (eds.) *Biological Measures of Human Experience Across the Lifespan: Making Visible to Invisable* (Berlin, Springer): 13–28.

Reid, K. (2007), *Gender, Crime and Empire: Convicts, Settlers and the State in Early Colonial Australia* (Manchester, Manchester University Press).

Riley, J.C. (2001), *Rising Life Expectancy: A Global History* (Cambridge, Cambridge University Press).

Roberts, D. (2011), 'The "Knotted Hands That Set us High": Labour History and the Study of Convict Australia', *Labour History*, 100: 33–50.

Rogers, H. (2015), '"A Very Fair Statement of His Past Life": Transported Convicts, Former Lives and Previous Offences', *Open Library of Humanities*, 1, 1.

Rose, M.E. and Cherpitel, C. (2011), *Alcohol: Its History, Pharmacology and Treatment* (Minnesota, Haselden).

Smith, B. (2008), *Australia's Birthstain: The Startling Legacy of the Convict Era* (Sydney, Allen and Unwin).

Steckel, R.H. (2009), 'Heights and Human Welfare: Recent Developments and New Directions', *Explorations in Economic History*, 46, 1: 1–23.

van de Weijer, S.G.A.; Bijleveld, C. and Blokland, A.A.J. (2014), 'The Intergenerational Transmission of Violent Offending', *Journal of Family Violence*, 29, 2: 109–118.

Ward, R. and Williams, L. (2016), 'Initial Views from the Digital Panopticon: Reconstructing Penal Outcomes in the 1790s', *Law and History Review*, 34, 4.

Williams, L. and Godfrey, B. (2015), 'Familial and Intergenerational Offending in Liverpool and the North West of England, 1850–1914', *History of the Family*, 20, 2.

Williams, L. and Godfrey, B. (2016), 'Bringing the Prisoner into View: English and Welsh Census Data and the Victorian Prison Population', *Australian Historical Studies*, 47, 3: 398–413.

Chapter 5

Intergenerational transmission of antisocial behaviour in childhood

Findings from the New South Wales Child Development Study

Stacy Tzoumakis, Melissa J. Green, Kristin R. Laurens, Kimberlie Dean, and Vaughan J. Carr

The intergenerational transmission of antisocial behaviour is increasingly acknowledged as beginning in the earliest development periods (DeLisi and Vaughn 2014: 15, Tremblay 2015: 44). This chapter presents findings on parental offending and early childhood psychosocial development from a large Australian multi-agency, intergenerational record linkage study of a population cohort of children and their parents: the New South Wales Child Development Study (NSW-CDS; http://nsw-cds.com.au; Carr et al. 2016). We provide a brief review of criminal justice in Australia, an overview of the NSW-CDS, describe a middle childhood survey of mental health and wellbeing, and introduce our plans to enhance the study by adding police contact data for the children in 2018.

Criminal justice in Australia

The Australian criminal justice system is founded on English law, but there is no single criminal justice system in Australia; the eight states and territories have separate systems of courts, prisons, police, and corrective institutions and services (Australian Bureau of Statistics 1997, Castles 1963: 1). The New South Wales (NSW) Criminal Justice System consists of the Lower Courts (Local Court and Children's Court), which deal with most criminal charges, and Higher Courts (District Court and Supreme Court), which deal with more serious offences (Australian Bureau of Statistics 1997). The Local Court deals mainly with adult offenders, while the Children's Court deals with juveniles aged 10 to 17 years (the age of criminal responsibility in NSW is 10 years). NSW is the most populous state in Australia (representing 32 per cent of the resident national population aged 10 and over) and in 2015–16 had the highest number of offenders across all states and territories (n = 128,397; 30 per cent) (Australian Bureau of Statistics 2017b). The most common offence nationally in 2015–16 was illicit drug offences (20 per cent), followed by acts intended to cause injury (18 per-cent), theft (18 per cent), and public order offences (15 percent) (Australian

Bureau of Statistics 2017b). The most common offence in NSW was theft (27 per cent), followed by acts intended to cause injury (23 per cent), illicit drug offences (14 per cent), and public order offences (14 per cent) (Australian Bureau of Statistics 2017b). Australia's crime rates are similar to the UK and Canada, and much lower than the US. For example, homicide rates per 100,000 of the population in 2015 were 0.98 for Australia, 0.92 for the UK, 1.68 for Canada, and 4.88 for the US (United Nations Office on Drugs and Crime 2015). In terms of imprisonment rates, Australia ranks 85th in the world, higher than the UK (105th) and Canada (139th), but much lower than the US (2nd) (Institute for Criminal Policy Research 2017). At the state level, NSW had the largest 2016 adult prisoner population, comprising one-third (33 per cent) of the total Australian adult prisoner population (Australian Bureau of Statistics 2017a).

Establishment of the NSW-CDS

The lead investigator of the NSW-CDS, Vaughan Carr, initiated the study in 2008. The main goal of the study was to identify life-course pathways to the development of severe mental disorders, including risk and protective factors that may be operating in early life. To be able to determine developmental pathways associated with severe, low-prevalence disorders such as schizophrenia, a large-scale longitudinal study of children's mental health was needed. The resulting population scope of the study provided the potential to broaden the mental health outcomes of interest, and to encompass other adverse outcomes such as antisocial behaviour. Moreover, considering the strong heritability of severe mental illnesses (Lichtenstein et al. 2009: 236) and antisocial behaviour (Rhee and Waldman 2002: 513), the intergenerational nature of the study facilitated the consideration of parental risk factors (such as parental mental illness history, or criminal offending history). While perinatal and other health indicators are all important in understanding the development of mental illness, the NSW-CDS aimed to include a wide range of factors other than those of health over the life-course. Thus, a multidisciplinary scientific committee was formed to comprise researchers from psychiatry, education, epidemiology and public health, psychology, child protection, and criminology. Government partnerships were also established with NSW Departments of Health, Education, and Family and Community Services to facilitate the research, given the linkage of administrative data from these agencies as a core feature of the methodology.

In 2009, a census of all children entering kindergarten in the state of NSW (*N* = 87,026) was conducted (the Australian Early Development Census, AEDC) as part of a nationwide initiative (Brinkman et al. 2014: 1089). The AEDC indexes early childhood developmental functioning across five domains, as shown in Table 5.1. The main purpose of the AEDC is to provide population-level data that allows profiles of child development to be generated for local communities and thereby inform the development of local policies and programmes to improve early childhood development. The AEDC data are also

Table 5.1 Australian Early Development Census (AEDC): five domains of developmental functioning

1 **Physical health and wellbeing**
   - Physical readiness for school, physical independence, gross and fine motor skills
2 **Social competence**
   - Overall social competence, approaches to learning, readiness to explore new things, responsibility, and respect
3 **Emotional maturity**
   - Pro-social and helping, anxious/fearful, aggressive, hyperactive, and inattentive behaviours
4 **Language and cognitive skills**
   - Basic and advanced literacy, basic numeracy, interest in literacy/numeracy, memory
5 **Communication and general knowledge**

made available to researchers for record-linkage studies. New capacities in NSW for multi-agency linkage of administrative records were developed contemporaneously, enabling linkage of the 2009 AEDC data for use in research studies. In 2010, a pilot study by the NSW-CDS team was conducted to determine the feasibility of linking education records (childhood literacy and numeracy assessments) to birth and perinatal records (Moore et al. 2014: 236). High linkage rates were achieved (i.e., 89 per cent of records were linked accurately), demonstrating that linking health data with other administrative datasets was viable. The NSW-CDS team sought research ethics approval to link child protection and criminal justice records to birth, perinatal, and other health records under the waiver of consent provisions of the National Statement on Ethical Conduct in Human Research in accordance with state and federal privacy protection legislation (NHMRC 2007: 21). The NSW-CDS thus commenced with linkage of health, education, child protection, and criminal justice data collections relating to the 87,026 children for whom 2009 AEDC data were available. The researchers are not privy to the identities of these participants, according to the strict privacy protocols by which record linkages are conducted.

Overview of the NSW-CDS

The NSW-CDS adopts a life-course epidemiological approach to examine the risk and protective factors associated with the development of mental illnesses and antisocial behaviours from birth to adolescence and early adulthood. More specifically, we are interested in how psychosocial development and academic achievement in childhood are influenced over time by social and environmental factors, and develop into later patterns of health and wellbeing on the one hand, or mental disorders and antisocial behaviours on the other. Research findings in criminology, psychology, and psychiatry concur that adult mental illness and criminal offending are typically preceded by child and juvenile precursors (Costello et al. 2003: 840, Kim-Cohen et al. 2003: 713, Loeber and Farrington 2000: 738). Moreover, it is well established that both mental illness and antisocial behaviour tend to co-occur (Fazel and Seewald 2012: 366, Teplin et al. 2002: 1135), and mental illness is sometimes linked to violence (Arseneault et al. 2000: 981, Fazel et al. 2009: 4). Furthermore, mental illness and offending co-occur from an intergenerational perspective; parental mental illness is associated with offending in adult offspring (Dean et al. 2012: 573). The NSW-CDS provides detailed information on both mental health and criminal justice contacts to further elucidate this relationship in an intergenerational developmental context. In addition, the study includes key pregnancy- and birth-related factors, such as low birth weight and prenatal maternal smoking, which are themselves linked to the development of severe mental illness and early onset offending (Cannon et al. 2002: 1086; Laurens et al. 2015: 8; Tibbetts and Piquero 1999: 859; Wakschlag et al. 2002: 968).

NSW-CDS record linkage I procedures

The NSW-CDS cohort is defined by the AEDC cross-sectional assessment that captured 99.9 per cent (N = 87,026) of the eligible NSW children in 2009. The AEDC was conducted when the children were in their first year of formal schooling (in kindergarten, at approximately five years of age). The children were assessed by their kindergarten teachers who had been in contact with the child for a minimum of one month; however, most of the assessments were completed by teachers with approximately five months' knowledge of the child. The AEDC was originally developed in Canada and is a population measure of children's developmental readiness for school and estimates the extent to which children have gained the necessary psychosocial competencies to engage effectively in school-based learning (Janus and Offord 2007: 6). It includes 96 items contributing to 16 subdomains within the 5 broad domains of: (1) physical health and wellbeing, (2) social competence, (3) emotional maturity, (4) language and cognitive development, and (5) communication and general knowledge (for individual items within each domain see Brinkman et al. 2014: 1092). The psychometric properties of the AEDC have been examined internationally (Canada, Australia, US, Jamaica, and Sweden) (Janus et al. 2011: 292), and have been established using Rasch modelling (Andrich and Styles 2004: 11; Hagquist and Hellström 2014: 306). The AEDC's predictive validity has also been demonstrated in association with middle childhood literacy and numeracy, wellbeing, and peer relations (Brinkman et al. 2013: 703; Guhn et al. 2016: 81). Children were considered *developmentally vulnerable* on any subdomain if they scored in the bottom 10 per cent of the national AEDC population distribution. Descriptive statistics for the AEDC domains and subdomains for the NSW-CDS cohort are presented in Table 5.2.

Table 5.2 Characteristics of the NSW Child Development Study

		Mean	SD
Demographic variables			
Child age (years) in 2009		5.63	0.38
Maternal age (years) at child's birth		29.80	5.53
Paternal age (years) at child's birth		33.27	6.38
		%	*n*
Child sex			
	Male	51.4	37,116
	Female	48.6	35,129
Child English as a second language			
	Yes	16.0	11,594
	No	84.0	60,651
Socio-Economic Index for Areas			
	Quintile 1 (Most disadvantaged)	23.6	17,067
	Quintiles 2–5	76.4	55,168
Accessibility/Remoteness Index of Australia			
	Major cities	73.6	53,171
	Regional/remote	26.4	19,074
Pregnancy and birth			
Prenatal smoking		14.2	10,167
Maternal pregnancy complications		10.9	7,872
Prematurity (< 37 weeks)		6.4	4,569
Low birth weight (< 2,500 g)		5.5	3,955
Parental mental health			
Any maternal mental disorders		8.1	5,826
Maternal substance use disorders		3.1	2,216
Any paternal mental disorders		5.0	3,614
Paternal substance use disorders		3.5	2,545
Child maltreatment			
Any child maltreatment		3.3	2,408
Child placed in out of home care		1.2	902
Offspring outcomes at age five years			
Vulnerability (lowest 10% of national population) on AEDC Domains and subdomains			
Physical health and wellbeing		8.2	5,639
	Physical readiness for school day	8.3	5,734
	Physical independence	7.3	5,046
	Gross and fine motor skills	6.3	4,335

		Mean	SD
Social competence		8.3	5,750
	Overall social competence	5.5	3,767
	Responsibility and respect	8.5	5,869
	Approaches to learning	7.6	5,209
	Readiness to explore new things	8.5	5,856
Emotional maturity		7.1	4,906
	Prosocial and helping behaviour	7.4	4,985
	Anxious and fearful behaviour	10.7	7,326
	Aggressive behaviour	8.3	5,729
	Hyperactive and inattentive behaviour	10.5	7,231
Language and cognitive skills		5.4	3,707
	Basic literacy	5.9	4,086
	Interest in literacy/numeracy and memory	6.0	4,104
	Advanced literacy	4.7	3,203
	Basic numeracy	8.6	5,916
Communication and general knowledge		8.3	5,689

Note: AEDC, Australian Early Development Census. *n* = 72,245 children for whom linked parental records were available for demographic, pregnancy and birth, parental mental health, and child maltreatment variables; *n* = 69,116 children for offspring outcome variables; excludes 3,129 children with special needs (medically diagnosed physical, intellectual or chronic medical condition which requires additional assistance) for whom AEDC developmental indices are unavailable.

In the NSW-CDS, the cross-sectional AEDC data were linked to other administrative data collections in 2014 by an independent agency, the Centre for Health Record Linkage (CHeReL; www.cherel.org.au). Linked records included children's birth, mortality, health, school, and child protection records; their mothers' perinatal records; and both parents' mortality, health, and criminal records. This record linkage brought together records from pre-birth up to when the children were approximately five years old. Child and parent records were matched by the CHeReL using name, date of birth, residential address, and sex. To protect participants' privacy, researchers never have access to these personal identifiers. The linkage was conducted using probabilistic linkage methods via ChoiceMaker software, which uses automated algorithms and machine learning techniques for assigning weights to personal information. Matches with probabilities above 0.75 were considered as 'true matches', and those below 0.25 were considered as 'false matches'. Clerical reviews were performed on all pairs with probabilities between 0.75 and 0.25. Moreover, once the clerical review was completed, a random sample of 5 per cent of those records that were reviewed was also completed (further information regarding quality assurance procedures can be found at www.cherel.org.au/quality-assurance). False-positive linkages in the NSW-CDS were low with a rate of 3/1,000 persons (0.3 per cent) for linkage of child data collections, and 5/1,000 persons (0.5 per cent) for linkage of parents to their children. Linkage procedures adhered to strict privacy protocols, and researchers received de-identified records only. Parents were identified via linkage of the child's AEDC record with data from the NSW Birth Registration records; as a result, it was possible to link parental records for 72,245 children (83.0 per cent of the cohort) whose births were registered in NSW.

Sample description

Descriptive statistics for record linkage of the NSW-CDS based on the children with linked parental records (N = 72,245) are provided in Table 5.2. The children in the NSW-CDS were on average 5.6 years old (SD = 0.4) when the AEDC was completed in 2009. Mothers were on average 29.8 years of age (SD = 5.5) and fathers 33.3 years (SD = 6.4) at the birth of their child. Just over half of the children were male (51.4 per cent; n = 37,116), and 16.0 per cent (n = 11,594) spoke English as a second language. A postcode-based measure of socio-economic status, the Socio-Economic Index for Areas (SEIFA), was available from the AEDC for the children in the cohort. Postcodes vary in size in Australia, with rural postcodes covering larger geographic areas compared to urban postcodes. SEIFA is derived from census information and measures the average income and employment status for each postcode in Australia (Pink 2013: 9). SEIFA provides an indicator of collective socio-economic status (relative disadvantage) that is likely to misclassify some individuals (Pink 2013: 3). A dichotomous socio-economic status indicator was created by recoding the national quintiles into the most disadvantaged (Quintile 1) and less disadvantaged (Quintiles 2–5 – four remaining quintiles). Approximately one-quarter of the children (23.6 per cent; n = 17,067) resided in the most disadvantaged areas (Quintile 1). Nearly three-quarters (n = 53,171) of the cohort lived in a major city according to the Accessibility/Remoteness Index of Australia (ARIA) (Department of Health and Aged Care [Australian Government] 2001: 3). The representativeness of the NSW-CDS to NSW and Australian populations of comparable age has been demonstrated in terms of sex, SEIFA, and ARIA (Carr et al. 2016: 2). Furthermore, comparisons (age, sex, English as second language, ARIA, SEIFA, and AEDC measures) were conducted between the full cohort (n = 87,026) and the cohort with linked parental data (n = 72,245), and no substantive differences were found (see Carr et al. 2016, Supplementary Tables 1-X and 2-X). The largest difference was between those children for whom English is a second language, which consisted of 17.9 per cent in the full cohort and 16.1 per cent in the cohort with linked parents, suggesting that we are likely excluding some migrant children by limiting our analyses to those whose births are registered in NSW.

Several data collections available in the NSW-CDS are of particular interest to the development of antisocial behaviour. Perinatal data from the *NSW Ministry of Health Perinatal Data Collection* (2000–2006) indicate that 14.2 per cent (n = 10,167) of the children in the cohort were exposed to maternal smoking during pregnancy, 6.4 per cent (n = 4,569) were born prematurely, 5.5 per cent (n = 3,955) had a low birth weight, and approximately 11 per cent (n = 7,872) of the mothers experienced pregnancy complications (maternal diabetes, gestational diabetes, hypertension, and preeclampsia). Data from the *NSW Ministry of Health Mental Health Admitted Patients* (public and private hospitals) and *Mental Health Ambulatory* (public only) records (2001–2009) were used to determine parental mental disorders; 8.1 per cent (n = 5,826) of the children had a mother, and 5.0 per cent (n = 3,614) had a father, with a contact for any type of mental disorder. Indicators were also computed for parental substance use disorders; similar proportions were observed for mothers (3.1 per cent; n = 2,216) and fathers (3.5 per cent; n = 2,545). Children with substantiated records of childhood maltreatment were identified from the Department of Family and Community Services (FACS) *Case Management System – Key Information Directory System* (2000–2009); 3.3 per cent (n = 2,408) of the children had a substantiated child maltreatment record, and 1.2 per cent (n = 902) were placed in out-of-home care (i.e., foster care). Further details on additional variables available in the NSW-CDS can be found in Carr et al. (2016).

Parental offending data was obtained from the *NSW Bureau of Crime Statistics Reoffending Database* for the period spanning 1994 to 2009. This includes information on each parent who was convicted of a criminal offence in NSW and the parent's subsequent criminal court appearance data (all charges proven and unproven) for charges before the Local, District, Supreme, and Children's Criminal Courts. The mothers in the cohort were born between 1947 and 1990, and the fathers were born between 1925 and 1989. In 1994, the parents in the cohort were, on average, in their early 20s (at January 1994, mean ages of fathers and mothers were 23.0 [SD = 6.4] and 20.1 [SD = 5.5] years, respectively). Therefore, the full criminal careers will only be available for the youngest parents in the cohort, and the records for many of the parents capture offending from early adulthood but not adolescence. Moreover, it is likely we are underestimating parental offending and tend to capture the more seriously offending parents. For each individual charge at a court appearance, categorical indicators were created for offspring with offending mothers (8.6 per cent) and fathers (25.7 per cent) for frequency and type of offending. Due to the skewed distribution of the data, we created the following indicator for offending frequency: no offences, one offence, two to five offences, and six or more offences. To compute offending type, all mothers and fathers were hierarchically assigned to one of the following categories based on their most serious type of offence: (0) none: no offences; (1) minor: at least one offence of minor type (e.g., traffic and vehicle offences, public health, and safety offences); (2) nonviolent: at least one offence of nonviolent type (e.g., theft, burglary, fraud, and drug offences); and (3) violent: at least one violent offence (e.g., homicide, assault, aggravated robbery, and sexual assault). The most frequent offending category (six or more offences) was observed in 1.8 per cent of mothers (n = 1,282) and 6.8 per cent of fathers (n = 4,877). Violent offending was observed in 2.6 per cent of mothers (n = 1,870) and 10.0 per cent of fathers (n = 7,237).

Table 5.3 provides further details regarding the distribution of offence types based on the 16 categories in the Australian and New Zealand Standard Offence Classification (ANZSOC) (Pink 2011: 5). The most frequent ANZSOC offence category was traffic and vehicle offences (mothers: 3.8 per cent, *n* = 2,781; fathers: 15.3 per cent, *n* = 11,020). Data regarding adult custody were also available from 2000. A small number of children in the cohort had parents who received an adult prison sentence; 326 mothers (0.5 per cent) and 1,940 (2.7 per cent) of fathers were imprisoned. These rates are likely to be underestimates because the custody data were only available since 2000.

Table 5.3 Parental crime indicators in the NSW Child Development Study

		Mothers		*Fathers*	
		%	*n*	%	*n*
Any offending		8.6	6,180	25.7	18,540
Offending frequency					
	0 offences	91.4	66,065	74.3	53,705
	1 offence	3.6	2,610	9.2	6,632
	2 to 5 offences	3.2	2,288	9.7	7,031
	6 or more offences	1.8	1,282	6.8	4,877
Offending type					
	None	91.5	66,065	74.3	53,705
	Minor	2.1	1,522	6.7	4,817
	Nonviolent	3.8	2,778	9.0	6,478
	Violent	2.6	1,870	10.0	7,237
Adult prison sentence		0.5	326	2.7	1,940
Australian and New Zealand Standard Offence Classification					
Homicide and related offences		0.0	26	0.1	89
Acts intended to cause injury		2.5	1,793	9.5	6,853
Sexual assault and related offences		0.0*	7*	0.6	443
Dangerous or negligent acts endangering persons		0.8	556	4.2	3,044
Abduction, harassment and other offences against the person		0.3	212	1.7	1,229
Robbery, extortion, and related offences		0.2	123	0.7	530
Unlawful entry with intent/burglary, break and enter		0.4	309	2.0	1,419
Theft and related offences		2.6	1,870	4.9	3,519
Fraud, deception, and related offences		1.2	877	2.3	1,637
Illicit drug offences		1.2	842	4.9	3,514
Prohibited and regulated weapons and explosive offences		0.1	81	1.2	848

	Mothers		Fathers	
	%	n	%	n
Property damage	1.0	742	4.5	3,218
Public order offences	1.6	1,125	5.5	3,945
Traffic and vehicle regulation	3.8	2,781	15.3	11,020
Offences against justice procedures, government security, and operations	1.8	1,302	6.3	4,532
Miscellaneous offences	0.4	273	1.0	753

Note: N = 72,245 children for whom linked parental records were available.
* Ethical restrictions on the reporting of data for cell-sizes <15 have precluded reporting data that would otherwise exist in these cells.

Findings

Describing the developmental course of mental illness is one of the main research themes of the NSW-CDS. Data to date have allowed us to examine early childhood vulnerabilities at age five years as measured by the AEDC domains and subdomains (see Table 5.2). Initial papers on the NSW-CDS cohort examined the effects of early childhood infections requiring hospitalisation (Kariuki et al. 2016) and the effects of parental schizophrenia spectrum disorders and child maltreatment (Matheson et al. 2016) on early childhood developmental vulnerabilities. Kariuki et al. (2016: 4) found consistent associations of low magnitude between single and multiple childhood hospitalisations for infections with vulnerability on all five AEDC developmental domains. Matheson et al. (2016: 6) found medium-sized associations between maltreatment and children's poor social competency, aggressive behaviour, and hyperactive/inattentive behaviour, and small associations between maltreatment and poor prosocial and anxious behaviour. A parental history of schizophrenia spectrum disorders was also associated with these social-emotional outcomes at age five years (including after adjustment for the effects of maltreatment), though the magnitude of these associations were smaller than those observed between maltreatment and social-emotional outcomes (Matheson et al. 2016: 7). Two recent papers have examined associations between parental offending and offspring outcomes (Laurens et al. 2017b; Tzoumakis et al. 2017).

The first of the latter two papers aimed to determine the relationship between parental offending and a range of early childhood developmental vulnerabilities. Laurens et al. (2017b) examined the association between mothers' and fathers' offending on the five broad domains of the AEDC (i.e., social, emotional, physical, cognitive, and communication), including any type of offending and violent offending for mothers, fathers, and both parents. These analyses showed that having a parent with a history of offending was associated with offspring vulnerability on the full range of developmental outcomes (as assessed by the AEDC), with the greatest influence on cognitive functioning, rather than social or emotional functioning. Mothers' offending had a larger magnitude of association on children's vulnerability across the five domains compared to fathers, even though mothers were less frequently involved in offending. Moreover, the findings suggested that when both parents had a history of offending, children were more likely to be vulnerable on all five AEDC domains and to show vulnerabilities on multiple AEDC domains. The magnitude of the associations observed between history of any and violent parental offending and AEDC outcomes increased in the following pattern: paternal < maternal < both parents' offending. The magnitudes of the associations between violent parental offending and the AEDC vulnerabilities were greater than those observed for any offending. While prior research has focused on how parental offending is associated with emotional-behavioural offspring outcomes, our findings suggest that the effects may be pervasive in early childhood, with multiple developmental outcomes affected, especially cognitive functioning.

The second of these papers focusing on parental offending (Tzoumakis et al. 2017) further disaggregated the measures of parental offending to account for differences in offending type (i.e., violent, nonviolent, minor) and frequency (i.e., no offences, one offence, two to five offences, and six or more offences). This paper used the AEDC aggression subdomain as the outcome, since high levels of aggression at school entry are early indicators of continuity of such behaviour in later developmental periods (Broidy et al. 2003; DeLisi and Vaughn 2014). The results showed an association between frequency of maternal offending and increased likelihood of other risk factors (Tzoumakis et al. 2017). As maternal offending frequency increased, so did the likelihood of paternal offending and parental mental illness. Offending mothers tended to be more disadvantaged than non-offending mothers, but this effect was more prominent for frequently offending mothers (i.e., six or more offences), who were also more likely to be younger at their child's birth, to experience mental illness and socio-economic disadvantage, and to have a partner with a criminal history. In examining the association between maternal offending frequency and child aggression, we found that maternal history of one offence was not significantly associated with child aggression when accounting for other risk factors (i.e., child sex, child English as second language, socioeconomic disadvantage, paternal offending). However, mothers with more frequent offending (i.e., two to five offences and six or more offences) were more likely to have children showing high levels of aggression at school entry after accounting for the other risk factors. Maternal involvement in frequent offending and violent offending had similar magnitudes of association. This study also showed that associations between mothers' and fathers' offending and offspring aggression were similar. No gender-specific effects were observed between parental offending and aggressive behaviour in early childhood, although it is possible such patterns may emerge at a later developmental period. Sensitivity analyses were completed for both papers and findings remained unchanged when limiting parental offending to proven offences.

NSW-CDS contributions

The NSW-CDS is the largest Australian child sample for which successive waves of record linkage are being undertaken longitudinally. Intergenerational studies using administrative records have largely been dominated to date by Scandinavian countries where national data registers have been kept since the 1950s. By combining record linkage with cross-sectional data, the NSW-CDS represents a unique and powerful methodological innovation of international significance. The design avoids recall biases, minimises selection and attrition biases, and allows the consideration of exposures and outcomes in a temporal context, including the statistical power for detecting relatively rare outcomes (i.e., serious offending and low-prevalence mental disorders).

Much research showing the intergenerational continuity of antisocial behaviour and criminal offending has focused primarily on the role of fathers rather than mothers, although studies are increasingly including both parents (van de Rakt et al. 2009: 99; van de Weijer et al. 2014: 113). Often, the small number of offending mothers and their daughters makes it difficult to draw conclusions about female intergenerational continuity of antisocial behaviour. There is some evidence suggesting that there are gender differences in the effects of parental offending and incarceration on offspring behavioural problems and offending (Auty et al. 2017: 227; Wildeman and Turney 2014: 1058). The NSW-CDS cohort will enable exploration of questions about potential gender-specific pathways into offending given the large sample size. Moreover, as the NSW-CDS is an interdisciplinary study, it is also possible to investigate a wide range of risk and protective factors as well as outcomes. For example, few studies have examined the impact of parental offending on other outcomes such as physical health or educational achievement, which the NSW-CDS has the capacity to do.

NSW-CDS findings to date have highlighted the extent and overlap of risk factors that influence several outcomes among offspring of offending parents. Owing to the nature of the parental offending and mental illness data in the study (i.e., administrative records), we are capturing the more serious offending behaviours and mental health problems requiring secondary-level care. Importantly, we have observed high levels of co-occurrence between parental offending and mental ill health (54 per cent of parents with a history of mental illness also had a history of criminal offending; 30 per cent of parents with offending histories also had a history of mental illness). Children of these parents are therefore subject to multiple parental risk factors for later adverse outcomes.

Additionally, we have found that there is considerable overlap among offending mothers and fathers, suggesting the presence of some degree of assortative mating in the cohort. Other studies have also found substantial assortative mating among individuals with a history of arrests and antisocial behaviour (Beaver 2013: 151; Krueger et al. 1998: 180). However, few intergenerational studies include sufficient numbers of offending mothers to be able to examine the role of assortative mating in the intergenerational continuity of antisocial behaviour. In the NSW-CDS cohort, assortative mating appeared to be especially prevalent for frequent and violent offenders. More specifically, close to 60 per cent of frequently offending mothers (six or more offences) also had a frequently offending partner, and this overlap was just over 50 per cent for violent offending. Strong evidence for assortative mating for violence was also found by Frisell et al. (2011: 100) using Swedish register data, whereby a person convicted for a violent offence was five times more likely to have children with a violent partner. This type of assortative mating can significantly impact children in multiple ways, by compounding genetic risk as well as contributing to social and environmental risk factors (Beaver 2013: 152). Intergenerational studies need to further examine assortative mating and consider the increased risk to offspring of having both parents involved in antisocial behaviour and/or experiencing mental illness. Intervening with such high-risk families is likely to present particular challenges. Desistance research has found that romantic relationships can be positive and contribute to discontinuity in offending (Rhule-Louie and McMahon 2007: 86), but prosocial partners for women in disadvantaged communities may not be available, and assortative mating of antisocial partners is likely to be higher among vulnerable women (Giordano et al. 2002: 1027).

Children whose parents are involved in offending represent a high-risk population. Disrupting the intergenerational transmission of antisocial behaviour needs to start early, prior to the birth of offspring, and target mothers as well as fathers. While women are traditionally less involved in offending and antisocial behaviour than men, it is important to support female offenders when they become mothers, particularly those involved in frequent or serious offending. These mothers experience multiple and compounding disadvantages, and there is evidence indicating that we should devise gender-specific support strategies for them (Covington and Bloom 2006: 12). Such interventions are a worthy subject for development and evaluation, given that rates of criminal justice system involvement of females in Australia and internationally have been steadily increasing in the last 10 years, with the number of incarcerated females growing at a faster rate than male prisoners (Australian Bureau of Statistics 2017a, Minton and Zeng 2015: 1).

Future directions

In late 2016, a second record linkage was conducted by the CHeReL to bring data up to age 12 years for the children, covering the period from birth to middle childhood. The NSW-CDS research team began to receive data from the various government agencies in early 2017 and will hold all the data by late 2017. These should be prepared and ready for analysis by early 2018. New sources of data were added for this record linkage (e.g., Pharmaceutical Drugs of Addiction data collection for child and parents; National Assessment Program Literacy and Numeracy for children) and additional variables have been included in the data collections we previously received for the first record linkage. For the criminal offending data, it has been possible to obtain more comprehensive criminal offence codes, and this will allow us to create indicators of parental domestic violence that were not previously possible to determine. In addition, children's school enrolment records will be linked, which will allow us to develop individual-level indicators of socio-economic status based on parental occupation and education. A key feature of this second record linkage is the addition of a cross-sectional self-report assessment of the children's psychological functioning for a subset of the sample; the Middle Childhood Survey.

Survey of mental health and wellbeing

The 2015 Middle Childhood Survey (MCS) is a unique aspect of the NSW-CDS which enabled the combination of both administrative records and a cross-sectional assessment of mental health and wellbeing. This statewide follow-up of the initial AEDC cohort aimed to survey as many of the 87,026 original children as possible. Owing to the large number of potential participants, active consent procedures were not feasible. Moreover, active parental consent would have biased the sample because it tends to reduce the participation of those most disadvantaged, reduce response rates, and underrepresent those involved in antisocial behaviour (Courser et al. 2009: 387). An opt-out consent model was therefore used where parents had the opportunity to opt-out their children from the MCS, and children could choose not to participate.

The MCS was an online self-report measure of children's mental health and wellbeing (Laurens et al. 2017a) that was administered to students in Year 6 (their final year of elementary school) during class time. All NSW schools with Year 6 enrolments (n = 2,371) were targeted for participation. Among these, 829 schools administered the MCS, and a total of 27,808 children completed the survey (31.4 per cent of eligible children); opt-outs were received from 816 children and 573 parents. The children who completed the survey were on average 11.5 years old (SD = 0.5) and 50.5 per cent were male. The sample is representative of the NSW population based on a range of demographic indices (including the proportions of government and non-government schools); all figures reported for the MCS participating schools are within ~2 per cent of NSW rates (Laurens et al. 2017a: 10). The survey consisted of 116 items reflecting children's demographics and social, emotional, and behavioural competencies; for a complete list see Laurens et al. (2017a: 5). Items relevant to the development of antisocial behaviour include: conduct problems and hyperactivity-inattention, as measured by the Strengths and Difficulties Questionnaire (Goodman 1997), as well as aggression and impulsivity (i.e., inhibitory control), as measured by the Early Adolescent Temperament Questionnaire (Ellis and Rothbart 2001). Importantly, this survey also includes several potential protective factors (e.g., family, school, and community supports; social integration; and temperament) that could contribute to the intergenerational discontinuity of antisocial behaviour. Low extraversion and low neuroticism among troublesome boys have been identified as protective factors for the development of offending (Farrington and Ttofi 2012: 81), and may operate similarly to disrupt the link between parental offending and offspring antisocial behaviour.

Police contact data

To date, criminal justice data in the NSW-CDS have been limited to conviction and subsequent court appearance data, which are likely to reflect the most serious offences, or those for whom there is the most evidence for prosecution to proceed. However, police contact data are available in NSW, and in 2018 we plan to add this more detailed source of crime data. NSW police records include all police contacts as a person of interest, witness, or victim. This will enable us to examine the temporal ordering of these types of contact (e.g., whether victimisation occurs prior to offending). The addition of police contacts in early adolescence will also permit examination of developmental pathways of antisocial behaviour and will help to inform preventative interventions. Beyond these immediate plans, ethical and data custodian liaison is currently under way to support a third record linkage when the offspring are adolescents. We intend to continue to follow-up with the cohort using successive waves of record linkage into adulthood.

Conclusion

Planned future record linkages will allow us to examine outcomes for children with early involvement in antisocial behaviour, and the degree of stability in their offending over time. We will be able to determine how risk factors in the prenatal and childhood (e.g., maltreatment, externalising behaviour problems) periods interact with potential protective factors (e.g., family and community support, positive peer relationships, educational achievement) in influencing the development of offending. While these childhood risk factors are known to be associated with negative adolescent and adult outcomes, less is known about their distribution and development at a population level. The NSW-CDS thus provides a unique opportunity to examine the intergenerational transmission of antisocial behaviour in a large population cohort of children, and to develop the necessary knowledge to effectively identify children and youth at risk of antisocial outcomes. The large size of the cohort will allow for the investigation of developmental pathways of both boys and girls. Having detailed police contact data, including victimisation records will enable us to better understand girls' antisocial behaviour and offending. This is particularly salient as girls tend to experience high levels of victimisation, and their victimisation experiences are often not accounted for in theoretical models of antisocial development (Lanctôt 2015).

Future intergenerational studies should examine both mothers and fathers, and both male and female offspring. This will allow researchers to examine gender-specific transmission and to better understand the impact of assortative mating. To disentangle the genetic and environment effects of parental assortative mating and other risk factors of antisocial behaviour, a genetically informed study design is required. Children of mothers with a history of antisocial behaviour and substance abuse, for example, may have alterations in gene expression associated with neurodevelopmental, self-control, and aggressive behaviour problems (Tremblay 2015). The NSW-CDS does not currently include genetic information, and with current methodology it is not possible to identify siblings (other than those who may also have been members of the NSW 2009 AEDC cohort). However, the study does include data from a wide variety of sources covering a wide variety of domains, which is important given the likely complexity of relationships underpinning intergenerational patterns of antisocial behaviour.

The NSW-CDS adopts a life-course epidemiological approach to examine associations at a population level. Large population-based epidemiological studies can help to elucidate relationships between predictors and rare outcomes. Moreover, these types of studies also enable the identification of population attributable risk (or fractions). This is the incidence in a population of an outcome that is associated with a particular risk factor, which could be prevented by an effective intervention that eliminated that risk factor, assuming an unconfounded association is identified. This can be informative to policymakers to help decide where to focus more efficiently certain prevention and intervention approaches. One of the advantages of using administrative data is that findings are translatable to the services from which data have been obtained (e.g., government health, family and community services, and, police). The NSW-CDS has strong working relationships with several government partners, which have been important in ensuring that the research conducted is relevant to the development of policy and practice. Closer working relationships with government and community sectors can better inform research, and lead to more effective translation of research findings. While we know that early family and parent training programs are an effective evidence-based strategy for preventing antisocial behaviour and delinquency (Piquero et al. 2016: 237), by working closely with government agencies, early detection practices might also be implemented at optimal points of contact with health (e.g., during pregnancy, postnatal care, and/or vaccination contacts) and other services to reduce the impact of early cumulative risk that adversely and disproportionately affects the most vulnerable families.

Acknowledgements

This research was conducted by UNSW Sydney with financial support from the Australian Institute of Criminology (Research Grant CRG 19/14–15), the Australian Research Council (Linkage Project LP110100150, with the New

South Wales (NSW) Ministry of Health, NSW Department of Education, and the NSW Department of Family and Community Services representing the Linkage Project Partners); the National Health and Medical Research Council (NHMRC; Project Grant APP1058652); the Australian Rotary Health (Mental Health Research Grant RG104090 and RG162302); a 2016 NARSAD Young Investigator Grant from the Brain & Behavior Research Foundation; and MJG was supported by a NHMRC RD Wright Biomedical Career Development Fellowship (APP1061875). The research was conducted using population data owned by the Commonwealth Department of Education; the NSW Bureau of Crime Statistics and Research; the NSW Department of Family and Community Services; the NSW Ministry of Health; the NSW Registry of Births, Deaths and Marriages; and the Australian Bureau of Statistics. The information and views contained in this study do not necessarily, or at all, reflect the views held by these departments. Linkage of NSW Police data to the cohort will be undertaken with financial support from the Australian Research Council (Discovery Project DP170101403). We would like to acknowledge the contributions of the NSW-CDS Scientific Committee: Dr Maina Kariuki, Ms Felicity Harris, Dr Miles Bore, Professor Allyson Holbrook, Professor Max Smith, Dr Sally Brinkman, Associate Professor Michael Tarren-Sweeney, Dr Megan Williams, Dr Katherine Dix, Dr Robert Stevens, Dr Titia Sprague, and Ms Marilyn Chilvers.

References

Andrich, D. and Styles, I. 2004. Final report on the psychometric analysis of the Early Development Instrument (EDI) using the Rasch Model: A technical paper commissioned for the development of the Australian Early Development Instrument (AEDI). Australia: School of Education, Murdoch University.

Arseneault, L., *et al.* 2000. Mental disorders and violence in a total birth cohort: Results from the Dunedin study. *Archives of General Psychiatry*, 57(10): 979–986.

Australian Bureau of Statistics. 1997. *Australian Social Trends (4th Edition) – Cat. No. 4102.0.* Canberra: Commonwealth of Australia.

Australian Bureau of Statistics. 2017a. *Prisoners in Australia, 2016, Cat. No. 4517.0.* Canberra: Commonwealth of Australia.

Australian Bureau of Statistics. 2017b. *Recorded Crime – Offenders, 2015–16, Cat. No. 4519.0.* Canberra: Commonwealth of Australia.

Auty, K. M., Farrington, D. P. and Coid, J. W. 2017. The intergenerational transmission of criminal offending: Exploring gender-specific mechanisms. *British Journal of Criminology*, 57(1): 215–237.

Beaver, K. M. 2013. The familial concentration and transmission of crime. *Criminal Justice and Behavior*, 40(2): 139–155.

Brinkman, S. A., *et al.* 2013. Associations between the early development instrument at age 5, and reading and numeracy skills at ages 8, 10 and 12: A prospective linked data study. *Child Indicators Research*, 6(4): 695–708.

Brinkman, S. A., *et al.* 2014. Data resource profile: The Australian Early Development Index (AEDI). *International Journal of Epidemiology*, 43(4): 1089–1096.

Broidy, L. M., *et al.* 2003. Developmental trajectories of childhood disruptive behaviors and adolescent delinquency: A six-site, cross-national study. *Developmental Psychology*, 39(2): 222.
Cannon, M., Jones, P. B. and Murray, R. M. 2002. Obstetric complications and schizophrenia: Historical and meta-analytic review. *The American Journal of Psychiatry*, 159(7): 1080–1092.
Carr, V. J., *et al.* 2016. New South Wales Child Development Study (NSW-CDS): An Australian multiagency, multigenerational, longitudinal record linkage study. *BMJ Open*, 6(2): e009023.
Castles, A. C. 1963. The reception and status of English law in Australia. *Adelaide Law Review*, 2: 1–31.
Costello, E. J., *et al.* 2003. Prevalence and development of psychiatric disorders in childhood and adolescence. *Archives of General Psychiatry*, 60(8): 837–844.
Courser, M. W., *et al.* 2009. The impact of active consent procedures on nonresponse and nonresponse error in youth survey data: Evidence from a new experiment. *Evaluation Review*, 33(4): 370–395.
Covington, S. S. and Bloom, B. E. 2006. Gender responsive treatment and services in correctional settings. *Women & Therapy*, 29(3–4): 9–33.
Dean, K., *et al.* 2012. Criminal conviction among offspring with parental history of mental disorder. *Psychological Medicine*, 42(3): 571–581.
DeLisi, M. and Vaughn, M. G. 2014. Foundation for a temperament-based theory of antisocial behavior and criminal justice system involvement. *Journal of Criminal Justice*, 42(1): 10–25.
Department of Health and Aged Care [Australian Government]. 2001. Measuring Remoteness: Accessibility/Remoteness Index of Australia (ARIA) Occasional Papers: New series No. 14. Canberra: Commonwealth of Australia.
Ellis, L. K. and Rothbart, M. K. 2001. Revision of the Early Adolescent Temperament Questionnaire. *Poster presented at the biennial meeting of the Society for Research in Child Development.* Minneapolis, MN.
Farrington, D. P. and Ttofi, M. M. 2012. Protective and promotive factors in the development of offending. *In:* Bliesener, T., Beelman, A. and Steemler, M. eds. *Antisocial behavior and crime: Contributions of developmental and evaluation research to prevention and intervention.* Cambridge, MA: Hogrefe Publishing, 71–88.
Fazel, S., *et al.* 2009. Schizophrenia and violence: Systematic review and meta-analysis. *PLoS Medicine*, 6(8): e1000120.
Fazel, S. and Seewald, K. 2012. Severe mental illness in 33 588 prisoners worldwide: Systematic review and meta-regression analysis. *The British Journal of Psychiatry*, 200(5): 364.
Frisell, T., Lichtenstein, P. and Långström, N. 2011. Violent crime runs in families: A total population study of 12.5 million individuals. *Psychological Medicine*, 41(1): 97–105.
Giordano, P. C., Cernkovich, S. A. and Rudolph, J. L. 2002. Gender, crime, and desistance: Toward a theory of cognitive transformation 1. *American Journal of Sociology*, 107(4): 990–1064.
Goodman, R. 1997. The strengths and difficulties questionnaire: A research note. *Journal of Child Psychology and Psychiatry*, 38(5): 581–586.
Guhn, M., *et al.* 2016. Associations of teacher-rated social, emotional, and cognitive development in kindergarten to self-reported wellbeing, peer relations, and academic test scores in middle childhood. *Early Childhood Research Quarterly*, 35: 76–84.
Hagquist, C. and Hellström, L. 2014. The psychometric properties of the Early Development Instrument: A Rasch analysis based on Swedish pilot data. *Social Indicators Research*, 117(1): 301–317.

Institute for Criminal Policy Research. 2017. *Highest to Lowest: Prison Population Rate, World Prison Brief* [online]. Available from: www.prisonstudies.org/highest-to-lowest/prison_population_rate?field_region_taxonomy_tid=All [Accessed 28 August 2017].

Janus, M., Brinkman, S. A. and Duku, E. K. 2011. Validity and psychometric properties of the early development instrument in Canada, Australia, United States, and Jamaica. *Social Indicators Research*, 103(2): 283–297.

Janus, M. and Offord, D. R. 2007. Development and psychometric properties of the Early Development Instrument (EDI): A measure of children's school readiness. *Canadian Journal of Behavioural Science/Revue canadienne des sciences du comportement*, 39(1): 1.

Kariuki, M., *et al.* 2016. Hospital admission for infection during early childhood influences developmental vulnerabilities at age 5 years. *Journal of Paediatrics and Child Health*, 52(9): 882–888.

Kim-Cohen, J., *et al.* 2003. Prior juvenile diagnoses in adults with mental disorder: Developmental follow-back of a prospective-longitudinal cohort. *Archives of General Psychiatry*, 60(7): 709–717.

Krueger, R. F., *et al.* 1998. Assortative mating for antisocial behavior: Developmental and methodological implications. *Behavior Genetics*, 28(3): 173–186.

Lanctôt, N. 2015. Development of antisocial behavior in adolescent girls. *In:* Morizot, J. and Kazemian, L. eds. *The development of criminal and antisocial behavior.* London: Springer, 399–412.

Laurens, K. R., *et al.* 2015. Common or distinct pathways to psychosis? A systematic review of evidence from prospective studies for developmental risk factors and antecedents of the schizophrenia spectrum disorders and affective psychoses. *BMC Psychiatry*, 15(1): 205.

Laurens, K. R., *et al.* 2017a. Cohort profile: The 2015 Middle Childhood Survey (MCS) of mental health and wellbeing at age 11 years in an Australian population cohort. *BMJ Open*, 7: e016244.

Laurens, K. R., *et al.* 2017b. Pervasive influence of maternal and paternal criminal offending on early childhood development: A population data linkage study. *Psychological Medicine*, 47(5): 889–901.

Lichtenstein, P., *et al.* 2009. Common genetic determinants of schizophrenia and bipolar disorder in Swedish families: A population-based study. *The Lancet*, 373(9659): 234–239.

Loeber, R. and Farrington, D. P. 2000. Young children who commit crime: Epidemiology, developmental origins, risk factors, early interventions, and policy implications. *Development and Psychopathology*, 12(4): 737–762.

Matheson, S., *et al.* 2016. Effects of maltreatment and parental schizophrenia spectrum disorders on early childhood social-emotional functioning: A population record linkage study. *Epidemiology and Psychiatric Sciences*: 1–12.

Minton, T. D. and Zeng, Z. 2015. Jail inmates at midyear 2014. Washington, DC: U.S. Department of Justice, Office of Justice Programs, Bureau of Justice Statistics.

Moore, E. A., *et al.* 2014. Birth outcomes and academic achievement in childhood: A population record linkage study. *Journal of Early Childhood Research*, 12(3): 234–250.

Australian National Health and Medical Research Council (NHMRC). 2007. *National statement on ethical conduct in human research (2007): Updated May 2015 (the national statement).* Canberra: Commonwealth of Australia.

Pink, B. 2011. *Australian and New Zealand Standard Offence Classification (ANZSOC).* Catalogue No. 1234.0. Canberra: Australian Bureau of Statistics, Commonwealth of Australia.

Pink, B. 2013. *Socio-Economic Indexes for Areas (SEIFA) 2011: Technical paper* (ed. Australian Bureau of Statistics). Catalogue No. 2039.0. Canberra: Commonwealth of Australia.

Piquero, A. R., *et al.* 2016. A meta-analysis update on the effects of early family/parent training programs on antisocial behavior and delinquency. *Journal of Experimental Criminology*, 12(2): 229–248.

Rhee, S. H. and Waldman, I. D. 2002. Genetic and environmental influences on antisocial behavior: A meta-analysis of twin and adoption studies. *Psychological Bulletin*, 128(3): 490.

Rhule-Louie, D. M. and McMahon, R. J. 2007. Problem behavior and romantic relationships: Assortative mating, behavior contagion, and desistance. *Clinical Child and Family Psychology Review*, 10(1): 53–100.

Teplin, L. A., *et al.* 2002. Psychiatric disorders in youth in juvenile detention. *Archives of General Psychiatry*, 59(12): 1133–1143.

Tibbetts, S. G. and Piquero, A. R. 1999. The influence of gender, low birth weight, and disadvantaged environment in predicting early onset of offending: A test of Moffitt's interactional hypothesis. *Criminology*, 37(4): 843–878.

Tremblay, R. E. 2015. Antisocial behavior before the age-crime curve: Can developmental criminology continue to ignore developmental origins? *In:* Morizot, J. and Kazemian, L. eds. *The development of criminal and antisocial behavior*. Switzerland: Springer, 39–49.

Tzoumakis, S., *et al.* 2017. The impact of parental offending on offspring aggression in early childhood: A population-based record linkage study. *Social Psychiatry and Psychiatric Epidemiology*, 52(4): 445–455.

United Nations Office on Drugs and Crime. 2015. *Homicide Counts and Rates (2000–2015)* [online]. Available from: https://data.unodc.org/ [Accessed 28 August 2017].

van de Rakt, M., Nieuwbeerta, P. and Apel, R. 2009. Association of criminal convictions between family members: Effects of siblings, fathers and mothers. *Criminal Behaviour and Mental Health*, 19(2): 94–108.

van de Weijer, S. G., Bijleveld, C. C. and Blokland, A. A. 2014. The intergenerational transmission of violent offending. *Journal of Family Violence*, 29(2): 109–118.

Wakschlag, L. S., *et al.* 2002. Maternal smoking during pregnancy and severe antisocial behavior in offspring: A review. *American Journal of Public Health*, 92(6): 966–974.

Wildeman, C. and Turney, K. 2014. Positive, negative, or null? The effects of maternal incarceration on children's behavioral problems. *Demography*, 51(3): 1041–1068.

Chapter 6

The Transfive Study

Five generations of crime?

Steve van de Weijer and Catrien Bijleveld

This chapter describes the Dutch Transfive Study and its most important findings. The Transfive Study was initiated by Catrien Bijleveld in 2003. She collected data on 198 high-risk boys who were born at the end of the nineteenth century, their parents, and all their descendants. This resulted in an internationally unique dataset with offending data on five consecutive generations. In this chapter, we will first describe the historical context of the dataset, the sample, and the available measurements. Next, we discuss the key findings from studies using the Transfive data and what these findings tell us about the possible mechanisms behind intergenerational continuities in crime. Finally, research topics that we think are important to address with multigenerational datasets will be discussed.

198 High-risk boys

Data collection of the Transfive Study started with the first 198 boys who were placed in a Dutch Catholic reform school at the beginning of the twentieth century. In 1907, the *Centrale Vereeniging voor Kinderbescherming* (Central Association for Childcare) was founded. It was a private organization, established at the initiative of Catholic civil society. Amongst others, it was commissioned to establish a reform school for Catholic children. On the 14th of September in 1911 the Catholic St. Vincentius reform school 'Harreveld' was officially opened in Harreveld, a small town in the Netherlands near the German border in the province of Gelderland. It could accommodate 200 children, which was a relatively high capacity for that time period (Bijleveld, Wijkman and Stuifbergen 2007).

Harreveld's registration book is one of the few documents that survives from its archives. This tome contains the handwritten registrations of all boys who were housed at the reform school since 1911. This includes background information for the first 198 boys, who were registered at the reform school between the 19th of June in 1911 and the 23rd of February in 1914. The problems and home situations of the boys were mixed. Some boys were placed in the reform school because of concerns about their character and problem

Table 6.1 Risk factors of the boys placed at the institution

Risk factor	*Prevalence*
Delinquent parent(s)	22%
Deceased parent(s)	29%
Alcohol abuse of parent(s)	26%
Poverty	4%
Neglect	10%
Behavioural problems of child	6%
Behavioural problems of sibling(s)	11%
Low morality of parent(s)	24%
Divorced parent(s)	8%

Source: Bijleveld et al. (2007: 17)

behaviour, including delinquency. Others were institutionalized because of the behaviour of their parents (including crime, prostitution, and alcohol abuse), who were, according to guardian organizations, unable to properly care of their children. In some cases, the problems that were described are not viewed as problematic nowadays, such as having a Protestant father or reading too many novels (Bijleveld et al. 2007). However, for most boys, several severe problems were described. Table 6.1 summarizes the risk factors for criminal development to which these boys were exposed according to the registration book. It is remarkable that most of these risk factors resemble the risk factors of boys who are treated in juvenile justice institutions nowadays. An important difference, however, is that boys nowadays are usually only dispatched to such institutions after actually showing serious problem behaviour, while most of the boys in this sample seemed 'at risk' for problem behaviour rather than actually exhibiting problem behaviour. The high prevalence rates of risk factors in Table 6.1 indicate that these 198 boys constituted a high-risk sample in terms of offending.

The 198 boys were, on average, 13 years and 2 months old when they were placed in the reform school, and stayed at this institution, on average, for 4 years and 8 months (Bijleveld et al. 2007). This average length of stay was much longer for these boys than it is for boys who are placed at similar institutions nowadays. For example, boys who were placed in the juvenile justice institution that was built on the grounds of the old reform school between 1989 and 1996 stayed at the institution for two years on average (Van der Geest, Bijleveld and Wijkman 2005). After leaving the reform school, the first 198 boys were usually put to work for a patron, usually an entrepreneur or a farmer, easing their way back into society and into employment. They remained under supervision of guardian organizations until the age of 21, when they had reached legal adulthood.

Bijleveld and van Poppel (2011) studied the societal adaption in later life of these 198 men. They found that they held occupations with significantly higher social status than their fathers, and their upward mobility exceeded the average in the Netherlands in that period. Their marriage chances were approximately normative, but they were at increased risk to divorce. Moreover, half of them were delinquent, among which one in six was a chronic or serious offender.

The multigenerational sample

In order to build a multigenerational dataset, the parents and all descendants of the 198 boys were traced in Dutch genealogical and municipal records up to 2007, with a retrieval rate of 100 per cent. Those sample members who emigrated during the course of the observation period were considered to be lost to follow-up and their descendants were not traced. All legal partners (i.e., from marriages or registered partnerships) of the sample members were also traced in municipal records and included in the dataset so that information on both parents is available for each sample member. Figure 6.1 summarizes the sample.

The 367 parents of the 198 boys are referred to as 'Generation 1' (G1) since they are the oldest generation in the sample. On average, members of G1 were born in 1870. The 198 institutionalized boys are referred to as G2, and were born on average in 1899. G2 married a total of 207 partners. From these marriages, 621 children were born and are referred to as G3. G3 were born, on average, in 1932 and had a total of 585 partners. G4 are the 1,315 children of G3 and their partners, who were born in 1960 on average. G4 married or cohabited with 1,130 partners and had 1,982 children who are referred to as G5. These G5 were, on average, born in 1986. Although some of the older G5 have partners and children (G6), this generation is not included in the current

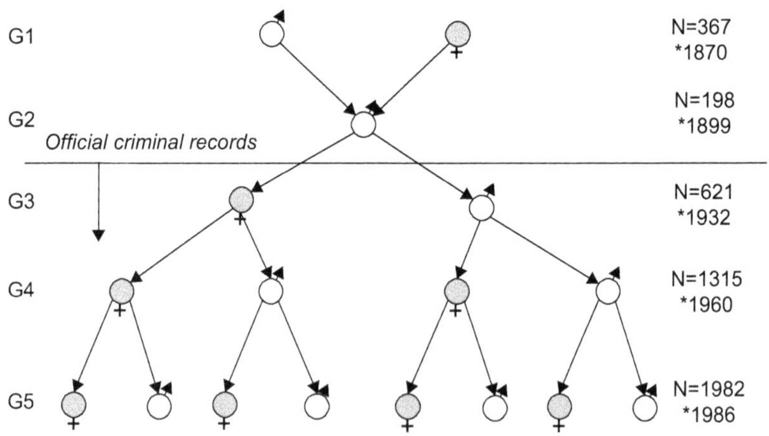

Figure 6.1 Study design of the Transfive Study

sample because the *N* is low and these children are still almost all below the age of legal responsibility (i.e., younger than 12 years old). G1 were studied retrospectively, while G2 (from adolescence onwards) and all subsequent generations were followed prospectively. G1 and G2 had all died at the moment of data collection, while surviving G3, G4, and G5 were on average 76 years, 48 years, and 22 years old, respectively. The sample members are predominantly ethnic Dutch, from a Catholic background, and from families that were part of the lower social strata of Dutch society around the 1900s. They are therefore not representative of the entire Dutch population, and results from studies using the Transfive dataset may therefore not be generalizable to the general population in the Netherlands.

A control group was constructed to compare the criminal behaviour of the descendants of the original 198 boys with criminal behaviour in the general population. For each sample member, a random member of the Dutch population, matched by age, was identified (for the procedure, see Bijleveld et al. 2007). The individuals in the control groups, however, are not family members of one another. Previous analyses using the control group (Bijleveld 2005) revealed that while offending rates remained relatively stable over generations G3–G5, those in the control group generations increased, showing that the descendants of the original 198 boys resembled average Dutch citizens increasingly over time.

Study characteristics

Information on the respondents is derived from three different sources. Information from the municipal administration records (in Dutch: *Gemeentelijke Basis Administratie* [GBA]) was used to obtain demographic variables. Official judicial documentation was used to measure offending behaviour. Data from the Ministry of Defence Archives and Registration Information Center (in Dutch: *Defensie Archieven en Registratie Informatie Centrum* [DARIC]) were used to derive variables on physical and mental health, family members, sexuality, education, employment, and leisure time for those men contacted for medical screening.

The municipal administration records

The demographic variables for sample members from each generation were obtained from Dutch municipal administration records. These data include the dates of birth, death, marriage, and divorce or separation. Based on these dates, demographic variables such as marriage, divorce, parenthood, parental divorce, and parental mortality could be constructed. Moreover, it can be inferred from these data whether the sample member had a stepparent. The gender of the sample members is available from the municipal administration records until 1994. From the records after 1994, gender is unknown but could be clearly determined from the given name in all cases but one, which was coded as a male. All residential addresses of the sample members are known from 1994 onwards. Based on this information we can measure residential mobility and we know whether family members live in the same household, neighbourhood, or city. Moreover, it makes it possible to add information about the neighbourhoods where sample members live.[1]

Offending information

Information on offending for sample members born before 1916 was retrieved from provincial and regional archives, the *Police Gazette* (a biweekly journal with lists of people sought by the police for crimes and escaped prisoners), and prison registries. In the original registration book, it had been indicated for some parents that they were criminal (e.g., some held brothels, one father was a burglar). While we scanned all major jurisdictions for the relevant years, not all archives could be scanned, and therefore information on offending for G1 and G2 is incomplete. Information on offending for those born after 1912 was sought from the computerized, paper, and microfilmed archives of the Dutch Criminal Records Documentation Service ('judicial documentation') in December 2007. This judicial documentation does not contain data on individuals born before 1912 and may miss people born between 1912 and 1916. The records are complete for all sample members born after 1916 except for sample members born before 1967 in the arrondissement (i.e., a judicial jurisdiction, comprising a number of communes) of Almelo (which applies to around 3 per cent of G3 and G4), as some data from the paper and microfilm archives for a number of years were accidentally destroyed in this region. The electronic records give complete coverage.[2]

Registrations that resulted in a conviction were counted. Acquittals and so-called 'technical dismissals' (i.e., dismissal of a case by the public prosecutor because of insufficient evidence and the case being expected to result in acquittal) were not counted. Cases that never received a disposition or that resulted in a policy dismissal (i.e., dismissal of a case because the prosecutor deemed it unfeasible to prosecute, for instance, because the perpetrator had already paid damages), were counted as convictions.

Offenses have been classified, based on the 'CBS standard classification for offenses' (Eggen and Van der Heide 2005). Crimes in this standard classification are divided into nine main categories of crime. First, the violent crimes in this classification include all hands-on sex crimes (i.e., rape, sexual assault, sexual abuse), crimes against life (i.e., murder and manslaughter), threats, assaults, physical injury, robbery, and extortion. Second, property crimes include theft, forgery, fraud, embezzlement, and handling stolen goods. Third, the category vandalism and public order includes crimes against public order, discrimination, indecent exposure, and vandalism. The other categories of crime are traffic offenses (including driving under the influence and hit-and-run accidents), economic crimes (including environmental crimes), drug laws, weapons offenses, crimes under military law, and other offenses. Besides these main categories, the exact types of crimes (i.e., the criminal code articles) are also known. Offenses were timed to the date the crimes were committed. If the date of commission was unknown, it was estimated as one year before the conviction date. If the conviction date was also missing, the commission date was timed as July 1 of the year of registration.

Ministry of Defence archives and registration information center

Data from the medical examinations prior to the mandatory military service were obtained from the Ministry of Defence for most of the men born after 1928. These medical examinations were usually carried out when conscripts were around age 18. The reports contain a wide range of variables based on the examination of physical and mental health and on questions about the conscript's family, sexuality, education, employment, and leisure activities. Not all of these variables were measured consistently and often there are missing values. Until now, only measurements of resting heart rates (Van de Weijer, De Jong, Bijleveld, Blokland and Raine 2017), occupational status, and educational level (Ramakers, Bijleveld and Ruiter 2011) have been used in analyses. In addition to these three variables, measurements of height, weight, and recovering heart rate were also measured among almost all conscripts and suitable to use in statistical analyses.[3]

These data are not available for all men as the medical screening could be abolished when it was clear that a conscript would be exempted from military service. Possible reasons to be exempted include indispensability in family businesses, being the main provider in families, extensive prior criminal behaviour, or 'brother service'.[4] In 1992, the Dutch government decided to suspend mandatory military service, and medical examinations stopped. As a consequence, data from the Ministry of Defence archives and registration information center are available for 227 G3 men, 542 G4 men, and 190 G5 men.

Key findings

Transmission of crime between family members

Due to the unique design of the Transfive Study, it is possible to examine the intergenerational transmission of offending over a much longer time period (approximately 1890–2007) and more consecutive generations than most other intergenerational studies.[5] Across the five generations, children with a criminal father were approximately twice as likely to be convicted themselves, compared to children without a criminal father. In addition, maternal offending was associated with offspring criminality across these five generations, although the degree of intergenerational transmission was more variable and not always significant because of the lower prevalence of offending in women (Bijleveld and Wijkman 2009). However, most studies using the Transfive dataset only focus on the three most recent generations (G3–G5) because the conviction data of G1 and G2 were collected from different and less complete archival sources.

Among sample members from these three most recent generations, crime was shown to be highly concentrated within nuclear families (Van de Weijer, Bijleveld and Blokland 2014). About 10 per cent of the families in the sample were responsible for approximately 65 per cent of the offenses committed by all families in the sample, and 80 per cent of all offenses were committed by only 20 per cent of the families. This concentration of crime within families was shown to be stronger for violent crimes than for non-violent crimes: about 80 per cent of the violent offenses were committed by only 11 per cent of the families. The intergenerational transmission of violent crime from father to son was also shown to be stronger than the intergenerational transmission of non-violent crime. Children with a violent father were 2.3 to 3.4 times more likely to be convicted for a violent crime themselves than children without a violent father. Sex offenses, a specific type of violent offenses, were also found to be concentrated within families and to be transmitted from father to son in the Transfive Study (Van de Weijer, Besemer, Bijleveland and Blokland 2015).

The design of the Transfive Study additionally also makes it possible to study similarity in offending between family members other than parents and their children. For example, a significant degree of similarity in criminal offending was found between marital partners. Partners were found to be similar in offending behaviour prior to their marriage as well as after their marriage (Van de Weijer and Beaver 2016). The first finding may point to the mechanism of assortative mating (i.e., people seek out partners who are similar to themselves), while the latter may be attributable to behavioural contagion (i.e., one mate socializes the other mate so that they become more similar to each other over time). Empirical evidence for 'intra'generational transmission of criminal offending between siblings was also found in the Transfive Study (Beijers, Bijleveld, Van de Weijer and Liefbroer 2017). Remarkably, not only were those with offending siblings more likely to be convicted than those with non-offending siblings, but children without siblings were also at increased risk to become criminal offenders. The intragenerational transmission of offending was found to be the strongest between sisters. Age differences between siblings did not influence the relationship between sibling offending and offending risk. Moreover, in a model in which the offending of both parents, one set of grandparents, and siblings were all used to simultaneously predict an individual's offending risk, the offending of each of these family members, except the grandmother, increased the risk of a conviction. Finally, sex offending also was shown to be associated with both sex offending by brothers and extended family members (Van de Weijer et al. 2015).

Mechanisms

Several mechanisms that could explain the intergenerational transmission of crime have been proposed in the literature (e.g., Farrington 2011), such as social learning mechanisms, mediation through risk factors for offending, genetic influences, and official bias towards known criminal families. At this moment, the Transfive Study lacks detailed measurements to directly test all these mechanisms. However, studying factors that mediate or moderate the intergenerational transmission of crime does provide us with insights about the possible mechanisms behind this transmission. For example, Ramakers et al. (2011) used data from the Ministry of Defence archives to show that a substantial part of the intergenerational transmission of offending was mediated by low occupational status and particularly by low educational attainment, which is in line with Farrington's (2011) risk factor mechanism.

Moreover, the degree of intergenerational transmission in the Transfive Study as described above is not the same for all families. For example, a significant intergenerational transmission of violence was only found in families in which the father committed at least one of his violent offenses during the son's youth (0–18 years). In families in which the father only committed violent offenses prior to the son's birth or during the son's adulthood, no intergenerational transmission of violence was found (Van de Weijer et al. 2014). A possible explanation for this finding is that exposure to the violent behaviour of the parent plays an important role in the intergenerational transmission of violent behaviour. In line with this, intergenerational transmission of violence was only found in families in which the parents were married during the entire youth of the child, but not in families in which the parents divorced (Van de Weijer et al. 2015). This might show the importance of exposure to violent fathers because children in the Netherlands usually live with their mother after parental divorce and, consequently, contact with the father and exposure to his violent behaviour after the divorce decreases.

These results, that suggest that exposure to parental offending is an important condition for intergenerational transmission of offending to occur, seem to be most in line with social learning theories (e.g., Burgess and Akers 1966; Sutherland 1947). Such theories assume that criminal behaviour and attitudes regarding crime are learned from other people. This, however, does not mean that genetic and biological factors do not contribute to the intergenerational transmission of crime. For example, Van de Weijer and colleagues (2017) showed that a low resting heart rate of children also moderates the intergenerational transmission of violent crime. A low resting heart rate has been argued to be a marker for fearlessness (Raine 1993, 1997), as well as stimulation-seeking behaviour (Zuckerman 1979), both of which may lead to antisocial or violent behaviour. Ortiz and Raine (2004: 154) concluded that "low resting heart rate appears to be the best-replicated biological correlate to date of antisocial and aggressive behaviour in children and adolescents". In the Transfive Study, a low resting heart rate was indeed found to be related to violent offending. Moreover, intergenerational transmission of violent offending was only found when the son had a low resting heart rate (Van de Weijer et al. 2017).

Development over time

Since the Transfive Study spans such a long time period it is possible to study how the degree of intergenerational transmission of crime develops over time. In almost all studies using the Transfive data, the intergenerational associations that were found were less strong between G3 and G4 compared to other generations. It is remarkable that stronger intergenerational transmission of crime was found between G4 and G5 than between G3 and G4 given the fact that class differences became smaller, state benefits increasingly provided for the unemployed, and higher education became available to all; intergenerational mobility of occupational status, social class (Ganzeboom and Luijkx 1995), and educational level (Ganzeboom and De Graaf 1989) also increased in this period. A child's future thus became less determined by his or her social origins, and young generations had more opportunities than before. One would expect that such a more socially mobile and secure society would also increase opportunities for children of criminal parents not to follow in their parents' footsteps.

This remarkable finding may be the consequence of prosecution trends in the Netherlands. After World War II, conviction rates in the Netherlands stayed relatively low until the mid-1960s when they started to increase. At the beginning of the twenty-first century, the number of criminal court case dispositions was about twice as high as during the 1960s (Dennison, Bijleveld and Van de Weijer 2017). As a consequence of these low conviction rates during the 1950s, 1960s, and 1970s, G3 and G4 in the sample may have been less likely to incur a conviction for the crimes they committed, especially for crimes committed at a young age. Consequently, intergenerational transmission between G3 and G4 may be underestimated.

Parental incarceration

Because the Transfive Study not only contains data on criminal offending but also on the type of punishment that the offenders received, it is also possible to study the intergenerational consequences of parental imprisonment. Bijleveld and colleagues (2014) showed that children who experienced parental incarceration were more likely to commit any offense, a serious offense, and a violent offense compared to children of criminal but not incarcerated or non-criminal parents. Moreover, intergenerational transmission of incarceration was found between G2 and G3, G3 and G4, and G4 and G5, which suggested that men with a father who was ever incarcerated were at increased risk to be imprisoned themselves. Similar to the results for the intergenerational transmission of offending, intergenerational transmission of incarceration was only found when the father was incarcerated during the son's youth (Dennison et al. 2017). Moreover, parental incarceration was found to be associated with offspring outcomes in other life domains, too. For example, children who experienced parental incarceration were found to be less likely to marry (Bijleveld, Van de Weijer, Besemer and Huschek 2014) and more likely to become a teen parent (Van de Weijer, Smallbone, Bouwman and Meyer 2016) or to die prematurely (Van de Weijer, Smallbone and Bouwman 2018).

Future research

All research using the Transfive Study has been carried out on data collected in 2007. Currently we are updating the data and will thereby add another 10 years of demographic and conviction data to the existing dataset. This is particularly important for our analyses concerning G5. Because the sample members from this generation were on average born in 1986, we only have conviction data for G5 until they are, on average, 21 years old. Although the age–crime curve shows that most criminal behaviour is committed during adolescence and early adulthood, this relatively short follow-up period for G5 limits the possibilities to examine criminal careers over the whole life course and to examine, for example, the associations between criminal offending and life events during adulthood (e.g., marriage, divorce, parenthood). Moreover, in previous studies often only G5 sample members that reached a certain age at the moment of data collection (e.g., 18 or 30 years old) were selected. As a consequence, families in which multiple generations had children at a young age were overrepresented in these analyses, which limits the generalizability of the results.

Adding 10 more years to the data also means that the sample size will increase. Children born after 2007 will be included to the sample, and in a considerable number of families a sixth generation (G6) can be added to the dataset. In addition, partners who married with sample members after 2007 will be added to the sample. Moreover, in 2007, existing sample members born after 1995 had not yet reached the age of legal responsibility (i.e., 12 years old, in the Netherlands). An update of the conviction data, therefore, also makes it possible to measure criminal behaviour of these young sample members, after they have reached the age of 12. This increased sample size will improve the possibilities to study relatively rare phenomena, such as sex offending or violent offending by women.

We also aim to link the data from the Transfive Study to data from Statistics Netherlands (as described in Chapter 3). The registers that Statistics Netherlands holds contain information on all Dutch inhabitants, which can be linked to the individual sample members of the Transfive Study through their personal identification number. This would enable us to enrich the Transfive Study with information from various life domains, such as employment, educational performance, social welfare benefits, health, and disease-specific mortality. Combining these datasets makes it possible to control for relevant background characteristics (e.g., socioeconomic status) when studying the intergenerational transmission of offending. Furthermore, other possible outcomes of parental crime and parental imprisonment than offspring offending can be examined, such as educational attainment and poor health.

After updating the Transfive Study and linking the dataset to the Statistics Netherlands registers, new research questions can be addressed. Below we describe a number of topics that we think should be of interest for researchers that use the Transfive Study data or other intergenerational data.

Genetic confounding

We believe that one strength of intergenerational datasets that is often ignored in criminological research is the fact that these are genetically informed datasets, containing data on sample members with different degrees of genetic similarity. Genetic explanations of criminal behaviour have thus far received relatively little attention from life-course criminologists. This may be due to the dominance of sociological thinking within criminology (Beaver 2009) and because biological theories were previously linked to immoral eugenic policies (Wright and Miller 1998). Although the validity of heritability studies for criminology is still debated (Burt and Simons 2014, 2015; Barnes et al. 2014), studies on genetic influences have gained increasing recognition recently. A recent meta-analysis of virtually all twin studies in behavioural genetics over the past 50 years showed that all human traits are to some extent heritable (Polderman et al. 2015). Overall, 49 per cent of the variance in human traits appears to be attributable to genetic influences, with the remaining 51 per cent attributable to shared and non-shared environmental influences (shared environments are the same between relatives and make them more similar to each other, while non-shared environments are unique to each relative and make them different from each other). Similar influences of genetic factors were found in meta-analyses that focus specifically on antisocial or criminal behaviour (Ferguson 2010; Mason and Frick 1994; Miles and Carey 1997; Rhee and Waldman 2002).

Intergenerational datasets like the Transfive Study are less suitable to estimate the heritability of criminal behaviour than twin studies because the equal environment assumption (i.e., that relatives with a different degree of genetic relatedness are equally correlated for their exposure to environmental influences of etiological importance) is likely to be violated when analysing non-twin siblings. Nevertheless, information on the genetic relatedness of sample members can be utilized for family-based, quasi-experimental designs. These designs can control for confounding by genetic and shared environmental factors when estimating the association between criminal behaviour and environmental variables (e.g., marriage, divorce, parenthood, employment, and educational performance). D'Onofrio, Lahey, Turkheimer, and Lichtenstein (2013) describe a large number of family-based, quasi-experimental designs that can be used to (partly) control for genetic confounding, and their advantages and limitations.

For example, comparing an employed sibling with an unemployed sibling in a fixed effects model excludes all selection factors that make siblings similar to each other, including genetic and environmental factors that are shared by siblings. See also Chapter 1 of this volume for an example of the use of such a fixed-effects model using siblings in Finnish register data. Similarly, a comparison between children of siblings (i.e., cousins) can be used to examine the relationship between crime and those risk factors that almost always are shared between siblings. For example, the effects of parental imprisonment could be examined by comparing a cousin who experienced parental imprisonment with a cousin who did not.

Intergenerational discontinuity

Studies using multigenerational datasets usually focus on the intergenerational transmission of crime, describing and explaining patterns of continuity of crime across generations. However, little research has been devoted to explain intergenerational *discontinuity* in offending. Who are the children that do not follow their parent's criminal behaviour? And why do they not become criminal against the odds?

Results from the Transfive Study have shown that intergenerational transmission of violent crime is reduced significantly when the father does not commit the violent crimes during the child's youth, when the parents are divorced during the child's youth, and when the son has a high heart rate. It would be an interesting topic for future studies to examine which other characteristics of parents, children, or families moderate the intergenerational transmission of crime and could lead to discontinuity in criminal behaviour. Results from such studies could give insights on the mechanisms behind both the continuity and discontinuity of criminal behaviour across generations. Moreover, it would help to identify which children of criminal parents are most at risk and which are least at risk to continue their parent's behaviour.

Intergenerational transmission of crime among subgroups

Another interesting research topic for future intergenerational studies is to examine the intergenerational transmission of criminal offending among specific subgroups. First of all, it might be interesting to focus on the transmission between female family members. Many studies using the Transfive dataset only utilized data on the male sample members because the number of convicted women was relatively low, even in this high-risk sample. Not all results discussed above can therefore be generalized to women. Research suggests that the share in the total amount of officially registered crime committed is rising for females (e.g., Slotboom, Hoeve, Ezinga and Van der Helm 2013). Therefore, it is increasingly important to gain knowledge about the intergenerational transmission of crime among women. In addition, women as wives, mothers, grandmothers, and daughters, play a pivotal role in the family, the upbringing of children, and the upholding and transmission of family values and norms. It is imperative that the impact of women's criminality in intergenerational patterns of offending is better understood.

Moreover, the above described results from the Transfive Study cannot be generalized to ethnic minorities in the Netherlands, because these groups were underrepresented or even absent in the predominantly ethnic Dutch sample of the Transfive Study. Because individuals with an Antillean, Surinamese, Moroccan, or Turkish background are overrepresented in offender populations in the Netherlands (Statistics Netherlands 2017), it would be important to study intergenerational transmission among these ethnic subgroups as well. Cultural differences and differences in family formation between these ethnic minorities and the ethnic Dutch population might influence the intergenerational transmission of crime and its underlying mechanisms among these ethnic minorities. Antillean and Surinamese families in the Netherlands, for example, are characterized by relatively high rates of single mothers (Statistics Netherlands 2017). Consequently, Antillean and Surinamese children might have less contact with their fathers. Social learning mechanisms might therefore explain the intergenerational transmission of crime among Antillean and Surinamese men to a lesser extent than among ethnic Dutch families. Moreover, ethnic minorities in the Netherlands more often live in deprived neighbourhoods and have higher unemployment rates than ethnic Dutch citizens (Statistics Netherlands 2017). Consequently, intergenerational transmission of crime among these ethnic minorities might be mediated in a different way by risk factors for criminal offending (such as living in bad neighbourhoods and unemployment). However, studying intergenerational transmission of crime among ethnic minorities poses significant data collection challenges, especially when people migrated recently to the Netherlands, or from countries where valid data on offending are harder to obtain.

It would also be interesting to focus on intergenerational transmission of specific types of criminal behaviour. For example, Dutch studies using small samples of families have shown that almost all sons of fathers who are involved in organized crime are involved in criminal offending themselves as well (Moors and Spapens 2017; Van Dijk 2016). Studies using larger samples of families involved in organized crime would be necessary to get a better understanding of the mechanisms behind the transmission of this specific type of crime. Moreover, as the prevalence of cybercrime has been increasing sharply during this century, it would be interesting to study how this relatively new type of crime is influenced by intergenerational factors. Although an intergenerational transmission of cybercrime might be unlikely because of intergenerational differences in information technology knowledge and use, it would be interesting to see whether children of parents who commit 'traditional' crimes are also more often involved in cybercrime.

Contextual factors

Finally, we argue that it is important to examine the impact of contextual factors on the intergenerational transmission of crime. Elder (1998: 304) argued that the life course of individuals "is shaped by the historical times and events they experience". These historical times and events that happen during the lives of individuals are, however, seldom taken into account when the intergenerational transmission of crime is studied. As described previously, research using the Transfive Study without exception finds that the degree of transmission is larger for the most recent generations (G4 and G5) than for the previous generations (G3 and G4). This may be due to differences in crime and incarceration rates, but could also be the consequence of different generations being exposed to different circumstances during their life course. G3 participants in the Transfive Study were born, on average, in 1932 and most experienced World War II. This experience may have shaped their life course differently than subsequent generations who grew up in the post–World War II period, when society was relatively affluent in comparison. In order to study the influence of such historical circumstances and events, large samples are necessary with sufficient individuals born in each year. Moreover, multigenerational datasets that span long historical periods are necessary to be able to investigate the impact of both sudden societal changes (e.g., wars, economic crises, famines, Spanish flu) and slower-moving trends (e.g., improved schooling, better hygiene, changes in child labour laws, increased social mobility).

Notes

1 Permission for building the sample was granted by the Frentrop Foundation (legal successor to the Harreveld reform school) and Bureau Registratie Persoonsgegevens, responsible for the GBA.
2 Permission for the collection of prosecution information was granted by the Ministry of Justice.
3 Permission for the collection of military screening data was granted by the Ministry of Defence.
4 'Brother service' implies that not all brothers from larger families had to serve. Until 1966, only the three oldest brothers had to serve in the armed forces. From 1966 onwards, only the two oldest brothers had to serve.
5 With the term 'intergenerational transmission of offending' we mean that criminal behavior occurs in both the parent and the child. It is also referred to as 'intergenerational continuity in offending'.

References

Barnes, J.C., Wright, J.P., Boutwell, B.B., Schwartz, J.A., Connolly, E.J., Nedelec, J.L. and Beaver, K.M. (2014) 'Demonstrating the validity of twin research in criminology', *Criminology*, 52(4), 588–626.

Beaver, K.M. (2009) *Biosocial criminology: A primer*, Dubuque, IA: Kendall/Hunt Publishing.

Beijers, J.E.H., Bijleveld, C.C.J.H., van de Weijer, S.G.A. and Liefbroer, A.C. (2017) ' "All in the family?" The relationship between sibling offending and offending risk', *Journal of Developmental and Life-Course Criminology*, 3(1), 1–14.

Bijleveld, C.C.J.H. (2005) 'Delinquency over five generations', Cambridge University Lecture Series, 20 October.

Bijleveld, C.C.J.H., Van de Weijer, S.G.A., Besemer, S. and Huschek, D. (2014) 'Parental imprisonment and offspring outcomes: A study on offending and marriage chances', in J. Murray, C.C.J.H. Bijleveld, D.P. Farrington and R. Loeber (eds.), *Effects of parental incarceration on children: Cross-national comparative studies*, Washington, DC: American Psychological Association.

Bijleveld, C.C.J.H. and van Poppel, F. (2011) 'The success of the civilization offensive: Societal adaptation of reformed boys in the early twentieth century in the Netherlands', *Journal of Social History*, 44(4), 1173–1194.

Bijleveld, C.C.J.H. and Wijkman, M.D.S. (2009) 'Intergenerational continuity in convictions: A five-generation study', *Criminal Behaviour and Mental Health*, 19(2), 142–155.

Bijleveld, C.C.J.H., Wijkman, M.D.S. and Stuifbergen, J.A.M. (2007) *198 Boefjes?*, Leiden: NSCR.

Burgess, R.L. and Akers, R.L. (1966) 'A differential association-reinforcement theory of criminal behavior', *Social Problems*, 14(2), 128–147.

Burt, C.H. and Simons, R.L. (2014) 'Pulling back the curtain on heritability studies: Biosocial criminology in the postgenomic era', *Criminology*, 52(2), 223–262.

Burt, C.H. and Simons, R.L. (2015) 'Heritability studies in the postgenomic era: The fatal flaw is conceptual', *Criminology*, 53(1), 103–112.

Dennison, S., Bijleveld, C.C.J.H. and Van de Weijer, S.G.A. (2017) 'Intergenerational continuity in incarceration: Evidence from a Dutch multi-generation cohort', in A.A.J. Blokland and V.R. Van der Geest (eds.), *Routledge international handbook of life-course criminology*, New York: Routledge.

D'onofrio, B.M., Lahey, B.B., Turkheimer, E. and Lichtenstein, P. (2013) 'Critical need for family-based, quasi-experimental designs in integrating genetic and social science research', *American Journal of Public Health*, 103(S1), S46–S55.

Eggen, A.T.J. and Van der Heide, W. (2005) *Criminaliteit en rechtshandhaving 2004*, Den Haag: Boom juridische uitgevers.

Elder, G.H. (1998) *Children of the great depression*, Boulder: Westview Press.

Farrington, D.P. (2011) 'Families and crime', in J.Q. Wilson and J. Petersilia (eds.), *Crime and public policy*, New York: Oxford University Press.

Ferguson, C.J. (2010) 'Genetic contributions to antisocial personality and behavior: A meta-analytic review from an evolutionary perspective', *The Journal of Social Psychology*, 150(2), 160–180.

Ganzeboom, H.B.G. and Graaf, D.P.M. (1989) 'Intergenerationele opleidingsmobiliteit in Nederland van geboortecohorten 1891–1960', *Sociale Wetenschappen*, 32, 263–278.

Ganzeboom, H.B.G. and Luijkx, R. (1995) 'Intergenerationele beroepsmobiliteit in Nederland: patronen en historische veranderingen', in J. Dronkers and W.C. Ultee (eds.), *Verschuivende ongelijkheid in Nederland: Sociale gelaagdheid en mobiliteit*, Assen: Van Gorcum.

Mason, D.A. and Frick, P.J. (1994) 'The heritability of antisocial behavior: A meta-analysis of twin and adoption studies', *Journal of Psychopathology and Behavioral Assessment*, 16(4), 301–323.

Miles, D.R. and Carey, G. (1997) 'Genetic and environmental architecture on human aggression', *Journal of Personality and Social Psychology*, 72(1), 207–217.

Moors, H. and Spapens, T. (2017) *Criminele families in Noord-Brabant: Een verkenning van generatie-effecten in de georganiseerde misdaad*, Amsterdam: Politie & Wetenschap.

Ortiz, J. and Raine, A. (2004) 'Heart rate level and antisocial behavior in children and adolescents: A meta-analysis', *Journal of the American Academy of Child and Adolescent Psychiatry*, 43(2), 154–162.

Polderman, T.J., Benyamin, B., de Leeuw, C.A., Sullivan, P.F., van Bochoven, A., Visscher, P.M. and Posthuma, D. (2015) 'Meta-analysis of the heritability of human traits based on fifty years of twin studies', *Nature Genetics*, 47(7), 702–709.

Raine, A. (1993) *The psychopathology of crime: Criminal behavior as a clinical disorder*, San Diego, CA: Academic Press Inc.

Raine, A. (1997) 'Antisocial behavior and psychophysiology: A biosocial perspective and a prefrontal dysfunction hypothesis', in D.M. Stoff, J. Breiling and J.D. Maser (eds.), *Handbook of antisocial behavior*, New York: John Wiley & Sons Inc.

Ramakers, A.A., Bijleveld, C.C.J.H. and Ruiter, S. (2011) 'Escaping the family tradition: A multi-generation study of occupational status and criminal behaviour', *The British Journal of Criminology*, 51(5), 856–874.

Rhee, S.H. and Waldman, I.D. (2002) 'Genetic and environmental influences on antisocial behavior: A meta-analysis of twin and adoption studies', *Psychological Bulletin*, 128(3), 490–529.

Slotboom, A., Hoeve, M., Ezinga, M. and Van der Helm, P. (2013) *Criminele meisjes en vrouwen: Achtergronden en aanpak*, Den Haag: Boom Lemma Uitgevers.

Statistics Netherlands (2017) *CBS Statline*. Online. Available http://statline.cbs.nl/Statweb/ (accessed 30 May 2017).

Sutherland, E.H. (1947) *Principles of Criminology*, 4th edn, Philadelphia: J.B. Lippincott Company.

Van der Geest, V.R., Bijleveld, C.C.J.H. and Wijkman, M.D.S. (2005) *Delinquentie na behandeling. Een verkennend onderzoek naar geregistreerde justitiecontacten, persoonlijke en omgevingskenmerken van jongeren uit een behandelinrichting*, Leiden: NSCR.

Van de Weijer, S.G.A. and Beaver, K.M. (2016) 'An exploration of mate similarity for criminal offending behaviors: Results from a multi-generation sample of Dutch spouses', *Psychiatric Quarterly*, 1–11.

Van de Weijer, S.G.A., Besemer, S., Bijleveld, C.C.J.H. and Blokland, A.A.J. (2015) 'The concentration of sex offenses within British and Dutch families', in A.A.J. Blokland and P. Lussier (eds.), *Sex offenders: A criminal career approach*, Oxford: Wiley-Blackwell.

Van de Weijer, S.G.A., Bijleveld, C.C.J.H. and Blokland, A.A.J. (2014) 'The intergenerational transmission of violent offending', *Journal of Family Violence*, 29(2), 109–118.

Van de Weijer, S.G.A., De Jong, R., Bijleveld, C.C.J.H., Blokland, A.A.J. and Raine, A. (2017) 'The role of heart rate levels in the intergenerational transmission of crime', *Societies*, 7(3).

Van de Weijer, S.G.A., Smallbone, H.S., and Bouwman, V. (2018) 'Parental imprisonment and premature mortality in adulthood', *Journal of Developmental and Life-Course Criminology*, 4(2), 148–161.

Van de Weijer, S.G.A., Smallbone, H.S., Bouwman, V. and Meyer, I. (2016) 'The long term consequences of parental imprisonment: Mortality, family formation, and offending', paper presented at Annual Conference of the American Society of Criminology, New Orleans, November 2016.

Van de Weijer, S.G.A., Thornberry, T.P., Bijleveld, C.C.J.H. and Blokland, A.A.J. (2015) 'The effects of parental divorce on the intergenerational transmission of crime', *Societies*, 5(1), 89–108.

Van Dijk, M. (2016) 'Kinderen van Beroepscriminelen: Valt de appel ver van de boom?', paper presented at Annual Conference of Nederlandse Vereniging voor Criminologie, Leiden, June.

Wright, R.A. and Miller, J.M. (1998) 'Taboo until today? The coverage of biological arguments in criminology textbooks, 1961 to 1970 and 1987 to 1996', *Journal of Criminal Justice*, 26(1), 1–19.

Zuckerman, M. (1979) *Sensation seeking: Beyond the optimal level of arousal*, Hillsdale, NJ: Lawrence Erlbaum Associates.

Part III

Studies using survey data

Chapter 7

Intergenerational transmission of self-reported offending in the Cambridge Study in Delinquent Development

David P. Farrington, Maria M. Ttofi, and Rebecca V. Crago

The Cambridge Study in Delinquent Development (CSDD) is a prospective longitudinal survey of 411 London males who were first studied in 1961 at age 8. They were last interviewed at age 48, and they have been followed up in criminal records from age 10 to age 56. Between 2004 and 2013, 551 adult children of these males were interviewed at the average age of 25. This chapter summarizes results on the intergenerational transmission of self-reported offending. In the interests of clarity, the original 411 males are termed generation 2 (G2), their parents are termed generation 1 (G1), and their children are termed generation 3 (G3).

The CSDD was begun by Professor Donald West in 1961. He had been impressed by the seminal work of the Gluecks (e.g., Glueck and Glueck 1950) and the McCords (e.g., McCord, McCord, and Zola 1959) in the US, and he wanted to mount a similar study in the UK. He contacted both the Gluecks and the McCords to ask for their questions and measures, but only the McCords gave him clear definitions and explicit criteria for variables such as parental supervision, attitude, and discipline. Consequently, many of the early family variables in the CSDD were based on the measures of the McCords. Professor David Farrington joined Professor West to work on the CSDD in 1969, and took over the direction of the CSDD in 1981. There will soon be another intergenerational transmission of the direction of the CSDD, as Dr. Maria Ttofi will be responsible for future data collections.

There appear to have been no previous prospective longitudinal publications on the self-reported offending of adults in two successive generations. Retrospective studies have a number of problems, because retrospective reports are likely to be biased by the knowledge of later events. Also, in retrospective studies, it may be very difficult to calculate valid prospective probabilities (e.g., the probability that offending fathers have offending sons).

Thornberry (2009) reviewed studies of intergenerational transmission and recommended that children in successive generations should be followed up prospectively over the same ages. In the Rochester Intergenerational Study, Thornberry, Freeman-Gallant, and Lovegrove (2009) prospectively followed up adolescents, first assessed at age 13–14 in 1988, and their children up to 2004.

They showed that the self-reported delinquency of the parents at age 14–18 predicted the externalizing behaviour of their children at age 8–9. Also, Kim et al. (2009) in the Oregon Youth Study carried out a similar study of externalizing behaviour, while Dubow, Huesmann, and Boxer (2003) in the Columbia County Longitudinal Study prospectively investigated the intergenerational transmission of aggression.

Other intergenerational research in criminology has been reviewed by Farrington, Ttofi, and Crago (2017). Also, a systematic review of intergenerational research in criminology was recently published by Besemer et al. (2017). Based on 21 studies, they concluded that children with criminal parents were more likely than others to become criminals themselves (weighted mean odds ratio = 2.38). Interestingly, the effect size was greater (2.86) for studies where the parental offending clearly preceded the child offending, but this applied to only four studies.

The only published study of self-reported offending in two successive generations seems to be by Johnson, Morris, and Menard (2015). They investigated self-reported offending in adolescence in the US National Youth Survey Family Study, and concluded that strain variables had the same effects on adolescent delinquency across the two generations. Only the CSDD, however, seems to have prospectively studied offending from childhood to adulthood in two successive generations.

It is important to investigate risk factors that might mediate the relationship between parent and child offending, because these might be possible targets for intervention efforts to prevent intergenerational transmission. For example, there could be individual, parental, child-rearing, or socio-economic mediators. Convicted fathers could be impulsive, with antisocial attitudes or alcohol problems; young parents, separated or divorced, or in conflict with their partners; using physical punishment or poor parental supervision; or they could have low income, frequent unemployment, and could be living in poor housing in a bad area. Mediators were chosen in this chapter based on knowledge about risk factors that lead to child offending (see e.g., Farrington 2015b).

Little is known about mediators between parent and child offending. However, in the Pittsburgh Youth Study, Farrington et al. (2001) suggested that a young mother, a bad neighbourhood, and low guilt feelings of the boy were mediators in the causal chain between arrested fathers and delinquent boys. In the Dutch Transfive study, Ramakers, Bijleveld, and Ruiter (2011) concluded that a large part of the intergenerational transmission of offending from fathers to sons was mediated by the son's low occupational status and low educational attainment. Possible mediators between parent and child offending are studied in the present chapter.

Previous findings in the CSDD

The results of the CSDD have been summarized in six books (Farrington, Piquero, and Jennings 2013; Piquero, Farrington, and Blumstein 2007; West 1969, 1982; West and Farrington 1973, 1977) and in five summary articles

(Farrington and West 1981, 1990; Farrington 1995, 2003; Farrington, Coid, and West 2009b). In addition, over 250 articles have been published describing results from the CSDD (listed on the Cambridge University Institute of Criminology website). The main topics that have been addressed are the development of offending and antisocial behaviour, risk and protective factors, and the effects of life events on the course of offending.

As an example of CSDD research on the development of offending, Farrington et al. (2014) documented prevalence and frequency, ages of onset and desistance, and criminal career duration, for the G2 males from age 8 to age 48, according to self-reports and convictions. They found that, according to self-reports, the number of offenses was over 30 times greater, the age of onset was earlier, and the career duration was longer, compared with conviction data.

As an example of CSDD research on risk factors, Farrington et al. (2015) compared 20 comparable risk factors for predicting G2 convictions and G3 convictions. Remarkably, G2 effect sizes correlated .80 with G3 effect sizes, showing the replicability of risk factors from one generation to the next. As an example of CSDD research on the effects of life events, Theobald and Farrington (2009) showed that convictions decreased after the G2 males got married, and Theobald and Farrington (2011) found that the effects were much greater for marriage at earlier ages. Later, Theobald and Farrington (2013) demonstrated that convictions increased after G2 males separated from their wives.

The CSDD has also inspired the integrated cognitive antisocial potential (ICAP) theory, which was designed to explain the development of offending in males (see e.g., Farrington 2005). This theory proposes that long-term risk factors lead to long-term between-individual differences in antisocial potential, while immediate situational factors lead to short-term within-individual differences in antisocial potential and to the commission of criminal offenses. Farrington and McGee (2017) operationally defined and measured the key theoretical construct of antisocial potential using G2 antisocial attitude measures at ages 18, 32, and 48, and showed that most of the predictions from the theory were confirmed.

Previous findings on intergenerational transmission

In the CSDD, Farrington, Gundry, and West (1975) and West and Farrington (1977) found that convicted G1 fathers and mothers tended to have convicted G2 sons and daughters. These results were based on criminal record searches up to 1973, when the majority of sons were aged 20. A convicted G1 parent by the G2 boy's age 10 was consistently one of the best predictors of a G2 boy's own convictions. The prevalence of convictions of sons did not vary according to whether the father was last convicted before the boy's birth, suggesting that there was no direct behavioural influence of criminal fathers on criminal sons.

Also, little intergenerational transmission was attributable to co-offending, since very few fathers co-offended with their sons (Reiss and Farrington 1991).

Later analyses of the CSDD by Farrington, Barnes, and Lambert (1996) and Rowe and Farrington (1997) were based on convictions of the G2 males up to age 40 and convictions of all their biological relatives (up to 1993). They found that offending was strongly concentrated in families (since 6 per cent of the families accounted for half of all convictions) and was transmitted from parents to children. About three-quarters of G1 convicted fathers had a convicted G2 son, compared with 45 per cent of unconvicted G1 fathers. Same-sex relationships (e.g., father to son) were stronger than opposite-sex relationships (e.g., father to daughter). Later analyses by Farrington and Crago (2016) compared the concentration of offending in G1–G2 families and G2–G3 families. While 6 per cent of G1–G2 families accounted for half of all convictions of family members, this was true for 8 per cent of G2–G3 families.

Further CSDD analyses of intergenerational transmission were carried out by Smith and Farrington (2004), Farrington, Coid, and Murray (2009a), and Besemer and Farrington (2012). Farrington et al. (2009a) published the first analysis of intergenerational transmission from the G2 males to their G3 sons and daughters, based on convictions up to 2006 of G3 children interviewed up to 2007. They concluded that the strength of intergenerational transmission was similar from G1 fathers to G2 sons and from G2 fathers to G3 sons. Smith and Farrington (2004) showed that convictions of G1 fathers and mothers predicted convictions of the G2 males and of their female partners. They suggested that parental authoritarianism and poor parental supervision may have been mediating factors. Besemer and Farrington (2012) studied the conviction trajectories of G2 males, their siblings, and their G1 fathers. Besemer (2012) also carried out a number of other studies of intergenerational transmission from G1 parents to G2 males and their siblings.

The most recent analyses of the intergenerational transmission of convictions in the CSDD was published by Farrington, Ttofi, and Crago (2017). They investigated intergenerational transmission from G2 males to their G3 sons. They found that there was significant intergenerational transmission of burglary, serious theft, minor theft, violence, carrying an offensive weapon, threatening behaviour, and serious motoring offenses. They also concluded that the most important mediators between parent and child convictions were the family renting rather than owning their own home, poor parental supervision, an anti-establishment attitude of the father, parental physical punishment of the child, and separation of the son from his father. The current chapter is modelled on that previous article, but it studies the intergenerational transmission of self-reported offending rather than of convictions.

The intergenerational transmission of convictions from G2 males and females to G3 males and females was studied by Auty, Farrington, and Coid (2017). They found significant intergenerational transmission, especially from mothers to daughters. They also concluded that the father's drug use and harsh parental discipline were important mediators. In addition, Auty, Farrington, and Coid (2015) investigated the intergenerational transmission of psychopathy from G2 males to G3 males and females. G3 females are not studied in this chapter because of time and space limitations; they will be studied in future analyses.

Method

The sample of G2 boys

At the time they were first contacted in 1961–62, the G2 boys were all living in a working-class area of South London. The vast majority of the sample was chosen by taking all the boys who were then aged 8–9 and on the registers of six state primary schools within a one-mile radius of a research office which had been established. In addition to 399 boys from these six schools, 12 boys from a local school for educationally subnormal children were included in the sample, in an attempt to make it more representative of the population of boys living in the area. Therefore, the boys were not a probability sample drawn from a population, but rather a complete population of boys of that age in that area at that time.

Most of the G2 boys (357, or 87 per cent) were White in appearance and of British origin, in the sense that they were being brought up by parents who had themselves been brought up in England, Scotland, or Wales. Of the remaining 54 boys, 12 were Afro-Caribbean, having at least one parent of West Indian (usually) or African origin. Of the remaining 42 boys of non-British origin, 14 had at least one parent from the North or South of Ireland, 12 had parents from Cyprus, and the other 16 boys were White and had at least one parent from another Western industrialized country.

On the basis of their fathers' occupations when they were aged 8, 94 per cent of the G2 boys could be described as working-class (categories III, IV, or V on the Registrar General's scale, describing skilled, semi-skilled, or unskilled manual workers), in comparison with the national figure of 78 per cent at that time. The majority of the boys were living in conventional two-parent families with both a father and a mother figure; at age 8, only 6 per cent of the boys had no operative father and only 1 per cent had no operative mother. This was, therefore, overwhelmingly a traditional White, urban, working-class sample of British origin.

Interviews with the G2 males

The G2 males have been interviewed nine times, at ages 8, 10, 14, 16, 18, 21, 25, 32, and 48. At ages 8, 10, and 14, they were assessed in their schools. The tests in schools measured individual characteristics such as intelligence, attainment, personality, and psychomotor impulsivity. In addition, the boys' teachers completed questionnaires when the G2 boys were aged about 8, 10, 12, and 14.

These questionnaires furnished data about the boys' troublesome and aggressive school behaviour, their lack of concentration or restlessness, their school attainments, and their truancy. Ratings were also obtained from the boys' peers when they were in the primary schools at ages 8 and 10 about such topics as their daring, dishonesty, troublesomeness, and popularity.

At all ages except 21 and 25, the aim was to interview all the G2 males who were still alive, and it was always possible to interview a high proportion of those who were still alive: 405 (99 per cent) at age 14; 399 (97 per cent) at age 16; 389 (95 per cent) at age 18; 378 (94 per cent) at age 32; and 365 (93 per cent) at age 48. At age 48, 17 males had died, 5 could not be traced, and 24 refused, which meant that 365 out of 394 who were alive were interviewed (Farrington et al. 2006). Because of inadequate funding, only about half of the males were interviewed at age 21, and about a quarter at age 25. At age 21, the aim was to interview all the convicted males and an equal number of randomly chosen unconvicted males, and 218 of the 241 target males (90 per cent) were interviewed. At age 25, only 85 males were interviewed.

Interviews with the G2 females

At age 32, 289 of the 378 interviewed G2 males (76 per cent) were living with a wife or female cohabitee, and 268 of these G2 females (93 per cent) filled in a questionnaire about child-rearing. At age 48, 299 of the 365 interviewed G2 males (82 per cent) were living with a female partner, and 254 of these G2 females (85 per cent) were interviewed.

Interviews with the G1 parents

Interviews with the G1 parents were carried out by female social workers who visited their homes. These interviews took place about once a year from when the G2 boy was about 8 until he was aged 14–15 and was in his last year of compulsory education. The primary informant was the mother, although many fathers were also seen. The G1 parents provided details about such matters as family income; family size; their employment histories; their child-rearing practices (including attitudes, discipline, and parental disharmony); their degree of supervision of the boy; and his temporary or permanent separations from them. The parents of 22 boys at age 8 (5 per cent) were considered to be uncooperative.

Interviews with the G3 children

Only G3 children aged at least 18 (born up to 1995) were targeted. We knew about and had identifying information for 691 G3 children. The ethical requirements of the South-East Region Medical Ethics Committee required that we contact the G2 male and/or his female partner in trying to interview the G3 children. Therefore, 20 G3 children whose G2 fathers refused at age 48, and 7 children whose fathers were dead at age 48 (and where no female partners were available) were not eligible to be interviewed. An additional six G3 males who had died and three who were disabled (one Down's syndrome, one mental health problems, one severe attention deficit-hyperactivity disorder), together with two who did not know that the G2 male was their father, were considered to be not eligible.

Of the 653 eligible G3 children, 551 were interviewed (84 per cent) at the average age of 25: 291 of the 343 G3 males (85 per cent) and 260 of the 310 G3 females (84 per cent). Of the remainder, 39 children refused, 33 parents refused, 13 children could not be traced, 14 were elusive (agreeing or not refusing but never being available to interview), and 3 were aggressive or problematic. Of the 29 eligible children living abroad since birth, 17 were interviewed, usually by telephone.

Self-reported offending of the G2 males

At age 18, the G2 males were asked to admit how many times they had committed specified offenses in the previous three years. These offenses were burglary, theft of vehicles, theft from vehicles, shoplifting, theft from slot machines, vandalism, assault (defined according to involvement in fights), marijuana use, class A drug use (heroin and LSD), and class B drug use (amphetamines and barbiturates). They were also asked about driving after drinking at least 10 units of alcohol, which would have caused them to fail the breathalyser test (1 unit = 10 mL of pure alcohol). This is approximately a half-pint of beer or cider, a small glass of wine, or a single measure of spirits. At age 32, they were asked to admit the same offenses, committed in the previous five years, together with theft from work and fraud (check, credit card, and tax). The questions about class A drug use at age 32 were more detailed, specifying heroin, cocaine, LSD, and magic mushrooms.

Self-reported offending of the G3 children

The G3 children were asked about the same offenses that the G2 males had been asked about at age 32, again referring to the previous five years. However, the questions about class A drugs now included crack cocaine and ecstasy. This chapter compares self-reported offending (SRO) of G2 males and G3 males. A SRO score for G2 males at age 18 and a comparable score for G3 males was based on the number of acts admitted out of the 11 enquired about for G2 males at age 18. The SRO score for G2 males at age 32 and a comparable score for G3 males was based on the number of acts admitted out of the 13 enquired about for G2 males at age 32.

Possible mediators between G2 and G3 male offending

Based on the classic work of Baron and Kenny (1986), there are three necessary conditions to establish a mediator: (1) the father's offending significantly predicts the mediator; (2) the mediator significantly predicts the son's offending; and (3) the strength of the relation between the father's offending and the son's offending decreases after controlling for the mediator. In general, the mediator should be measured after the father's offending and before the son's offending.

For comparability and for ease of understanding the results, all possible mediators were dichotomized, as far as possible, into the "worst" quarter versus the remainder (Farrington and Loeber 2000). These variables were mostly measured in two, three, or four categories when the G2 male was age 32 (see Farrington 1989; Smith and Farrington 2004, for more information about all these variables). In most cases, the mediators were measured after the father's offending and before the son's offending.

Parental (eight variables): Convictions of G2 fathers and G2 mothers were measured up to age 32. (For information about criminal record searches of all three generations, see Farrington, Ttofi, and Crago 2017.) Young fathers referred to G2 males who were under age 23 at the time of the birth of their first child, and young mothers referred to G2 mothers who were under age 21 at the birth of their first known child. (We only have records of children that the G2 female had with the G2 male.) Parental conflict was based on the G2 father's report of frequent rows with his female partner, and he also reported whether he had been divorced in the previous five years (up to age 32). The G2 father also reported whether he had hit his female partner and whether he had a biological child living elsewhere, both at age 32.

Child-rearing (two variables): The G3 male reported retrospectively about the physical punishment and supervision that he had received in childhood (under age 12).

Socio-economic (six variables): Low take-home pay was reported by the G2 male at age 32, and large family size referred to five or more people living in the G2 male's household at that time. Low social class at age 32 indicated that the G2 male had a semi-skilled or an unskilled manual job. The G2 male also reported whether he was currently unemployed at age 32, and how many months he had been unemployed in the previous five years. High unemployment was defined as 10 or more months unemployed. The G2 male also reported the longest time that he had spent in one job in the previous five years. The men with the shortest time had spent two years or less in one job.

Housing (five variables): Poor housing of the G2 male at age 32 was rated by the interviewer, based on whether the home was dirty, smelly, damp, neglected, overcrowded, inadequately furnished, had vermin, or had structural problems. The interviewer also rated the immediate area of residence, according to whether it was dirty, noisy, or lacked amenities. The G2 male reported whether his home was owner occupied or rented, and whether he was living in London or out of London. Generally, the upwardly mobile families had moved out of London. The G2 male also reported how many addresses he had lived at in the previous five years, and four or more addresses indicated residential mobility.

Individual (three variables): A measure of impulsiveness at age 32 was based on the G2 male's endorsement of items such as "I often do things without thinking" (see Farrington 1991). Similarly, a measure of the anti-establishment attitude of the G2 male at age 32 was based on his endorsement of negative attitudes to police, bosses, school, rich people, and public servants, and a measure of aggressive attitude was based on his positive endorsement of items such as "Anyone who insults me is asking for a fight" and negative endorsement of items such as "I try to keep out of fights" (see West and Farrington 1977).

Behaviour (five variables): At age 32, the G2 male reported whether he spent four or more evenings out per week. A measure of alcoholism at age 32 was based on CAGE questionnaire items such as "Have you ever had guilty feelings about your drinking?" and "Have you ever started off the day with a drink?" (Mayfield, McLeod, and Hall 1974). Heavy drinking of the G2 male at age 32 was based on his consumption of at least 40 units of alcohol per week, while binge drinking was based on his consumption of at least 13 units in one evening. Heavy gambling was based on his expenditure of large amounts of money on betting.

Plan of analyses

The analyses are designed to address the following questions:

1. To what extent does self-reported offending of the G2 males predict self-reported offending of the G3 males? The intergenerational transmission of different types of offenses is studied. Self-reported offending of the G2 males at ages 18 and 32 is compared with self-reported offending of the G3 males (at the average age of 25).
2. What variables were significantly related to high SRO scores of the G2 males and to high SRO scores of the G3 males? These variables are potential mediators between G2 and G3 self-reported offending.
3. To what extent does the predictive power of G2 high SRO scores decrease after controlling for these potential mediators? If G2 high SRO scores no longer predict G3 high SRO scores after controlling for a particular variable X, this is evidence that X is a mediator.

Statistical methods

The odds ratio (OR) was used to measure the strength of relationships between possible mediators and self-reported offending. Logistic regression analyses were used to investigate whether G2 offending predicted G3 offending after controlling for possible mediators.

Because the G3 children are not all independent, it is necessary to adjust the variance of the OR to take account of the clustering of G3 children in G2 families (i.e., the fact that there can be more than one G3 child in a family). It is easiest to do this by referring to the standardized mean difference, *d*. Clustering has no material effect on the value of *d* but it increases the variance of *d* (see e.g., Hedges and Hedberg 2007). This variance is increased by [1 + (*n* – 1) ⋆ ICC], where *n* is the number of individuals in a cluster and ICC is the intraclass correlation. This correction has been known for many years and has been called the design effect (e.g., Kish 1965) or the variance inflation factor (e.g., Donner, Birkett, and Buck 1981).

It is well known (see e.g., Lipsey and Wilson 2001: 202) that

Ln(OR) = pi⋆*d*/sqrt(3)

or

Ln(OR) = 1.81⋆*d*

Therefore,

SE[Ln(OR)] = 1.81⋆SE(*d*)

Since SE[Ln(OR)] increases in direct proportion to SE(*d*), it follows that the variance of Ln(OR), like the variance of *d*, needs to be increased by [1 + (*n* – 1)⋆ICC] to take account of clustering.

For the dichotomized measure of G3 self-reported offending based on 13 acts, the ICC was .196; the comparable figure for convictions was .27 (Farrington, Ttofi, and Crago 2017). Since there were 291 boys in 192 families, the average number of G3 boys in a family was 1.52. Therefore, the variance of Ln(OR) was increased by [1 + 0.52 ⋆ 0.196], or by 10.1 per cent, to take account of the clustering of self-reported offending in families. This is equivalent to increasing the standard error of Ln(OR) by 4.9 per cent.

Results

Intergenerational transmission of self-reported offending

In light of the varying ages at which the G3 males were interviewed, the relation between age and self-reported offending was investigated. Five types of offenses varied significantly with age: theft from vehicles (r = .14), minor theft (r = .18), theft from work (r = .19), fraud (r = .16), and marijuana use (r = –.20). In order to bring out the results more clearly, the G3 males were classified into four age categories: 18–22 (N = 75), 23–24 (N = 69), 25–27 (N = 76), and 28 or above (N = 71). The percentage admitting marijuana use generally decreased with age; it was 61.3 per cent at age 18–22, 65.2 per cent at age 23–24, 48.7 per cent at age 25–27, and 35.2 per cent at age 28 or older (chi-squared = 15.78, 3 df,

$p < .001$). The percentage admitting the other four offenses generally increased with age. For example, for theft from work, it was 16.0 per cent at age 18–22, 29.0 per cent at age 23–24, 39.5 per cent at age 25–27, and 43.7 per cent at age 28 or older (chi-squared = 15.51, 3 df, $p < .001$).

In light of these variations, age at interview was controlled (in logistic regression analyses) in investigating the relation between G2 and G3 self-reported offending. However, this only made a substantial difference for marijuana use. For the relation between G2 marijuana use at age 18 and G3 marijuana use, the OR increased from 1.88 (CI = 1.14 to 3.10) without controlling for age to 2.12 (CI = 1.27 to 3.55) with controlling for age. For the relation between G2 marijuana use at age 32 and G3 marijuana use, the OR increased from 3.64 (CI = 1.76 to 7.51) without controlling for age to 4.21 (CI = 2.00 to 8.84) with controlling for age. Unadjusted ORs are presented in Tables 7.1 and 7.2 for all other offenses.

Tables 7.1 and 7.2 summarize the intergenerational transmission of self-reported offending. (One-tailed tests are used throughout this chapter because of clear directional predictions.) It might be expected that the prevalence of most types of offending would decrease steadily from age 18 to age 32, so that (if there were no changes in offending during the time period) G3 offending would be less prevalent than G2 offending at age 18 but more prevalent than G2 offending at age 32. Comparing G2 at age 18 with G3 at the average age of 25, the prevalence of self-reported burglary, theft of vehicles, and theft from vehicles decreased considerably. However, comparing G2 at age 32 with G3 at the median age of 25, the prevalence of these offenses was greater for the G3 males. The greatest increases in prevalence from G2 to G3 were for the drug

Table 7.1 Self-reported offending: G2 males at age 18 versus G3 males

Offense	*% prevalence*		*% G3-S*		*OR*	*CI*
	G2	*G3*	*G2-NS*	*G2-S*		
Burglary	16.7	7.2	4.9	16.4	3.77	1.65–8.59
Theft of vehicle	25.4	13.4	13.7	12.3	0.89	0.44–1.80
Theft from vehicle	19.8	10.0	7.7	21.1	3.20	1.57–6.51
Shoplifting	29.3	42.6	41.1	50.0	1.43	0.91–2.24
Theft from machine	29.6	6.2	6.2	7.1	1.15	0.47–2.80
Vandalism	39.3	40.2	35.7	45.5	1.50	0.97–2.31
Assault	71.7	60.5	41.7	67.0	2.84	1.75–4.61
Marijuana	28.5	52.6	48.8	64.2	2.12	1.27–3.55
Class A drug	7.7	42.3	41.9	45.0	1.14	0.51–2.54
Class B drug	12.6	10.7	11.4	6.3	0.52	0.14–1.90
Drunk driving	21.9	23.4	21.5	30.1	1.58	0.93–2.68
High SRO (11)	23.4	23.4	17.2	42.0	3.48	2.06–5.88

Notes: OR = odds ratio; CI = 90% confidence interval, corrected for clustering; SRO = self-reported offending; G3-S = G3 self-reported; G2-S = G2 self-reported; G2-NS = G2 did not self-report.

Table 7.2 Self-reported offending: G2 males at age 32 versus G3 males

Offense	*% prevalence*		*% G3-S*		*OR*	*CI*
	G2	*G3*	*G2-NS*	*G2-S*		
Burglary	2.6	7.2	NA	NA	NA	NA
Theft of vehicle	3.7	13.4	13.1	16.7	1.33	0.34–5.24
Theft from vehicle	2.9	10.0	NA	NA	NA	NA
Shoplifting	5.6	42.6	41.5	52.9	1.59	0.67–3.79
Theft from machine	2.6	6.2	NA	NA	NA	NA
Theft from work	30.7	32.0	31.6	34.0	1.12	0.70–1.78
Fraud	55.6	47.1	46.7	47.3	1.02	0.68–1.54
Vandalism	1.1	40.2	NA	NA	NA	NA
Assault	37.8	60.5	54.9	70.5	1.96	1.25–3.08
Marijuana	18.3	52.6	49.0	77.8	4.21	2.00–8.84
Class A drug	7.4	42.3	41.4	57.1	1.89	0.73–4.91
Class B drug	5.8	10.7	10.5	16.7	1.70	0.43–6.78
Drunk driving	43.4	23.4	19.5	28.3	1.63	1.00–2.64
High SRO (13)	20.1	23.7	20.1	43.8	3.09	1.74–5.49

Notes: OR = odds ratio; CI = 90% confidence interval, corrected for clustering; SRO = self-reported offending; G3-S = G3 self-reported; G2-S = G2 self-reported; G2-NS = G2 did not self-report; NA = not applicable (based on fewer than 10 cases).

offenses. The most common class A drugs that were admitted by the G3 males were cocaine (104 out of 291 males, or 35.7 per cent) and ecstasy (62 out of 291 males, or 21.3 per cent).

Of the individual types of crimes, G2 and G3 self-reports were significantly related for burglary, theft from vehicles, assault, and marijuana use (for G2 at age 18) and for assault, marijuana use, and drunk driving (for G2 at age 32). G2 and G3 self-reports were not significantly related for theft of vehicles, shoplifting, theft from machines, theft from work, fraud, vandalism, or class A or B drug use. Comparing the transmission of self-reported offending with the previous results for convictions (Farrington, Ttofi, and Crago 2017), burglary and assault were strongly transmitted in both cases, while shoplifting and fraud were not strongly transmitted in both cases.

The total SRO scores were dichotomized into the worst quarter versus the remainder. This was done in order to compare with the results for convictions (e.g., 27 per cent of the G3 males were convicted up to age 32) and also because the relationship between SRO scores and convictions seemed to be nonlinear. For example, for the G3 SRO score based on 11 acts, 36 per cent of 44 males scoring 4 were convicted and 32 per cent of 25 males scoring 5, compared with 53 per cent of 15 males scoring 6 and 67 per cent of 18 males scoring 7 or more. For the G3 SRO score based on 13 acts, 33 per cent of 40 males scoring

4 were convicted, 37 per cent of 38 males scoring 5, 31 per cent of 39 males scoring 6–7, but 67 per cent of 21 males scoring 8 or more.

Table 7.1 shows that the total G2 SRO score at age 18 significantly predicted the total G3 SRO score based on 11 acts (OR = 3.48, CI = 2.06 to 5.88). Similarly, the total G2 SRO score at age 32 significantly predicted the total G3 SRO score based on 13 acts (OR = 3.09, CI = 1.74 to 5.49). Controlling for G3 age did not affect these odds ratios. The corresponding figure for the intergenerational transmission of convictions was very similar (OR = 3.46, CI = 2.04 to 5.86; see Farrington, Ttofi, and Crago 2017). Therefore, there is strong evidence for the intergenerational transmission of self-reported offending as well as convictions.

Mediation analysis

Table 7.3 shows the relationship between 29 risk factors and high G2 (at age 18) and G3 SRO scores. The strongest correlates of G2 SRO scores were current unemployment of the G2 male (OR = 9.36), binge drinking of the G2 male (OR = 6.93), high unemployment of the G2 male (OR = 6.30), convictions of the G2 male (OR = 6.16), his heavy drinking (OR = 5.95), and his separation from a child at age 32 (OR = 5.17). The strongest predictors of G3 SRO scores were binge drinking of the G2 male (OR = 4.11), living in London (OR = 3.14), poor housing of the family (OR = 2.85), a convicted mother (OR = 2.85), and his separation from a child (OR = 2.86). Seventeen variables were significantly related to both G2 and G3 self-reports, and therefore are prime candidates for the mediation analysis. However, in the interests of studying causal processes, five variables that measured antisocial behaviour by the G2 male (convicted father, hit wife, alcoholic, heavy drinking, binge drinking) were not included because they were (at least to some extent) measuring the same underlying theoretical construct as the G2 SRO score.

Table 7.4 shows the results of the mediation analyses. As mentioned, a high G2 SRO score at age 18 significantly predicted a high G3 SRO score (OR = 3.48, CI = 2.06 to 5.88). The 12 potential mediators were then controlled one by one in logistic regressions. Table 7.4 shows that the greatest decrease in the OR (from 3.48 to 2.71) occurred after controlling for renting (as opposed to home ownership) at age 32. Further analyses showed that the most important mediators were parental conflict, poor parental supervision, an anti-establishment attitude, living in London, and poor housing. After controlling for these five variables, the relation between G2 high SRO scores at age 18 and G3 high SRO scores was reduced to 1.73 and became nonsignificant (CI = 0.89 to 3.36).

It was interesting that the relationship between G2 and G3 SRO scores became stronger after controlling for a convicted mother. This was affected by the small number of criminal mothers ($N = 17$) and the very strong relationship between G2 and G3 SRO scores for those with convicted mothers. Of the eight cases where G2 males had high SRO scores, G3 males also had high SRO scores

Table 7.3 Possible mediators: G2 males at age 18 and G3 males

Variable	*% G2 SRO*			*% G3 SRO*		
	NR	*R*	*OR*	*NR*	*R*	*OR*
Parental						
Convicted father	12.2	46.2	6.16*	18.1	33.6	2.30*
Convicted mother	22.2	47.1	3.12*	21.9	44.4	2.85*
Young father	21.4	36.5	2.11*	21.7	29.2	1.49
Young mother	24.1	28.3	1.24	21.4	30.6	1.62
Parental conflict	19.2	33.7	2.15*	19.3	31.4	1.91*
Divorced	21.3	38.1	2.27*	20.6	34.4	2.02*
Hit wife	20.1	47.2	3.56*	20.8	38.9	2.42*
Child elsewhere	20.7	57.4	5.17*	20.0	41.7	2.86*
Child-rearing						
Physical punishment (G3)	25.1	22.7	0.88	18.6	33.7	2.23*
Poor supervision (G3)	17.5	32.6	2.28*	15.3	31.9	2.59*
Socio-economic						
Low take-home pay	16.7	37.2	2.95*	19.0	33.3	2.14*
Large family size	22.8	31.9	1.59	22.5	26.9	1.27
Low SES	21.7	39.6	2.37*	22.2	29.8	1.49
Currently unemployed	20.2	70.4	9.36*	21.9	40.7	2.45*
High unemployment	19.6	60.5	6.30*	21.8	36.8	2.10*
Short time in one job	21.8	45.0	2.94*	22.3	32.5	1.69
Housing						
Poor housing (Int)	20.5	48.0	3.57*	20.3	42.0	2.85*
Bad area (Int)	24.1	34.1	1.63	22.5	34.1	1.79
Frequent moves	25.1	25.3	1.01	20.6	32.1	1.82*
Renting	13.5	40.7	4.41*	16.5	33.3	2.54*
In London	16.1	36.0	2.93*	14.6	34.9	3.14*
Individual						
Impulsive	22.2	37.7	2.13*	22.7	27.8	1.31
Anti-establishment	18.8	43.1	3.26*	19.6	35.6	2.27*
Aggressive	18.9	49.1	4.14*	23.0	26.2	1.19
Behaviour						
Frequently out	22.4	43.9	2.72*	22.5	34.1	1.79
Alcoholic	19.0	45.3	3.52*	18.6	38.9	2.78*
Heavy drinking	17.1	55.2	5.95*	20.4	36.1	2.21*
Binge drinking	11.8	48.0	6.93*	14.0	40.2	4.11*
Heavy gambling	21.6	32.6	1.75*	21.3	28.9	1.50

Notes: SRO = self-reported offending at age 18; NR = nonrisk category; R = risk category; OR = odds ratio; SES = socio-economic status; Int = based on interviewer rating; G3 = derived from G3; other variables derived from the G2 male at age 32.

* $p < .05$, one-tailed, corrected for clustering.

Table 7.4 Mediation analyses for age 18 SRO scores

Mediators	*OR*	*CI*
No mediators	3.48	2.06–5.88
Renting	2.71	1.56–4.71
In London	2.76	1.60–4.76
Poor housing	2.90	1.68–5.02
Anti-establishment	2.96	1.72–5.10
Child elsewhere	2.99	1.68–5.31
Poor supervision	3.08	1.80–5.27
Currently unemployed	3.13	1.79–5.49
High unemployment	3.14	1.80–5.49
Parental conflict	3.15	1.78–5.55
Divorced	3.15	1.84–5.37
Low take-home pay	3.35	1.82–6.16
Convicted mother	3.65	2.08–6.40
Renting, parental conflict	2.43	1.33–4.44
Renting, parental conflict, child elsewhere	2.19	1.16–4.13
Renting, parental conflict, child elsewhere, poor supervision	2.07	1.08–3.95
Renting, parental conflict, child elsewhere, poor supervision, anti-establishment	2.00	1.04–3.86
Parental conflict, child elsewhere, poor supervision, anti-establishment, in London	1.90	0.98–3.69
Parental conflict, poor supervision, anti-establishment, in London, divorced	1.89	0.99–3.60
Parental conflict, poor supervision, anti-establishment, in London, divorced, poor housing	1.73	0.89–3.36
All 12 mediators	2.89	1.25–6.67

Notes: OR = odds ratio: CI = 90% confidence interval, corrected for clustering.

in seven cases. Of the nine cases where G2 males did not have high SRO scores, G3 males also did not have high SRO scores in eight cases. When all 12 potential mediators were entered into a logistic regression analysis, the relationship between G2 and G3 SRO scores was still significant (OR = 2.89, CI = 1.25 to 6.67). This shows the value of studying possible mediators in a stepwise fashion.

Table 7.5 shows the possible mediators between G2 SRO scores at age 32 and G3 SRO scores (based on 13 items). Nine nonbehavioural variables were significantly related to both G2 SRO scores and G3 SRO scores: a convicted mother,

Table 7.5 Possible mediators: G2 males at age 32 and G3 males

Variable	*% G2 SRO*			*% G3 SRO*		
	NR	*R*	*OR*	*NR*	*R*	*OR*
Parental						
Convicted father	6.9	34.3	7.09*	18.6	33.6	2.21*
Convicted mother	13.7	50.0	6.29*	22.7	38.9	2.17*
Young father	15.6	20.6	1.40	22.6	27.7	1.31
Young mother	14.7	27.1	2.15*	21.8	30.6	1.58
Parental conflict	9.1	22.1	2.84*	21.6	29.1	1.49
Divorced	14.8	23.4	1.76	22.0	31.3	1.61
Hit wife	9.7	36.1	5.24*	22.1	36.1	1.99*
Child elsewhere	12.9	37.5	4.07*	21.4	39.6	2.40*
Childrearing						
Physical punishment (G3)	15.1	20.7	1.47	20.2	31.5	1.82*
Poor supervision (G3)	14.1	17.5	1.30	16.0	31.9	2.46*
Socio-economic						
Low take-home pay	11.8	25.0	2.48*	19.4	31.3	1.88*
Large family size	17.7	14.1	0.76	23.0	26.9	1.24
Low SES	17.0	15.8	0.92	23.5	26.3	1.16
Currently unemployed	15.0	33.3	2.83*	22.3	40.7	2.39*
High unemployment	14.1	34.2	3.16*	22.2	36.8	2.05*
Short time in one job	13.0	40.0	4.48*	22.7	32.5	1.64
Housing						
Poor housing (Int)	14.5	30.0	2.52*	21.1	40.0	2.49*
Bad area (Int)	17.4	17.1	0.98	21.6	41.5	2.57*
Frequent moves	16.7	16.7	0.99	20.6	33.3	1.93*
Renting	9.1	26.8	3.64*	17.7	32.5	2.24*
In London	10.8	24.0	2.62*	16.5	33.3	2.54*
Individual						
Impulsive	16.7	16.7	0.99	23.2	27.8	1.27
Anti-establishment	11.2	32.9	3.88*	20.1	35.6	2.20*
Aggressive	13.5	27.7	2.45*	22.5	29.2	1.42
Behaviour						
Frequently out	14.8	31.7	2.67*	23.3	31.7	1.53
Alcoholic	15.3	20.8	1.45	19.5	37.5	2.47*
Heavy drinking	11.1	37.7	4.87*	20.4	37.7	2.37*
Binge drinking	11.2	26.2	2.80*	14.0	41.1	4.27*
Heavy gambling	15.7	18.9	1.25	20.3	32.2	1.87*

Notes: SRO =self-reported offending at age 32; NR = nonrisk category, R = risk category; OR = odds ratio; SES = socio-economic status; Int = based on interviewer rating; G3 = derived from G3; other variables derived from the G2 male at age 32.

* $p < .05$, one-tailed, corrected for clustering.

a child elsewhere, low take-home pay, current unemployment, high unemployment, poor housing, renting, living in London, and an anti-establishment attitude of the G2 male. As before, these were investigated in mediation analyses.

The nine potential mediators were first studied one by one in logistic regression analyses (see Table 7.6). The four mediators that reduced the G2–G3 OR the most were renting (as opposed to home ownership), an anti-establishment attitude, living in London, and poor housing. Remarkably, those were also the most important four mediators in the previous analysis for G2 SRO scores at 18. Further analyses showed that the greatest reduction in the OR came after controlling for living in London, poor housing, and low take-home pay. However, the OR was still significant (OR = 2.20, CI = 1.10 to 4.39). When all nine mediators were entered into the analysis, the OR was substantial and significant (OR = 2.78, CI = 1.23 to 6.31), again showing the value of entering potential mediators stepwise.

Tables 7.3 and 7.5 report the results of many statistical tests (116 in total). It might be argued that the large number of tests increases the risk of Type I errors (concluding that there is a relationship when in fact there is not), and that some form of *p*-value adjustment might be desirable. However, 80 of the tests (69 per cent) were statistically significant, far in excess of the chance expectation of 5 per cent. Also, the use of *p*-value adjustments is controversial for many reasons, including the fact that they tend to increase the risk of Type II errors

Table 7.6 Mediation analyses for age 32 SRO scores

Mediators	*OR*	*CI*
No mediators	3.09	1.74–5.49
Renting	2.59	1.43–4.69
Anti-establishment	2.64	1.45–4.79
In London	2.65	1.47–4.77
Poor housing	2.71	1.50–4.88
Low take-home pay	2.79	1.44–5.40
High unemployment	2.84	1.58–5.10
Currently unemployed	2.88	1.61–5.16
Convicted mother	2.95	1.58–5.49
Child elsewhere	2.98	1.61–5.51
Renting, anti-establishment	2.39	1.30–4.37
Renting, anti-establishment, poor housing	2.27	1.23–4.18
In London, anti-establishment, poor housing	2.21	1.20–4.08
In London, poor housing, low take-home pay	2.20	1.10–4.39
All 9 mediators	2.78	1.23–6.31

Notes: OR = odds ratio; CI = 90% confidence interval, corrected for clustering.

(concluding that there is not a relationship when in fact there is; see e.g., Feise 2002). In light of the very large number of statistically significant results, we think that the risk of Type I errors is very small, and therefore we consider that the disadvantages of a *p*-value adjustment would outweigh its advantages.

Conclusions

The main aim of this chapter was to study the intergenerational transmission of self-reported offending in the CSDD. This chapter described the intergenerational transmission from G2 fathers to G3 sons.

The main conclusions are:

1 High SRO scores of G2 males at ages 18 and 32 significantly predicted high SRO scores of G3 males at the average age of 25. The strength of intergenerational transmission was similar for self-reported offending and for convictions.
2 Intergenerational transmission was particularly strong and replicable for assault and marijuana use. It was also strong for burglary, theft from vehicles, and drunk driving. These results replicate the previous findings on the intergenerational transmission of convictions, where transmission was especially strong for burglary, violence, and serious motoring offenses (Farrington, Ttofi, and Crago 2017).
3 The intergenerational transmission of SRO scores was reduced or eliminated after controlling for important mediators that were mostly measured when the G2 male was aged 32.
4 The most important mediators reflected socio-economic deprivation (renting, living in London, poor housing, low take-home pay); relationship problems (parental conflict, divorce, separation of the father from a child); poor child-rearing (poor parental supervision); and an anti-establishment attitude. Once again, these results replicated the findings for convictions, where the most important mediators were renting, poor parental supervision, an anti-establishment attitude, physical punishment of the child, and separation of the father from a child.

It is important to extend developmental and life-course criminology theories to explain the intergenerational transmission of offending, as Thornberry and Krohn (2018) have done. Farrington et al. (2001) proposed several possible explanations: intergenerational continuities in exposure to multiple risk factors, direct influences of one family member on another, environmental mediators, genetic mechanisms, and criminal justice system biases. The present analyses mainly advance knowledge about mediating variables, but they are also compatible with intergenerational continuities in exposure to multiple risk factors. They show that criminal justice system biases cannot explain intergenerational transmission, since the strength of transmission is similar for self-reported and official offending.

Our conclusion is that the intergenerational transmission of offending can be partly explained by the fact that offending fathers tend to have socio-economic deprivation, relationship problems, poor child-rearing, and anti-establishment attitudes, and these risk factors are all likely to contribute to offending by their sons.

In order to reduce the intergenerational transmission of offending, it is desirable to identify families who are at high risk of having a delinquent child. Tables 7.3 and 7.5 specify many important risk factors for offending by the G3 male. It is then important to offer interventions to families at high risk, and especially to criminal parents and their children. These interventions could include parent training (to improve parental supervision and child-rearing), cognitive-behavioural skills training (to reduce antisocial attitudes and increase self-control), vocational training (to reduce unemployment and socioeconomic deprivation), and relationship education (to improve family relationships). In addition, other programs designed to reduce offending (e.g., alcohol and drug programs) would be highly desirable (see Farrington 2015a; Farrington and Welsh 2007; Lipsey 2009, for reviews of effective programs).

The intergenerational transmission of offending is extremely important. It is essential to intervene to interrupt the cycle and prevent the next generation becoming offenders. The CSDD has significantly advanced knowledge about the transmission of both convictions and self-reported offending. Where results are replicated in both methods, this increases confidence that they reflect real offending behaviour rather than criminal justice system or self-report biases.

It is hoped that further data on the CSDD can be collected under the direction of Dr. Maria Ttofi. It would be particularly desirable to reinterview the G2 males at about age 65, in order to construct a full picture of their life course from age 8 to age 65 (involving 10 face-to-face interviews). It would also be desirable to reinterview the G3 children at about age 35, 10 years after their previous interview. It would also be desirable to begin interviewing the G4 children, to make this one of the few prospective studies of the development of offending and antisocial behaviour in four successive generations.

The new G2 interviews would yield unique information about the development of offending and antisocial behaviour from childhood to old age in a large sample, and about the importance of risk and protective factors, and life events, at different ages. For example, it is important to measure self-reported and official offending after age 60, because some people may continue to offend until they die or become disabled. In addition, the new G3 interviews would advance knowledge on the neglected topic of grandparental (G1) influences on (G3) grandchildren's offending and antisocial behaviour. It is to be hoped that the CSDD will continue to produce useful results for many years to come.

Acknowledgements

For funding the CSDD, we are very grateful to the Home Office, the Department of Health, the Department for Education, the Rayne Foundation, the Barrow-Cadbury Trust, and the Smith Richardson Foundation.

References

Auty, K. M., Farrington, D. P., and Coid, J. W. (2015) 'Intergenerational transmission of psychopathy and mediation via psychosocial risk factors', *British Journal of Psychiatry*, 206: 26–31.

Auty, K. M., Farrington, D. P., and Coid, J. W. (2017) 'The intergenerational transmission of criminal offending: Exploring gender-specific mechanisms', *British Journal of Criminology*, 57: 215–237.

Baron, R. M. and Kenny, D. A. (1986) 'The moderator-mediator variable distinction in social psychological research: Conceptual, strategic and statistical considerations', *Journal of Personality and Social Psychology*, 51: 1173–1182.

Besemer, S. (2012) *Intergenerational Transmission of Criminal and Violent Behaviour*, Leiden, Netherlands: Sidestone Press.

Besemer, S., Ahmad, S. I., Hinshaw, S. P., and Farrington, D. P. (2017) 'A systematic review and meta-analysis of the intergenerational transmission of criminal behavior', *Aggression and Violent Behavior*, 37: 161–178.

Besemer, S. and Farrington, D. P. (2012) 'Intergenerational transmission of criminal behaviour: Conviction trajectories of fathers and their children', *European Journal of Criminology*, 9: 120–141.

Donner, A., Birkett, N., and Buck, C. (1981) 'Randomization by cluster', *American Journal of Epidemiology*, 114: 906–914.

Dubow, E. F., Huesmann, L. R., and Boxer, P. (2003) 'Theoretical and methodological considerations in cross-generational research on parenting and child aggressive behavior', *Journal of Abnormal Child Psychology*, 31: 185–192.

Farrington, D. P. (1989) 'Later adult life outcomes of offenders and non-offenders', in M. Brambring, F. Lösel and H. Skowronek (eds.) *Children at Risk: Assessment, Longitudinal Research, and Intervention* (pp. 220–244), Berlin: De Gruyter.

Farrington, D. P. (1991) 'Antisocial personality from childhood to adulthood', *The Psychologist*, 4: 389–394.

Farrington, D. P. (1995) 'The development of offending and antisocial behaviour from childhood: Key findings from the Cambridge Study in Delinquent Development', *Journal of Child Psychology and Psychiatry*, 36: 929–964.

Farrington, D. P. (2003) 'Key results from the first 40 years of the Cambridge Study in Delinquent Development', in T. P. Thornberry and M. D. Krohn (eds.) *Taking Stock of Delinquency: An Overview of Findings from Contemporary Longitudinal Studies* (pp. 137–183), New York: Kluwer/Plenum.

Farrington, D. P. (2005) 'The Integrated Cognitive Antisocial Potential (ICAP) theory', in D. P. Farrington (ed.) *Integrated Developmental and Life-Course Theories of Offending* (pp. 73–92), New Brunswick, NJ: Transaction.

Farrington, D. P. (2015a) 'The developmental evidence base: Prevention', in D. A. Crighton and G. J. Towl (eds.) *Forensic Psychology* (2nd ed., pp. 141–159), Chichester, UK: Wiley.

Farrington, D. P. (2015b) 'The developmental evidence base: Psychosocial research', in D. A. Crighton and G. J. Towl (eds.) *Forensic Psychology* (2nd ed., pp. 161–181), Chichester, UK: Wiley.

Farrington, D. P., Barnes, G., and Lambert, S. (1996) 'The concentration of offending in families', *Legal and Criminological Psychology*, 1: 47–63.

Farrington, D. P., Coid, J. W., Harnett, L., Jolliffe, D., Soteriou, N., Turner, R., and West, D. J. (2006) *Criminal Careers Up to Age 50 and Life Success Up to Age 48: New Findings from the Cambridge Study in Delinquent Development*, London: Home Office (Research Study No. 299).

Farrington, D. P., Coid, J. W., and Murray, J. (2009a) 'Family factors in the intergenerational transmission of offending', *Criminal Behaviour and Mental Health*, 19: 109–124.

Farrington, D. P., Coid, J. W., and West, D. J. (2009b) 'The development of offending from age 8 to age 50: Recent results from the Cambridge Study in Delinquent Development', *Monatsschrift fur Kriminologie und Strafrechtsreform (Journal of Criminology and Penal Reform)*, 92: 160–173.

Farrington, D. P. and Crago, R. V. (2016) 'The concentration of convictions in two generations of families', in A. Kapardis and D. P. Farrington (eds.) *The Psychology of Crime, Policing and Courts* (pp. 7–23), Abingdon, UK: Routledge.

Farrington, D. P., Gundry, G., and West, D. J. (1975) 'The familial transmission of criminality', *Medicine, Science and the Law*, 15: 177–186.

Farrington, D. P., Jolliffe, D., Loeber, R., Stouthamer-Loeber, M., and Kalb, L. M. (2001) 'The concentration of offenders in families, and family criminality in the prediction of boys' delinquency', *Journal of Adolescence*, 24: 579–596.

Farrington, D. P. and Loeber, R. (2000) 'Some benefits of dichotomization in psychiatric and criminological research', *Criminal Behaviour and Mental Health*, 10: 100–122.

Farrington, D. P. and McGee, T. R. (2017) 'The Integrated Cognitive Antisocial Potential (ICAP) theory: Empirical testing', in A. A. J. Blokland and V. R. Van Der Geest (eds.) *The Routledge International Handbook of Life-Course Criminology* (pp. 11–28), London: Routledge.

Farrington, D. P., Piquero, A. R., and Jennings, W. G. (2013) *Offending from Childhood to Late Middle Age: Recent Results from the Cambridge Study in Delinquent Development*, New York: Springer.

Farrington, D. P., Ttofi, M. M., and Crago, R. V. (2017) 'Intergenerational transmission of convictions for different types of offenses', *Victims and Offenders*, 12: 1–20.

Farrington, D. P., Ttofi, M. M., Crago, R. V., and Coid, J. W. (2014) 'Prevalence, frequency, onset, desistance and criminal career duration in self-reports compared with official records', *Criminal Behaviour and Mental Health*, 24: 241–253.

Farrington, D. P., Ttofi, M. M., Crago, R. V., and Coid, J. W. (2015) 'Intergenerational similarities in risk factors for offending', *Journal of Developmental and Life-Course Criminology*, 1: 48–62.

Farrington, D. P. and Welsh, B. C. (2007) *Saving Children from a Life of Crime: Early Risk Factors and Effective Interventions*, Oxford, UK: Oxford University Press.

Farrington, D. P. and West, D. J. (1981) 'The Cambridge Study in Delinquent Development (United Kingdom)', in S. A. Mednick and A. E. Baert (eds.) *Prospective Longitudinal Research* (pp. 137–145), Oxford, UK: Oxford University Press.

Farrington, D. P. and West, D. J. (1990) 'The Cambridge Study in Delinquent Development: A long-term follow-up of 411 London males', in H.-J. Kerner and G. Kaiser (eds.) *Kriminalitat: Personlichkeit, Lebensgeschichte und Verhalten (Criminality: Personality, Behavior and Life History)* (pp. 115–138), Berlin, Germany: Springer-Verlag.

Feise, R. J. (2002) 'Do multiple outcome measures require p-value adjustment?', *BMC Medical Research Methodology*, 2: 8.

Glueck, S. and Glueck, E. T. (1950) *Unraveling Juvenile Delinquency*, New York: Commonwealth Fund.

Hedges, L. V. and Hedberg, E. C. (2007) 'Intraclass correlations for planning group randomized experiments in rural education', *Journal of Research in Rural Education*, 22: 1–15.

Johnson, M. C., Morris, R. G., and Menard, S. (2015) 'Historical invariance in delinquency causation: A test of equivalent models of delinquency for two generations of adolescents', *Crime and Delinquency*, 61: 1283–1310.

Kim, H. K., Capaldi, D. M., Pears, K. C., Kerr, D. C. R., and Owen, L. D. (2009) 'Intergenerational transmission of internalizing and externalizing behaviours across three generations: Gender-specific pathways', *Criminal Behaviour and Mental Health*, 19: 125–141.

Kish, L. (1965) *Survey Sampling*, New York: Wiley.

Lipsey, M. W. (2009) 'The primary factors that characterize effective interventions with juvenile offenders: A meta-analytic overview', *Victims and Offenders*, 4: 124–147.

Lipsey, M. W. and Wilson, D. B. (2001) *Practical Meta-Analysis*, Thousand Oaks, CA: Sage.

Mayfield, D., McLeod, G., and Hall, P. (1974) 'The CAGE questionnaire: Validation of a new alcoholism screening instrument', *American Journal of Psychiatry*, 131: 1121–1123.

McCord, W., McCord, J., and Zola, I. K. (1959) *Origins of Crime: A New Evaluation of the Cambridge-Somerville Youth Study*, New York: Columbia University Press.

Piquero, A. R., Farrington, D. P., and Blumstein, A. (2007) *Key Issues in Criminal Career Research: New Analyses of the Cambridge Study in Delinquent Development*, Cambridge, UK: Cambridge University Press.

Ramakers, A. A. T., Bijleveld, C. C. J. H., and Ruiter, S. (2011) 'Escaping the family tradition: A multi-generation study of occupational status and criminal behaviour', *British Journal of Criminology*, 51: 856–874.

Reiss, A. J. and Farrington, D. P. (1991) 'Advancing knowledge about co-offending: Results from a prospective longitudinal survey of London males', *Journal of Criminal Law and Criminology*, 82: 360–395.

Rowe, D. C. and Farrington, D. P. (1997) 'The familial transmission of criminal convictions', *Criminology*, 35: 177–201.

Smith, C. A. and Farrington, D. P. (2004) 'Continuities in antisocial behaviour and parenting across three generations', *Journal of Child Psychology and Psychiatry*, 45: 230–247.

Theobald, D. and Farrington, D. P. (2009) 'Effects of getting married on offending: Results from a prospective longitudinal survey of males', *European Journal of Criminology*, 6: 496–516.

Theobald, D. and Farrington, D. P. (2011) 'Why do the crime-reducing effects of marriage vary with age?', *British Journal of Criminology*, 51: 136–158.

Theobald, D. and Farrington, D. P. (2013) 'The effects of marital breakdown on offending: Results from a prospective longitudinal survey of males', *Psychology, Crime and Law*, 19: 391–408.

Thornberry, T. P. (2009) 'The apple doesn't fall far from the tree (or does it?): Intergenerational patterns of antisocial behavior: The American Society of Criminology 2008 Sutherland address', *Criminology*, 47: 297–325.

Thornberry, T. P., Freeman-Gallant, A., and Lovegrove, P. J. (2009) 'Intergenerational linkages in antisocial behaviour', *Criminal Behaviour and Mental Health*, 19: 80–93.

Thornberry, T. P. and Krohn, M. D. (2018) 'Interactional theory', in D. P. Farrington, L. Kazemian, and A. R. Piquero (eds.) *The Oxford Handbook on Developmental and Life-Course Criminology*, New York: Oxford University Press, in press.

West, D. J. (1969) *Present Conduct and Future Delinquency*, London: Heinemann.

West, D. J. (1982) *Delinquency: Its Roots, Careers and Prospects*, London: Heinemann.

West, D. J. and Farrington, D. P. (1973) *Who Becomes Delinquent?*, London: Heinemann.

West, D. J. and Farrington, D. P. (1977) *The Delinquent Way of Life*, London: Heinemann.

Chapter 8

The Oregon Youth Study – Three Generational Study

A review of design, theory, and findings

Deborah M. Capaldi, David C. R. Kerr, and Stacey S. Tiberio

Whereas much can be learned regarding intergenerational associations between adult parents' behaviours and those of their offspring from cross-sectional and shorter-term longitudinal studies, such studies give relatively poor estimates of intergenerational associations in antisocial behaviour due to the potential for recall bias in retrospective reports (e.g., parental reports of their own delinquency during adolescence) and the inability to examine intergenerational associations for differing developmental periods (e.g., from parental antisocial behaviour in adolescence to offspring antisocial behaviour in childhood vs. adolescence). This is particularly important for antisocial behaviour – including delinquency and crime – as well as associated problem behaviours such as substance abuse. These are highly related to age and development (Capaldi, Kerr, Eddy and Tiberio 2016*; Steffensmeier and Allan 2000) and manifest in numerous ways across developmental periods (e.g., prevalence, frequency, severity, types of crime, and substance use) that cannot be reliably recollected in cross-sectional and shorter-term longitudinal studies. Thus, for a better understanding of both the magnitude and developmental characteristics of risk to offspring from parental problem behaviours, prospective, long-term longitudinal intergenerational studies are critical. The size of the association across generations includes all sources of continuity, including genetic, broader contextual, and social aspects of transmission. Thus, unbiased and reliable estimates of these associations are needed in order to understand issues such as the upper bound on direct genetic contributions. Furthermore, mechanisms of transmission can only be examined properly by using developmentally accurate estimates of association of the behaviour of interest in each generation.

In this chapter, we review intergenerational study findings and their implications from the Oregon Youth Study – Three Generational Study, and also methodological issues using data from parents (Generation 1 [G1]) and their school-age sons (Generation 2 [G2]) who originally participated in the Oregon Youth Study (OYS), as well as from the now grown G2 men, their G2 female partners, and their Generation 3 (G3) offspring who participate in the ongoing Three Generational Study (3GS).

Oregon Youth Study design (G1 and G2)

The Oregon Youth Study (OYS) approach was based in a social learning model, which focused particularly on parenting (e.g., discipline, monitoring) practices and peer influences associated with the development of antisocial behaviour, including delinquency (Patterson 1986; Patterson, Reid and Dishion 1992). The model focused on a coercion process, whereby a child may learn to use aversive responses either during aggressive interchanges with parents or to get their own way – for example, by responding aggressively when parents ask them to tidy their room, which they have learned results in their parent backing down (Patterson 1982). Boys and their families were recruited into the OYS by inviting the entire fourth grade (ages 9–10 years) of boys from schools in neighbourhoods with a higher-than-usual incidence of delinquency to participate. Thus, the boys were at elevated risk for delinquency due to neighbourhood characteristics, but were not necessarily showing conduct problems at the time of recruitment. Furthermore, as the recruitment area was a medium-sized town in Oregon, United States, it did not include very high-crime neighbourhoods such as might be found in inner cities of major metropolitan areas. Families were home visited for recruitment, and the face-to-face contact with a friendly individual who could answer their questions and alleviate any concerns about participation was valuable for attaining strong participation rates (Capaldi, Chamberlain, Fetrow and Wilson 1997; Capaldi and Patterson 1987). The original OYS family recruitment rate was 74.4 per cent, and retention rates of G2 men were 98 per cent through high school, 97 per cent through the mid-20s, and 93 per cent through the mid-30s.

Data collection for OYS began in 1984 and was yearly from ages 9–10 years through 31–32 years, with additional assessments at ages 35–36 and 37–38 years. All these assessments involved data on the G2 men; data on the G1 parents also were collected through their son's age 17–18 year assessment. Assessments of the G2 men with their romantic partners (regardless of whether they had children) were collected every two to three years from men's age 17–18 through 31–32 years assessments. Crime measures included official juvenile court records and police records of arrests throughout the study, and self-reported crime from age 12 years on.

Risk nature of the Oregon Youth Study sample

Regarding the level and range of risk in the OYS sample, we compared means and variance for a scale of 14 externalizing items from the Child Behaviour Checklist, Parent Report (Achenbach 1991) for the OYS men from the first five waves of OYS (childhood and early adolescence) with those of a nationally representative sample of boys (National Longitudinal Survey of Youth–Child; Bureau of Labour Statistics, 2010) at similar ages. Means were higher for the OYS than for the National Longitudinal Survey of Youth at ages 9–10 and

10–12 years (M = .60 vs. .51 and .61 vs. .50, respectively) but not at later ages, and the variances did not significantly differ between the samples at any wave (e.g., SD = .37 vs. .39; and .37 vs. .38 at ages 9–10 and 10–12 years, respectively; F = 1.11 and 1.04, $p > .10$). Thus, although the OYS youth showed higher levels of externalizing behaviours in the early waves, there was no evidence of restricted range on this key construct. Therefore, the OYS sample includes a mixture of men with and without externalizing problems as youth.

Understanding the risk level of the target G2 boys who later became the fathers of G3 children provides a basis for interpreting findings of the intergenerational study. Recruitment and retention of risky individuals is an important advantage of the OYS. We have argued that due to relatively low recruitment and retention rates, or to selection strategies (e.g., studies recruiting from high schools that miss dropouts, studies using phone recruitment), many studies are missing individuals at the more severe levels of behaviour problems and thus have problematic restriction of range in that respect (Capaldi and Eddy 2005). As an illustration of this, in the OYS 13 per cent of the families had no phone at the time of recruitment and were recruited by personal visits with no prior call, which often required staff to make several visits to catch them at home. Of these boys, 62 per cent had three or more police referrals prior to age 18 years, compared with 19 per cent of boys from families with a phone. Of the no-phone-family boys, 23 per cent had between three and five referrals for violence, compared with 1 per cent of the rest of the boys.

Ethnicity of OYS G2 fathers and mothers

Of the 155 OYS men (and partners) who are biological parents of G3 children in the study/dataset, 85.4 per cent (73.3 per cent of partners) are White, 5.1 per cent (7.1 per cent of partners) African American, 4.5 per cent (5.3 per cent of partners) Latino, 3.8 per cent (10.7 per cent of partners) Native American, and 1.2 per cent (3.6 per cent of partners) Asian or Pacific Islander. Although the G2 parents are predominantly White, approximately one-fourth are ethnic minority. In 1980, in the childhood of the G2 parents, approximately 75 per cent of the U.S. population was White, 12 per cent African American, 9 per cent Hispanic, and the remainder Asian and American Indian (Sandefur et al. 2001). Thus, the sample is relatively comparable in ethnic composition to the U.S population at the time. There are other major longitudinal studies across a similar developmental span of antisocial behaviour in other ethnic populations, including African American (e.g., Chicago Youth Development Study: Gorman-Smith, Tolan, Zelli and Huesmann 1996; Rochester Youth Development Study: Thornberry, Smith and Howard 1997), but few others with an *at-risk* predominantly White population. Therefore, a predominantly working-class and White sample, such as the OYS, is relatively rare and of great importance in studying the aetiology and intergenerational transmission of antisocial behaviour.

Three Generational Study design

The Oregon Youth Study–Three Generational Study (OYS–3GS) was initiated in 1995 to examine the intergenerational transmission of antisocial behaviour and related problem behaviours using a fully prospective design. The study involved the children (G3) born to men who were recruited at ages 9–10 years (in 1984–85), along with their parents, into the OYS.[1] The study has expanded to examine issues related to intergenerational associations in substance use and other risk behaviours, including sexual risk behaviours. In this chapter, we will focus on the work related to antisocial behaviour and on intergenerational transmission via fathers.

One question that must be resolved when designing a three generational study concerns which children in G3 should be included. Individuals often have multiple children with multiple partners (see Guzzo 2014), and this can occur across a very wide reproductive span (e.g., our G3 sample ranges from toddlers to young adults), all of which can impose budgetary, feasibility, and statistical challenges. The OYS – 3GS included up to two children from each of the G2 men's female partners who were mothers of his biological children. Originally, G3 stepchildren were included; however, recruitment of new stepchildren was ended early on to reduce costs. Recruiting only first-born children has some disadvantages, including that they may have characteristics related to being a first born, which makes them not fully representative of G3 (Paulhus, Trapnell and Chen 1999). Furthermore, men who fathered their first child in adolescence are more likely to lose touch with the child, limiting study of mechanisms of transmission via the fathers' parenting. Thus, to avoid some of the problems of including only first-born children, there are advantages to including multiple children of each G2 target parent. A further advantage is that aspects of intergenerational transmission affecting more than one G3 sibling, versus differential effects for siblings, can be examined.

From inception of the OYS, the combined studies have now been underway, and continually ongoing, for 33 years. Collecting data on G3, if on a developmental schedule (e.g., an assessment at age 3 years, a further assessment at age 5 years), can stretch out over many years of G2 fertility. Undertaking prospective intergenerational studies is not for the faint of heart! Of course, the study was not originally intended as intergenerational, but the opportunity to pursue such questions became apparent when the OYS boys matured to young adulthood. Maintaining study funding, which is always a challenge, is particularly a challenge for intergenerational studies where some of the main study goals may not be achieved within the usual funding periods of 5 years or less.

One must also consider how design characteristics specific to intergenerational studies can affect methodological and statistical approaches. For example, having multiple G3 children of the G2 man in the OYS–3GS is not problematic for data analysis so long as such dependence among siblings' scores is appropriately accounted for in the model. The modelling of non-independence of nested data within families can be achieved using a variety of statistical methods – including, but not limited to, hierarchical linear modelling/mixed effects modelling (Raudenbush and Bryk 2002), dyadic data analysis techniques (Kenny, Kashy and Cook 2006), and by estimating standard errors using a sandwich estimator (Muthén and Muthén 1998–2015). Furthermore, as mentioned above, a developmental design dictates that children will mature into each developmental period over a wide array of years. Thus, the G3 children born to younger OYS men will complete the 3GS many years prior to G3 children born to older OYS men. As a result, G3 child sample size by assessment age will be larger at the younger than older ages. Missing data at the older G3 child ages for children born to older OYS men can be explicitly incorporated into the statistical model by including child's age at his/her last completed assessment as a missing data correlate (e.g., by using the AUXILLARY option in Mplus versions 7.3; Muthén and Muthén 1998–2015). Thus, the added complexities associated with intergenerational, developmental designs can be addressed by using appropriate and more innovative statistical models.

Three Generational Study child participation

The OYS–3GS involves G2 mothers and fathers, even if they have separated. Of the 200 living OYS men (currently aged 41 to 43 years), 155 (78 per cent) are biological fathers. Data have been collected on a total of N = 307 biological offspring of N = 142 G2 OYS men and N = 196 G2 mothers to date (27 stepchildren also were assessed prior to a decision not to include further stepchildren). Child participation rates are excellent. Only 20 children (7 per cent) who were eligible have not participated (6 refusals of the G2 parents; 14 fathers had no contact and G3 could not be located). Regarding sample retention, only 22 children no longer participate (8 adopted out of the family; 6 cannot be located; 8 have a parent who died, dropped out, or cannot be located). Shown in Table 8.1 are current G3 child sample sizes by assessment age, which are larger at the younger than older-aged assessments due to the developmental design. In addition, we have parallel constructs for the G2 mothers to those of the G2 fathers for each of the 3GS waves and also retrospective data on G2 mothers' families of origin.

Table 8.1 Projected completion rates (current to 2017)

	*T1** *18–24 months*	*T2* *36–42 months*	*T3* *Age 5*	*T4* *Age 7*	*T5** *Age 9*	*T6* *Grade 6*	*T7* *Grade 8*	*T8* *Grade 10*	*T9* *Grade 12*	*T10* *Age 19*
6/30/17	231	300	300	268	114	205	181	148	111	73

* These assessments were dropped, thus yielding smaller sample sizes at these assessments.

Oregon Youth Study–Three Generational Study assessment and measures

Each wave of OYS–3GS involves an assessment with the G2 father and mother and, in some cases, an additional assessment (e.g., with a peer). In addition to interviews and questionnaires to parents and children, the study involved teacher questionnaires and included observational data with parents through mid-adolescence. Measures of externalizing were comprehensive, and self-reported delinquency was collected from age 7 years on. The observations focused on the quality of parent–child interaction, social teaching (e.g., subtle encouragement of antisocial behaviours and substance use), as well as parent–child problem solving. Peer interaction tasks were initiated at age 5 years to study peer influences from an early age, including rule-breaking talk and behaviour and the reinforcement of such talk by the other child (Dishion, Spracklen, Andrews and Patterson 1996). The assessment also has included innovative measurement of executive functioning (e.g., the GoStop Impulsivity Task; Dougherty, Mathias and Marsh 2003) and a series of computerized tasks designed to test working memory and inhibitory control. At ages 15–16 years, G3 children also complete the computerized version of the Diagnostic Interview Schedule for Children-Version 4 (DISC-IV; National Institute of Mental Health 1997) that yields DSM-IV diagnoses. For a complete list of constructs assessed see Appendix A.

Overview of findings and theoretical development of the Oregon Youth Study for G1 and G2: the foundation of the intergenerational study

Although not a high-risk sample (e.g., if participants had been sampled from a population already showing behaviour problems in childhood or were all children of men with arrest histories), the G2 OYS men showed relatively high levels of self-reported offending behaviour and also arrests. Through ages 23–24 years, 66 per cent of the study men self-reported committing at least one Federal Bureau of Investigation (FBI) index offense, with 40 per cent reporting committing six or more such offenses (Wiesner, Capaldi and Kim 2007). Arrest data were collected regularly from juvenile authorities and in adulthood from police records. As reported by Wiesner, Capaldi and Kim (2007), by ages 26–27 years 71 per cent of the men had been arrested at least once (excluding minor traffic violations and contempt of court); among those who were arrested, the number of arrests ranged from 1–39 (mean = 6.97; mode = 1; median = 3). Relatively few studies collect arrest data regularly from juvenile court and the relevant police record jurisdictions. Findings for OYS G2 suggest that most men who in childhood lived in relatively risky neighbourhoods, at least in their historical cohort, have been arrested at least once at some time during the juvenile and early adult period.

Furthermore, for the purposes of this chapter, we examined intergenerational transmission of risk for arrests in adulthood for G1 parents and G2 men. Prevalence of adult arrests was 35.4 per cent (n = 73 of 206) for G1 (denoting arrests for either or both G1 parents – collected from police records) and 73.3 per cent (n = 151 of 206) for OYS men. The prevalence of two or more adult arrests was 24.3 per cent (n = 50 of 206) for G1 and 55.3 per cent (n = 114 of 206) for G2. Regarding transmission, G2 OYS men were 2.79 ($\chi^2_{(1)} = 7.82, p = 0.005$) times more likely to have been arrested at least once (vs. never arrested) as adults, provided one or more of their G1 parents had also been arrested at least once (vs. G1 never arrested); for transmission of two or more adult arrests, estimates of G2 men's risk was considerably higher (OR = 6.13, $\chi^2_{(1)} = 21.944, p < 0.001$; see Table 8.2 for cross tabulations). Estimating associations for G1 parents and only those G2 OYS men who had at least one biological G3 child participate in 3GS resulted in odds ratio estimates of 5.98 ($\chi^2_{(1)} = 11.96, p < 0.001$) for transmission of one or more adult arrests, and 10.66 ($\chi^2_{(1)} = 19.17, p < 0.001$) for transmission of two or more adult arrests (see Table 8.3 for cross tabulations). Thus, there is a high degree of concordance between the adult arrest behaviours of the G1 parents and G2 men. Of the 50 G1 parents who had been arrested twice or more in adulthood, 42 of the OYS men (84 per cent) had also been arrested two or more times as adults. In comparison, 46 per cent (n = 72 of 156) of the OYS men were arrested twice or more if their G1 parents had never been arrested or were only arrested once as adults. In sum, intergenerational transmission of risk for multiple arrests for criminal behaviour in adulthood was

Table 8.2 Contingency table of two or more adult arrests for G1 and for all G2 OYS men (N = 206)

	G2 arrested 0 or 1 time	*G2 arrested 2 or more times*	*Total*
G1 arrested 0 or 1 time	84	72	156
G1 arrested 2 or more times	8	42	50
Total	92	114	206

Table 8.3 Contingency table of two or more adult arrests for G1 and for only those G2 men who had biological children participate in 3GS (*N* = 149)

	G2 arrested 0 or 1 time	*G2 arrested 2 or more times*	*Total*
G1 arrested 0 or 1 time	53	58	111
G1 arrested 2 or more times	3	35	38
Total	56	93	149

highly supported, with OYS men being more than six times more likely to have multiple arrests (vs. no or only one adult arrest), provided their G1 parents had also been arrested multiple times. This concordance is considerably higher than findings regarding more general measures of externalizing that we have found from G2 to G3 (Thornberry, Hops, Conger and Capaldi 2003b*). It is important to note, however, that there were still a substantial number of G2 men who had been arrested two or more times in adulthood despite the lack of similar behaviours in their G1 parents. Thus, it is vital to understand moderators and mediators of intergenerational transmission of arrests for criminal behaviour.

Numerous publications by Patterson and colleagues addressed the development of antisocial behaviour from childhood to adolescence for G2 based on the coercion model (Dishion and Patterson 2006; Patterson 1982, 2005; Wiesner, Capaldi and Patterson 2003). As the OYS evolved, both theoretical and methodological advances in the field led to expansion of approaches to study a more comprehensive lifespan systems model to examine heterogeneity in the course of delinquency and crime, including issues of persistence and desistance (Capaldi, Kim and Owen 2008; Capaldi and Wiesner 2009; Wiesner and Capaldi 2003; Wiesner, Capaldi and Kim 2007). Key aspects of these studies involved an extension of the social learning and coercion models to a dynamic developmental systems approach, whereby development, including the development of problem behaviours, is viewed as multifaceted and attributable to ongoing processes of influence and interaction among multiple systems, including the individual's prior disposition and experiences, contextual factors (including proximal and distal factors), physiological factors, and interactions with key influential figures across the lifespan (including parents, peers, and partners) (Capaldi, Kerr, Eddy and Tiberio 2016). Age or stage of development is a particularly important factor in determining risk for problem behaviours. For example, age is arguably the strongest predictor of violence, crime, and other problem behaviours (Steffensmeier and Allan 2000).

An influential age-related crime theory focuses on lifespan-persistent crime committed by (1) more serious offenders – hypothesized to involve enduring individual differences that emerge across childhood and adolescence and are thought to be lifespan persistent – and (2) adolescent-limited less serious offenders – thought to be due to developmentally related factors, including emulating older peers and hypothesized to account for the adolescent peak in offending (Moffitt, Caspi, Harrington and Milne 2002). Rather than supporting this two-group model, findings from our work in adolescence and adulthood with the OYS boys indicated that more serious offenders accounted for the adolescent peak in offending, and most offenders, including the most serious offenders, showed declines in problem behaviour in early adulthood (Monahan, Steinberg, Cauffman and Mulvey 2009; Wiesner, Capaldi and Kim 2007).

An important implication of the association of age and crime is that children born to adolescent and young-adult parents are more likely to be born into a context involving parental criminal involvement than are children who are born to older parents. This is particularly the case because antisocial behaviour is a risk factor for becoming a parent at a younger age. In line with this argument, OYS boys who became adolescent fathers had an average of 5.5 juvenile arrests versus 2.2 for those who were not fathers at this age (Fagot et al. 1998*).

Interestingly, becoming a father can improve men's antisocial behaviour, even after accounting for the protective effect of marriage, which is known to be associated with a reduction in antisocial behaviour (Sampson and Laub 1990). Kerr et al. (2011*) found that, following the birth of a first biological child, men's crime trajectories showed slope decreases beyond those attributable to age alone; thus, fatherhood was associated with reduced rates of criminal behaviour over time. Timing of first fatherhood, however, was a key moderator. The older the men were when they became fathers, the greater the decreases were in crime (note that all men were age 31 years or younger at the time of the study). These findings raise a number of prevention possibilities and suggest that timing may be important; fathers with conduct problem histories may be motivated to desist from criminal behaviours around the time of their first child's birth, with fathers who become parents at older ages being the most susceptible to improvement, and such desistance may reduce intergenerational transmission of conduct problems.

Theory and findings of the Three Generational Study

The first publication from the OYS–3GS study, which addressed intergenerational associations in antisocial behaviour, was published as one of a set of four articles from different prospective three generational studies, each of which addressed three key intergenerational questions using prospective data from three generations, to attempt replication of findings (Capaldi, Pears, Patterson and Owen 2003;* Conger, Neppl, Kim and Scaramella 2003; Hops, Davis, Leve and Sheeber 2003; Thornberry et al. 2003a*). These questions were whether, first, parenting experienced in childhood or adolescence in the family of origin would predict parenting practices in adulthood in the family of procreation; second, externalizing behaviour assessed in adolescence for G2 would predict externalizing behaviour in early childhood for G3; and third, such intergenerational associations in externalizing behaviour would be mediated by G2 parenting practices. As discussed by Thornberry, Hops, Conger and Capaldi (2003b*), the weight of evidence from the four studies indicated that G1 and G2 adults engaged in similar styles of parenting, and antisocial or externalizing behaviours in G2 and G3 were associated. Intergenerational associations (which at the time concerned differing ages or developmental stages for G2 and G3) were modest in magnitude. The OYS–3GS (Capaldi, Conger, Hops and Thornberry 2003*) was still in a relatively early stage of data collection at that time; thus, the sample size was low, at around G3 $N = 100$; the G3 children were young (aged 16–30 months); and externalizing was assessed by temperamental risk (activity level and anger). In the full model, a marginal association was found between G1 and G2 poor parenting (poor discipline, low enjoyment of parenting), and – whereas G1 poor parenting predicted G2 adolescent antisocial behaviour – the association of the latter with the G2 father's poor parenting practices in early adulthood was marginal and the indirect association of G1 to G2 parenting via G2 antisocial behaviour was marginal. A significant association was found between the G2 father's antisocial behaviour at ages 13–16 years and G3 temperamental risk.

It became clear from findings of the 2003 replication studies that it would be important to test intergenerational association across similar developmental stages for G2 and G3. Furthermore, findings from those and other intergenerational studies indicated that although there is significant continuity across generations, the size of such associations is modest. Therefore, an important question to address is how to explain discontinuity across generations (Thornberry 2016). Understanding discontinuity is critical for prevention as it will lead to improved interventions to reduce intergenerational transmission of antisocial behaviour. Research on discontinuity will be discussed later in the chapter. Since the 2003 publications, we have progressed both to examining further questions regarding the intergenerational transmission of antisocial behaviour and to being able to address these issues at older ages in childhood and adolescence for G3 – thus at more similar ages for G2 and G3.

Gender-specific intergenerational associations

In a later study, we examined the transmission of externalizing and internalizing behaviours across three generations (from G1 parents to G2 boys in adolescence, and from G2 as parents to G3 at ages 18–21 months), and we examined maternal versus paternal effects (Kim et al. 2009*). As there is robust evidence that externalizing and internalizing behaviours are associated or tend to co-occur in childhood and adolescence (Angold, Costello and Erkanli 1999; Capaldi and Kim 2014; Wolff and Ollendick 2006), examination of transmission of both within the same model helps clarify effects related to each. In line with this evidence, dimensions of both temperament risk and behaviour were used to assess G3 externalizing – including activity level, anger, poor soothability, impulsivity, and poor inhibitory control, along with aggressive and destructive behaviours – and G3 internalizing was assessed by shyness, fear, sadness, discomfort, anxiety, and withdrawal. Findings for G1 and G2 (see Figure 8.1) indicated that whereas the G2 adolescent boys' internalizing behaviour was predicted (additively) by both G1 maternal and paternal internalizing behaviour (as might be expected), G2 adolescent externalizing behaviour was predicted by both maternal externalizing and internalizing behaviours but not by either father behaviour. This indicated a considerable influence of maternal behaviour on the boy's antisocial behaviour in adolescence, but a nonsignificant influence of paternal behaviour. Note that, for both G1 parents and for G2 in adolescence, externalizing and

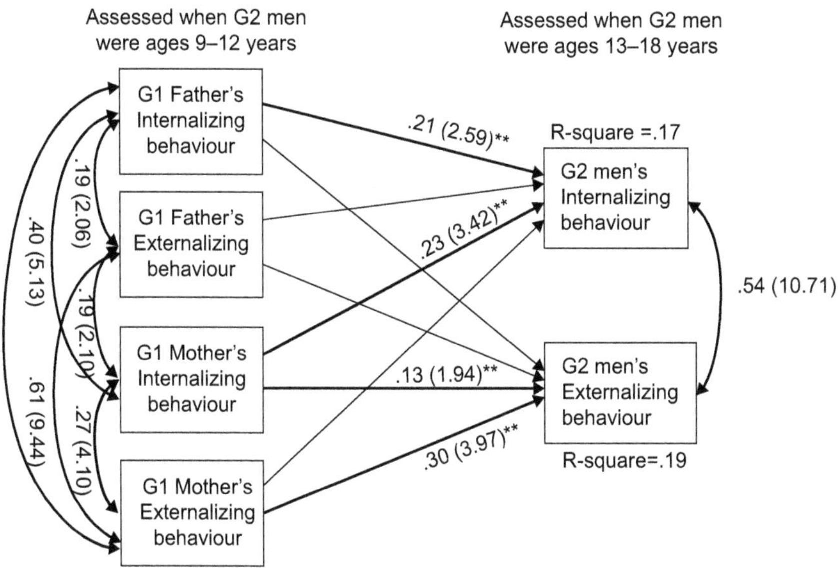

Figure 8.1 Intergenerational transmission from G1 to G2

Note: Boldfaced paths indicate significant paths ($p < .01$). Values in the parentheses indicate *t*-values. For simplicity, coefficients and *t*-values for nonsignificant paths are not presented.

internalizing behaviours were significantly associated, and there was also evidence of assortative partnering (i.e., partner similarities that may reflect selection) in G1 by both externalizing and internalizing behaviours (Merikangas 1982).

Regarding relations between G2 mothers' and fathers' behaviours and G3 toddlers' behaviours, fathers' internalizing behaviours had a significant association with G3's internalizing behaviours for girls but not for boys, and father's externalizing behaviour predicted G3 externalizing behaviour also for girls only (Figure 8.2). On the other hand, G2 mothers' internalizing behaviour was significantly related to G3 internalizing behaviour of both boys and girls. Thus, the father's psychopathology symptoms (i.e., internalizing and externalizing behaviour) may be more strongly predictive of similar internalizing and externalizing temperament risk in early childhood, although for girls only, whereas the mother's internalizing symptoms may be predictive of internalizing in both boys and girls. Note also that a difference between the two models is that there were only boys in G2 but both boys and girls in G3. Again, both internalizing and externalizing behaviours showed significant co-occurrence for mothers, fathers, and children, and there was evidence of assortative partnering in G2 by both internalizing and externalizing behaviours. Findings indicate that there may be more risk for offspring from maternal externalizing (and internalizing)

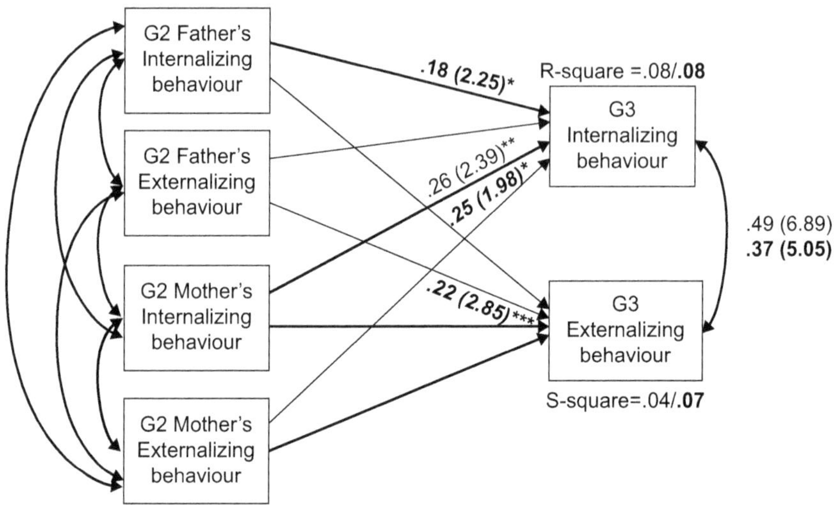

Figure 8.2 Intergenerational transmission from G2 to G3

Note: Boldfaced paths represent significant paths. Values in bold represent estimates for girls and unbolded values are estimates for boys. Values in parentheses indicate *t*-values. Covariance between G2 fathers' internalizing and externalizing behaviour was .54 (8.54) for boys and .48 (6.68) for girls. Covariance between G2 fathers' and mothers' internalizing behaviour was .28 (2.86) for boys and .22 (3.46) for girls. Covariance between G2 fathers' externalizing and G2 mothers' internalizing behaviour was .34 (3.51) for boys and .34 (3.81) for girls. Covariance between G2 mothers' internalizing and externalizing behaviour was .40 (3.31) for boys and .52 (7.20) for girls. Covariance between G2 fathers' and mothers' externalizing behaviour was .29 (2.59) for boys and .27 (2.52) for girls. $p < .05$*; $p < .01$**; $p < .001$***.

behaviours than is often assumed to be the case. Men show higher levels of externalizing behaviours and criminal offending than do women (Steffensmeier 1996), which may lead to an assumption that their behaviour in these areas is more influential. These findings challenge such views. Differences in findings for the prediction models from G1 to G2 versus from G2 to G3 may also have been due to the fact that in the former model G2's symptoms of psychopathology were measured in adolescence, whereas in the latter model they were measured in toddlerhood.

Whereas early studies established intergenerational associations in levels of antisocial behaviour, the contribution of intergenerational risk to changes over time or growth in antisocial behaviour across childhood has been little addressed. Capaldi et al. (2012★) examined intergenerational prediction models of growth in the third generation's (G3) externalizing problems across ages 3 to 9 years. Antisocial behaviour of both the G2 father and mother, along with father contact with the child and mother age at birth, were included in the models. Paternal intergenerational associations again were found to be modest or nonsignificant with all predictors in the model. Transmission was primarily to the intercept rather than slope (i.e., predictions to level at age 3 years but not to changes over ages 3 to 9 years), with mother's young age at the birth of the G3 child being a risk factor, particularly for boys. These findings indicate that to understand intergenerational influences on growth or change in externalizing behaviours across childhood we must look beyond parental antisocial behaviour during their offspring's preschool years. It is possible that changes in parental antisocial behaviour across G3's childhood – particularly lack of desistance (as improvement or desistance is normative in adulthood; Blumstein, Cohen, Roth and Visher 1986); G3 child temperament risk; and key aspects of socialization, including parenting, would predict growth or change in externalizing behaviour across ages 3 to 9 years.

Findings from these studies indicate that the ways in which mothers compared to fathers contribute to psychopathology in their sons and daughters may be quite complex, and these findings need further replication tests and examination in other intergenerational studies.

G3 externalizing behaviours given G1 grandparents' and G2 fathers' arrests in adulthood

For the purposes of this chapter, we examined how G3 risk for greater levels of and linear increases in externalizing behaviours across two developmental periods in early childhood (ages 3, 5, 7, and 9 years) and adolescence (ages 11–12, 13–14, 15–16, and 17–18 years) differed due to G1 to G2 transmission of risk for arrests in adulthood. Two or more arrests by a grandparent or father were considered as particularly indicative of risk, as being an indicator of repeat offending that has come to official attention. Specifically, at each of the four early childhood and four adolescent assessments, child externalizing behaviours were reported by parents using 33 items from the Child Behaviour Checklist (Achenbach 1991). Two linear hierarchical linear models (HLMs) were separately estimated for each developmental period, which accounted for the nesting of repeated observations across time and siblings' scores within families. Data from N = 285 biological G3 children of N = 146 G2 OYS men and N = 193 G3 children from N = 104 G2 OYS men were included in early childhood and adolescence, respectively. Of the N = 285 total G3 children, n = 65 (22.3 per cent) were at the greatest risk, having both G1 grandparent(s) and G2 fathers who had been arrested two or more times as adults; n = 123 (42.1 per cent) had only G2 fathers (not G1 grandparents) with two or more adult arrests; and n = 98 (33.6 per cent) were at the lowest risk, with neither G1 grandparents nor G2 fathers having been arrested two or more times as adults. Note that given the high degree of association between two or more adult arrests in G1 and G2, only n = 6 (2.1 per cent) G3 children had G1 grandparent(s) but not a G2 father who had had two or more adult arrests; data from these G3 children were not included in the HLMs due to insufficient sample size.

A series of models was used to test group differences in G3 externalizing intercepts and slopes, given G1 and G2 adult arrest behaviours. Specifically, we examined four group comparisons for G3 children at (1) little or no risk (i.e., neither G1 nor G2 was arrested two or more times) versus any risk (i.e., two or more arrests in both G1 and G2, or only G2 fathers); (2) no risk versus the greatest risk (i.e., two or more arrests in both G1 and G2); (3) no risk versus risk due to only G2 fathers having been arrested two or more times; and finally, (4) the greatest risk (i.e., arrests in both generations) versus risk due to only G2 fathers.

Results (shown in Table 8.4) indicated that linear changes in G3 externalizing behaviours across early childhood and adolescence were not significantly different for any of the group comparisons. However, G3 child and adolescent levels of externalizing behaviours (i.e., intercepts) were found to significantly differ, given G1 and G2 arrests. First, for group comparisons between little or no versus any risk, G3 offspring whose G1 grandparents and G2 fathers had zero or one arrests as adults had significantly lower externalizing behaviours at each assessment in early childhood (at ages 3, 5, 7, and 9 years) and adolescence (at ages 11, 13, 15, and 17 years) compared with G3 children for whom only G2 fathers, or both G2 fathers and G1 grandparents, had had two or more adult arrests. No significant differences were found for comparisons two or three. For the fourth comparison, at all eight assessments – except for age 11 years – G3 offspring whose fathers, but not grandparents, had been arrested two or more times were found to have significantly greater externalizing behaviours than G3 children whose fathers and grandparents had been arrested zero or one time. In sum, this pattern of results supports that externalizing behaviours were significantly lower for G3 offspring whose G1 grandparents and G2 fathers had not been arrested multiple times in adulthood compared to G3 offspring at higher risk – whether it be due to two or more adult arrests in both generations or only for G2 fathers.

Protective factors: transmission of positive parenting

An important source of protection against developing antisocial behaviour is positive parenting. Transmission of positive parenting is hypothesized to relate to intergenerational transmission of strong adjustment in children. Kerr, Capaldi, Pears, and Owen (2009*) examined the degree to which constructive or positive parenting was transmitted across generations, and how this influenced the intergenerational transmission of antisocial and externalizing behaviour (Figure 8.3). Constructive parenting was assessed by monitoring (supervision and tracking of child), positive discipline, parental warmth toward the child, and parental involvement with the child. Findings indicated that G1 constructive parenting was predictive of the G2 sons' constructive parenting of their G3 children in

Table 8.4 Parameter estimates of group differences for G3 intercept and slope parameters given G1 to G2 intergenerational transmission of two or more adult arrests

Effects on G3 Externalizing in Early Childhood					
Group comparison for G3 children	*Intercept (age 3 years)*	*Intercept (age 5 years)*	*Intercept (age 7 years)*	*Intercept (age 9 years)*	*Slope (ages 3–9 years)*
Any risk (1) vs. No risk (−1)	2.02(.69), p = .003	2.00(.61), p = .001	2.00(.69), p = .004	1.94(.86), p = .025	0.03(.14), p = .858
Both G1 and G2 risk (1) vs. No risk (−1)	1.72(.90), p = .057	1.48(.76), p = .052	1.24(.78), p = .110	1.00(.94), p = .284	–0.12(.18), p = .497
Only G2 risk (1) vs. No risk (−1)	2.29(.79), p = .004	2.35(.71) p = .001	2.41(.81), p = .003	2.47(1.02), p = .015	0.03(.18), p = .864
Both G1 and G2 risk (1) vs. Only G2 risk (−1)	0.57(0.98), p = .559	0.87(.81), p = .284	1.17(.82), p = .153	1.47(.99), p = .137	0.15(.19), p = 0.437
Effects on G3 Externalizing in Adolescence					
Group comparison for G3 children	*Intercept (age 11 years)*	*Intercept (age 13 years)*	*Intercept (age 15 years)*	*Intercept (age 17 years)*	*Slope (ages 11–18 years)*
Any risk (1) vs. No risk (−1)	3.07(1.36), p = .024	3.02(1.10), p = .006	2.97(1.01), p = .003	2.90(1.12), p = .010	0.03(.23), p = .906
Both G1 and G2 risk (1) vs. No risk (−1)	3.76(2.15), p = .081	3.06(1.80), p = .090	2.37(1.55), p = .126	1.68(1.44), p = .245	–0.35(0.26), p = .179
Only G2 risk (1) vs. No risk (−1)	2.57(1.47), p = .079	2.97(1.13), p = .008	3.37(1.12), p = .003	3.77(1.45), p = .009	0.20(0.33), p = .541
Both G1 and G2 risk (1) vs. Only G2 risk (−1)	1.19(2.28), p = .603	0.09(1.84), p = .961	1.00(1.67), p = .547	2.10(1.85), p = .256	0.55(.39), p = .163

Note: "No risk" = G1 grandparents and G2 fathers were not arrested two or more times as adults (n = 98); "Only G2 risk" = G2 fathers, but not G1 grandparents, were arrested two or more times as adults (n = 123); "Both G1 and G2 risk" = G1 grandparents and G2 fathers were arrested two or more times as adults (n = 65). "Any risk" = G1 grandparents and G2 fathers, or only G2 fathers, were arrested two or more times as adults (n = 188). Tabled numbers denote $b(se)$.

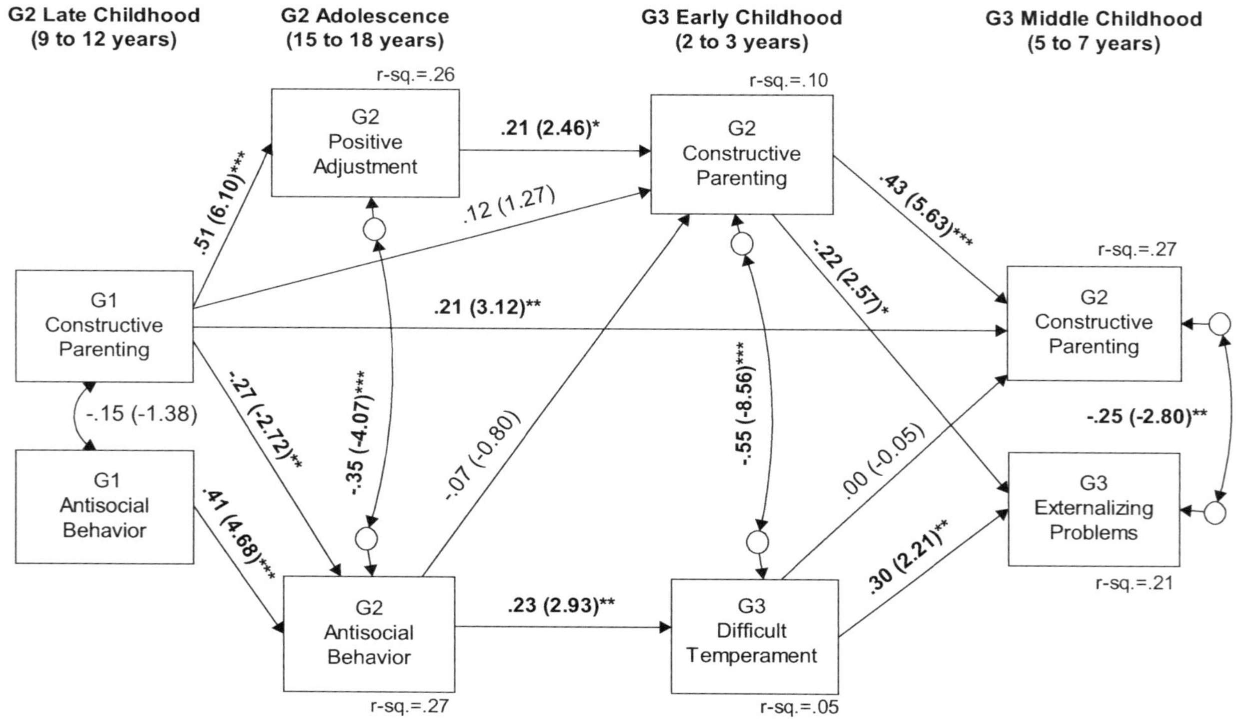

Chi-Sq=14.55 P=0.27 (12 df)
CFI=0.989 TLI=0.976 AIC=3701.36
RMSEA=.034 Free Parameters=32
N=181 3GS, 102 OYS
*p < .05. **p < .01. ***p<.001

Summary of key indirect effects:
G1 Parenting to G2 Parenting in Early Childhood = .12**
G1 Parenting to G2 Parenting in Middle Childhood = .10***
G1 Parenting to G3 Externalizing in Middle Childhood = -.07*
G1 Antisocial Behavior to G3 Difficult Temperament = .09*

Figure 8.3 Final path model of intergenerational transmission of constructive parenting

middle childhood approximately 20 years later; intergenerational transmission of constructive parenting in G3 children's early childhood was mediated by the G2 son's positive adolescent adjustment (academic skill, peer relations, and self-esteem in adolescence).

At the same time as establishing a pathway via positive adjustment for the intergenerational transmission of constructive parenting, the model test indicated intergenerational associations in antisocial behaviour from G1 to G2, and the prediction from G2 antisocial behaviour to G3 externalizing at ages 5–7 years was mediated via G3 children's difficult temperament in childhood. Intergenerational associations in constructive parenting and difficulties in child adjustment were also supported. G1 constructive parenting was associated with lower levels of G2 antisocial behaviour; likewise, G2 constructive parenting was associated with lower levels of G3 difficult temperament in early childhood and G3 externalizing behaviours in middle childhood (see Figure 8.3). Consistent with prior intergenerational studies, G1 constructive parenting explained only a modest amount of variance in G2 constructive parenting, again emphasizing the need to consider intergenerational associations and processes along with other factors of influence, particularly related to intergenerational discontinuity.

Sources of discontinuity across generations

Intergenerational studies almost always have prospective data from only one G2 parent's development (although public records data can provide an exception). Yet children have two biological parents (as well as possibly stepparents), and the other parent therefore influences G3 in a number of ways – including via genetics, their own parenting, and indirectly via the influence they have on their partner. We examined women's influence on men's discipline practices using OYS–3GS. Poor discipline practices are a known risk factor for antisocial behaviour in children, and we examined both intergenerational and partner influences on fathers' poor and harsh discipline (Capaldi, Pears, Kerr and Owen 2008*). That is, in a model in which the young father's discipline of G3 was the outcome variable, we included hypothesized direct effects from G1 poor discipline to G2 poor discipline, a mediated effect via father risk behaviour (antisocial behaviour and substance use; not shown in Figure 8.4), additional effects of risk context (G2 socioeconomic status and the father's age at birth of his first child), and effects of the G2 mother's risk behaviours and of her discipline of G3.

Findings (shown in Figure 8.4) indicated a significant direct effect of the G2 men's experience of discipline in their family of origin with discipline practices they used with their young G3 children. There was no significant additional prediction to the G2 men's poor and harsh discipline from socioeconomic status, father's age at first birth, or from the G2 father's risk behaviour (and no mediated effect of parenting from G1 to G2 via his risk behaviour). As hypothesized,

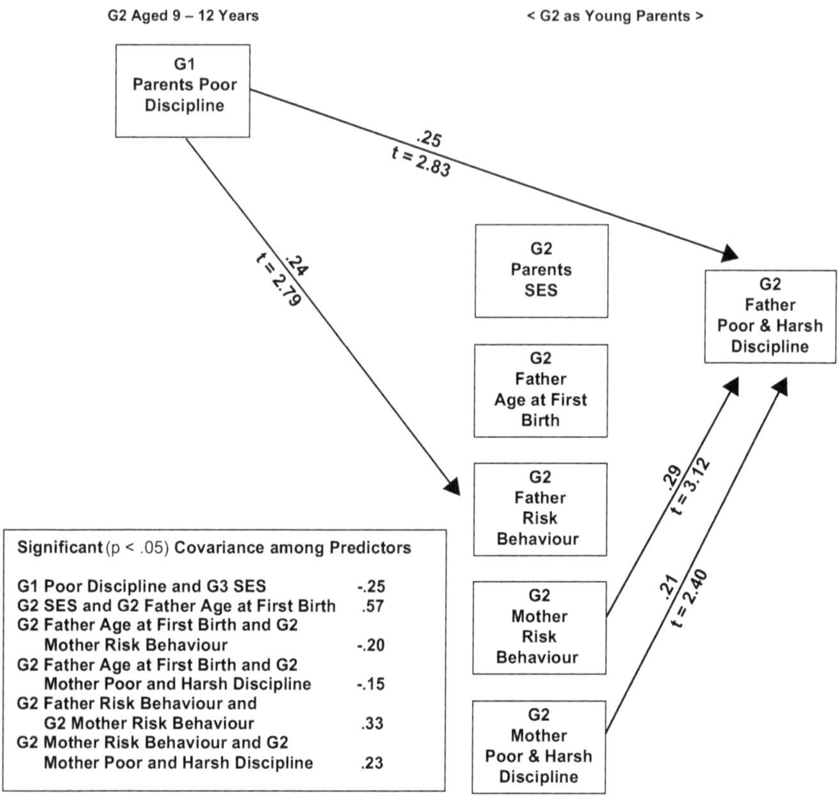

Figure 8.4 Findings for path coefficients and significant covariances among predictor variables

however, the young G2 female partner influenced fathers' discipline practices, such that both her own risk behaviour and her poor/harsh discipline predicted the young father's parenting behaviours. The findings of this study indicate that the men's partners (their children's mothers) are influential in affecting the men's parenting practices, over and above influences from his experience of parenting from his own parents. Thus, the behaviour of the young mother may further reinforce the behaviour of the young father if her risk behaviour and parenting are similar to his, or may be a source of discontinuity if her behaviours differ from his. It is also likely that the young father affects the parenting of the young mother over and above experiences in her family of origin. However, we did not have the fully prospective data on young mothers to test this hypothesis. Note that as there is relatively robust evidence of assortative partnering by antisocial behaviour, this may increase the likelihood of intergenerational transmission of antisocial behaviour.

Parenting and child effortful control: a transactional model

Not all our work pertaining to understanding the development of antisocial behaviour using the 3GS dataset involves intergenerational examination of antisocial behaviour. The dynamic developmental systems model views development as part of a continual ongoing process, yet as stated by Tiberio et al. (2016):

> Most research on parenting and child behaviors defaults to unidirectional prediction models; in most longitudinal models, parent behaviors temporally precede child behaviors, and cross-sectional associations are commonly interpreted as likely reflecting effects of parenting on child behavior. Nevertheless, most researchers assume parents and children have bidirectional influences on one another over the short and long term.
>
> (838)

Tiberio et al. (2016) tested a model of the transactional association of G2 parenting (for positive parenting and poor discipline) and G3 child effortful control from ages 3 to 13–14 years using five time points of data. Poor effortful control is a temperamental factor that is related to poor behaviour regulation and underlies externalizing behaviour problems (Olson et al. 2005; Ormel et al. 2005; Prior, Smart, Sanson and Oberklaid 2001). Although poor effortful control is theorized to have some genetic basis, it also is believed to be responsive to caregiver behaviours (Calkins 1994). Models were tested separately for G2 fathers and mothers and included possible effects of earlier G2 parenting on later G3 behaviour, and vice versa.

Findings indicated, first, significant stability of both parenting and effortful control from early childhood to early adolescence. Second, as hypothesized, concurrent associations between parenting and effortful control were found that were significantly weaker at older ages. Third, bidirectional effects were found that were consistent with a view of child temperament having evocative effects on parenting; that is at younger ages, children's effortful control influenced later parenting, whereas at older child ages parenting influenced later effortful control. Finally, a transactional effect was found such that maternal parenting in late childhood was a mechanism explaining children's development of effortful control from mid-childhood to adolescence. Overall, findings of this relatively stringent test of associations of parenting practices and the child temperament dimension of poor effortful control across 10 years of childhood indicated that the association is bidirectional. As stated by Tiberio et al. (2016: 851), 'The long-term effects on the child's adjustment of evocative child effects could be of large magnitude as influences accumulate across development.' Findings indicate that child evocative effects may be a source of discontinuity in both child behaviour and in parenting across generations, if the child's temperamental characteristics differ from those of the parent. Findings also emphasize the importance of addressing child evocative effects in parenting interventions for both mothers and fathers.

Emerging theoretical approach: intergenerational developmental congruence

Based in the dynamic developmental systems approach where the emphasis is on the role of development, a key hypothesis of the study is now intergenerational developmental congruence (vs. discontinuity). In geometry, congruence refers to figures of a similar shape and size. Here we use this term to posit that ages of onset of use and patterns of growth across development will show similarity across generations (Capaldi, Kerr and Tiberio 2017*). Some evidence suggests that genetic and temperamental factors increase an individual's risk when they are expressed at sensitive developmental periods (Witt 2010). Thus, the timing of vulnerability (e.g., susceptibility to deviant peer influences) and behaviours (e.g., poorly controlled aggression with peers) is expected to be similar across generations. Such similarity is also expected to be more likely when there are continuities in social risk contexts (Capaldi et al. 2012*; Gavin, Hill, Hawkins and Maas 2011; Lipman, Georgiades and Boyle 2011; Scaramella, Neppl, Ontai and Conger 2008; Schofield et al. 2011; Thornberry, Freeman-Gallant and Lovegrove 2009) and family mechanisms, such as parenting (Capaldi, Pears et al. 2003*; Kerr, Capaldi, Pears and Owen 2009*), that also are made more probable by shared genetic and temperamental factors. Prospective intergenerational study designs are necessary to examine congruence in the timing and patterns of antisocial behaviours. Approaches such as comparing growth models across generations can be used to test such hypotheses. We have not as yet undertaken such work regarding antisocial behaviour, but have recently addressed this issue regarding intergenerational associations in adolescent substance use onset (Tiberio, Kerr and Capaldi, under review*).

Conclusions and future directions

Replication approaches

Collaborations among researchers with longitudinal studies of G2 who initiated studies of G3 have led to the recognition that stronger tests of intergenerational questions can be achieved through tests of replications across samples with differing characteristics, including differing levels of risk, ethnic and gender composition, and country of origin (Capaldi, Conger, Hops and Thornberry 2003*; Thornberry, Hops, Conger and Capaldi 2003b*). The frame of Schmidt (2009) that replication may be "direct" versus "conceptual" has become influential in psychology. Direct replication is defined as a test that is as similar as possible to the original, whereas in a conceptual replication some elements of the original test differ or are altered to see if associations might be found to generalize across a variety of conditions. In fact, these forms of replication represent opposite ends of a continuum, with many replications containing design elements (e.g., samples, measures) that vary along this dimension (Asendorpf et al. 2013; Earp and Trafimow 2015). Particular types of between-study variance, such as differences in sample characteristics, can be advantageous in testing whether findings are robust. It is typical that intergenerational studies do differ along a number of dimensions, including ethnic makeup, risk context, cohort or historical time when the participants were of a certain age, and measurement (e.g., two studies may have measured antisocial behaviour but with different instruments). Future replication efforts will strengthen the contributions of intergenerational studies to our understanding of factors relating to continuity and discontinuity in antisocial behaviour and crime, as well as other risk behaviours.

Other important future goals for prospective intergenerational studies are to integrate a broader range of dynamic system influences within the same study. Thus, integrated study of physiological systems as well as psychological and social systems would be ideal. This is difficult to do as many aspects of each of these systems are relevant – and dynamic. For example, some key aspects of physiological functioning include genetic inheritance, gene expression and factors which influence that, the functioning of the stress response system, and brain growth and modification due to developmental and environmental influences.

Findings from OYS G1 and G2, and from OYS–3GS G1, G2, and G3 reviewed in this chapter indicate that the magnitude of intergenerational associations in crime and antisocial behaviour differ considerably depending on the developmental stages examined and measures used. Thus large associations are found across G1 to G2 for official adult arrest records and relatively large associations of G2 arrests with G3 child externalizing behaviours. Associations of broader constructs of antisocial behaviour in G2 and temperamental risk and externalizing in G3 however were modest. This discrepancy may be due to the fact that problem behaviours are more common in adolescence when such behaviour is at a peak, than in adulthood, when many have desisted, indicating that adult arrests may be a measure of more severe antisocial behaviour. Overall these discrepant findings indicate the need for further theorizing and study regarding the meaning of and mechanisms of intergenerational transmission of antisocial behaviours at differing developmental stages.

For an intergenerational study such as OYS–3GS, which began in the 1980s for the target G2 parent and in the 1990s for the target G3 children, this is an exciting time for examining questions regarding antisocial and associated problem behaviours, including substance use, as many of the G3 offspring are maturing into their teens and thus reaching a "critical mass" sample in G3. This allows for examining continuity across similar developmental periods in G2 (who were usually recruited in late childhood or adolescence) and G3, and for addressing key questions related to mediation (i.e., mechanisms explaining intergenerational associations) and to discontinuity or moderation (i.e., factors that exacerbate or ameliorate intergenerational associations), including by parent and child gender. This work will be valuable for informing prevention programs, especially if replication efforts across intergenerational projects continue to test the robustness of such findings.

Note

1 The original principal investigator of the Oregon Youth Study was Dr. Gerald R. Patterson. Dr. Beverly Fagot initiated the Three Generational Study.

References

Note: References marked with an asterisk are from the Oregon Youth Study–Three Generational Study.

Achenbach, T.M. (1991) *Manual for the Child Behavior Checklist/4–18 and 1991 Profile*, Burlington, VT: University of Vermont, Department of Psychiatry.

Angold, A., Costello, E.J. and Erkanli, A. (1999) 'Comorbidity', *Journal of Child Psychology and Psychiatry*, 40: 57–87.

Asendorpf, J.B., Conner, M., De Fruyt, F., De Houwer, J., Denissen, J.J.A., Fiedler, K., . . . Wicherts, J.M. (2013) 'Recommendations for increasing replicability in psychology', *European Journal of Personality*, 27: 108–119. doi:10.1002/per.1919

Blumstein, A., Cohen, J., Roth, J.A. and Visher, C.A. (eds.). (1986) *Criminal Careers and Career Criminals*, vol. 1. Washington, DC: National Academy Press.

Bureau of Labor Statistics. (2010) *Department of Labor and National Institute for Child Health and Human Development: Children of the NLSY79, 1986–2010*, Columbus, OH: Center for Human Resource Research.

Calkins, S.D. (1994) 'Origins and outcomes of individual differences in emotional regulation', *Monographs of the Society for Research in Child Development*, 59: 53–72. doi:10.1111/j.1540-5834.1994.tb01277.x

Capaldi, D.M., Chamberlain, P., Fetrow, R.A. and Wilson, J. (1997) 'Conducting ecologically valid prevention research: Recruiting and retaining a "whole village" in multimethod, multiagent studies', *American Journal of Community Psychology*, 25: 471–492.

*Capaldi, D.M., Conger, R.D., Hops, H. and Thornberry, T.P. (2003) 'Introduction to special section on three-generational studies', *Journal of Abnormal Child Psychology*, 31: 123–125.

Capaldi, D.M. and Eddy, J.M. (2005) 'Oppositional defiant disorder and conduct disorder', in T.P. Gullotta and G.R. Adams (eds.) *The Handbook of Adolescent Behavioral Problems: Evidence-Based Approaches to Prevention and Treatment*, 283–308, New York, NY: Springer Science+Business Media.

Capaldi, D.M., Kerr, D.C.R., Eddy, J.M. and Tiberio, S.S. (2016) 'Understanding persistence and desistance in crime and risk behaviors in adulthood: Implications for theory and prevention', *Prevention Science*, 17: 785–793. doi:10.1007/s11121-015-0609-0

*Capaldi, D.M., Kerr, D.C.R. and Tiberio, S.S. (2017) 'Intergenerational transmission of risk for behavioral problems including substance use', in O. Braddick (ed.) *Oxford Research Encyclopedia of Psychology* (Online doi:10.1093/acrefore/9780190236557.013.42), New York, NY: Oxford University Press.

Capaldi, D.M. and Kim, H.K. (2014) 'Comorbidity of depression and conduct disorder', in C.S. Richards and M.W. O'Hara (eds.) *The Oxford Handbook of Depression and Comorbidity*, 186–199. New York, NY: Oxford University Press.

Capaldi, D.M., Kim, H.K. and Owen, L.D. (2008) 'Romantic partners' influence on men's likelihood of arrest in early adulthood', *Criminology*, 46: 401–433. doi:10.1111/j.1745-9125.2008.00110.x

Capaldi, D.M. and Patterson, G.R. (1987) 'An approach to the problem of recruitment and retention rates for longitudinal research', *Behavioral Assessment*, 9: 169–177.

*Capaldi, D.M., Pears, K.C., Kerr, D.C.R. and Owen, L.D. (2008) 'Intergenerational and partner influences on fathers' negative discipline', *Journal of Abnormal Child Psychology*, 36: 347–358. doi:10.1007/s10802-007-9182-8

*Capaldi, D.M., Pears, K.C., Kerr, D.C.R., Owen, L.D. and Kim, H.K. (2012) 'Growth in externalizing and internalizing problems in childhood: A prospective study of psychopathology across three generations', *Child Development*, 833: 1945–1959. doi:10.1111/j.1467-8624.2012.01821.x

*Capaldi, D.M., Pears, K.C., Patterson, G.R. and Owen, L.D. (2003) 'Continuity of parenting practices across generations in an at-risk sample: A prospective comparison of direct and mediated associations', *Journal of Abnormal Child Psychology*, 31: 127–142. doi:10.1023/A:1022518123387

Capaldi, D.M. and Wiesner, M. (2009) 'A dynamic developmental systems approach to understanding offending in early adulthood', in J. Savage (ed.) *The Development of Persistent Criminality*, 374–388, New York, NY: Oxford University Press.

Conger, R.D., Neppl, T., Kim, K.J. and Scaramella, L. (2003) 'Angry and aggressive behavior across three generations: A prospective longitudinal study of parents and children', *Journal of Abnormal Child Psychology*, 31: 143–160.

Dishion, T.J. and Patterson, G.R. (2006) 'The development and ecology of antisocial behavior in children and adolescents', in D. Cicchetti and D.J. Cohen (eds.) *Developmental Psychopathology: Risk, Disorder and Adaptation*, vol. 3, 503–541, New York, NY: Wiley.

Dishion, T.J., Spracklen, K.M., Andrews, D.W. and Patterson, G.R. (1996) 'Deviancy training in male adolescent friendships', *Behavior Therapy*, 27: 373–390. doi:10.1016/S0005-7894(96)80023-2

Dougherty, D.M., Mathias, C.W. and Marsh, D.M. (2003) *Go Stop Impulsivity Paradigm (Version 1.0)*, Houston, TX: Neurobehavioral Research Laboratory and Clinic, University of Texas Health Science Center.

Earp, B.D. and Trafimow, D. (2015) 'Replication, falsification and the crisis of confidence in social psychology', *Frontiers in Psychology*, 6: 1–11. doi:10.3389/fpsyg.2015.00621

*Fagot, B.I., Pears, K.C., Capaldi, D.M., Crosby, L. and Leve, C.S. (1998) 'Becoming an adolescent father: Precursors and parenting', *Developmental Psychology*, 34: 1209–1212.

Gavin, A.R., Hill, K.H., Hawkins, J.D. and Maas, C. (2011) 'The role of maternal early life and later life risk factors on offspring low birth weight: Findings from a three-generational study', *Journal of Adolescent Health*, 49: 166–171. doi:10.1016/j.jadohealth.2010.11.246

Gorman-Smith, D., Tolan, P.H., Zelli, A. and Huesmann, L.R. (1996) 'The relation of family functioning to violence among inner-city minority youth', *Journal of Family Psychology*, 10: 115–129.

Guzzo, K.B. (2014) 'New partners, more kids: Multiple-partner fertility in the United States', *The ANNALS of the American Academy of Political and Social Science*, 654: 66–86.

Hops, H., Davis, B., Leve, C. and Sheeber, L. (2003) 'Cross-generational transmission of aggressive parent behavior: A prospective, mediational examination', *Journal of Abnormal Child Psychology*, 31: 161–169. doi:10.1023/A:1022522224295

Kenny, D.A., Kashy, D.A. and Cook, W.L. (2006) *Dyadic Data Analysis*, New York, NY: Guilford Press.

*Kerr, D.C.R., Capaldi, D.M., Owen, L.D., Wiesner, M. and Pears, K.C. (2011) 'Changes in at-risk American men's crime and substance use trajectories following fatherhood', *Journal of Marriage and Family*, 73: 1101–1116. doi:10.1111/j.1741-3737.2011.00864.x

*Kerr, D.C.R., Capaldi, D.M., Pears, K.C. and Owen, L.D. (2009) 'A prospective three generational study of fathers' constructive parenting: Influences from family of origin,

adolescent adjustment and offspring temperament', *Developmental Psychology*, 45: 1257–1275. doi:10.1037/a0015863

*Kim, H.K., Capaldi, D.M., Pears, K.C., Kerr, D.C.R. and Owen, L.D. (2009) 'Intergenerational transmission of internalising and externalising behaviors across three generations: Gender specific pathways', *Criminal Behaviour and Mental Health*, 19: 125–141. doi:10.1002/cbm.708

Lipman, E.L., Georgiades, K. and Boyle, M.H. (2011) 'Young adult outcomes of children born to teen mothers: Effects of being born during their teen or later years', *Journal of the American Academy of Child and Adolescent Psychiatry*, 50: 232–241. doi:10.1016/j.jaac.2010.12.00

Merikangas, K.R. (1982) 'Assortative mating for psychiatric disorders and psychological traits', *Archives of General Psychiatry*, 39: 1173–1180.

Moffitt, T.E., Caspi, A., Harrington, H. and Milne, B.J. (2002) 'Males on the life-course-persistent and adolescence-limited antisocial pathways: Follow-up at age 26 years', *Development and Psychopathology*, 14: 179–207.

Monahan, K.C., Steinberg, L., Cauffman, E. and Mulvey, E.P. (2009) 'Trajectories of antisocial behavior and psychosocial maturity from adolescence to young adulthood', *Developmental Psychology*, 45: 165–168. doi:10.1037/a0015862

Muthén, L.K. and Muthén, B.O. (1998–2015) *Mplus User's Guide*, 7th edn, Los Angeles, CA: Muthén and Muthén.

National Institute of Mental Health. (1997) *Diagnostic Interview Schedule for Children-Version IV-Parent and Youth (NIMH DISC-IV)*, Washington, DC: Author.

Olson, S.L., Sameroff, A.J., Kerr, D.C.R., Lopez, N.L. and Wellman, H.M. (2005) 'Developmental foundations of externalizing problems in young children: The role of effortful control', *Development and Psychopathology*, 17: 25–45. doi:10.1017/S0954579405050029

Ormel, J., Oldehinkel, A.J., Ferdinand, R.F., Hartman, C.A., De Winter, A. F., Veenstra, R., . . . Verhulst, F.C. (2005) 'Internalizing and externalizing problems in adolescence: General and dimension-specific effects of familial loadings and preadolescent temperament traits', *Psychological Medicine*, 12: 1825–1835. doi:10.1017/S0033291705005829

Patterson, G.R. (1982) *Coercive Family Process: A Social Learning Approach to Family Intervention*, vol. 3, Eugene, OR: Castalia.

Patterson, G.R. (1986) 'Performance models for antisocial boys', *American Psychologist*, 41: 432–444.

Patterson, G.R. (2005) 'Coercive cycles in families', in M. Hersen, G. Sugai and R. Horner (eds.) *Encyclopedia of Behavior Modification and Cognitive Behavior Therapy: Educational Applications*, vol. 3, 1224–1226, Thousand Oaks, CA: Sage.

Patterson, G.R., Reid, J.B. and Dishion, T.J. (1992) *A Social Learning Approach: Antisocial Boys*, vol. 4, Eugene, OR: Castalia.

Paulhus, D.L., Trapnell, P.D. and Chen, D. (1999) 'Birth order effects on personality and achievement within families', *Psychological Science*, 10: 465–469.

Prior, D., Smart, D., Sanson, A. and Oberklaid, F. (2001) 'Longitudinal predictors of behavioural adjustment in pre-adolescent children', *Australian and New Zealand Journal of Psychiatry*, 35: 297–307.

Raudenbush, S.W. and Bryk, A.S. (2002) *Hierarchical Linear Models: Applications and Data Analysis Methods*, 2nd edn, Newbury Park, CA: Sage.

Sampson, R.J. and Laub, J.H. (1990) 'Crime and deviance over the life course: The salience of adult social bonds', *American Sociological Review*, 55: 609–627.

Sandefur, G.D., Martin, M., Eggerling-Boeck, J., Mannon, S.E. and Meier, A.M. (2001). 'An overview of racial and ethnic demographic trends', in N.J. Smelser, W.J. Wilson and F. Mitchell (eds.) *American Becoming: Racial Trends and Their Consequences*, vol. 1, 40–102, Washington, DC: National Research Council.

Scaramella, L.V., Neppl, T.K., Ontai, L.L. and Conger, R.D. (2008) 'Consequences of socioeconomic disadvantage across three generations: Parenting behavior and child externalizing problems', *Journal of Family Psychology*, 22: 725–733. doi:10.1037/a0013190

Schmidt, S. (2009) 'Shall we really do it again? The powerful concept of replication is neglected in the social sciences', *Review of General Psychology*, 13: 90–100. doi:10.1037/a0015108

Schofield, T.J., Martin, M., Conger, R.D., Neppl, T.K., Donnellan, M.B. and Conger, K.J. (2011) 'Intergenerational transmission of adaptive functioning: A test of the interactionist model of SES and human development', *Child Development*, 82: 33–47.

Steffensmeier, D. (1996) 'Gender and crime: Toward a gendered theory of female offending', *Annual Review of Sociology*, 22: 459–487.

Steffensmeier, D. and Allan, E. (2000) 'Looking for patterns: Gender, age and crime', in J. Sheley (ed.) *Criminology: The Contemporary Handbook*, 85–127, Belmont, CA: Wadsworth.

Thornberry, T.P. (2016) 'Three generation studies: Methodological challenges and promise', in M.J. Shanahan, J.T. Mortimer and M.K. Johnson (eds.) *Handbook of the Life Course*, 1st edn, vol. 2, 571–598, New York, NY: Springer.

Thornberry, T. P., Freeman-Gallant, A., Lizotte, A. J., Krohn, M. D. and Smith, C. A. (2003a) 'Linked lives: The intergenerational transmission of antisocial behavior', *Journal of Abnormal Child Psychology*, 31: 171–184.

Thornberry, T.P., Freeman-Gallant, A. and Lovegrove, P.J. (2009) 'Intergenerational linkages in antisocial behaviour', *Criminal Behaviour and Mental Health*, 19: 80–93.

*Thornberry, T.P., Hops, H., Conger, R.D. and Capaldi, D.M. (2003b) 'Replicated findings and future directions for intergenerational studies: Closing comments', *Journal of Abnormal Child Psychology*, 31: 201–203. doi:10.1023/A:1022530426113

Thornberry, T.P., Smith, C.A. and Howard, G.J. (1997) 'Risk factors for teenage fatherhood', *Journal of Marriage and the Family*, 59: 505–522.

*Tiberio, S.S., Capaldi, D.M., Kerr, D.C.R., Bertrand, M., Pears, K.C. and Owen, L.D. (2016) 'Parenting and the development of effortful control from early childhood to early adolescence: A transactional developmental model', *Development and Psychopathology*, 28: 837–853. doi:10.1017/S0954579416000341

*Tiberio, S.S., Kerr, D.C.R. and Capaldi, D.M. (under review) *Adolescent onset of alcohol, tobacco and marijuana use: Tests of developmental congruence across generations*, Manuscript under review.

Wiesner, M. and Capaldi, D.M. (2003) 'Relations of childhood and adolescent factors to offending trajectories of young men', *Journal of Research in Crime and Delinquency*, 40: 231–262.

Wiesner, M., Capaldi, D.M. and Kim, H.K. (2007) 'Arrest trajectories across a 17-year span for young men: Relation to dual taxonomies and self-reported offense trajectories', *Criminology*, 45: 835–863.

Wiesner, M., Capaldi, D.M. and Patterson, G.R. (2003) 'Development of antisocial behavior and crime across the life-span from a social interactional perspective: The coercion model', in R.L. Akers and G.F. Jensen (eds.) *Social Learning Theory and the Explanation of Crime: A Guide for the New Century: Advances in Criminological Theory*, vol. 11, 317–337, New Brunswick, NJ: Transaction.

Witt, E.D. (2010) 'Research on alcohol and adolescent brain development: Opportunities and future directions', *Alcohol*, 44: 119–124. doi:10.1016/j.alcohol.2009.08.011

Wolff, J.C. and Ollendick, T.H. (2006) 'The comorbidity of conduct problems and depression in childhood and adolescence', *Clinical Child and Family Psychology Review*, 9: 201–220. doi:10.1007/s10567-006-0011-3

Chapter 9

Aggression and criminality over three generations

Eric F. Dubow, L. Rowell Huesmann, Paul Boxer, Cathy Smith, and Aaron E. Sedlar

The Columbia County Longitudinal Study began in 1960 and has culminated so far in the collection of four waves of data over a 40-year span on children who were living in Columbia County, New York, in 1960. The entire population of third-graders – Generation 2, whom we refer to as our original participants (and most of their parents, Generation 1) – participated in the first wave of this project in 1960; follow-up assessments were conducted on Generation 2 in 1970 when the participants were approximately 19 years of age; in 1981 when the participants were approximately 30 years of age; and between 1999 and 2002 when the participants were approximately 48 years of age. We also have interviewed children of the original participants – Generation 3.

This is a unique, long-term, prospective study of an entire population of third-graders in a socioeconomically heterogeneous county in the United States. Methodological strengths of the study include: the 40-year prospective design; assessment points on the focal participants at four developmental periods (childhood, late adolescence, early adulthood, middle adulthood), their parents, and their offspring; and multiple methods of data collection (e.g., parent reports, peer nominations, self-reports, official criminal records).

Published findings have informed the literature on child and parental factors related to the development of aggression and other important social behaviours in school-age children. Perhaps the most path-breaking results concerned the relation between early TV violence viewing and later aggression, which have had a substantial impact on the field's understanding of the reality of observational learning as well as on social policy. We also have documented moderate continuity from ages 8 to 48 in aggression both for males and for females, and we have expanded our analyses to investigate what contextual (e.g., family relationships, media influences) and personal (e.g., gender, self-concept) factors predict specific later competent outcomes (e.g., educational and occupational success) and problematic outcomes (e.g., aggression, substance use, psychopathology) within and across generations. Most recently, we have used the first three waves of data to examine what early childhood and adolescent factors predict adult criminality (Dubow, Huesmann, Boxer and Smith 2014, 2016; Huesmann, Eron and Dubow 2002).

The Columbia County Study has also made important theoretical contributions to our understanding of how aggression develops within and across generations. Our thinking has evolved from a behavioural model emphasizing observational learning (i.e., exposure to aggressive models) to a social-cognitive model which emphasizes the processes (e.g., patterns of thinking about – and our emotional reactions to – the world, the self, and others) by which exposure to aggressive models leads to an enduring pattern of aggressive behaviour.

In this chapter, we begin by describing the Columbia County Longitudinal Study (the background, sample characteristics, the longitudinal design, and the key measures relevant to aggression and criminality). Next, we explicate the theoretical model that has informed the evolving study design. We call this model the "social-cognitive ecological model." In that section of the chapter, we describe four modes of cross-generational transmission of aggression and violence, and the aggression-supporting social cognitions and emotional dysregulation through which these modes of transmission produce a characteristic pattern of aggression. Then, as a test of the theoretical model, we summarize our study's findings on cross-generational relations of aggression, violence, and offenses, and we link the findings back to our model. We conclude with a brief discussion of the implications of our findings for prevention and intervention programs, as well as potential future plans for research.

The Columbia County Longitudinal Study

Background

The Columbia County Longitudinal Study was pioneered by Leonard Eron. In 1955, Eron, a professor at Yale University, joined the Rip Van Winkle Foundation, a privately funded community health centre in nearby Columbia County, New York, as the Director of Research. His interests were in the epidemiology of mental health problems in rural areas. Eron narrowed his interests to the development of aggression ("an act which injures or irritates another person"), and for five years, piloted and refined parent report and peer nomination measures of child aggression and potential predictor variables (e.g., child-rearing measures). In 1960, with funding from the National Institute of Mental Health, Eron and his colleagues, Monroe Lefkowitz and Leopold Walder (clinical psychologists at the Rip Van Winkle Foundation and the local hospital), launched the project, which has become known as the Columbia County Longitudinal Study (CCLS). The cohort was re-interviewed in 1970 when Rowell Huesmann joined the research team (funded by the National Institute of Mental Health), in 1980 when Eric Dubow joined the research team (funded by the National Institutes of Health), and in 2000 when Paul Boxer joined the research team (again funded by the National Institutes of Health).

Sample characteristics

The CCLS has so far culminated in the collection of 40 years of data on 856 children (436 boys, 420 girls; 95 per cent Caucasian) who were living in Columbia County, a semi-rural area of New York State, in 1960. According to the U.S. Census Bureau, in 1960, the county's population was approximately 47,000, with approximately 11,000 residing in the largest town, Hudson; by 2000, the most recent wave of data collection, the size of the county had grown to approximately 63,000, although Hudson's population had decreased to approximately 7,500 (U.S. Decennial Census, 1960/2000). In terms of ethnicity, the sample is not representative of the U.S. population as a whole. However, in terms of other important demographic characteristics, the sample was representative of 40 per cent of the counties in the United States in terms of social and economic characteristics, population density, urban–rural characteristics, and the system of school administration (Eron, Walder and Lefkowitz 1971; Eron, Walder, Toigo and Lefkowitz 1963; Toigo 1965). Families reported a broad range of socioeconomic backgrounds, with fathers' occupations averaging the equivalent of jobs such as craftsmen, foremen, and skilled tradesmen. The sample displayed a wide range of intelligence, with an average IQ of 104.

Longitudinal study design

Figure 9.1 shows the number of participants in each generation who were interviewed in each phase of the study (1960, 1970, 1981, and 2000). In the first phase of this project, the entire population of the county's third-graders (Generation G2, $N = 856$) participated (Eron et al. 1971). At that time, 85 per cent of their mothers (mean age = 36.02 years, $SD = 6.39$) and 71 per cent of their fathers (mean age = 39.30 years, $SD = 7.43$) also were interviewed (Generation G1). Youth were interviewed in their classrooms (through peer nomination procedures) and parents were interviewed in person.

In 1970, 10 years after the initial data collection period, we obtained complete in-person interviews from 427 of the original G2 subjects (198 males, 211 females), who were then 19 years old (Eron, Huesmann, Lefkowitz and Walder 1972; Lefkowitz, Eron, Walder and Huesmann 1977).

In 1981, we conducted a third-stage interview with the G2 subjects, whose modal age was 30. We interviewed 295 of the original subjects in person and another 114 by mail and telephone for a total of 409 subjects (198 males, 211 females). Furthermore, we interviewed the spouses of 165 of the interviewed subjects and 82 of the subjects' children (Generation G3) who were approximately the same age as the subjects in 1960. We also obtained archival data from the New York State Divisions of Criminal Justice and Motor Vehicles (Huesmann, Eron, Lefkowitz and Walder 1984).

Between 2000 and 2002, we completed a fourth wave of data collection (Huesmann, Dubow, Eron and Boxer 2006; Dubow, Huesmann, Boxer,

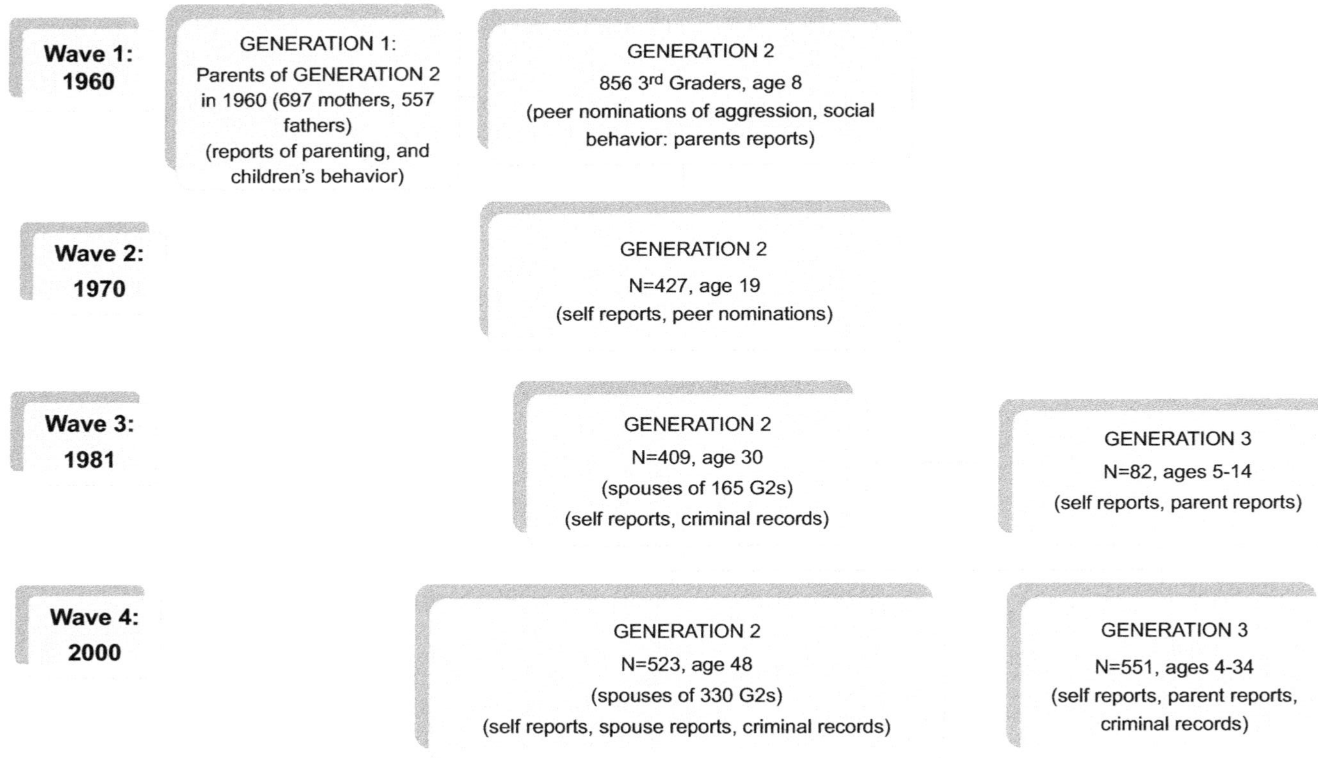

Figure 9.1 Columbia County Longitudinal Study participants interviewed in each wave and methods of data collection

Pulkkinen and Kokko 2006; Dubow, Boxer and Huesmann 2008; Huesmann, Dubow and Boxer 2009). We re-interviewed 523 (61 per cent) of the original G2 subjects (268 males, 255 females; 284 in person and 239 by mail and telephone) and again obtained data from their spouse/person who knows them well (n = 330) and from criminal and traffic archives. In this fourth wave, we also interviewed 551 of the G3 children (269 males, 282 females) of the G2 subjects. These children represented 195 pairs of siblings and 161 single children. For these children, we also obtained teacher reports of academic and behavioural functioning, as well as their criminal records.

G2 sample attrition from wave 1 to wave 4

For the 523 of the 856 G2 participants re-interviewed during the 2000 phase, the mean age was 48.85 years (SD = .81); the average education level was between "some college" and a college degree; the average occupational attainment reflected a middle-class status (i.e., mean occupational prestige code using Stevens and Hoisington's (1987) occupational prestige ratings indicated jobs such as salespeople, bookkeepers, and secretaries). Sixty-nine percent of the original participants were living with their spouses. Most of the re-interviewed subjects (63 per cent) were living in New York State at the time of recruitment; many of those were living in, or in close proximity to, Columbia County. By far, the majority (77 per cent) of the re-interviewed participants were living in the mid-Atlantic or northeastern regions of the United States. Only two of the original participants were residing outside of the United States.

In any longitudinal study, there is a loss of participants over time. In Figure 9.1, we show that among Generation 2 at the start of the study there were 856 participants; 10 years later, we interviewed 427 (participants were now one year out of high school, and many could not be located); in 1981, we interviewed 409; but in 2000, we interviewed 523 (individuals were easier to locate through internet searches). At age 48, we collected some type of data (archival, interview, or other report) on 683 (80 per cent) of the original sample of 856 (as noted, actual interviews were conducted with 523 of them). Of the non-interviewed participants, 37 had died, 112 had disappeared and could not be found despite intense efforts, 40 could not be interviewed because of distance and scheduling difficulties, and 144 refused. The number who refused to be interviewed (despite substantial financial incentives) was higher than expected, but the completed re-interview rate of 61 per cent and data collection rate of 80 per cent over 40 years still provided us with a sizeable sample for analysis. Dubow et al. (2006) showed that a comparison of means on age 8 scores revealed that compared to participants who were re-interviewed at age 48, participants who were not re-interviewed had higher levels of aggression, lower levels of popularity, and lower IQ at age 8, but many of the high aggressive *were* re-sampled. Analyses for this chapter showed that in terms of criminal arrests 17 per cent of those re-interviewed had been arrested at least once in their lifetimes compared to 23 per cent of those not re-interviewed ($\chi^2(1) = 3.78, p < .10$). There was no significant difference in age 8 father's occupational status between re-sampled participants and dropouts.

Measures

Figure 9.1 shows our multimethod approach to assessments at each wave (i.e., self-reports, peer nominations, reports by parents and spouses, official criminal records). In terms of the content of the measures, when the project began, the principal goal was to investigate child individual-personal (e.g., intelligence) and parenting (e.g., harsh physical punishment) factors contributing to the development and maintenance of aggression in school-aged children. Since that time, the goals of the study have expanded to investigate the factors accounting for continuity or discontinuity in aggression and related behaviours over time and across generations.

Many of the core measures were developed for the first wave of the project by Leonard Eron, Leo Walder, Monroe Lefkowitz, and colleagues in 1960 (Eron et al. 1971) and used continuously throughout. Because the project began primarily as a study of aggression in children, and the environmental conditions under which it is learned, most measures relate either directly or indirectly to aggressive behaviour. By the 1981 wave, however, the areas of assessment broadened considerably. Many of the original participants were married or had been married at one time, and a sizeable minority of them were parents as well. Measurement thus was expanded to include important domains of adult functioning, including depression, spousal conflict, beliefs about parenting, and alcoholism. At the same time, the theoretical model underlying the Columbia County Study also was undergoing expansion and refinement (Huesmann and Eron 1984; Huesmann 1988), leading to the incorporation of detailed cognitive measures into the interview battery. The expansion of measurement continued into the 2000 wave, with the addition of numerous measures of internal (e.g., emotion regulation, social cognitions related to aggression, self-competence) and contextual (e.g., social support, life experience, neighbourhood characteristics) phenomena. In the Appendix, we present a summary of the measures.

At wave 1 when the participants were 8 years old, their parents (G1) were interviewed mostly about child-rearing practices (physical punishment, nurturance, rejection) and the child's behaviour. Our best measure of G1's aggression is the extent to which G1 endorsed hitting G2 as a form of punishment ("spank your child until he/she cries?" and "slap your child in the face"). We also computed a parent delinquency score in response to an item whether the parent was "occasionally in trouble with the police when a youth." If both parents were interviewed, their scores were averaged. However, G2 child aggression at age 8 was not based on parent report, but on peer nominations of aggression (10 classroom-administered peer nomination items such as "Who pushes and shoves other children?", "Who starts fights over nothing?", "Who says mean things?"). It is worth noting that peer-nominations are more valid and reliable than "peer-ratings" because each of *N* peers can only contribute 1/*N*th of any child's score.

At age 19, peer nominations were administered again to G2s, as well as two self-report measures of aggression that we continued to include at ages 30 and 48 and for the G3 participants in 2000 (severe physical aggression: how often in the last year they engaged in each of four behaviours such as choked someone, slapped or kicked someone, punched or beaten someone, knifed or shot at someone or threatened to do it; and aggressive personality: the sum of scales 4, 9, and F from the Minnesota Multiphasic Personality Inventory (MMPI; Hathaway and McKinley 1940), which we have shown to be a reliable and valid measure of antisocial-aggressive behaviour (e.g., Huesmann et al. 1984; Huesmann, Lefkowitz and Eron 1978). G2 at ages 19, 30, and 48 and G3 also provided self-reports of whether they had been in trouble with the law and whether they had been arrested.

Finally, during the 1981 and 2000 data collections, criminal history data were obtained from the New York State Criminal Justice Archive for G2 participants; in 2000, we also collected criminal data for G3 participants. For each arrest, we coded whether it was a violent offense (one involving physical force against a person) as well as a violence seriousness rating (Rossi, Bose and Berk 1974).

Other key domains of measures include psychopathology, depression, and substance abuse (G2 and G3); parenting behaviours and beliefs of G1 and G2 and other contextual factors, such as exposure to violence as witness or victim and interspousal conflict/aggression; and emotional and social-cognitive mediators of the effects of contextual factors on the development of aggression (e.g., G2's and G3's hostile attribution bias, repertoire of aggressive scripts, aggressive fantasy, normative beliefs justifying aggression).

The social-cognitive ecological model of the development of aggression over time and across generations

Overview of the social-cognitive ecological model

The theoretical framework guiding our understanding of within- and cross-generational influences on aggression and violence has focused on understanding the psychological processes through which predisposing individual-personal factors (e.g., genetic and epigenetic factors, neurophysiology, innate temperament) and environmental contextual factors combine to produce a characteristic pattern of aggressive behaviour. Our model has evolved from concentrating on the powerful role of observational learning (e.g., exposure to violent environments) to an expanded social-cognitive ecological model of the development of aggression. Social-cognitive and emotional mediating mechanisms in our model (scripts for behaviour, schema about the world and oneself, beliefs about aggression/violence, emotional dysregulation) represent the enduring psychological structures that link predispositions (e.g., genetic and epigenetic, neurophysiology, temperament) and environmental contextual inputs (e.g., observation of violence across contexts of the social ecology in which the child is nested) to subsequent aggressive and violent behaviour. The model is illustrated in Figure 9.2. Thus, the model can be applied both to continuity of aggression and violence *within* and *across* generations. Regarding within-generation continuity, repeated exposure to violence in the macro- and micro-environments, as well as situational factors, lead to the development of aggression-supporting social-cognitive processes that, once crystallized, account for a stable pattern of aggression within an individual. Regarding cross-generational transmission, exposure to parental violence at the micro-level and genetic inputs promote aggression-supporting social cognitions in the offspring, which influence the offspring's aggressive behaviour.

This model draws on ideas developed in several other social-cognitive information processing models over the past three decades to explain how children's interactions with the environment lead to enduring patterns of aggressive and violent behaviour (e.g., Anderson and Bushman 2002; Crick and Dodge 1994; Huesmann and Eron 1984; Huesmann 1988, 1997, 1998). These models draw heavily on the work of cognitive psychologists and information processing theory, in particular from Bandura's (1977, 1986) earlier formulations of cognitive processing in social learning as well as Berkowitz's (1990) neoassociationist thinking. According to Bandura's (1986) social-cognitive formulations, social behaviour is under the control of internal self-regulating cognitive processes. What is important is the cognitive evaluation of events taking place in the child's environment, how the child interprets these events, and how competent the child feels in responding in different ways. These cognitions provide a basis for stability of behaviour tendencies across situations. Internalized standards for behaviour are developed from information conveyed through a variety of ecological contexts, including the observation of others' behaviours (e.g., parents, peers, characters in the mass media).

This cognitive-ecological model for explaining behaviour choices in social problem-solving situations was first described in detail in Huesmann (1998) and Guerra and Huesmann (2004). The model focuses on the central role of three core sets of cognitive processes that have been linked to social behaviours including aggression and violence: (1) encoding and interpretation of cues in a social situation, (2) search for a script to follow, and (3) evaluation of the script and its outcomes.

Several factors have been found to influence cue attention and interpretation among aggressive youths. First, the child may enter the situation with a preexisting emotional state (e.g., anger, irritability), which influences selective attention to situational cues. Compared to nonaggressive children, aggressive children attend to fewer situational cues (Dodge and Newman 1981). Also, schemas about the world influence cue interpretation. Aggressive children exhibit a tendency to perceive hostile intent in others even in ambiguous situations (Dodge and Frame 1982).

Next, after interpreting the situational cues, the child searches his or her repertoire of relevant scripts (i.e., internalized guides for behaving in a social conflict situation) for potential responses. Script search is an automatic process; once learned, a script is easily accessed. Aggressive scripts are developed through observational learning (e.g., interparental conflict; peer conflict; violent media portrayals) and enactive learning (e.g., parent or peer support for "standing up for oneself" by fighting). Dubow and Reid (1994) found that compared to nonaggressive children, aggressive children are more likely to generate aggressive strategies in response to hypothetical provocation situations. Huesmann and Kirwil (2007) described ways in which script search is affected by emotional factors. For example, anger specifically primes aggressive scripts. High emotional arousal "short circuits" information processing and leads to selection of simple responses which are often aggressive. Conversely, individuals who experience less arousal and anxiety from exposure to aggression are also more at risk for aggression because when they cognitively evaluate aggressive scripts, they experience insufficient negative affect to inhibit aggression. When they behave aggressively, they experience insufficient negative affect, and they achieve a more desirable level of arousal which is reinforcing.

Third, once a script is retrieved, the child evaluates it using several criteria that reflect beliefs about oneself. We have focused on normative beliefs about behaving aggressively; that is, does aggressing in the situation meet his or her standards for personal behaviour? Several researchers have found a link between such normative beliefs and aggressive behaviour (e.g., Crane-Ross, Tisak and Tisak 1998; Huesmann and Guerra 1997; Slaby and Guerra 1988). Other beliefs include one's perceived ability to enact an aggressive response successfully (e.g., Erdley and Asher 1996) and one's perceptions of expected outcomes from behaving aggressively (e.g., Egan, Monson and Perry 1998; Guerra and Slaby 1990; Perry, Perry and Rasmussen 1986).

Given this model for social problem solving, an important question becomes: how are the relevant social cognitions that influence the outcome of the social problem-solving process acquired? Our view is that they are acquired through multiple processes, including genetic influences and macro- and micro-environmental factors that exert their influence through observational learning or conditioning.

Applying the social-cognitive ecological model to understanding processes involved in cross-generational transmission

As Figure 9.2 illustrates, we hypothesize that genetic predispositions for aggressive behaviour and repeated exposure to aggression and violence across ecological contexts (Bronfenbrenner 2005) lead to the development of aggressive scripts (mental representations of how to behave in certain situations), hostile schemas (ways of viewing the world and the self), and normative beliefs justifying aggression, as well as emotional dysregulation (e.g., arousal or desensitization to aggression-related stimuli). Because our focus here is on cross-generational influences, we focus on the role of the parental context in the micro-environment, but as Figure 9.2 shows, and as noted earlier, the model also shows how, within individuals, exposure to violence in the media, peer groups, neighbourhood, and culture are other aggression socializers.

We have put forth a model describing four modes of cross-generational transmission of aggression and violence, and the aggression-supporting social cognitions and emotional dysregulation through which these modes of transmission produce a characteristic pattern of aggression (Huesmann, Dubow and Boxer 2011). First, we highlight the mode of genetic and epigenetic

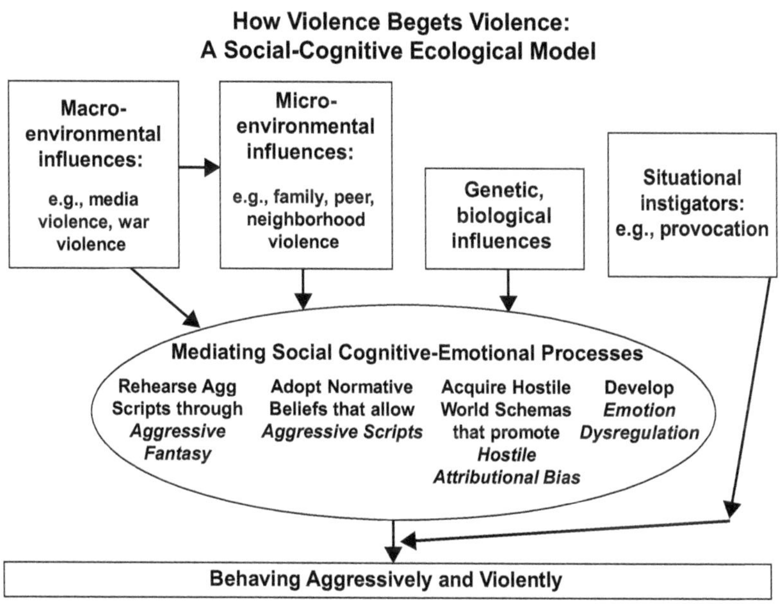

Figure 9.2 A social-cognitive ecological model of the development of aggression

transmission, which has been supported through genetically informed designs (e.g., Caspi et al., 2002; Deater-Deckard and Plomin 1999; Miles and Carey 1997). Neurobiological factors that have been implicated in early aggression (e.g., neurophysiology, neurotransmitters, hormones) are influenced by genetic and epigenetic factors (e.g., Knoblich and King 1992; Raine and Jones 1987), early environment, and gene-by-environment interactions as in the Caspi et al. (2002) study. We argue that these factors influence aggression and violent behaviours by influencing aggression-supporting social cognitions and emotional dysregulation.

The three remaining modes of intergenerational transmission involve environmental influences. Parents not only pass down genes to their offspring, but also may perpetuate a stable environment (for better or worse) across generations. For example, there is evidence of continuity in parenting behaviours across generations (see *Journal of Abnormal Child Psychology*, 2003, volume 31, where five prospective cross-generational studies on parenting and aggression, including the CCLS, reported significant cross-generational parenting correlations; see Dubow, Huesmann and Boxer 2003). Other risk factors in the environment (e.g., poverty, neighbourhood violence, peer violence; see for example Tolan, Gorman-Smith and Henry 2003) also promote aggression and violence; to the extent that there is cross-generational continuity in these environmental factors, one might expect cross-generational continuity in aggression. Of course, environments can drastically change from one generation to the next in positive ways (e.g., parents moving to a more highly resourced neighbourhood, educational opportunities for the parent or child) and in negative ways (e.g., parents moving to a more disadvantaged neighbourhood due to financial troubles, war or ethnic-political conflict breaks out), so these changes in environmental influences can account for discontinuities across generations in aggression.

A major way in which the parenting environment influences the child's behaviour and promotes cross-generational continuity of behaviour is through observational learning. Children observe parents' behaviours and are influenced by what they observe. However, it is not just the observed behaviours that are immediately mimicked or imitated in the future. As we have noted (Huesmann 2017; Huesmann in press), observational learning means that when children observe others, they infer the scripts, schemas, and beliefs that are behind the others' behaviours and encode those social cognitions, which then influence the children's behavior. We know that observational learning effects are stronger when the child identifies with the actor, and the child generally identifies with the parent. For example, if a parent generally behaves aggressively, the child is more likely to encode these scripts for behaviours that the child observes the parent using in social interactions, as well as schemas about the world (e.g., "it is unsafe and hostile") and normative beliefs justifying aggression. These long-term learning effects of observation serve to maintain aggression over time, and provide the foundation for cross-generational transmission of aggressive behaviour and aggression-supporting cognitive structures and processes.

A final mode of intergenerational transmission of aggression is through parents conditioning their children (Eron et al. 1971). Parents may intentionally positively reinforce the child's aggression as a response to peer conflict (e.g., "stand up for yourself and fight back"), or they may unintentionally negatively reinforce it (e.g., the classic example of the parent "giving in" to stop a tantrum; see Patterson 1982). Again, the parent is conditioning not only behaviours, but also scripts, schema, beliefs, and emotional reactions.

Cross-generational transmission findings from the Columbia County Longitudinal Study

Cross-generational relations of aggression, violence, and offenses

Our study has provided evidence of cross-generational transmission of aggression, violence, and antisocial behaviour across two and three generations. In terms of two-generation findings, as noted above, our best measure of G1's aggression was their physical punishment of G2 when G2 was 8 years old. Indeed, G1's self-reported endorsement of physical punishment was significantly related to G2's peer-nominated aggressive behaviour at age 8 (e.g., Dubow et al. 2003; Huesmann et al. 1984; Huesmann et al. 2011). A new analysis for this chapter shows that by age 48, G2 participants who were offenders (a self-report of having been in trouble with the law sometime during their lives, or an arrest sometime during their lives, n = 236) compared to non-offenders (n = 325) were more likely to have parents at age 8 who endorsed physical punishment, $t(559) = 2.79, p < .01$, consistent with our model illustrating the importance of exposure to parental violence in the micro-environment.

We also have reported that aggressive behaviour of G2, including severe physical aggression across the lifespan (at ages 8, 19, 30, and 48) is significantly related to their G3 children's aggressive behaviour when G3 children were late adolescents, on average (Huesmann et al. 2011). Because two G3 children were interviewed for 195 of the participants, to avoid issues of dependency, we restricted our analyses to one child per participant. In these cases, we selected the younger child for these analyses so that the G3 sample could be characterized as a late adolescent, rather than an early adulthood, sample, and thus close to the age of the G2 participant in wave 2; the average age of the G3 children in these analyses was 18.74 years (SD = 5.66). We presented these analyses in Huesmann et al. (2011). We found significant correlations between G2's latent aggression score (based on up to four aggression measures) at each age (8, 19, 30, and 48) and their G3 children's aggressive personality and severe physical aggression. G2's age 8 aggression was more highly correlated with G3's aggressive personality

(r = .24) than severe physical aggression (r = .09), but both correlations are statistically significant. The correlations are consistent with transmission across generations of genetic, biological predispositions in our model, but could also be due to a combination of continuity of aggression within the G2 generation and later influence of G2's behaviour on G3 (exposure to parental violence in the micro-environment). At older G2 ages, correlations with G3's severe physical aggression increased up to r = .26 at age 48, and this is consistent with cross-generational transmission models that focus on children observing parents' aggression and parent's conditioning children's behaviour.

We expanded these analyses to examine the correspondence between G2 and G3 official arrest records. First, we focused on the youngest or only G3 child of the G2s interviewed in 2000 who were residents in New York State. We only included G3s who were 18 years old or older because we did not have arrest records for those under 18. Of these 149 G3s, 19 had an arrest record. A chi-square analysis showed a significant association between whether G2 had a lifetime arrest record and whether G3 had an arrest record ($\chi^2(1) = 4.94, p < .05$, Cramer's V = .18, small to medium effect). Of the G2s who did not have an arrest record, 10 per cent of their G3 children had an arrest record, whereas of the G2s who did have an arrest record, 26 per cent of their G3 children had an arrest record. Next, we created a score for G2 and G3 participants reflecting a combination of whether they had an arrest record and whether they had self-reported as having been in trouble with the law; a "yes" to either item classified the participant as an "offender" (34 per cent of G2 and 46 per cent of G3 participants). A chi-square analysis showed a significant association between whether G2s and G3s were classified as an offender ($\chi^2(1) = 4.60, p < .05$, Cramer's V = .18, small to medium effect); of the G2s who were non-offenders, 39 per cent of their G3 children were offenders, whereas of the G2s who were offenders, 58 per cent of their G3 children were offenders.

We repeated these analyses on the sample of G3s who were the older or only child in the family. This sample, as expected, was somewhat older (mean age = 21.75 years, SD = 5.44), and 34 of the 205 G3s who were 18 and older had an arrest record. A chi-square analysis showed a significant association between whether G2 had an arrest record and whether G3 had an arrest record ($\chi^2(1) = 12.92, p < .001$, Cramer's V = .25, medium effect); of the G2s who did not have an arrest record, 13 per cent of their G3 children had an arrest record, whereas of the G2s who did have an arrest record, 38 per cent of their G3 children had an arrest record. Next, a chi-square analysis showed a significant association between whether G2s and G3s were classified as an offender ($\chi^2(1) = 9.51, p < .01$, Cramer's V = .21, small to medium effect); of the G2s who were non-offenders, 38 per cent of their G3 children were offenders, whereas of the G2s who were offenders, 61 per cent of their G3 children were offenders.

Taken together, these findings on cross-generational consistency between G2 and G3 in aggressive personality, physical aggression, and offending "are consistent with the concept that characteristically aggressive personalities are influenced by predisposing genetic and biological factors modified by learning experiences during the early child-rearing years" (Huesmann et al. 2011: 134), the latter illustrated in Figure 9.2 as violence exposure in the micro-environment.

The role of social cognitions in the cross-generational transmission of aggression and violence

As described earlier, in the most recent wave of data collection, we have expanded our measurement of social cognitions related to aggression. Examining the *processes* that account for cross-generational transmission is a unique contribution of our study. Relevant to cross-generational transmission from parent to child, we examined the degree to which G2's aggression while the G3 child was growing up predicted subsequent aggression-related social cognitions of G3. For these analyses, we again used the G3 sample that included G2's youngest or only child (n = 349). We categorized G2 as high in aggression during G3's childhood years if the G2 parent (the original CCLS participant) or spouse (n = 112 were interviewed) was in the top quartile of the distribution on age 30 (wave 3) severe physical aggression, or if the G2 parenting environment for G3 during childhood was in the top quartile on the parental punishment by hitting variable (slapped in face, spanked or beat with a stick or belt, punched or kicked; composite score at wave 4 of retrospective reports from G2 parents [both if interviewed] and the G3 child, about the amount of hitting G2 received from both parents before G3 was 8 years old); 37 per cent of G2s were thus categorized as high in aggression, and all others were categorized as low in aggression. We compared G3s in these two groups on their social cognitions related to aggression when they were, on average, late adolescents at wave 4. The social cognition variables included: *aggressive fantasy* (4 items, such as "Do you sometimes have daydreams about hitting or hurting somebody that you don't like?"); *hostile attribution bias* (responses to 4 vignettes, such as "Imagine you are standing on the playground and you get hit hard in the back by a ball thrown by another kid. Why do you think this happened?" 0 = by accident, 1 = on purpose); *normative beliefs supporting aggression* (12 items asking youth how right or wrong it is to engage in retaliatory aggression in response to 12 situations); *persecution beliefs* (7 items asking youth how much they agree with each item such as, "People want to be mean to me"); and *aggressive script responses* (open-ended responses to 4 social-conflict vignettes asking youth to list their likely responses, coded for aggression). We standardized the scores for each of these social-cognitive variables for presentation purposes in Figure 9.3. The results show that youth who were exposed to G2s who were high in aggression during childhood were significantly more likely than those exposed to low G2 aggression to have higher levels of hostile attribution bias, normative beliefs supporting aggression, persecution beliefs, and aggressive script responses.

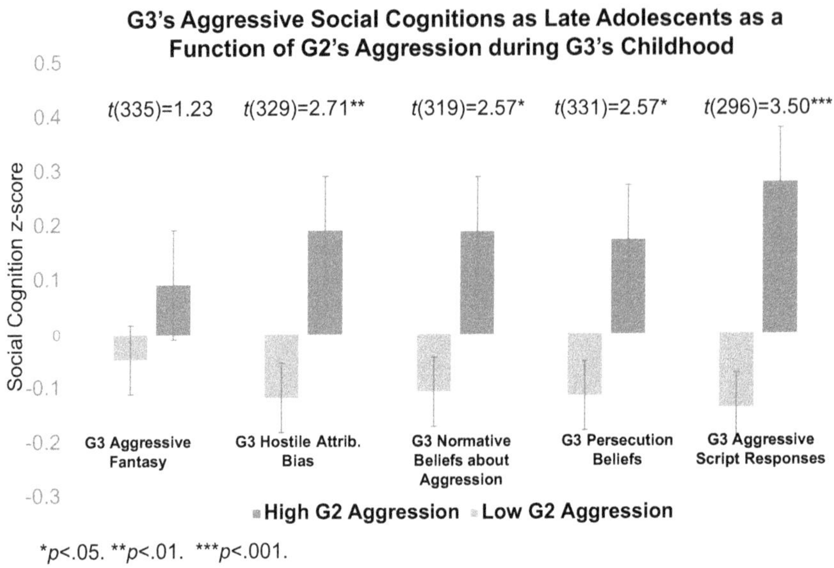

Figure 9.3 G3's aggressive social cognitions as a function of G2's aggression during G3's childhood

All five social cognition scores correlated significantly with the G3's contemporaneous report of aggressive personality (*r*s ranged from .34 to .47, all *p*s < .01) and severe physical aggression (*r*s ranged from.25 to .40, all *p*s < .01). In addition, recall that we classified G3s as offenders if they ever had an arrest record or had self-reported that they had been in trouble with the law. Figure 9.4 shows that compared to non-offenders, offenders had higher levels on four of the five aggression-supporting social cognitions – higher levels of fantasizing about aggression, hostile attribution bias, normative beliefs supporting aggression, and persecution beliefs. Taken together, these results are consistent with our social-cognitive model of cross-generational transmission; aggressive parental models provide opportunities for their youth to develop, through long-term learning, a set of scripts, beliefs, and ways of viewing the world that support a characteristically aggressive pattern of behaviour.

We then created a structural equation model in MPlus to examine the direct effect of G2's aggression/aggressive parenting and the effect of the mediation of G2's aggression/aggressive parenting through G3's wave 4 aggressive social cognitions on the dichotomous outcome of G3's offending by wave 4. The model is diagrammed in Figure 9.4. The model includes two latent variables – G2 aggression/aggressive parenting (made up of three manifest variables: G2's own and spouse's severe physical aggression at wave 3 and the score for the G2 parenting environment reflecting hitting of G3, reported retrospectively at wave 4); and G3's aggressive social cognitions (made up of the five G3 aggressive social

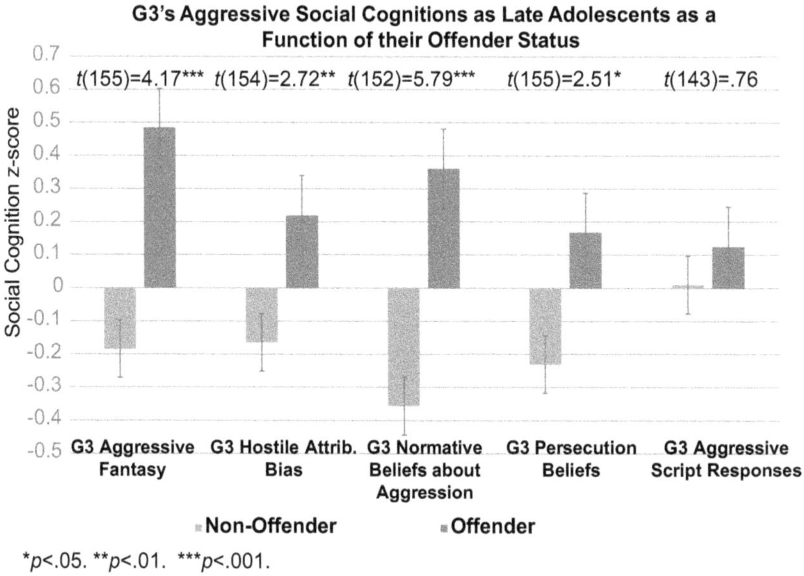

Figure 9.4 G3's aggressive social cognitions as a function of their offender status

cognition variables at wave 4). G3's age and sex were included as covariates. We used the G3 sample that included G2's youngest or only child, and the child had to be 18 years old or older. The parameters were estimated using weighted least squares probit regression for a binary dependent variable. Missing values were treated as pairwise present, meaning that the covariance matrix was estimated using all available data, leaving us with $n = 201$. Correlations among the error terms for G3 social cognitive variables were chosen based on modification indices in order to achieve the best fit. Figure 9.5 shows that this resulted in a well-fitted model ($\chi^2(35) = 45.04$, $p > .11$, RMSEA = .038, with 90 per cent CI = (.00,.067), CFI =1.00). We found that both the direct and indirect effects of G2's aggression independently increased G3's chances of offending by wave 4 (direct $\beta = .30$, $p < .01$; indirect $\beta = .11$, Sobel $z = 1.961$, $p < .05$). These results are consistent with the hypothesis that the intergenerational transmission of aggression and antisocial behaviour, whether originating in continuity of predispositions or continuity of environment, is mediated by the development of aggressive social cognitions that have a lasting influence on behaviour within a generation.

Continuity over three generations

In Huesmann et al. (2011), we presented a three-generational model that includes the within-generation continuity of G2's aggression (Figure 9.6). In this model, G1's hitting of G2 when G2 was 8 years old is correlated with

G3's Aggressive Social Cognitions as Mediators of the Relation between G2's Aggression and G3's Offending

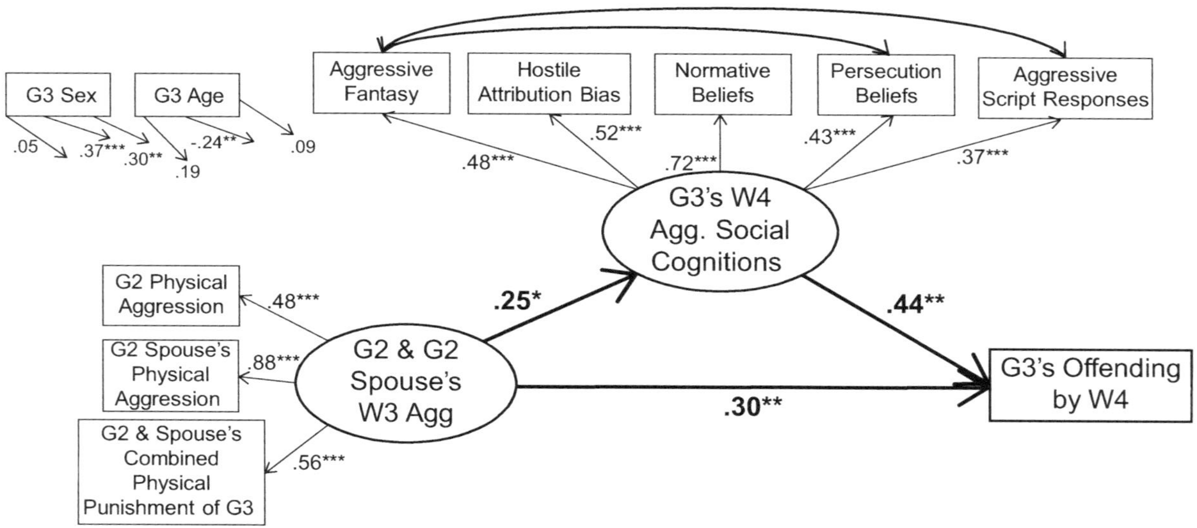

***n*=201, *X*2(35) =45.04, *p* > .11, RMSEA =.038 with 90% CI = (.00, .067), CFI =1.00**

***p* < .05 ***p*<.01 ****p*<.001**

Standardized path coefficients (β's) are shown. β's were estimated in Mplus using weighted least squares regressions with missing values handled by using a covariance matrix with pairwise deletions. Indirect effect of G2's Aggression in W3 on G3's offending in W4 is β=.11* .

Figure 9.5 G3's aggressive social cognitions as mediators of the relation between G2's aggression and G3's offending

Intergenerational Transmission of Aggression in the CCLS

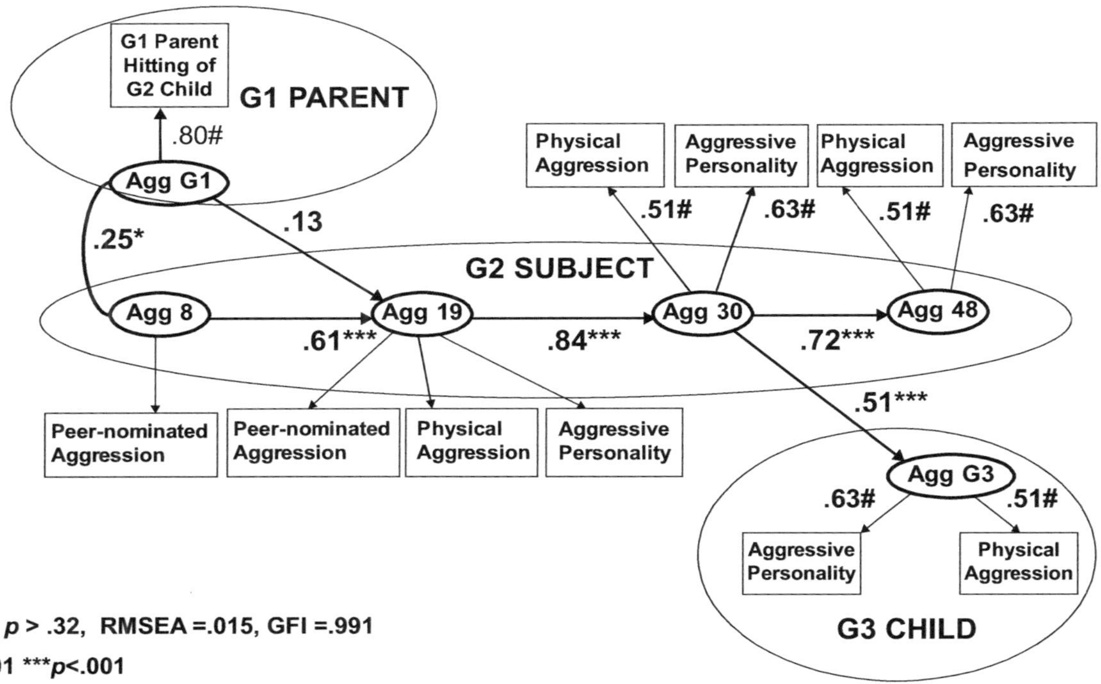

$\chi 2(52) = 56.1$, $p > .32$, RMSEA =.015, GFI =.991

$*p < .05$ $**p<.01$ $***p<.001$

 # indicates that the measurement parameter was fixed at the value estimated for the within-generation model.

Correlated errors were specified for same measures across ages.

Adapted from Huesmann et al. (2011).

Figure 9.6 Transmission of aggression across three generations

G2's age 8 aggression. G2's aggression is then stable over time, and by age 30, G2's aggression as a young parent predicts G3's subsequent aggression during late adolescence, on average. These results again are consistent both with the hypothesis that cross-generational continuity is influenced by the continuity of innate predispositions and the continuity of environmental influences.

Because we did not collect data on G1's social cognitions or G2's social cognitions in wave 1 when they were 8 years old, we could not estimate this model with social cognitions as a mediating variable. However, because of the results found in examining continuity from G2 to G3 in Figure 9.5, we are confident in suggesting that the same social cognitions mediate the three generation, cross-generational effects shown in Figure 9.6.

Limitations, conclusions, and future directions

In this chapter, we reviewed findings on cross-generational transmission of aggression, violence, and criminality that come from our Columbia County Longitudinal Study, a 40-year, four-wave prospective study of youth in the 1952 birth cohort (Generation G2) in that county in New York State and their parents (Generation G1) and children (Generation G3). The study has many unique methodological features, has contributed to our knowledge base of continuity within- and cross-generational transmission of aggression and violence, and has expanded theory, especially social-cognitive models, of the mechanisms accounting for continuity. At the same time, as with any research study, especially with those involving multiple sources of data collected over long timespans, our study has methodological limitations that must be considered. Missing data in longitudinal studies is a significant concern. Regarding attrition over the 40-year period in our study, and in most long-term studies, higher-risk participants are more likely to be lost to follow-up assessments. Another reason for missing data in our study was that we chose to assess some constructs at a given point by multiple measures (e.g., for physical punishment of G3, we used a composite of the child's self-report and both parents' reports), but in some cases, both parents were not interviewed. Fortunately, modern data analytic techniques aid in understanding and taking into account the effects of missing data. Another critical issue to consider in longitudinal studies is the fact that the manifestation of underlying constructs changes across development (see Kagan and Moss 1962; Schulenberg and Maslowsky 2009); this refers to the concept of heterotypic continuity: "continuity in underlying purpose or function, but discontinuity in manifest behaviour over time" (Schulenberg and Maslowsky 2009: 123). We measured the underlying construct of aggression in childhood with peer nominations of behaviour in the classroom, but in adult years with self-reports of being in trouble with the law, self-reports and spouse reports of marital aggression, and official criminal records – so the specific manifest behaviour is not the same from childhood through adulthood.

Despite these limitations, by combining previously published results with new analyses, we showed that there is intergenerational continuity of aggressive and violent behaviour across three generations from grandparent to parent to child. We also showed that there is intergenerational continuity of criminality, based both on official records and self-reports, across generations from parent to child. Based on theoretical extrapolations and our findings about aggressive behaviour, we believe continuity of criminality would also extend over three generations, but we did not have criminality data on the G1 generation in this study; so we could not test that. Perhaps our most important finding, however, is that cross-generational continuity of aggressive, violent, and criminal behaviour is mediated by cross-generational continuity of the social cognitions supporting aggression; that is, aggressive scripts and their rehearsal, hostile attributional bias and persecution beliefs, and probably most importantly, aggressive normative beliefs. Regardless of whether the origins or the aggressive behaviour reside more in innate predisposing factors (e.g., genetic, neurophysiology, birth trauma) or in observational learning of and conditioning by the environment, these social cognitions seem to mediate cross-generational continuity of aggressive and criminal behaviour.

Future work with the CCLS will continue our examination of how environmental influences outside of the family context – such as peer behaviours, neighbourhood experiences, and interpersonal conflict and violence – increase aggressive responding over time by promoting and reinforcing social-cognitive styles that support aggression. In addition, we would like to further our exploration of social-cognitive and emotional factors in the transmission and continuity of aggressive behaviour, including potentially the assessment of these processes and criminality of the next generation (Generation 4). In the Columbia County Longitudinal Study, we have not yet assessed a key proposed mediator of the relation between violence exposure and aggressive behaviour – emotional arousal. As described earlier, youth who are exposed to high levels of violence during critical periods in their childhood may become "desensitized" to violence; they may experience lower levels of anxious arousal to violence which can lead to a higher likelihood of engaging in aggressive and violent behaviour (e.g., see Huesmann and Kirwil 2007; Krahe et al. 2011). In a recent field study, we have conducted physiological assessments of emotional desensitization by examining participants' skin conductance levels in response to viewing violent video clips. We found that youth who were low in anxious arousal were more likely to increase in aggressive and violent behaviour as a result of growing up in a context of high levels of ethnic-political violence (Huesmann, Dubow, Boxer and Shikaki 2016). These types of assessments, as well as other biological markers of the stress response system, will further our understanding of key features of our model.

Finally, it should be noted that in addition to undergirding our understanding of how aggressive, criminal behaviour maintains within and across generations, longitudinal research on aggression and the social-cognitive ecological model has produced robust insights into prevention and intervention programming. Generally speaking, longitudinal, cross-generational research on the development of aggression has drawn critical attention to the importance of preventive intervention during childhood, and particularly middle childhood (Huesmann et al. 2006). Findings from our CCLS as well as similar long-term studies have highlighted the role of parenting and other social influences during childhood on the emergence and maintenance of aggressive and antisocial behaviour well into adulthood. This evidence base supports policy approaches to crime reduction that hinge on promoting positive parenting skills during those crucial childhood years. Further, research on intervention approaches derived specifically from the social-cognitive ecological framework that has emerged in part from our work (Huesmann 1988, 1998) has shown that this model has great utility for program design and application to reducing and preventing aggression in children (Boxer and Dubow 2002; Boxer, Goldstein, Musher-Eizenman, Dubow and Heretick 2005). A variety of intervention packages relying on social-cognitive content have been identified as best-practice approaches (Thornton, Craft, Dahlberg, Lynch and Baer 2002) and the broad, social-cognitive ecological framework has long been recognized as the foundation for effective aggression reduction and prevention (Guerra, Boxer and Kim 2005).

References

Anderson, C.A., and Bushman, B.J. (2002) 'Human aggression', *Annual Review of Psychology*, 53: 27–51.

Bandura, A. (1977) *Social Learning Theory*, Englewood-Cliffs, NJ: Prentice Hall.

Bandura, A. (1986) *Social Foundations of Thought and Action: A Social-Cognitive Theory*, Englewood-Cliffs, NJ: Prentice-Hall.

Berkowitz, L. (1990) 'On the formation and regulation of anger and aggression: A cognitive-neoassociationistic analysis', *American Psychologist*, 45: 494–503.

Boxer, P., and Dubow, E.F. (2002) 'A social-cognitive information-processing model for school-based aggression reduction and prevention programs: Issues for research and practice', *Applied & Preventive Psychology*, 10: 177–192.

Boxer, P., Goldstein, S.E., Musher-Eizenman, D., Dubow, E.F., and Heretick, D. (2005) 'Developmental issues in the prevention of school aggression from the social-cognitive perspective', *Journal of Primary Prevention*, 26: 383–400.

Bronfenbrenner, U. (Ed.) (2005) *Making Human Beings Human: Bioecological Perspectives on Human Development*, Thousand Oaks, CA: Sage.

Caspi, A., McClay, J., Moffitt, T. E., Mill, J., Martin, J., Craig, I. W., Taylor, A., and Poulton, R. (2002) 'Role of genotype in the cycle of violence in maltreated children', *Science*, 297: 851–854.

Crane-Ross, D., Tisak, M.S., and Tisak, J. (1998) 'Aggression and conventional rule violation among adolescents: Social-reasoning predictors of social behavior', *Aggressive Behavior*, 24: 347–365.

Crick, N.R. and Dodge, K.A. (1994) 'A review and reformulation of social information processing mechanisms in children's adjustment', *Psychological Bulletin*, 115: 74–101.

Deater-Deckard, K., and Plomin, R. (1999) 'An adoption study of the etiology of teacher and parent reports of externalizing behavior problems in middle childhood', *Child Development*, 70: 144–154.

Dodge, K.A., and Frame, C.L. (1982) 'Social cognitive biases and deficits in aggressive boys', *Child Development*, 53: 620–635.

Dodge, K.A., and Newman, R.J. (1981) 'Biased decision-making processes in aggressive boys', *Journal of Abnormal Psychology*, 90: 375–379.

Dubow, E.F., Boxer, P., and Huesmann, L.R. (2008) 'Childhood and adolescent predictors of early and middle adulthood alcohol use and problem drinking: The Columbia County Longitudinal Study', *Addiction*, 103: 36–47.

Dubow, E.F., Huesmann, L.R., and Boxer, P. (2003) 'Theoretical and methodological considerations in cross-generational research on parenting and child aggressive behavior', *Journal of Abnormal Child Psychology*, 31: 185–192.

Dubow, E.F., Huesmann, L.R., Boxer, P., Pulkkinen, L., and Kokko, K. (2006) 'Middle childhood and adolescent contextual and personal predictors of adult educational and occupational outcomes: A mediational model in two countries', *Developmental Psychology*, 42: 937–949.

Dubow, E.F., Huesmann, L.R., Boxer, P., and Smith, C. (2014) 'Childhood predictors and age 48 outcomes of self-reports and official records of offending', *Criminal Behaviour and Mental Health*, 24: 291–304.

Dubow, E.F., Huesmann, L.R., Boxer, P., and Smith, C. (2016) 'Childhood and adolescent risk and protective factors for violence in adulthood', *Journal of Criminal Justice*, 45: 26–31.

Dubow, E.F., and Reid, G.J. (1994) 'Risk and resource variables in children's aggressive behavior: A two year longitudinal study', in L.R. Huesmann (ed.) *Aggressive Behavior: Current Perspectives* (pp. 187–211), New York: Plenum.

Egan, S.K., Monson, T.C., and Perry, D.G. (1998) 'Social-cognitive influences on change in aggression over time', *Developmental Psychology*, 34: 996–1006.

Erdley, C.A., and Asher, S.R. (1996) 'Children's social goals and self-efficacy perceptions as influences on their responses to ambiguous provocations', *Child Development*, 67: 1329–1344.

Eron, L.D., Huesmann, L.R., Lefkowitz, M.M., and Walder, L.O. (1972) 'Does T. V. violence cause aggression?', *American Psychologist*, 27: 153–263.

Eron, L.D., Walder, L.O., and Lefkowitz, M.M. (1971) *Learning of Aggression in Children*, Boston: Little, Brown.

Eron, L.D., Walder, L.O., Toigo, R., and Lefkowitz, M.M. (1963) 'Social class, parental punishment for aggression, and child aggression', *Child Development*, 34: 849–867.

Guerra, N.G., Boxer, P., and Kim, T. (2005) 'A cognitive-ecological approach to serving students with emotional and behavioral disorders: Application to aggressive behavior', *Behavioral Disorders*, 30: 277–288.

Guerra, N.G., and Huesmann, L.R. (2004) 'A cognitive-ecological model of aggression', *International Review of Social Psychology*, 17: 177–203.

Guerra, N.G., and Slaby, R.G. (1990) 'Cognitive mediators of aggression in adolescent offenders: II. Intervention', *Developmental Psychology*, 26: 269–277.

Hathaway, S.R., and McKinley, J.C. (1940) *The MMPI Manual*, New York: Psychological Corporation.

Huesmann, L.R. (1988) 'An information processing model for the development of aggression', *Aggressive Behavior*, 14: 13–24.

Huesmann, L.R. (1997) 'Observational learning of violent behavior: Social and biosocial processes', in A. Raine, P.A. Brennen, D.P. Farrington and S.A. Mednick (eds.) *Biosocial Bases of Violence* (pp. 69–88), London: Plenum.

Huesmann, L.R. (1998) 'The role of social information processing and cognitive schema in the acquisition and maintenance of habitual aggressive behavior', in R.G. Geen and E. Donnerstein (eds.) *Human Aggression: Theories, Research, and Implications for Social Policy* (pp. 73–109), San Diego, CA: Academic Press.

Huesmann, L.R. (2017) 'An integrative theoretical understanding of aggression', in B. Bushman (ed.) *Aggression and Violence: A Social Psychological Perspective* (pp. 3–21), New York: Routledge.

Huesmann, L.R. (in press) 'The contagion of violence. Chapter 30', in A. Vazsonyi, D. Flannery and M. DeLisi (eds.) *The Cambridge Handbook of Violent Behavior and Aggression*, 2nd Edition, Cambridge: Cambridge University Press.

Huesmann, L.R., Dubow, E.F., and Boxer, P. (2009) 'Continuity of childhood, adolescent, and early adulthood aggression as predictors of adult criminality and life outcomes: Implications for the adolescent-limited and life-course-persistent models', *Aggressive Behavior*, 35: 136–149.

Huesmann, L.R., Dubow, E.F., and Boxer, P. (2011) 'The transmission of aggressiveness across generations: Biological, contextual, and social learning processes', in P. Shaver and M. Mikulincer (eds.) *Human Aggression and Violence: Causes, Manifestations, and Consequences* (pp. 123–142), Washington, DC: American Psychological Association.

Huesmann, L.R., Dubow, E.F., Boxer, P., and Shikaki, K. (2016, July) 'Consequences of exposure to war violence: Discriminating those with heightened risk for aggression from those with heightened risk for post-traumatic symptoms', In E.F. Dubow (chair) *A social-cognitive-ecological model of exposure to ethnic-political violence: Effects of exposure on Palestinian youths' aggressive and violent behavior.* Presented at the XXIInd World Meeting of the International Society for Research on Aggression, Sydney, Australia.

Huesmann, L.R., Dubow, E.F., Eron, L.D., and Boxer, P. (2006) 'Middle childhood family-contextual and personal factors as predictors of adult outcomes', in A.C. Huston and M.N. Ripke (eds.) *Developmental Contexts in Middle Childhood: Bridges to Adolescence and Adulthood* (pp. 62–86), New York: Cambridge University Press.

Huesmann, L.R., and Eron, L.D. (1984) 'Cognitive processes and the persistence of aggressive behavior', *Aggressive Behavior*, 10: 243–251.

Huesmann, L.R., Eron, L.D., and Dubow, E.F. (2002) 'Childhood predictors of adult criminality: Are all risk factors reflected in childhood aggressiveness?', *Criminal Behaviour & Mental Health*, 12: 185–208.

Huesmann, L.R., Eron, L.D., Lefkowitz, M.M., and Walder, L.O. (1984) 'The stability of aggression over time and generations', *Developmental Psychology*, 20(6): 1120–1134.

Huesmann, L.R., and Guerra, N.G. (1997) 'Children's normative beliefs about aggression and aggressive behavior', *Journal of Personality and Social Psychology*, 72: 408–419.

Huesmann, L.R., and Kirwil, L. (2007) 'Why observing violence increases the risk of violent behavior in the observer', in D.J. Flannery, A.T. Vazsonyi and I.D. Waldman (eds.) *The Cambridge Handbook of Violent Behavior and Aggression* (pp. 545–570), Cambridge, UK: Cambridge University Press.

Huesmann, L.R., Lefkowitz, M.M., and Eron, L.D. (1978) 'The sum of MMPI scales F, 4, and 9 as a measure of aggression', *Journal of Consulting and Clinical Psychology*, 46: 1071–1078.

Kagan, J., and Moss, H.A. (1962) *Birth to Maturity: A Study in Psychological Development*, New York: Wiley.

Knoblich, G., and King, R. (1992) 'Biological correlates of criminal behavior', in J. McCord (ed.) *Advances in Criminological Theory* (vol. 3, pp. 1–21). New Brunswick, NJ: Transaction.

Krahe, B., Moeller, I., Huesmann, L.R., Kirwil, L., Felber, J., and Berger, A. (2011) 'Desensitization to media violence: Antecedents, consequences, and content specificity', *Journal of Personality and Social Psychology*, 100: 630–646.

Lefkowitz, M.M., Eron, L.D., Walder, L.O., and Huesmann, L.R. (1977) *Growing Up to Be Violent*, New York: Pergamon.

Miles, D.R., and Carey, G. (1997) 'Genetic and environmental architecture of human aggression', *Journal of Personality and Social Psychology*, 72: 207–217.

Patterson, G.R. (1982) *Coercive Family Process*, Eugene, OR: Castalia.

Perry, D.G., Perry, L.C., and Rasmussen, P. (1986) 'Cognitive social learning mediators of aggression', *Child Development*, 57: 700–711.

Raine, A., and Jones, F. (1987) 'Attention, autonomic arousal, and personality in behaviorally disordered children', *Journal of Abnormal Child Psychology*, 15: 583–599.

Rossi, P., Bose, C., and Berk, R. (1974) 'The seriousness of crime, normative structure and individual differences', *American Sociological Review*, 39: 224–237.

Schulenberg, J.E., and Maslowsky, J. (2009) 'Taking substance use and development seriously: Developmentally distal and proximal influences on adolescent drug use', *Monographs of the Society for Research in Child Development*, 74: 121–130. http://doi.org/10.1111/j.1540-5834.2009.00544.x

Slaby, R.G., and Guerra, N.G. (1988) 'Cognitive mediators of aggression in adolescent offenders: Assessment', *Developmental Psychology*, 4: 580–588.

Stevens, G., and Hoisington, E. (1987) 'Occupational prestige and the 1980 U.S. labor force', *Social Science Research*, 6: 74–105.

Thornton, T.N., Craft, C.A., Dahlberg, L.L., Lynch, B.S., and Baer, K. (2002) *Best Practices of Youth Violence Prevention: A Sourcebook for Community Action' (Rev.)*, Atlanta, GA: Centers for Disease Control and Prevention, National Center for Injury Prevention and Control.

Toigo, R. (1965) 'Social status and schoolroom aggression in third grade children', *Genetic Psychology Monographs*, 71: 221–268.

Tolan, P.H., Gorman-Smith, D., and Henry, D. (2003) 'The developmental ecology of urban male's youth violence', *Developmental Psychology*, 39(2): 274–291.

'U.S. Decennial Census', United States Census Bureau. Census of population and housing, 1960/2000. Available HTTP: https://www.census.gov/prod/www/decennial.html. (accessed 3 January 2015).

Chapter 10

Seattle Social Development Project – The Intergenerational Project (SSDP–TIP)

Jennifer A. Bailey, Karl G. Hill, Marina Epstein, Christine Steeger, and J. David Hawkins

Study aims and origin

The Seattle Social Development Project (SSDP) and The Intergenerational Project (TIP) are two prospective, longitudinal studies that link three generations. The SSDP (principle investigators: J. David Hawkins, Karl G. Hill, Rick Kosterman, and Jennifer A. Bailey) is a study of prosocial and antisocial development that began in 1985, and followed a panel of 808 individuals (second generation, or G2) from age 10 to age 39 (in 2014); one parent (first generation, or G1) also was included in the SSDP study in the first six years. TIP (principal investigators: Karl G. Hill, Jennifer A. Bailey) began in 2000, and includes 411 SSDP G2 respondents who have become parents, their oldest child (third generation, or G3), and a second caregiver, when present. The TIP study has been supported by the U.S. National Institute on Drug Abuse (grant R01DA023089). It is broadly focused on understanding the effects of grandparent (G1) and parent (G2) substance use on child (G3) social, emotional, and cognitive development, as well as on child substance use and antisocial behaviour. Another important focus is understanding *how* (i.e., via what mechanisms or mediators) G1 and G2 substance use might affect G3 development and behaviour. In December 2012, the U.S. state of Washington, where the SSDP sample was originally recruited, legalized non-medical cannabis use by adults ages 21 and over. In response to this, funding was obtained for new aims more specific to cannabis legalization. Research questions include whether non-medical cannabis legalization predicts changes in the level or pattern of youth cannabis and other drug use across adolescence or predicts increases in risk factors for youth cannabis use (e.g., parent use, pro-use norms).

Theoretical grounding and conceptual models

Both the SSDP and TIP studies are grounded in the social development model (SDM). The SDM is a theory of the development of prosocial and antisocial behaviour across the life span (Catalano and Hawkins 1996; Hawkins and Weis 1985). This model builds on social control (Hirschi 1969), social learning (Akers 1977; Bandura 1977), and differential association theories (Sutherland and Cressey 1970). The SDM (Figure 10.1) hypothesizes that individuals learn

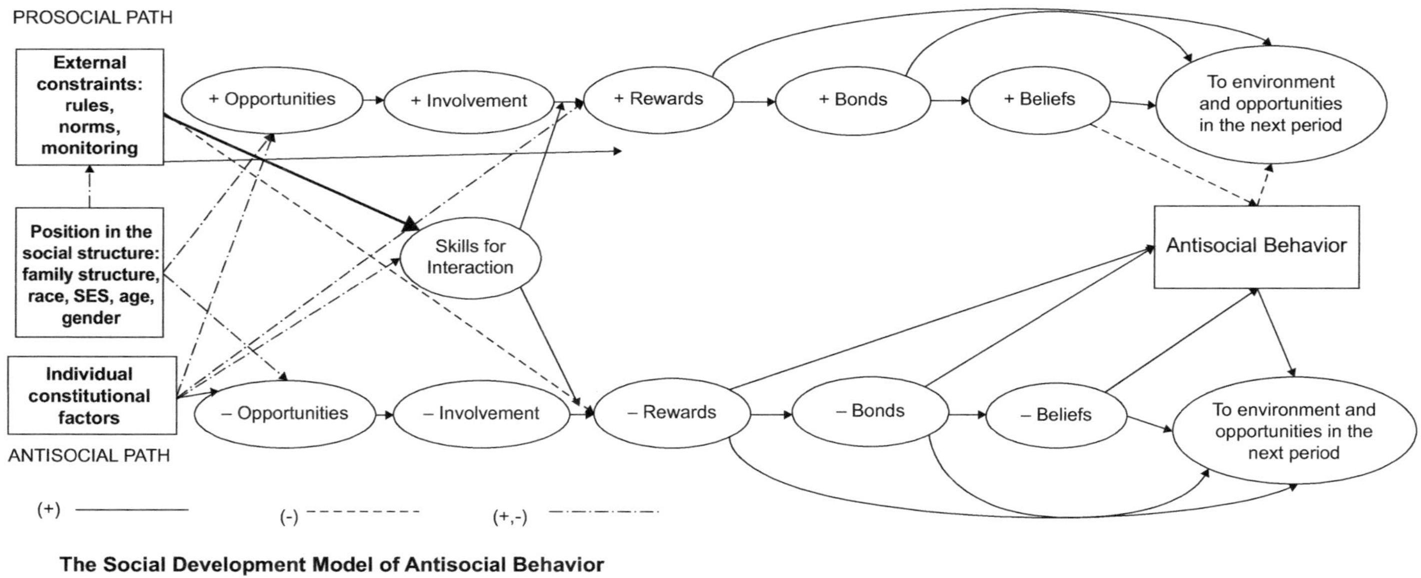

Figure 10.1 The social development model

patterns of behaviour, whether prosocial or antisocial, in different socializing units, including family, school, peers, and neighbourhoods. The model posits that people are socialized through perceived opportunities for involvement in activities and interactions with others, actual involvement and interaction, skills to participate in these involvements and interactions, and reinforcement perceived from these involvements and interactions. Skillful involvement that is rewarded encourages development of a social bond between individuals and the socializing unit; this bond influences behaviour because it motivates individuals to conform to the norms and values of the socializing unit. Thus, individuals will behave in a prosocial or antisocial manner, depending on the predominant behaviours and values of the socializing unit. Position in the social structure (socioeconomic status, gender, race/ethnicity), individual characteristics (e.g., impulsivity, sensation seeking, shyness), and external constraints (rules, norms, laws) affect behaviour by affecting the opportunities and rewards one experiences. Empirical studies have supported the SDM, which has explained between 9 per cent and 49 per cent of the variance in child and adolescent antisocial behaviours, including substance use, alcohol misuse, externalizing behaviour, and violence (Brown et al. 2005; Catalano and Hawkins 1996; Catalano et al. 1999; Huang et al. 2001; Lonczak et al. 2001). See Catalano and Hawkins (1996) and Hawkins and Weis (1985) for additional discussion of the SDM.

The TIP study also is guided by the conceptual model depicted in Figure 10.2. These hypotheses build on the SDM and past research, which has established parent–child transmission of both substance-specific tendencies to use (e.g., cannabis to cannabis, alcohol to alcohol) (Andrews et al. 1997; Chassin et al. 1993; Chassin et al. 1991; Hawkins et al. 1992a; Jennison and Johnson 1998; Merikangas and Avenevoli 2000) and a general tendency to use any substance (Merikangas and Avenevoli 2000; Merikangas et al. 1998).

Figure 10.2 shows a detailed set of hypotheses about the mechanisms by which G2 current and prior substance use might affect G3 developmental outcomes. Beginning from the left side of the figure, G2 socioeconomic status, neighbourhood disorganization, delinquency, mental health, and drug use prior to becoming a parent are thought to predict a poorer developmental environment for the G3 child that includes lower family socioeconomic status, higher mobility, and more changes in family structure. G2 substance use, criminal behaviour, and poor mental health are thought to persist after they become parents, and to negatively affect the G3 child's developmental environment and proximal social developmental processes. For example, substance-using parents are thought to engage in less monitoring and set fewer rules around risk behaviour, to provide fewer prosocial opportunities for involvement and more antisocial opportunities (i.e., increased substance availability), to have more family conflict and poorer discipline practices, to provide fewer rewards for prosocial behaviour and fewer costs for antisocial involvement, and to present norms favourable to substance use.

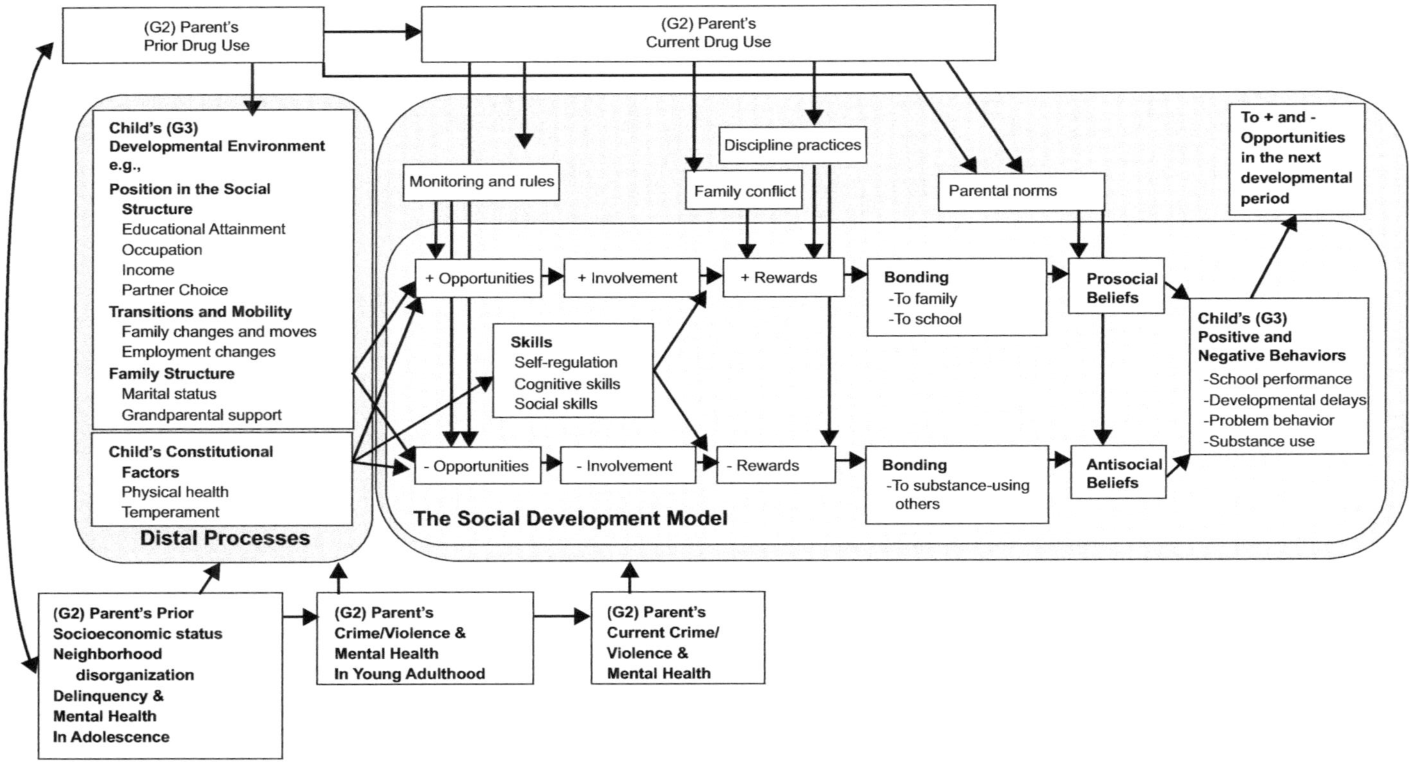

Figure 10.2 Detailed conceptual model of mechanisms linking parent substance use and child development

Methods

Participants

SSDP participants ($N = 808$) were recruited from 18 schools in an urban school district in the State of Washington, USA. Of the youth in Grade 5 classrooms in these schools in 1985, 77 per cent consented to participate and constitute the longitudinal panel. SSDP collected data from the G2 students, one of their parents (G1), and their teachers. SSDP G2 students were surveyed annually from ages 10–16 and at ages 18, 21, 24, 27, 30, 33, 35, and 39 (in 2014). G1 parents and teachers were surveyed annually when the G2 students were ages 10–16 and 10–14, respectively. The G2 respondents were 49 per cent female, 47 per cent European American, 26 per cent African American, 22 per cent Asian American, and 5 per cent Native American. Of these, 5 per cent reported Hispanic or Latino/a ethnicity. About 52 per cent of G2 students were eligible for the U.S. national Free and Reduced Price Lunch program (an indicator of poverty) in Grade 5, 6, or 7.

The SSDP study was a quasi-experimental evaluation of Raising Healthy Children, a universal intervention aimed at preventing youth substance use and other antisocial behaviour. Approximately 18 per cent of G2 students received the "full" intervention, receiving services in Grades 1–6, and 30 per cent received a "late" intervention in Grades 5 and 6 only. The intervention included child social and emotional skill development, teacher training in classroom management, and instruction in child development and family management for parents. Follow-up studies have found long-term benefits of the Raising Healthy Children intervention, including higher educational attainment and socioeconomic status, better mental and physical health, less teen pregnancy, and fewer sexually transmitted infections (Hawkins et al. 1999; Hawkins et al. 1992b; Hawkins et al. 2001; Hawkins et al. 2005; Hawkins et al. 2008). Additional details about Raising Healthy Children can be found in the cited publications.

In 2000, recognizing that the G2 "students" were now adults and many were having children (G3, or Generation 3), the founding principal investigator Karl G. Hill and his team implemented the TIP study. The TIP sample families include: the G2 parent who participated in SSDP (all SSDP participants with biological children were screened for eligibility), the eldest biological child with whom they had regular contact (G3), and an "other caregiver" (usually the G2 participant's spouse) identified by the G2 parent as sharing the greatest responsibility for raising the child. Teachers of school-aged children (ages 6–18 years) also were surveyed.

To date, the TIP sample includes 411 families. About 48 per cent of the G3 children were female, and about 60 per cent of the SSDP G2 parents were female. Children in the TIP sample were racially/ethnically diverse: 31 per cent European American, 20 per cent African American, and 35 per cent multi-ethnic, with the remainder being primarily Asian American/Pacific Islander or Native

American; 12 per cent of children were Latino/a. The median family income in 2015 was US $65,001–$70,000; 22 per cent of families received government financial assistance. We have located an average of 95 per cent of families at each wave; recruitment of eligible SSDP parents and their children has averaged 82 per cent across waves. Retention from wave to wave averaged 90 per cent. See Hill and colleagues (2015) for procedures used to maximize retention in our longitudinal studies. Eligibility, recruitment, and retention analyses have included G2 gender, marital status, receipt of government financial assistance, and cigarette use, cannabis use, and binge drinking at age 27 (TIP baseline); G2 free lunch eligibility in childhood; cigarette use, cannabis use, and binge drinking in high school; and race/ethnicity. Across waves, SSDP G2 mothers and G2s who were married were consistently more likely to meet eligibility criteria (regular, face-to-face contact with the child) than SSDP fathers and unmarried SSDP participants. Once eligible, families were slightly less likely to be recruited if the SSDP parent was Asian American or was eligible for free lunch in Grades 5–7; recruitment was not related to whether the G2 parent participated in the SSDP intervention during childhood. Retention was not consistently related to any of the variables tested.

TIP study design

Given that the SSDP parents were all in primary school Grade 5 during the same year, they are very close to one another in age. These G2 parents, however, did not all have their first child at the same time. Some G2 parents had their first child in their teens, as young as 15 years of age, whereas other G2 parents had their first child in their late 30s or early 40s. Thus, G3 participants come from multiple birth cohorts that have been followed longitudinally. TIP, then, has an accelerated longitudinal design, also called a cohort-sequential design. In 2002 when the first wave of data collection occurred, G3 children ranged in age from 1 to 13 years. In addition to following these families over time, new families were recruited as SSDP respondents became biological parents for the first time. Families were eligible to participate in TIP if SSDP G2 parents had face-to-face contact with the target child at least once a month. Data were collected annually around the child's birthday (+/−6 weeks) in order to maintain developmental comparability between children of the same age. For example, given the rapid developmental changes observed in young children, two children measured at "age 2" may not be developmentally comparable if one was measured just before their second birthday and the other was measured at age 2.5 years. To date, nine waves of annual data have been collected in 2002–2005, 2009–2011, 2015, and 2016; wave 10 began in 2017. Some intervening years were missed due to gaps in funding. By the end of the 2017 data collection effort, the G3 children will range in age from 1 to 28 years. Thus, this cost-efficient design allows examination of G3 development across ages 1–28 without requiring a 28-year study.

Procedures

TIP data were collected via face-to-face and phone interviews, web surveys, and observations. Reporters included the SSDP G2 parent, the other caregiver, and G3 children age 6 years or older; younger children were not interviewed directly, but their SSDP parent and other caregiver were interviewed. In the United States, adults ages 18 and older are able to consent to participation in research studies, but youth under age 18 are not legally able to give consent, and permission to include children in research must come from parents or legal guardians. SSDP parents, other caregivers, and children age 18 or older provided informed consent at each data collection. Parents provided permission for children under age 18. Once we had parental permission, we also asked the children whether they were willing to participate. Parents provided permission for teacher contact, and teachers were consented at each data collection. All procedures were approved by the University of Washington Human Subjects Internal Review Board.

Measures

Multi-method and multi-source measurement were emphasized, including G2 and other caregiver surveys, G3 surveys, teacher surveys, behavioural observations, and geographic information system (GIS) coding. TIP included six surveys designed for: (1) G3 children ages 6–9, (2) G3 children ages 10–17, (3) G3 children ages 18 and older, (4) G2 parents and other caregivers of G3 children ages 1–17, (5) G2 parents and other caregivers of G3 children ages 18 and older, and (6) teachers. Three versions of the G3 survey were needed to pair measures and response options with the developmental stage of the child. Similarly, two versions of the G2 parent/other caregiver survey were needed to reflect the fact that some G3 children are minors and in the care of their parents (ages 1–17), and some G3s are legally adults (ages 18 and older) and may be independent.

Parent, child, and teacher surveys covered the child's cognitive, affective, academic, and social development. SDM constructs in the family, peer, school/work, and neighbourhood domains were assessed. In addition, the G2/other caregiver interview assessed their relationship with their own parents (G1), and G1's current substance use and prosocial or antisocial behaviour. G2 parents, other caregivers, and children reported on their own alcohol, cigarette, cannabis, and other drug use and norms at each wave; child reports were phased in as was developmentally appropriate. G3 self-reports and teacher reports of G3 of externalizing problems were assessed from age 6 onward; parent reports of child externalizing began at age 2. G3 self-reported sexual behaviour and romantic relationship quality measures began at age 13. For school-age children (ages 6–18), the child's teacher completed the Teacher Survey, which included measures of G3 study and social skills, externalizing, and disciplinary actions. Appendix 10.A shows the scope of available measures by child age and reporter.

In addition to surveys, TIP included in-home observation of parent–child interactions, an important strength (Dishion and Granic 2004; Hops et al. 1995). For all children age 2 years and older, we conducted a parent–child interaction task with the target G3 child. For children 2–8 years we used the Parent–Child Interaction Task (PCIT) (Eyberg and Robinson 1983; Forehand and McMahon 1981). The child and parent played with assorted age-appropriate toys in three tasks in increasing order of constraint on the child: *Child's Game*, *Caregiver's Game*, and *Clean Up*. For children 9 years and older, we adapted the PCIT discussion tasks developed by Reid (1989) and modified and used by McMahon et al. in the Fast Track Project (McMahon and Estes 1993). The parent–child discussion tasks were: *Expectations and Guidelines*, *Solving Family Problems*, and *Recognition*. Four waves of observational data were collected between 2002 and 2005.

In waves 5–7 (2009–2011), the study included Stroop tasks and a Balloon Analog Risk Task (BART) (Lejuez et al. 2007; Lejuez et al. 2005) to measure response inhibition and risk aversion, respectively. Two Stroop tasks were used. G2 parents, other caregivers, and G3 children ages 6 years and older completed a computer-based colour-word Stroop task, and children ages 3–5 years completed the Day/Night Stroop task with interviewers (Passler et al. 1985; Simpson and Riggs 2005a; Simpson and Riggs 2005b). The BART was administered via laptop computer. Respondents pressed a keyboard button to inflate a virtual balloon. As the balloon inflated, the participants accumulated virtual money; however, the balloon became more likely to burst and cause the participant to lose the virtual money. Participants were allowed to stop inflating the balloon whenever they liked in order to bank their virtual money, which could then be used to buy small prizes from the interviewer.

Under new funding in 2015, we added additional substance use measures. In order to capture the accelerating use of electronic cigarettes or vapes, we added a small battery of questions on vape use and attitudes about vaping to surveys for parents and children ages 10 and older. As a part of our efforts to understand the effects of non-medical cannabis legalization on G3s and their families, we added a number of cannabis-related questions to the surveys in 2015. For G2 and G3 respondents ages 10+, we added questions about cannabis sources, modes of administration, type of cannabis (plant, resin, edibles, etc.), knowledge of the laws regulating cannabis use, cannabis-related parenting practices, and changes in personal use and attitudes in response to legalization. We also used GIS methods to geocode respondent addresses from waves 8–10 (2015–2017) and match them to the location of retail cannabis outlets and outlet sales data. Thus, the TIP data also include proximity to nearest cannabis outlet, number of nearby outlets, and sales volume of nearby outlets. Finally, we compiled information on local variability in statutes regulating non-medical cannabis businesses and tied them to the respondent's address; some municipalities and counties do not allow cannabis businesses, even though they are permitted under state law.

Analysing accelerated longitudinal data

Studying several age or birth cohorts longitudinally (accelerated longitudinal designs, see Figure 10.3) (Bell 1953) has become more feasible with the development of multilevel modelling, which allows examination of between-person differences in within-person change and accounts for nesting of youth within birth cohorts (Labouvie and Nesselroade 1985; Raudenbush and Chan 1993; Schaie and Baltes 1975). Many modern statistical software packages can perform multilevel modelling and can be used to analyse accelerated longitudinal data. Accelerated longitudinal designs allow for the disentangling of development (age) and history (e.g., cannabis legalization, the Great Recession) because multiple cohorts of youth that may differ in history are measured at the same developmental age. Thus, accelerated longitudinal designs are particularly strong for evaluating the impact of sudden historical events or policy changes. For example, in the TIP study, several G3 birth cohorts were measured at age 15 before non-medical cannabis legalization (Figure 10.3). Three later birth cohorts will be measured at age 15 after cannabis legalization. This design allows us to directly compare the cannabis use of youth who were measured at the same age before and after legalization was passed, providing a strong test of the impact of cannabis legalization on youth cannabis use. Age or birth cohorts can be combined at points of overlap to allow estimation of developmental trajectories across large age ranges. Figure 10.4 shows hypothetical data on G3 cannabis use frequency, and illustrates how combining birth cohorts allows estimation of an average developmental trajectory. Short, thin lines indicate the trajectory for each cohort. The long, heavy line indicates the average trajectory when the overlapping cohorts are combined. Because each child is measured multiple times, they contribute multiple "child years" to the study, which provides a great deal of statistical power (Moerbeek 2011). Moerbeek (2011) provides helpful syntax in *R* for estimating statistical power in accelerated longitudinal designs.

Care must be taken when analysing accelerated longitudinal data to account for its nested nature (observations nested within person) and to appropriately test for and model birth cohort differences. If, for example, some cohorts experienced an important historical event or experienced the event at a critical time in development, their trajectory of behaviour across ages may not be in line with those of the other cohorts – essentially an age ×cohort interaction effect (Miyazaki and Raudenbush 2000). In this case, combining cohorts into an average trajectory becomes inappropriate. Miyazaki and Raudenbush (2000) provide a method for testing cohort effects in a multilevel modelling framework; if cohort effects are not detected, then the cohorts can be combined for analysis. Further, failing to accurately model age, as happens when data are analysed using "wave" instead of G3 age to indicate time, can bias estimates of developmental trajectories, because each point in the trajectory is estimated based on averaged data from youth at a variety of ages. To illustrate, if we were to estimate

G3 birth cohort																												
1990													W1	W2	W3	W4				W5	W6	W7		L		W8	W9	W10
1991												W1	W2	W3	W4				W5	W6	W7		L		W8	W9	W10	
1992											W1	W2	W3	W4				W5	W6	W7		L		W8	W9	W10		
1993										W1	W2	W3	W4				W5	W6	W7		L		W8	W9	W10			
1994									W1	W2	W3	W4				W5	W6	W7		L		W8	W9	W10				
1995								W1	W2	W3	W4				W5	W6	W7		L		W8	W9	W10					
1996							W1	W2	W3	W4				W5	W6	W7		L		W8	W9	W10						
1997						W1	W2	W3	W4				W5	W6	W7		L		W8	W9	W10							
1998					W1	W2	W3	W4				W5	W6	W7		L		W8	W9	W10								
1999				W1	W2	W3	W4				W5	W6	W7		L		W8	W9	W10									
2000			W1	W2	W3	W4				W5	W6	W7		L		W8	W9	W10										
2001		W1	W2	W3	W4				W5	W6	W7		L		W8	W9	W10											
2002	W1	W2	W3	W4				W5	W6	W7		L		W8	W9	W10												
2003	W2	W3	W4				W5	W6	W7		L		W8	W9	W10													
2004	W3	W4				W5	W6	W7		L		W8	W9	W10														
2005	W4				W5	W6	W7		L		W8	W9	W10															
2006				W5	W6	W7		L		W8	W9	W10																
2007			W5	W6	W7		L		W8	W9	W10																	
2008		W5	W6	W7		L		W8	W9	W10																		
2009	W5	W6	W7		L		W8	W9	W10																			
2010	W6	W7		L		W8	W9	W10																				
2011	W7		L		W8	W9	W10																					
2012		L		W8	W9	W10																						
2013	L		W8	W9	W10																							
2014		W8	W9	W10																								
2015	W8	W9	W10																									
2016	W8	W10																										
2017	W10																											
	1	2	3	4	5	6	7	8	9	10	11	12	13	14	15	16	17	18	19	20	21	22	23	24	25	26	27	28

G3 age

Reading horizontally, waves 1 through 10 are shown from left to right. Gray boxes show years where no data were collected, and "L" shows the age at which cannabis legalization occurred for each cohort. Reading vertically shows the wave at which a birth cohort was measured at a given age.

Figure 10.3 Accelerated longitudinal design of the TIP study

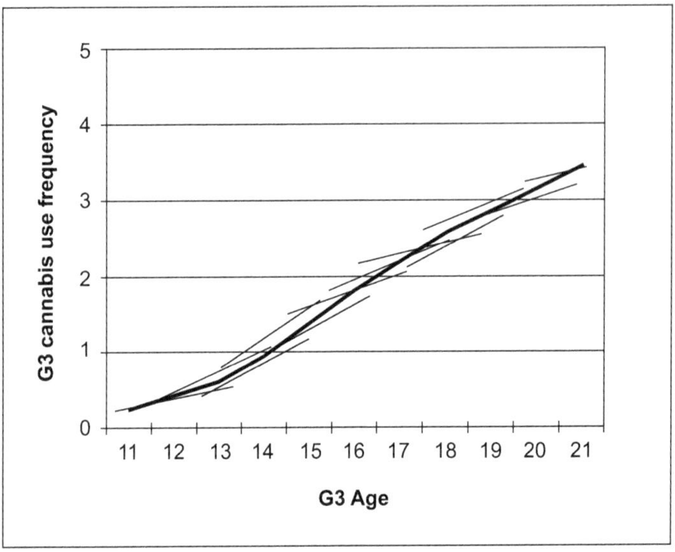

Figure 10.4 Hypothetical child cannabis use trajectory based on overlapping cohort data

the trajectory of alcohol use frequency for G3 children based on wave in our data, the estimate of alcohol use frequency at the wave 7 time point would be based on data from G3s ranging from 6 to 22 years of age. Yet, children age 6 have a dramatically different pattern of alcohol use from children age 22, and statistically controlling for age may not fully account for the vast developmental differences in alcohol use.

Conducting etiologic analyses in a sample exposed to an intervention

Although the G3 children in TIP did not experience an intervention, many of the G2 parents who participated in SSDP experienced the Raising Healthy Children intervention when they themselves were children. There are two ways that the intervention experienced by G2 parents could affect etiologic analyses in this project. First, the intervention could have affected levels of risk and protective factors experienced by G3. As noted above, for example, G2 parents who received the full Raising Healthy Children intervention reported higher educational attainment and fewer depressive symptoms in adulthood (Hawkins et al. 2005; Hawkins et al. 2008). Thus, their children might have a better developmental environment than children of G2 parents who did not receive the intervention. This difference in the *levels* of risk and protective factors can easily be accounted for with statistical controls for intervention status and any parent variables that were affected by the intervention. A second, more problematic way in which the intervention could affect etiologic analyses is by altering the etiologic processes themselves, or the strength of the association between risk or protective factors and outcomes. That is, the strength of the association between, for instance, G2 educational attainment and G3 substance use, may be different in families where G2 received Raising Healthy Children versus families where G2 did not receive the intervention. In this case, including a control for intervention status is insufficient, and tests of predictor-by-intervention status are required. Fortunately, tests of predictor-by-intervention status interactions are easily done in a multilevel framework. We routinely test for such interactions in order to guard against potential bias due to the intervention experienced by G2. We have not found evidence for such interactions in either our TIP studies (e.g., Bailey et al. 2006; Bailey et al. 2009) or our work with the G2 sample as part of the SSDP study (e.g., Catalano et al. 1996; Huang et al. 2001), therefore, we typically have combined intervention and control G2s in etiologic analyses with statistical controls for intervention status.

An overview of study findings

In addition to testing the Raising Healthy Children intervention, our work has sought to understand the developmental course and etiology of childhood, adolescent, and young adult substance use and related risk behaviours. We have produced a body of work motivated by the SDM and using both TIP and SSDP data identifying risk factors for youth problem behaviours, including individual, peer, and parent norms; parent and peer substance use; parenting practices; and drug availability (Bailey et al. 2006; Bailey et al. 2009; Beyers et al. 2004; Hill et al. 2005; Oesterle et al. 2012). We also have paid attention to development, studying sensitive periods and the changing roles of risk factors across childhood, adolescence, and young adulthood (Guo et al. 2002; Guttmannova et al. 2011; Epstein et al. 2017b). Findings to date related to intergenerational processes are based on the first seven waves of data collection (G3 children ages 1–22, M = 13 age years), and are described below.

Parent substance use and child development

One goal motivating the TIP study was to understand the implications of parent substance use for child social, emotional, behavioural, and cognitive development. We have found consistent support for links between parent substance use and deficits in child self-regulation. For example, we found that parent substance use predicted higher concurrent child externalizing behaviours in both G1–G2 and G2–G3 pairs (Bailey et al. 2006). We have found inconsistent support for a relationship between G2 substance use and G3 developmental delays. Guttmannova and colleagues (2016) found that G2 maternal adolescent alcohol use and paternal adult alcohol use both predicted increased developmental delays among G3 children; however, unpublished analyses have not found associations between parent cigarette, cannabis, or general substance use and G3 developmental delays. We also have not found evidence for links between G2 substance use and G3 internalizing or affective problems. Generally speaking, we were surprised not to observe stronger or more wide-ranging effects of G2 substance use on G3 developmental outcomes. Possible explanations include: (1) the negative effects of parent substance use may manifest later in development, particularly once youth enter mid to late adolescence; (2) parent substance use may need to be severe or involve abuse or dependence, such as is found in clinical rather than community samples, to be truly problematic for children; and (3) other aspects of parent health and functioning may play a more important role in predicting general child development, whereas parent substance use is mostly a risk in terms of child substance use (see below).

Parent–child transmission of substance use and problem behaviour

Better understanding the intergenerational transmission of substance use was also a motivating goal of the TIP study. Our findings have generally shown parent–child transmission of substance use (Bailey et al. 2013; Bailey et al. 2011; Bailey et al. 2009; Epstein et al. 2013). Specifically, we found a small but consistent link between a latent factor of G1 substance use, indicated by binge drinking, cigarette use, and cannabis use frequency, during G2's adolescence and a similar latent factor of G2 adolescent substance use (standardized estimate = .22) (Bailey et al. 2006). Once initiated in adolescence, G2 substance use remained quite stable into adulthood. In the G2–G3 pair, we found that G2 parent current (but not prior) cannabis use predicted an increased probability of G3 alcohol use and cannabis use between the ages of 10 and 18 (Bailey et al. 2016).

We have found particularly strong evidence for cross-generation continuity in cigarette use. Hill and colleagues (2005) found that G1 cigarette use predicted a higher hazard for onset of G2 adolescent daily smoking. In another study, G2s were more likely to smoke cigarettes if their G1 parents smoked, even after accounting for their increased risk of using any drug (Bailey et al. 2006). Epstein and colleagues (2013) found that G2 respondents were more likely to smoke at age 18 if their G1 parents smoked and had pro-cigarette norms. Further, G2s who smoked at age 18 were more likely to choose a smoking partner and develop nicotine dependence in adulthood. In the G2–G3 pair, G2 current cigarette use predicted a higher likelihood of G3 adolescent cigarette use (Bailey et al. 2016).

We also have found continuity between G2 and G3 in child/adolescent externalizing behaviour problems. Specifically, we found a small but consistent link between G2 externalizing problems at ages 13–14 and G3 externalizing 14 years later (standardized estimate ~.18) (Bailey et al. 2009). Our findings indicate that externalizing behaviour may play a key role in the intergenerational transmission of substance use. In our analyses, G2 early adolescent externalizing behaviour problems fully mediated the association between G1 substance use and G2 substance use (Bailey et al. 2006). Future analyses will test this mediational pathway in the G2–G3 pair as well.

Mechanisms through which parent substance use influences children

Key hypotheses underlying the TIP study are that parent substance use may compromise (1) parenting practices or (2) children's developmental environment; that is, the context in which they grow up (e.g., family socioeconomic status, parent physical and mental health). We have found mixed evidence as to whether substance use in the TIP sample impairs parenting practices. One study found that G2 early adult illicit drug use disorder predicted lower observer-rated parenting skills, which, in turn, predicted more child externalizing behaviour (Bailey et al. 2013). In another study, parent substance use was related to lower parental monitoring by both G1 and G2 parents; however, substance use did not predict harsh parenting practices in either generation (Bailey et al. 2009). In a study looking at alcohol use and parenting among mothers and fathers, stronger G2 maternal parenting skills predicted fewer G3 childhood developmental delays, but G2 mothers' alcohol use was not related to their parenting skills (Guttmannova et al. 2016). G2 fathers' alcohol use was indirectly related to child developmental delays: fathers' adolescent alcohol use predicted lower family socioeconomic status, which predicted lower maternal parenting skills and, finally, more G3 developmental delay.

G2 young adult substance use was linked to a range of adult functioning variables relevant to the healthy developmental environment of G3 (Bailey et al. 2013). G2 early adult illicit drug use disorder predicted lower G2 educational attainment, poorer physical health, greater depressive symptoms, lower income-to-needs ratio, and poorer social skills at age 27. Prior studies suggest that low parent socioeconomic status, poor physical and mental health, and social problems predict problems in child development (Hans 2002; McCarty et al. 2003; Shaw et al. 2009). Surprisingly, in our data, these factors did not predict G3 externalizing problems in childhood. Future research will test whether these G2 parent characteristics become important for G3 adolescent development or the emergence of G3 substance use.

Pregnancy, of course, constitutes a critical developmental environment for children. In TIP, 30 per cent of participating biological mothers reported any use of cigarettes, alcohol, cannabis, or other drugs during pregnancy; cigarettes (18 per cent) and alcohol (18 per cent) were by far the most common. G2 maternal adolescent substance use and maternal or paternal early adult illicit drug use disorder predicted an increased likelihood of prenatal drug exposure among G3 children (Bailey et al. 2013; Gavin et al. 2011; Guttmannova et al. 2016). Prenatal alcohol and cigarette use then predicted low G3 birth weight

(Gavin et al. 2011). In analyses using life history calendar data collected from G2 respondents, Bailey et al. (2008) found that mothers temporarily desisted from substance use during pregnancy, but quickly returned to pre-pregnancy levels of use after giving birth. Some mothers continued to use throughout their pregnancy, with about 2 per cent reporting binge drinking, 20 per cent smoking cigarettes, and 9 per cent using cannabis for the duration of their pregnancy. Fathers did not reduce their substance use while their partner was pregnant. Although many of our other analyses have tested for links between G2 maternal prenatal substance use and G3 outcomes, we have found little evidence of effects of prenatal exposure to cigarettes, alcohol, cannabis, or other drugs on child externalizing behaviour, internalizing behaviour, or developmental delays (Bailey et al. 2013; Guttmannova et al. 2016).

We also have investigated G3 children's attitudes as an explanation for the link between G2 cannabis use and G3 alcohol and cannabis use. In fact, this association was fully mediated by children's own pro-substance norms and their perception that their friends held pro-substance norms; G3's perception that their parents had pro-substance norms contributed to their likelihood of alcohol and cigarette use, but did not explain the link between G2 use and G3 use (Bailey et al. 2016).

The role of grandparent substance use

Very few prospective studies of links between grandparent and grandchild substance use exist because of the long study duration required. Several retrospective studies have shown that substance use by close relatives, including grandparents, raises the risk for grandchild substance use (Brook et al. 2012; Milne et al. 2009). We found little support, however, for direct links between G1 substance use and G3 child outcomes in our prospective analyses. Bailey et al. (2016) found no direct association between G1 current or past cannabis use and G3 cigarette, alcohol, or cannabis use. Similarly, Bailey et al. (2006) found no direct links between G1 substance use during G2's adolescence and G3 childhood externalizing behaviour. Taken together, our findings suggest that G1 substance use may affect G3 substance use and development indirectly via increased G2 substance use and poor self-regulation.

Future directions for the TIP study

As described above, G2 parents who received the Raising Healthy Children intervention experienced a wide range of benefits relevant to the development and well-being of G3 children. These benefits to G2 included delayed alcohol initiation, less heavy drinking, less early pregnancy, lower involvement in delinquency and crime, and stronger attachment and commitment to school during adolescence (Hawkins et al. 1992b; Hawkins et al. 1999; Hawkins et al. 2001; Lonczak et al. 2002), as well as less involvement in crime, higher educational attainment, higher socioeconomic status, and better mental health in adulthood (Hawkins et al. 2008; Hill et al. 2005). These beneficial outcomes of the Raising Healthy Children intervention experienced by parents may, in turn, positively affect the development of G3 children. Analyses are currently underway to test whether the benefits of the Raising Healthy Children intervention may be transmitted across generations. For example, G3 children whose parent received the intervention may have fewer emotional or behavioural problems because the intervention appears to have improved G2 adult mental health and socioeconomic status.

Current funding for the TIP study supports aims focused on understanding the impact on youth and families of legalization of non-medical cannabis use for adults ages 21 and older. Thus, we are planning analyses looking at whether cannabis legalization is associated with higher levels of youth cannabis and other drug use or with higher levels of risk factors that predict youth cannabis and other drug use. One set of analyses showing links between G2 current cannabis use and G3 alcohol and cannabis use was described above (Bailey et al. 2016). A second published paper investigated predictors of adult cannabis use among a general sample of adults (the SSDP sample), a sample of adults who are actively parenting (TIP G2 parents), and a sample of non-parents (SSDP sample members who did not have children) (Epstein et al. 2017a). Results showed that the levels of cannabis use were lower among parents than among non-parents, although many parents (~ 20 per cent) did report cannabis use. The predictors of current cannabis use among parents and non-parents, however, were similar, and included having a romantic partner who used cannabis, having used cannabis in adolescence or young adulthood, and having attitudes favourable toward cannabis use. Because we are still collecting post-legalization data, we have been unable as yet to conduct direct tests of any effects of legalization on G3 cannabis or other drug use or risk factors, however, these analyses will be forthcoming.

Future directions for intergenerational research

Intergenerational studies are rich sources for understanding how shared environment, biology, social context, and history affect human development. They link developmental processes in one generation to developmental processes in the next generation. Consequently, they enable strong tests of theories of development and socialization by allowing hypothesized processes to be tested in G1 and G2, and then tested again in G2 and G3, who often experience different social, legal, and historical contexts. So far, intergenerational studies have been underutilized for testing and refinement of developmental theories and furthering understanding of the role of historical context in human development.

Intergenerational studies also identify patterns of continuity and discontinuity across generations. They help us to understand how risk factors and problem behaviours are transmitted across generations, or conversely, to understand how this transmission might be interrupted by preventive interventions. Thus, in addition to informing traditional prevention approaches, which attempt to halt the development of problems by reducing risk and increasing protective factors, intergenerational studies hold great promise for *primordial prevention*, or prevention of the occurrence of risk factors themselves (Leupker and Leyasmeyer 1999; see also special issue of *Preventive Medicine*, vol. 29, on primordial prevention). The SSDP and TIP studies are presently the only U.S. intergenerational studies with the potential to examine long-term, intergenerational effects of a preventive intervention and test for interruption of risk processes and promotion of protective processes. Further studies examining long-term cross-generation effects of childhood preventive interventions are warranted. The full power of intergenerational research has not yet been brought to bear on informing prevention. Additional work is needed to understand factors that either contribute to or disrupt cross-generational continuity in order to allow development of programs aimed at disrupting the transmission of problem behaviours like substance use and poor parenting. We urge other researchers testing preventive interventions to follow up the next generation. If interventions are nested within longitudinal intergenerational studies, researchers can test hypothesized mechanisms for interrupting intergenerational transmission of health compromising behaviours and for perpetuating transmission of healthy behaviours.

References

Akers, R.L. (1977) *Deviant behavior: A social learning approach*, Belmont: Wadsworth Publishing Company.

Andrews, J.A., Hops, H. and Duncan, S.C. (1997) 'Adolescent modeling of parent substance use: The moderating effect of the relationship with the parent', *Journal of Family Psychology*, 11: 259–270.

Bailey, J.A., Hill, K.G., Guttmannova, K., Epstein, M., Abbott, R.D., Steeger, C.M. and Skinner, M.L. (2016) 'Associations between parental and grandparental marijuana use and child substance use norms in a prospective, three-generation study', *Journal of Adolescent Health*, 59: 262–268.

Bailey, J.A., Hill, K.G., Guttmannova, K., Oesterle, S., Hawkins, J.D., Catalano, R.F. and Mcmahon, R.J. (2013) 'The association between parent early adult drug use disorder and later observed parenting practices and child behavior problems: Testing alternate models', *Developmental Psychology*, 49: 887–899.

Bailey, J.A., Hill, K.G., Hawkins, J.D., Catalano, R.F. and Abbott, R.D. (2008) 'Men's and women's patterns of substance use around pregnancy', *Birth: Issues in Perinatal Care*, 35: 50–59.

Bailey, J.A., Hill, K.G., Meacham, M.C., Young, S.E. and Hawkins, J.D. (2011) 'Strategies for characterizing complex phenotypes and environments: General and specific family environmental predictors of young adult tobacco dependence, alcohol use disorder, and co-occurring problems', *Drug and Alcohol Dependence*, 118: 444–451.

Bailey, J.A., Hill, K.G., Oesterle, S. and Hawkins, J.D. (2006) 'Linking substance use and problem behavior across three generations', *Journal of Abnormal Child Psychology*, 34: 273–292.

Bailey, J.A., Hill, K.G., Oesterle, S. and Hawkins, J.D. (2009) 'Parenting practices and problem behavior across three generations: Monitoring, harsh discipline and drug use in the intergenerational transmission of externalizing behavior', *Developmental Psychology*, 45: 1214–1226.

Bandura, A. (1977) *Social learning theory*, Englewood Cliffs: Prentice Hall.

Bell, R.Q. (1953) 'Convergence: An accelerated longitudinal approach', *Child Development*, 24: 145–152.

Beyers, J.M., Toumbourou, J.W., Catalano, R.F., Arthur, M.W. and Hawkins, J.D. (2004) 'A cross-national comparison of risk and protective factors for adolescent substance use: The United States and Australia', *Journal of Adolescent Health*, 35: 3–16.

Brook, J.S., Zhang, C., Balka, E.B. and Brook, D.W. (2012) 'Pathways to children's externalizing behavior: A three-generation study', *The Journal of Genetic Psychology*, 173: 175–197.

Brown, E.C., Catalano, R.F., Fleming, C.B., Haggerty, K.P., Abbott, R.D., Cortes, R.C. and Park, J. (2005) 'Mediator effects in the social development model: An examination of constituent theories', *Criminal Behaviour and Mental Health*, 15: 221–235.

Catalano, R.F. and Hawkins, J.D. (1996) 'The social development model: A theory of antisocial behavior', in Hawkins, J.D. (ed.) *Delinquency and crime: Current theories*, New York: Cambridge University Press.

Catalano, R.F., Kosterman, R., Hawkins, J.D., Newcomb, M.D. and Abbott, R.D. (1996) 'Modeling the etiology of adolescent substance use: A test of the social development model', *Journal of Drug Issues*, 26: 429–455.

Catalano, R.F., Oxford, M.L., Harachi, T.W., Abbott, R.D. and Haggerty, K.P. (1999) 'A test of the social development model to predict problem behaviour during the elementary school period', *Criminal Behaviour and Mental Health*, 9: 39–56.

Chassin, L., Pillow, D.R., Curran, P.J. and Molina, B.S. (1993) 'Relation of parental alcoholism to early adolescent substance use: A test of three mediating mechanisms', *Journal of Abnormal Psychology*, 102: 3–19.

Chassin, L., Rogosch, F. and Barrera, M. (1991) 'Substance use and symptomatology among adolescent children of alcoholics', *Journal of Abnormal Psychology*, 100: 449–463.

Dishion, T.J. and Granic, I. (2004) 'Naturalistic observation of relationship processes', in Haynes, S.N. and Heiby, E.M. (eds.) *Comprehensive handbook of psychological assessment, vol 3: Behavioral assessment*, Hoboken: John Wiley & Sons.

Epstein, M., Bailey, J.A., Steeger, C.M., Hill, K.G. and Skinner, M.L. (2017a) 'Predictors of adult marijuana use among parents and nonparents', *Prevention Science*. Online. Available HTTP: https://link.springer.com/article/10.1007/s11121-017-0801-5 (accessed 8 November 2017).

Epstein, M., Hill, K.G., Bailey, J.A. and Hawkins, J.D. (2013) 'The effect of general and drug-specific family environments on comorbid and drug-specific problem behavior: A longitudinal examination', *Developmental Psychology*, 49: 1151–1164.

Epstein, M., Hill, K.G., Roe, S.S., Bailey, J.A., Iacono, W.G., Mcgue, M., Kristman-Valente, A., Catalano, R.F. and Haggerty, K.P. (2017b) 'Time-varying effects of families and peers on adolescent marijuana use: Person-environment interactions across development', *Development & Psychopathology*, 39: 887–900.

Eyberg, S.M. and Robinson, E.A. (1983) 'Dyadic parent-child interaction coding system: A manual', *Psychological Documents*, 13(2): Ms. No. 2582.

Forehand, R.L. and Mcmahon, R. (1981) *Helping the noncompliant child: A clinician's guide to parent training*, New York: Guilford Press.

Gavin, A.R., Hill, K.G., Hawkins, J.D. and Maas, C. (2011) 'The role of maternal early-life and later-life risk factors on offspring low birth weight: Findings from a three-generational study', *Journal of Adolescent Health*, 49: 166–171.

Guo, J., Hill, K.G., Hawkins, J.D., Catalano, R.F. and Abbott, R.D. (2002) 'A developmental analysis of sociodemographic, family, and peer effects on adolescent illicit drug initiation', *Journal of the American Academy of Child and Adolescent Psychiatry*, 41: 838–845.

Guttmannova, K., Bailey, J.A., Hill, K.G., Lee, J.O., Hawkins, J.D., Woods, M.L. and Catalano, R.F. (2011) 'Sensitive periods for adolescent alcohol use initiation: Predicting the lifetime occurrence and chronicity of alcohol problems in adulthood', *Journal of Studies on Alcohol and Drugs*, 72: 221–231.

Guttmannova, K., Hill, K.G., Bailey, J.A., Hartigan, L.A., Small, C.M. and Hawkins, J.D. (2016) 'Parental alcohol use, parenting, and child on-time development', *Infant and Child Development*. Online. Available HTTP: http://onlinelibrary.wiley.com/doi/10.1002/icd.2013/pdf (accessed 8 November 2017).

Hans, S.L. (2002) 'Studies of prenatal exposure to drugs: Focusing on parental care of children', *Neurotoxicology & Teratology*, 24: 329–337.

Hawkins, J.D., Catalano, R.F., Kosterman, R., Abbott, R. and Hill, K.G. (1999) 'Preventing adolescent health-risk behaviors by strengthening protection during childhood', *Archives of Pediatrics and Adolescent Medicine*, 153: 226–234.

Hawkins, J.D., Catalano, R.F. and Miller, J.Y. (1992a) 'Risk and protective factors for alcohol and other drug problems in adolescence and early adulthood: Implications for substance-abuse prevention', *Psychological Bulletin*, 112: 64–105.

Hawkins, J.D., Catalano, R.F., Morrison, D.M., O'donnell, J., Abbott, R.D. and Day, L.E. (1992b) 'The Seattle Social Development Project: Effects of the first four years on protective factors and problem behaviors', in Mccord, J. and Tremblay, R.E. (eds) *Preventing antisocial behavior: Interventions from birth through adolescence*, New York: Guilford Press.

Hawkins, J.D., Guo, J., Hill, K.G., Battin-Pearson, S. and Abbott, R.D. (2001) 'Long-term effects of the Seattle Social Development Intervention on school bonding trajectories', *Applied Developmental Science*, 5: 225–236.

Hawkins, J.D., Kosterman, R., Catalano, R.F., Hill, K.G. and Abbott, R.D. (2005) 'Promoting positive adult functioning through social development intervention in childhood: Long-term effects from the Seattle Social Development Project', *Archives of Pediatrics & Adolescent Medicine*, 159: 25–31.

Hawkins, J.D., Kosterman, R., Catalano, R.F., Hill, K.G. and Abbott, R.D. (2008) 'Effects of social development intervention in childhood 15 years later', *Archives of Pediatrics & Adolescent Medicine*, 162: 1133–1141.

Hawkins, J.D. and Weis, J.G. (1985) 'The social development model: An integrated approach to delinquency prevention', *The Journal of Primary Prevention*, 6: 73–97.

Hill, K.G., Hawkins, J.D., Catalano, R.F., Abbott, R.D. and Guo, J. (2005) 'Family influences on the risk of daily smoking initiation', *Journal of Adolescent Health*, 37: 202–210.

Hill, K.G., Woodward, D., Woelfel, T., Hawkins, J.D. and Green, M. (2015) 'Planning for long-term follow-up: Strategies learned from longitudinal studies', *Prevention Science*, 17: 806–818.

Hirschi, T. (1969) *Causes of delinquency*, Berkeley: University of California Press.

Hops, H., Davis, B. and Longoria, N. (1995) 'Methodological issues in direct observation: Illustrations with the Living in Familial Environments (LIFE) coding system', *Journal of Clinical Child Psychology*, 24: 193–203.

Huang, B., Kosterman, R., Catalano, R.F., Hawkins, J.D. and Abbott, R.D. (2001) 'Modeling mediation in the etiology of violent behavior and adolescence: A test of the social development model', *Criminology*, 39: 75–107.

Jennison, K.M. and Johnson, K.A. (1998) 'Alcohol dependence in adult children of alcoholics: Longitudinal evidence of early risk', *Journal of Drug Education*, 28: 19–37.

Labouvie, E.W. and Nesselroade, J.R. (1985) 'Age, period, and cohort analysis and the study of individual development and social change', in Nesselroade, J.R. and Von Eye, A. (eds) *Developmental and social change: Explanatory analysis*, New York: Academic Press.

Lejuez, C., Aklin, W.M., Bornovalova, M.A. and Moolchan, E.T. (2005) 'Differences in risk-taking propensity across inner-city adolescent ever-and never-smokers', *Nicotine & Tobacco Research*, 7: 71–79.

Lejuez, C., Aklin, W.M., Daughters, S., Zvolensky, M., Kahler, C. and Gwadz, M. (2007) 'Reliability and validity of the youth version of the Balloon Analogue Risk Task (BART-Y) in the assessment of risk-taking behavior among inner-city adolescents', *Journal of Clinical Child and Adolescent Psychology*, 36: 106–111.

Leupker, R.V. and Leyasmeyer, E. (1999) 'Proceedings from the international symposium on primordial prevention of cardiovascular disease risk factors: Introduction', *Preventive Medicine*, 29: s1–s2.

Lonczak, H.S., Abbott, R.D., Hawkins, J.D., Kosterman, R. and Catalano, R.F. (2002) 'Effects of the Seattle Social Development Project on sexual behavior, pregnancy, birth, and sexually transmitted disease outcomes by age 21 years', *Archives of Pediatrics and Adolescent Medicine*, 156: 438–447.

Lonczak, H.S., Huang, B., Catalano, R.F., Hawkins, J.D., Hill, K.G., Abbott, R.D., Ryan, J.A. and Kosterman, R. (2001) 'The social predictors of adolescent alcohol misuse: A test of the social development model', *Journal of Studies on Alcohol*, 62: 179–189.

Mccarty, D.A., Mcmahon, R. and Conduct Problems Prevention Research Group (2003) 'Mediators of the relation between maternal depressive symptoms and child internalizing and disruptive behavior disorders', *Journal of Family Psychology*, 17: 545–556.

Mcmahon, R.J. and Estes, A.M. (1993) *Fast Track parent-child interaction task: Observational data collection manuals*, Seattle: University of Washington.

Merikangas, K.R. and Avenevoli, S. (2000) 'Implications of genetic epidemiology for the prevention of substance use disorders', *Addictive Behaviors*, 25: 807–820.

Merikangas, K.R., Stolar, M., Stevens, D.E., Goulet, J., Preisig, M.A., Fenton, B., Zhang, H., O'malley, S.S. and Rounsaville, B.J. (1998) 'Familial transmission of substance use disorders', *Archives of General Psychiatry*, 55: 973–979.

Milne, B.J., Caspi, A., Harrington, H., Poulton, R., Rutter, M. and Moffit, T.E. (2009) 'Predictive value of family history on severity of illness', *Archives of General Psychiatry*, 66: 738–747.

Miyazaki, Y. and Raudenbush, S.W. (2000) 'Tests for linkage of multiple cohorts in an accelerated longitudinal design', *Psychological Methods*, 5: 44–63.

Moerbeek, M. (2011) 'The effects of the number of cohorts, degree of overlap among cohorts, and frequency of observation on power in accelerated longitudinal designs', *Methodology*, 7: 11–24.

Oesterle, S., Hawkins, J.D., Steketee, M., Jonkman, H., Brown, E.C., Moll, M. and Haggerty, K.P. (2012) 'A cross-national comparison of risk and protective factors for adolescent drug use and delinquency in the United States and the Netherlands', *Journal of Drug Issues*, 42: 337–357.

Passler, M.A., Isaac, W. and Hynd, G.W. (1985) 'Neuropsychological development of behavior attributed to frontal lobe functioning in children', *Developmental Neuropsychology*, 14: 349–370.

Raudenbush, S.W. and Chan, W.S. (1993) 'Application of a hierarchical linear model to the study of adolescent deviance in an overlapping cohort design', *Journal of Consulting and Clinical Psychology*, 61: 941–951.

Reid, J.R. (1989) *NIMH grant proposal*, Eugene, OR: Oregon Prevention Research Center.

Schaie, K.W. and Baltes, P.B. (1975) 'On sequential strategies in developmental research: Description or explanation', *Human Development*, 18: 384–390.

Shaw, D.S., Connell, A., Dishion, T.J., Wilson, M.N. and Gardner, F. (2009) 'Improvements in maternal depression as a mediator of intervention effects on early childhood problem behavior', *Development & Psychopathology*, 21: 417–439.

Simpson, A. and Riggs, K.J. (2005a) 'Factors responsible for performance on the day-night task: Response set or semantics?', *Developmental Science*, 8: 360–371.

Simpson, A. and Riggs, K.J. (2005b) 'Inhibitory and working memory demands of the day-night task in children', *British Journal of Developmental Psychology*, 23: 471–486.

Sutherland, E.H. and Cressey, D.R. (1970) *Criminology*, New York: Lippincott.

Appendix 10.A

Available study measures by age and data source

Construct	Data Source	G3 Child Age 1	2	3	4	5	6	7	8	9	10	11	12	13	14	15	16	17	18+
Constructs from parent/caregiver, child and teacher surveys																			
Child involvement in family members' substance use																			
Cigarettes	G2, G3						x	x	x	x	x	x	x	x	x	x	x	x	x
Alcohol	G2, G3						x	x	x	x	x	x	x	x	x	x	x	x	x
Cannabis (updated from wave 8 on)	G2, G3										x	x	x	x	x	x	x	x	x
Child's substance use																			
Tobacco	G3						x	x	x	x	x	x	x	x	x	x	x	x	x
Alcohol	G3						x	x	x	x	x	x	x	x	x	x	x	x	x
Binge drinking	G3										x	x	x	x	x	x	x	x	x
Cannabis use	G3										x	x	x	x	x	x	x	x	x
Other illicit drugs (cocaine, heroin, hallucinogens, etc.)	G3										x	x	x	x	x	x	x	x	x
E-cig/vape use and attitudes	G3										x	x	x	x	x	x	x	x	x
Substance use attitudes (cigarettes, alcohol, cannabis)	G3										x	x	x	x	x	x	x	x	x
Sources and availability	G3										x	x	x	x	x	x	x	x	x
Child's delinquency																			
Violence	G3						x	x	x	x	x	x	x	x	x	x	x	x	x
Relational aggression	G3						x	x	x	x	x	x	x	x	x	x	x	x	x
Bullying	G3						x	x	x	x	x	x	x	x	x	x	x	x	x

(*Continued*)

(Continued)

Construct	Data	G3 Child Age																	
	Source	1	2	3	4	5	6	7	8	9	10	11	12	13	14	15	16	17	18+
Constructs from parent/caregiver, child and teacher surveys																			
Theft	G3						x	x	x	x	x	x	x	x	x	x	x	x	x
Runaway	G3						x	x	x	x	x	x	x	x	x	x	x	x	x
Drug selling	G3										x	x	x	x	x	x	x	x	x
Trouble with the law	G3										x	x	x	x	x	x	x	x	x
School trouble	G3										x	x	x	x	x	x	x	x	x
Gang involvement	G3										x	x	x	x	x	x	x	x	x
Child sexual development and behavior																			
Pubertal development	G3										x	x	x	x	x	x	x	x	x
Dating (including dating violence)	G3										x	x	x	x	x	x	x	x	x
Sexual activity and risk behavior	G3													x	x	x	x	x	x
Pregnancy and prenatal care	G3										x	x	x	x	x	x	x	x	x
G3 have any children (G4)	G3										x	x	x	x	x	x	x	x	x
Gender identity and sexual orientation	G3										x	x	x	x	x	x	x	x	x
Child civic engagement	G3																		x
Child gender attitudes	G3										x	x	x	x	x	x	x	x	x
Child work/job	G3										x	x	x	x	x	x	x	x	x
Child educational aspirations	G3										x	x	x	x	x	x	x	x	x
Grandparent drug use and crime	G2	x	x	x	x	x	x	x	x	x	x	x	x	x	x	x	x	x	x
Parent drug use and norms (cigarettes, alcohol, cannabis, other drugs, e-cigs/vapes)	G2	x	x	x	x	x	x	x	x	x	x	x	x	x	x	x	x	x	x
Parent (maternal) prenatal substance use (reported by bio mom)	G2	x	x	x	x	x	x	x	x	x	x	x	x	x	x	x	x	x	x

Construct	*Data*	*G3 Child Age*																	
	Source	*1*	*2*	*3*	*4*	*5*	*6*	*7*	*8*	*9*	*10*	*11*	*12*	*13*	*14*	*15*	*16*	*17*	*18+*
Constructs from parent/caregiver, child and teacher surveys																			
Parent crime	G2	x	x	x	x	x	x	x	x	x	x	x	x	x	x	x	x	x	x
Parent gender identity and sexual orientation	G2	x	x	x	x	x	x	x	x	x	x	x	x	x	x	x	x	x	x
Parent and grandparent prosocial activities	G2	x	x	x	x	x	x	x	x	x	x	x	x	x	x	x	x	x	x
Parent health, exercise, and diet	G2	x	x	x	x	x	x	x	x	x	x	x	x	x	x	x	x	x	x
Child temperament																			
Effortful control (attention focusing, impulse control)	G2		x	x	x	x	x	x	x	x	x	x	x	x	x	x	x	x	x
Positive emotionality (surgency, extraversion)	G2		x	x	x	x	x	x	x	x	x	x	x	x	x	x	x	x	x
Negative emotionality (anger, frustration, depressed)	G2		x	x	x	x	x	x	x	x	x	x	x	x	x	x	x	x	x
Child self-regulation: Achenbach Child Behavior Checklist																			
Attention deficit/ hyperactivity	G2		x	x	x	x	x	x	x	x	x	x	x	x	x	x	x	x	x
Oppositional defiant	G2,T						x	x	x	x	x	x	x	x	x	x	x	x	x
Conduct problems	G2, G3						x	x	x	x	x	x	x	x	x	x	x	x	x
Full CBCL except for somatic complaints and thought problems subscales	T						x	x	x	x	x	x	x	x	x	x	x	x	x
Child health																			
Height and weight	G2, G3										x	x	x	x	x	x	x	x	x
Illness	G2	x	x	x	x	x	x	x	x	x	x	x	x	x	x	x	x	x	x
Disability	G2	x	x	x	x	x	x	x	x	x	x	x	x	x	x	x	x	x	x
General health (added in wave 5)	G2	x	x	x	x	x	x	x	x	x	x	x	x	x	x	x	x	x	x
Physical activity and diet (added in wave 5)	G3										x	x	x	x	x	x	x	x	x
Physical activity and diet (added in wave 5)	G2	x	x	x	x	x	x	x	x	x									

(*Continued*)

(Continued)

Construct	*Data Source*	*G3 Child Age*																	
		1	*2*	*3*	*4*	*5*	*6*	*7*	*8*	*9*	*10*	*11*	*12*	*13*	*14*	*15*	*16*	*17*	*18+*
Constructs from parent/caregiver, child and teacher surveys																			
External constraints																			
Family monitoring	G2					x	x	x	x	x	x	x	x	x	x	x	x	x	x
Family monitoring	G3										x	x	x	x	x	x	x	x	x
Family rules	G2,G3						x	x	x	x	x	x	x	x	x	x	x	x	x
Perceived norms (family and friends)	G3										x	x	x	x	x	x	x	x	x
Parents' attitudes toward drug use	G2	x	x	x	x	x	x	x	x	x	x	x	x	x	x	x	x	x	x
Opportunities for involvement																			
In family, school, neighborhood, peers	G3					x	x	x	x	x	x	x	x	x	x	x	x	x	x
Mentors	G3										x	x	x	x	x	x	x	x	x
Child degree of involvement																			
With family, boy/girlfriend, school/community	G3						x	x	x	x	x	x	x	x	x	x	x	x	x
Child rewards/costs of involvement																			
With family, boy/girlfriend, school/community	G3						x	x	x	x	x	x	x	x	x	x	x	x	x
Child bonding (family, siblings, friends, and school)																			
In family, school, neighborhood, peers	G3						x	x	x	x	x	x	x	x	x	x	x	x	x
Child prosocial beliefs	G3						x	x	x	x	x	x	x	x	x	x	x	x	x
Child antisocial beliefs	G3										x	x	x	x	x	x	x	x	x
Child prosocial and antisocial behavior of others (including partner/coworker)	G3						x	x	x	x	x	x	x	x	x	x	x	x	x
Child involvement in prosocial activities																			
Hobbies and clubs	G3						x	x	x	x	x	x	x	x	x	x	x	x	x

Construct	*Data Source*	*G3 Child Age* 1	2	3	4	5	6	7	8	9	10	11	12	13	14	15	16	17	18+
Constructs from parent/caregiver, child and teacher surveys																			
Work around the home	G3						x	x	x	x	x	x	x	x	x	x	x	x	x
Exercise	G3						x	x	x	x	x	x	x	x	x	x	x	x	x
Religious activities	G3						x	x	x	x	x	x	x	x	x	x	x	x	x
Volunteering	G3						x	x	x	x	x	x	x	x	x	x	x	x	x
Informal helping	G3						x	x	x	x	x	x	x	x	x	x	x	x	x
Rewards and costs for involvement in prosocial activity	G3						x	x	x	x	x	x	x	x	x	x	x	x	x
Rewards and costs for involvement in antisocial activity	G3						x	x	x	x	x	x	x	x	x	x	x	x	x
Child's skills/ competencies																			
Emotion regulation	G2, G3, T						x	x	x	x	x	x	x	x	x	x	x	x	x
Academic performance	G2, G3, T						x	x	x	x	x	x	x	x	x	x	x	x	x
Consequential thinking	G2, G3, T					x	x	x	x	x	x	x	x	x	x	x	x	x	x
Social competence	G2, G3, T					x	x	x	x	x	x	x	x	x	x	x	x	x	x
School cannabis, alcohol, cig, and e-cig trends	T						x	x	x	x	x	x	x	x	x	x	x	x	x
Disciplined for using or possessing substances at school	T						x	x	x	x	x	x	x	x	x	x	x	x	x
Student service need	T						x	x	x	x	x	x	x	x	x	x	x	x	x
Teaching style/ ability																			
Task-focused instructional learning strategies	T						x	x	x	x	x	x	x	x	x	x	x	x	x
Performance-focused instructional learning strategies	T						x	x	x	x	x	x	x	x	x	x	x	x	x
Teaching self-efficacy (discontinued W9)	T						x	x	x	x	x	x	x	x	x	x	x	x	x
Classroom environment																			
Peer support	T						x	x	x	x	x	x	x	x	x	x	x	x	x

(Continued)

(Continued)

Construct	*Data*	*G3 Child Age*																	
	Source	*1*	*2*	*3*	*4*	*5*	*6*	*7*	*8*	*9*	*10*	*11*	*12*	*13*	*14*	*15*	*16*	*17*	*18+*
Constructs from parent/caregiver, child and teacher surveys																			
Classroom involvement	T						x	x	x	x	x	x	x	x	x	x	x	x	x
Class behavior problems	T						x	x	x	x	x	x	x	x	x	x	x	x	x
Victimization	G2, G3						x	x	x	x	x	x	x	x	x	x	x	x	x
Discrimination based on race/ethnicity	G2, G3													x	x	x	x	x	x
Discrimination based on sexual orientation	G2, G3													x	x	x	x	x	x
Child positive personal characteristics																			
Positive life events	G3						x	x	x	x	x	x	x	x	x	x	x	x	x
Self-esteem	G3						x	x	x	x	x	x	x	x	x	x	x	x	x
Empathy	G3						x	x	x	x	x	x	x	x	x	x	x	x	x
Hopefulness	G3						x	x	x	x	x	x	x	x	x	x	x	x	x
Future orientation	G3						x	x	x	x	x	x	x	x	x	x	x	x	x
Self-efficacy	G3										x	x	x	x	x	x	x	x	x
Academic expectations	G3										x	x	x	x	x	x	x	x	x
Religiosity	G3										x	x	x	x	x	x	x	x	x
Family composition (brothers/sisters/ household roster)	G2	x	x	x	x	x	x	x	x	x	x	x	x	x	x	x	x	x	x
	G3						x	x	x	x	x	x	x	x	x	x	x	x	x
Family financial strain	G2	x	x	x	x	x	x	x	x	x	x	x	x	x	x	x	x	x	x
	G3																		x
Cannabis-related constructs (updated from wave 8 on)																			
Cannabis-specific G2 parenting practices/ behaviors	G2, G3										x	x	x	x	x	x	x	x	x
Retail cannabis store proximity	G2, G3										x	x	x	x	x	x	x	x	x
Norms and attitudes about cannabis	G2, G3										x	x	x	x	x	x	x	x	x
Medical and recreational cannabis laws	G2, G3										x	x	x	x	x	x	x	x	x

Construct	Data Source	G3 Child Age 1	2	3	4	5	6	7	8	9	10	11	12	13	14	15	16	17	18+
Constructs from parent/caregiver, child and teacher surveys																			
Cannabis use (additional items, including types and modes of use)	G2, G3										x	x	x	x	x	x	x	x	x
Other constructs/ measures from existing waves																			
G3 attachment style (Q-sort)	G2	x	x	x															
Risk aversion (Balloon Analog Risk Task)	G2	x	x	x	x	x	x	x	x	x	x	x	x	x	x	x	x	x	x
Risk aversion (Balloon Analog Risk Task)	G3						x	x	x	x	x	x	x	x	x	x	x	x	x
Response inhibition (Stroop)	G2	x	x	x	x	x	x	x	x	x	x	x	x	x	x	x	x	x	x
Response inhibition (Stroop)	G3						x	x	x	x	x	x	x	x	x	x	x	x	x
Observed parent–child interaction	G2, G3	x	x	x	x	x	x	x	x	x	x	x	x	x	x	x	x	x	x
Child developmental delay (Ages and Stages Questionnaire)	G2	x	x	x	x														
Cannabis-related constructs (updated from wave 8 on)																			
G2, G3 retail cannabis outlet proximity/ density/sales	GIS	x	x	x	x	x	x	x	x	x	x	x	x	x	x	x	x	x	x

Chapter 11

Key findings from the Rochester Intergenerational Study

Terence P. Thornberry, Kimberly L. Henry, Marvin D. Krohn, Alan J. Lizotte, and Emily L. Nadel

Intergenerational studies of crime, substance use, and related problem behaviours address two central questions. The first concerns the extent to which a parent's involvement in problem behaviours is a significant risk factor for, and potential cause of, their child also being involved in that same behaviour. The typical hypothesis is one of continuity: we expect that children will follow in the footsteps of their parents such that parental delinquency significantly increases the odds that the child will also be involved in delinquency. But, there are many cases in which parents and offspring are dissimilar with respect to delinquency and other problem behaviours; that is, intergenerational *dis*continuity also requires explanation. In addressing this question there is a growing consensus (Capaldi et al. 2012a; Knight et al. 2014) that intergenerational studies should have comparable measures of the parent's and the child's behaviours covering the *same ages* or the *same developmental stages*. Traditional longitudinal studies can examine contemporaneous effects (i.e., the effect of the parent's adult behaviour on the child's adolescent behaviour). Prospective intergenerational designs, however, can uniquely examine intergenerational effects by looking at continuity (or discontinuity) between the generations for the same behaviour at the same developmental stage and, importantly, doing so using prospective data (Thornberry 2016).

The second core question is explanatory. If parents and children are similar with respect to delinquent behaviour, the central question is: Why? What are the mediating processes by which the parent's involvement in delinquency increases the child's risk of also being involved in delinquency, some 20 to 30 years later? Several explanations have been examined, ranging from genetic models, to the negative consequences of the parent's earlier delinquency on their own life-course development and their ability to effectively socialize their children, to shared environments independently generating delinquency in both generations. Most likely, several of these influences are at play simultaneously. Correctly answering this question informs our theoretical understanding of the origins of delinquent behaviour and how a parent's earlier developmental history can have long-term consequences affecting the behaviour of their offspring. Understanding these processes also provides vital information for the development of prevention programs to enhance prosocial outcomes and to decrease antisocial outcomes.

In contrast, if the parent and child are dissimilar with respect to delinquency the central question is: What moderating influences account for the discrepancy? There are two forms of discontinuity: in some cases, the child is significantly less involved in delinquency than the parent was and the task is to explain intergenerational resilience. What are the protective factors that reduce the transfer of risk from the parent to the child? In other cases, the child is more delinquent than the parent was and the task is to explain intergenerational escalation.

Intergenerational studies, therefore, confront an interesting and difficult challenge – to account for *both* continuity *and* discontinuity across the generations. The Rochester Intergenerational Study (RIGS) investigates these issues using a prospective, three-generation study design. This project began in 1999 with a primary focus on general antisocial behaviour such as delinquency and aggression. As the participants have aged these interests remain but have expanded to other outcomes. Currently, the project is funded by the US National Institute on Drug Abuse and has a primary focus on understanding intergenerational patterns of adolescent substance use.

We have two objectives in this chapter. The first is to describe the research design of the RIGS and how the study has unfolded over the past 18 years. The second is to summarize major findings about the two core questions of study.

The design of the Rochester Intergenerational Study

As is true of most intergenerational studies (Thornberry 2016), RIGS began as an extension to an existing longitudinal study, the Rochester Youth Development Study (RYDS), which followed an adolescent participant and one of his or her parents over time. Thus, it followed two generations of the sample families: Generation 1, or G1, the original parent generation, and Generation 2, or G2, the adolescent generation. The study was designed to understand and explain the behaviour of the G2 adolescent.

The intergenerational extension, RIGS, added a third generation, a G3 child, to the overall study and is following them over time. RIGS is designed to investigate the problem behaviour of the G3 children and to incorporate the G2 parent's earlier development and involvement in problem behaviours as key explanatory variables.

The Rochester Youth Development Study

The original study began in 1988 with a sample of 1,000 G2 adolescents selected from the population of seventh and eighth graders in the public schools of Rochester, New York. Given the project's initial focus – investigating serious, chronic, and violent delinquency – a stratified sample was selected so that: (1) the entire public school population of seventh and eighth graders is represented in the sample, but (2) high-risk youth are overrepresented, and (3) the findings can be appropriately weighted to represent the target population. Overrepresentation was accomplished by disproportionately stratifying on gender (75 per cent males) and proportionately stratifying on residence in high arrest rate areas of the city (see Krohn and Thornberry 1999 for details). The initial sample of 1,000 accurately represents the cohort of all seventh and eighth graders in the Rochester public schools in 1988 (Farnworth et al. 1991). Attrition is discussed below.

Phase 1 of the RYDS covered G2's adolescent years, ages 14 to 18. We interviewed the G2 adolescents nine times at 6-month intervals, and, for each G2, one G1 parent at the first eight interviews. In 85 per cent of the cases, the G1 respondent is G2's biological mother, and in 10 per cent G1 is G2's stepmother. In Phase 2 we interviewed the G2 subjects and their parents at three annual intervals, at ages 21 to 23. Finally, during Phase 3 we interviewed the G2 participants at ages 29 and 31. In addition to face-to-face, hour-long interviews, we collected archival data about school performance, child maltreatment, and contact with the juvenile and adult justice systems.

The Rochester Intergenerational Study

The intergenerational study began in 1999, two years after Phase 2 of the RYDS ended. At that time, the G2 participants were, on average, 23 years of age, and 856 of them were still active in the study. These 856 respondents formed the pool from which we sampled the G3 children.

There are a variety of strategies for selecting G3 children in a prospective three-generation study (Thornberry 2016). We attempted to enrol *all firstborn biological children* of G2 participants. In Year 1 of the study we contacted the 856 active G2 participants to determine if they had an eligible G3 child and, if so, sought their cooperation with the study. A total of 370 G3 children and their families enrolled in the study in Year 1. The age range of the children was from 2 to 13 years with an average age of 6 years. In each subsequent year, we screened the remaining G2 participants to identify new firstborn biological children and attempted to enrol them in the study as they turned 2 years of age. By Year 17, a total of 531 G3 children had enrolled in the study. At Year 17 they ranged in age from 2 to 29 years (mean = 19 years) and the G2 parents were in their early 40s. The sample is evenly divided by sex and largely African American (62 per cent), with 17 per cent Hispanic, 12 per cent white, and 9 per cent mixed race. At this point, we are approximately 99 per cent of the way to our goal of identifying all firstborn biological children of the G2 participants.

To understand G3's development and behaviour we annually interview three participants: the G2 parent, the G3 child (at age 8 and older), and the child's other primary caregiver (OCG). For the children of G2 fathers, the OCG is almost always (93 per cent) the child's biological mother. For the children of G2 mothers, however, the OCGs are grandmothers (47 per cent), biological fathers (31 per cent), stepfathers (6 per cent), aunts (7 per cent), and others (9 per cent). In the early years of the study we also conducted videotaped observations of G3 interacting with G2 and, separately, with OCG and coded them using the Iowa Family Interaction Rating Scales (Melby et al. 1998). Finally, we collected data from official agencies such as police and social services.

Because of budget reductions, we had to eliminate some data collection. Since Year 8 we have not interviewed OCG respondents for the G2 mothers (except for G2 age 2) or the G2 parent for G3 ages 18+. We discontinued the videotaped observations after Year 7 and, unfortunately, they have lost considerable utility as they are only available for a portion of the total sample.

Over the course of the project the G3 participants range in age from toddlerhood to adulthood which requires that measures of core concepts be adapted to the respondent's developmental stage to accurately reflect the theoretical constructs of interest (Campbell 1990; Patterson 1993). Because of this, we have attempted to select standardized measures that have a broad developmental reach or that have different but comparable versions across this age range. We also used measures that are age-appropriate versions of scales we used in the original RYDS, and we have consistently added new measures as G3 moves across developmental milestones. For example, as G3s began the transition from adolescence to early adulthood, we added measures developed in our Phase 2 interviews, when G2 participants were in their early 20s. Also, to the extent possible, we use the same measures used in RYDS to assess G1 and G2, to now assess G2 and G3, allowing direct examinations of intergenerational similarities and dissimilarities. The measures used in the Rochester projects have acceptable validity and reliability. For example, we examined the reliability of core RIGS scales by type of respondent (e.g., G2 and OCG) and by G3 age groups. The average Cronbach's α is .85; they are quite stable over type of respondent and G3 age groups, and only four of the 141 alphas calculated were below .6. Major concept areas and illustrations of specific measures covered in the RIGS are presented in the Overview Table prepared for this volume (Appendix A). More detail about the specific measures and scales included in the dataset is available upon request.

Attrition analysis

Subject attrition is a concern in all longitudinal studies but it may be particularly acute in intergenerational studies since, first, there is attrition in the original longitudinal study and then in the intergenerational component itself. Figure 11.1 presents a flowchart of case loss from the initial sample of 1,000 G2 adolescents to those still retained in RIGS as of Year 17. Of the 1,000 participants, 856 were still actively involved in RYDS in 1999 when the intergenerational study began. The attrition of 144 participants was due to refusals,

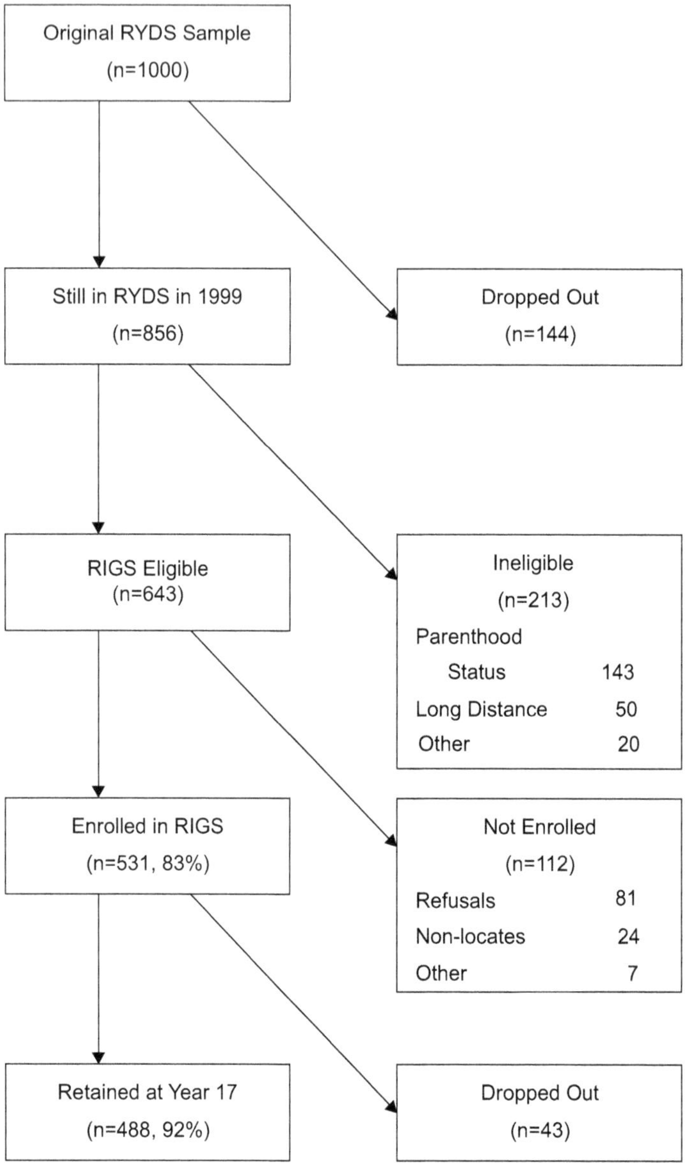

Figure 11.1 Flowchart of participant loss in the Rochester Intergenerational Study (RIGS) through Year 17

inability to locate, death, etc. Of the 856 participants who were active, 643 met our eligibility criteria for the RIGS; 213 were ineligible. There are a variety of reasons for ineligibility. The largest reason (n = 143) is the fact that the G2 is not a parent or, in more recent years, we had lost contact with them and could no longer determine parenthood status. Thus, this group is a combination of those who are not yet parents by their early 40s and those who, while lost to follow-up, may have become a parent at a rather late age. In addition, 50 cases were ineligible because they had moved from the Rochester area and the project did not have the financial resources to conduct long-distance interviews and video-taped observations. Families that moved from the Rochester area after enrolling were, however, followed. Another 20 cases were ineligible for a variety of idiosyncratic reasons (the oldest biological G3 child had died, G3 was adopted, a G2 female participant could not have children, etc.).

Of the 643 who became eligible at any point during Years 1–17 of RIGS, 531 (83 per cent) enrolled in the study. Of the G2 mothers, 186 (97 per cent) enrolled in the study and of the G2 fathers, 345 (76 per cent) did. Many G2 fathers had little or no contact with the G3 child or with the child's biological mother who is typically the caretaker. Securing cooperation required finding the biological mother who had no prior contact with RYDS and who often was in conflict with the G2 father and gaining their agreement. Of the 106 G2 father families not enrolled, refusals (either by the G2 father or the biological mother) accounted for 81 cases, inability to locate them accounted for 24, and "other" reasons for 7. Of the 531 families who enrolled in RIGS at some point, 488 (92 per cent) were retained as of Year 17 while 43 had dropped out of the study. The primary reasons for dropout are refusals and loss of contact.

The original stratified random sample of 1,000 adolescents selected in 1988 was an excellent representation of the population of seventh and eighth graders in Rochester schools (Farnworth et al. 1991). The central question here is whether the retained sample at each stage presented in Figure 11.1 continues to represent the full population. To assess this, we examine the sample on 45 characteristics, clustered in 11 conceptual areas and measured as early in the RYDS as possible (Table 11.1). In the interest of space, and because our primary interest here is in comparing the similarity of the groups and not in a substantive investigation, we do not provide details on the measurement of these variables. Instead, we refer the reader to two earlier publications (Thornberry et al. 2003b, 2014) that contain descriptions of each of these variables, their psychometric properties, and information on their range and variation.

The first column in Table 11.1 describes the full sample on these 45 variables. In the subsequent columns of Table 11.1 we assess whether the retained and lost sample members are significantly different from one another on each of these characteristics. For binary variables we use a chi-square test and for the other variables we use a t-test. Differences that are significant at $p < .05$ are indicated with an asterisk (*). Since we are conducting between 40 and 45 significance tests for each comparison we would expect two of them to be significant by chance alone.

The first comparison focuses on attrition in the original RYDS and contrasts those still in the RYDS in 1999 with those who left the study on 40 of the 45 variables. Because of when they are measured, precocious transitions are not included in this comparison. For six of the variables the differences are

Table 11.1 Attrition analysis for the Rochester Intergenerational Study (RIGS) through Year 17

	RYDS			*RIGS*						
	Original sample	*Still in RYDS in 1999*	*Dropped out*	*Eligible*	*Ineligible: parenthood status*	*Ineligible: long distance/ other*	*Males only:* enrolled	*Males only:* not enrolled	*Retained at year 17*	*Dropped out*
(Maximum n)[a]	(1000)	(856)	(144)	(643)	(143)	(70)	(345)	(106)	(488)	(43)
					(compared to eligible)					
Demographics										
African American	0.68	0.68	0.69	0.69	0.61*	0.67	0.65	0.57	0.73	0.60
Hispanic	0.17	0.17	0.19	0.16	0.16	0.21	0.17	0.21	0.15	0.21
Male	0.73	0.72	0.78	0.70	0.82*	0.69	–	–	0.66	0.58
Eighth grade	0.44	0.41	0.57*	0.44	0.32*	0.39	0.40	0.49	0.41	0.60*
Area characteristics										
Percent in poverty	0.33	0.33	0.34	0.34	0.29*	0.34	0.33	0.35	0.34	0.37
Neighbourhood disorganization	1.69	1.69	1.72	1.71	1.62	1.63	1.69	1.78	1.67	1.87
Neighbourhood integration	2.24	2.25	2.15	2.25	2.27	2.16	2.25	2.32	2.23	2.30
Neighbourhood drug use	2.19	2.20	2.13	2.24	2.00*	2.25	2.13	2.13	2.25	2.46
Family background/structure										
G1 education	11.35	11.38	11.16	11.20	12.15*	11.45	11.24	11.36	11.22	10.81
Poverty level income	0.32	0.32	0.32	0.34	0.22*	0.25	0.33	0.27	0.35	0.33
G1 age at first birth	19.07	19.08	19.02	18.86	20.12*	18.92	19.08	18.99	18.87	18.76
Lived with both biological parents	0.24	0.24	0.23	0.23	0.34*	0.17	0.27	0.17*	0.24	0.24

G1 parent stressors										
Depressive symptoms	1.69	1.69	1.66	1.70	1.62	1.75	1.73	1.64	1.70	1.85
Parental stress	2.17	2.17	2.15	2.18	2.15	2.09	2.21	2.16	2.18	2.26
Negative life events	1.04	1.05	0.95	1.06	1.00	1.14	1.13	0.94	1.08	1.13
Ever used marijuana	0.43	0.45	0.33*	0.46	0.35*	0.54	0.43	0.46	0.44	0.63*
Exposure to family violence										
Maltreatment victimization	0.20	0.20	0.22	0.20	0.15	0.26	0.15	0.23	0.18	0.26
Family hostility	1.61	1.62	1.55	1.64	1.58	1.58	1.69	1.56	1.64	1.80
Parent–child relationships										
G2 attachment to G1	3.40	3.39	3.45	3.39	3.42	3.38	3.42	3.39	3.39	3.38
G1 attachment to G2	3.47	3.47	3.43	3.46	3.54*	3.47	3.44	3.47	3.46	3.38
Consistent discipline	2.79	2.80	2.74	2.80	2.78	2.90	2.77	2.85	2.80	2.64
Parent involvement	2.60	2.62	2.43*	2.61	2.66	2.69	2.61	2.52	2.64	2.50
Supervision	3.63	3.63	3.63	3.62	3.65	3.70	3.60	3.58	3.63	3.67
Education										
Commitment to school	3.08	3.08	3.04	3.07	3.10	3.10	3.06	3.08	3.07	3.12
College aspirations	3.57	3.59	3.39*	3.57	3.67	3.64	3.57	3.52	3.57	3.64
College expectations	0.75	0.76	0.67	0.76	0.79	0.70	0.75	0.78	0.75	0.79
G1 college expectations for G2	0.52	0.53	0.45	0.51	0.63*	0.52	0.51	0.48	0.53	0.40
School grades	1.88	1.92	1.59*	1.83	2.30*	2.01	1.75	1.92	1.82	1.68
Peer relationships										
Gang membership	0.15	0.15	0.11	0.17	0.06*	0.12	0.13	0.20	0.17	0.13
Delinquent peers	1.41	1.41	1.41	1.42	1.41	1.36	1.40	1.44	1.42	1.34
Unsupervised time with friends	1.99	1.99	2.03	2.05	1.77*	1.91	2.06	2.15	2.01	2.16

(Continued)

Table 11.1 (Continued)

	RYDS			*RIGS*						
							Males only:			
	Original sample	*Still in RYDS in 1999*	*Dropped out*	*Eligible*	*Ineligible: parenthood status*	*Ineligible: long distance/ other*	*enrolled*	*not enrolled*	*Retained at year 17*	*Dropped out*
Adolescent stressors										
Negative life events	2.87	2.88	2.81	2.94	2.62	2.91	2.83	2.97	2.92	3.03
Depressive symptoms	2.13	2.15	2.00*	2.17	2.09	2.12	2.12	2.05	2.19	2.26
Low self-esteem	3.08	3.07	3.12	3.06	3.10	3.08	3.08	3.09	3.06	3.03
Internalizing problems	0.49	0.49	0.46	0.50	0.48	0.45	0.50	0.46	0.50	0.54
G2 antisocial behaviours										
Externalizing behaviours	0.46	0.47	0.45	0.48	0.43	0.42	0.50	0.49	0.48	0.47
Delinquent beliefs	1.25	1.25	1.25	1.26	1.23	1.24	1.27	1.29	1.25	1.24
General delinquency	0.53	0.53	0.55	0.55	0.42*	0.55	0.54	0.59	0.55	0.51
Problem marijuana use	0.03	0.03	0.02	0.03	0.01	0.04	0.03	0.06	0.03	0.05
Problem alcohol use	0.05	0.05	0.03	0.05	0.04	0.03	0.04	0.06	0.05	0.05
G2 precocious transitions										
Precocious sexual activity	0.32	–	–	0.34	0.26	0.34	0.36	0.38	0.34	0.21
Precocious parenthood	0.19	–	–	–	–	0.14	0.15	0.25*	0.22	0.33
Precocious cohabitation	0.10	–	–	0.12	0.05*	0.09	0.11	0.10	0.11	0.20
Living independently from parent	0.14	–	–	0.16	0.05*	0.09	0.11	0.12	0.15	0.32*
School dropout	0.27	–	–	0.31	0.13*	0.22	0.32	0.30	0.30	0.40

* $p < 0.05$.

a This is the maximum *n* for each group. The actual *n* varies across these variables because of the wave at which the variable was measured and missing data. More complete information including the *n* for each comparison, standard deviations, t-tests, and chi-square values is available upon request.

statistically significant but there is no strong pattern to the differences as they are scattered across five developmental domains. The retained sample still strongly represents the initial sample of 1,000 adolescents, as can be seen by comparing the values in column 1, the full sample, and in column 2, the retained sample. Even for the six variables that are significantly different, the averages are virtually identical for the two groups.

The next comparison is between the eligible RYDS participants and those who are ineligible because they are not yet a parent or because their parental status is uncertain. We add four of the five precocious transitions to this comparison, for a total of 44 variables. As the decision to become a parent is substantively meaningful, there are many significant differences between these two groups (19 of the 44 comparisons). Those who become parents were more likely to be African American, female, and in the eighth-grade cohort at the beginning of the RYDS. They were also more likely to come from disadvantaged backgrounds, have lower school performance and expectations, more likely to be gang members and to spend unsupervised time with friends, and to self-report more delinquency. The largest differences were associated with precocious transitions – cohabiting, living independently of parents while still of high school age, and school dropout. To explore this issue further we compared the eligible cases to those who were screened at least through the age of 35 (n = 85) and to those whose last screening was under age 35 (n = 58). The results are substantively the same to those reported in the combined group.

We next compared those eligible for RIGS to those ineligible because they were long-distance cases or for "other" reasons. None of the 45 comparisons are statistically significant. Similarly, there are few differences between those who actually enrolled in the intergenerational study and those who did not. We examine this issue only for the G2 fathers as only six of the G2 mothers did not enroll in the study. Only two significant differences are observed.

Finally, we compare those retained at Year 17 to those who left the panel. Only three significant differences are observed. Comparing the average scores on all of the 45 variables for those retained at Year 17 of RIGS with the full panel of adolescents (column 1) demonstrates that the retained sample still adequately represents the initial population of all seventh and eighth graders in the Rochester public schools in 1988.

G3 age heterogeneity

The G3 children in the RIGS currently range from toddlers to adults and, thus, the total sample size is divided across many birth cohorts. The most feasible way for intergenerational studies to gain adequate statistical power is to cluster G3 participants of the same ages, drawn from different birth cohorts, into synthetic cohorts of adequate size that represent meaningful segments of the overall life course, for example, the preschool years, late adolescence, and so forth. In other words, intergenerational studies are almost inevitably a special case of cohort sequential or accelerated longitudinal designs (Prinzie and Onghena 2005).

Combining different cohorts, however, is not necessarily straightforward. First, G3 participants of similar ages will be drawn from different birth cohorts that may be separated by as many as 20 years. Second, some G3 participants will be the children of teenage parents while others will be born to G2 participants who become parents in their early 40s. Finally, at the selected ages, some G3 participants will have been interviewed during the early waves of the intergenerational study while others will have been interviewed toward the end of the study. The most common response to the necessity of combining multiple birth cohorts in one analysis is to control either for G3 age (e.g., Bailey et al. 2013) or G2 age at the birth of G3 (e.g., Capaldi et al. 2012b; Thornberry et al. 2009a, 2009b).

A formal way of testing the appropriateness of combining multiple cohorts is to estimate a multilevel model examining whether constructs of interest vary as a function of birth cohort. The variance in the construct at each level is estimated and used to calculate the intraclass correlation coefficient (ICC). If we can safely combine cohorts, we would expect to see very small ICCs associated with birth cohort indicating that little variance is accounted for by differences across cohorts (Raudenbush and Bryk 2002).

Here we examine G3 involvement in externalizing problems, internalizing problems, and delinquent behaviour as reported by the parent using the Child Behavior Checklist (Achenbach 1991). These measures have been assessed a sufficient number of times – from ages 4 to 17 – and for a sufficient number of birth cohorts – 1986 to 2006 – to constitute a rigorous test of whether there are likely to be cohort differences.

We start with an unconditional model with three levels: repeated measures of G3 behaviour (Level 1), nested in G3 (Level 2), nested in birth cohort (Level 3). The unconditional models produced the following ICCs associated with Level 3, or birth cohort: delinquent behaviour 5.7 per cent, externalizing behaviour 1.3 per cent, and internalizing behaviour 0.9 per cent. Very little of the variance is due to G3 birth year differences. The highest Level 3 ICC is for delinquency, 5.7 per cent. We therefore examine how the unconditional ICC changes with the addition of control variables that we typically include in our models: G2 gender, G2 race/ethnicity, G2 birth year, G1 education, the arrest rate and poverty rate of the neighbourhood that G2 grew up in, G3 age, G3 gender, and family poverty at each year the outcome was measured. In this model, the ICC at Level 3 was reduced to 1.4 per cent, indicating that the birth cohort differences can be readily explained by a carefully chosen set of covariates.

Similarly, Loughran et al. (2017) assessed the extent to which the prevalence of adolescent drug use at ages 14 to 18 varied as a function of birth cohort. Level 1 represented the repeated measures of drug use, Level 2 the individual, and Level 3 birth cohort. Given the low prevalence in some years, Loughran et al. analysed 3-year cohorts by aggregating three consecutive birth years. The unconditional model produced a Level 3 ICC of 7.7 per cent while the results, conditional on G3 age, are 0.2 per cent. This decrease in the variance explained by the cohort after age is introduced is expected given what we know about the strong relationship between age and drug use.

Findings from the Rochester Intergenerational Study

In several publications we discussed broad theoretical and methodological issues related to intergenerational study. Thornberry presented our theoretical model of intergenerational continuity (2005, 2009) and discontinuity (2017) of delinquency; an intergenerational extension of interactional theory (Thornberry 1987; Thornberry and Krohn 2005, Forthcoming). Krohn et al. (2016) examined the generality of social control, social learning, and interactional theories and demonstrated that the impact of key explanatory variables on adolescent drug use is virtually identical for G3 drug use as for G2 drug use. In addition, Thornberry (2016) presented a general discussion of the methodological challenges associated with intergenerational designs, as well as the theoretical and methodological advantages offered by these studies.

Intergenerational continuity and discontinuity

The first core question of intergenerational study concerns continuity and discontinuity between parents and offspring with respect to a particular behaviour. Thornberry et al. (2006) examined prevalence measures of alcohol and marijuana use for G1 (primarily females ranging in age from 20 to 60), G2 (both males and females measured when they were in adolescence, emerging adulthood, and adulthood), and G3 (ranging in age from 9 to 15). Intergenerational continuity was found from G1 females to G2 females but not to G2 males. G2 fathers had no significant impact on the substance use of their G3 children but substance use by the G3 children of G2 mothers was significantly influenced by both G2 substance use and by G1 substance use. G1 grandmother and G2 mother substance use had independent effects on G3 use. The fact that few G2 fathers lived with G3 could have affected the lack of impact of their substance-using behaviour on their children's substance use. It also should be noted that G2 use in adolescence and emerging adulthood were more strongly related to G3 use than was concurrent adult G2 use, suggesting that it is necessary to consider the substance use history of parents to adequately assess their impact on their children's behaviour.

Henry and Augustyn (2017) investigated the role of a parent's use of cannabis during adolescence, as well as his/her subsequent abuse or dependence, on the G3 child's onset of cannabis use by age 15 for 442 parent–child dyads (274 father–child, 168 mother–child). Fathers who began using cannabis by age 15 were more likely to meet the criteria for a lifetime cannabis disorder.

The offspring of fathers who met the criteria for a disorder had higher odds of early initiation of cannabis use and early onset cannabis use by the father was indirectly associated with their child's onset of cannabis use via father's lifetime cannabis disorder. No significant effects for mothers were observed, although analyses were limited due to the low rate of mothers who met the criteria for a lifetime cannabis disorder.

Henry (2017) examined the unique influence of G2 fathers' alcohol and cannabis disorder on G3 children's onset of these same substances for 274 father–child dyads. Logistic regression models assessed the association between fathers' lifetime incidence of an alcohol and cannabis disorder and G3 onset of these same substances at or before age 15. The children of fathers who met criteria for a lifetime cannabis disorder were significantly more likely to initiate use of alcohol and cannabis by age 15, controlling for background covariates and presence of a lifetime alcohol disorder. No unique effect of fathers' alcohol disorder on children's onset of alcohol and cannabis use were observed.

Nadel and Thornberry (2017) extended this line of investigation to examine both homotypic continuity in substance use (the influence of a parent's adolescent substance use on their child's adolescent substance use) as well as heterotypic continuity (the influence of a parent's adolescent substance use on their child's involvement in other problem behaviours – delinquency, depressive symptoms, and risky sex behaviours). For G2 fathers, especially supervisory fathers, there was strong evidence of intergenerational continuity, both homotypic and heterotypic. For G2 mothers, however, there was no evidence of either type of intergenerational continuity. In contrast, the G2 mother's concurrent involvement in substance use was an important risk factor for the child's involvement in substance use and related problem behaviours, but for the fathers concurrent substance use was less important.

Examining intergenerational continuity for general antisocial behaviour Thornberry et al. (2003a) found significant correlations between G2 adolescent antisocial behaviour and G3 externalizing behaviour (as reported by the OCG) for both G2 fathers and for G2 mothers. For resident G2 fathers the same pattern was seen but for non-resident fathers the correlation was not statistically significant. This same pattern was evident in other analyses, including when G3 externalizing behaviours were measured by teacher reports (Thornberry 2005) and by biological mother reports (Thornberry et al. 2009a, 2009b). Thornberry (2009) estimated structural equation models with G2 adolescent antisocial behaviour (adolescent delinquency plus drug use) predicting G2 adult antisocial behaviour and both G2 measures predicting G3 externalizing behaviours (maternal reports), for mothers, supervisory fathers and, non-supervisory fathers, separately. For all three groups there were significant G2 stability effects from adolescence to adulthood. For mothers their antisocial behaviour at both stages was related to G3 behaviours, for the supervisory fathers only their adolescent antisocial behaviour was, but for the non-supervisory fathers neither coefficient was significant. Thus, the antisocial behaviour of non-supervisory fathers showed the same intragenerational stability as the other parents, but it was seemingly irrelevant with respect to their child's behaviour.

We have also investigated levels of intergenerational continuity for a variety of other behaviours. They include child maltreatment (Thornberry and Henry 2013), intimate partner violence (Smith et al. 2011), school disengagement (Thornberry 2009), teen parenthood (Pogarsky et al. 2006), and gang membership (Augustyn et al. 2014).

Overall, these analyses suggest some significant degree of intergenerational continuity in the behaviour investigated. At the same time, the results indicate that intergenerational continuity is somewhat more nuanced than is often expected. Whether intergenerational continuity is observed or not, and the magnitude of the relationship, often depends on how the behaviour is measured (e.g., the seriousness of the behaviour, dimensional measures versus diagnostic categories), the developmental stage at which it is measured (e.g., adolescence versus adulthood), and whether we are examining G2 mothers or G2 fathers. Moreover, these dimensions appear to interact in generating differences in relationships; compare, for example, Thornberry et al. (2006), Henry and Augustyn (2017), and Nadel and Thornberry (2017).

These results also highlight the importance of studying intergenerational discontinuity. While parental adolescent antisocial behaviour significantly increases child antisocial behaviour, the correlations, both in our study and in others, is typically in the .3 range. While there is a significant transfer of risk, clearly there is also a substantial degree of discontinuity. Many children do not follow in the footsteps of their parents, and that requires investigation as well.

Mediators of continuity

The second central issue in intergenerational study is to identify the mediating pathways that link the behaviour of parents and children. Thornberry et al. (2003a) examined the influence of G1 poverty and parenting styles on G2 financial stress and parenting behaviours and how these variables mediate the link between G2 adolescent antisocial behaviour and G3 antisocial behaviour. For G2 fathers, their parenting style mediated a sizeable part of the impact of G2 adolescent antisocial behaviour on G3 antisocial behaviour, but not all of it. G2 parenting also mediated the impact of G2 financial stress on G3 antisocial behaviour. G1 poverty and G1 parenting style exerted only indirect effects on G3, via G2 financial stress and G2 adolescent antisocial behaviour, respectively.

For G2 mothers, parenting style was a more important influence, mediating all of the impact of G2 antisocial behaviour on G3 antisocial behaviour. Parenting was affected by their current financial stress, their adolescent antisocial behaviour, and G1's earlier parenting of them. Also, G1 poverty increased G2 level of financial stress which, in turn, was related to G2 parenting style.

Given the importance of continuing contact between fathers and their children in examining intergenerational continuity, we identified a group of "supervisory fathers" who either live with or have frequent contact with the G3 child. The following mediational analyses were limited to G2 mothers and G2 supervisory fathers.

Thornberry (2005) examined a model that included G1 parenting behaviours, G2 adolescent drug use, G2 adult stressful life events, G2 parenting, and G3 delinquency as measured by teacher reports. For G2 parenting, separate indicators of positive parenting (e.g., warmth/support) and negative parenting (hostility; harsh discipline) were used based on videotaped observations of parent–child interactions.

For G2 mothers, positive aspects of parenting (but not negative aspects) lead to G3 delinquency; mothers who failed to provide warm and supportive parenting had more delinquent children. In turn, that parenting style was significantly influenced by G1 parenting, G2 adolescent drug use, and stressful life events. For supervisory fathers, however, it was the negative aspects of parenting (but not the positive aspects) that influenced G3 delinquency; delinquency was higher when fathers exhibited a hostile, irritable style of parenting. For these fathers, parenting was not influenced by G1 parenting or by their adolescent drug use; it was influenced by stressful life events which also had a direct impact of G3 delinquency. Parenting behaviours play an important role in explaining G3 delinquency and in accounting for intergenerational continuity in delinquency. Interestingly though the type of parenting (positive versus negative) differed for mothers and supervisory fathers and did so in ways that are consistent with basic gender differences in the parenting role (Lamb and Tamis-LeMonda 2004).

Thornberry et al. (2009a) focused on depressive symptoms as a key mediator of intergenerational continuity. The model also investigated the role of parent's age at the birth of G3 and parent's attachment to G3. For G2 mothers, adolescent delinquency and drug use, along with a young age at first birth, increased subsequent depressive symptoms and, in turn, depressive symptoms, both directly and indirectly via attachment, influenced G3 externalizing behaviour. For G2 supervisory fathers, adolescent delinquency and drug use increased depressive symptoms which indirectly influenced G3 behaviour via attachment. Depressive symptoms and parenting were influential mediators for both G2 mothers and fathers.

Little attention has been paid to the stress that arises from the parenting role itself in the intergenerational literature. Thornberry et al. (2009b) examined parenting stress as a mediator. For supervisory fathers their adolescent antisocial behaviour was associated with a lower age at first birth, increased their level of parenting stress, and reduced effective parenting (as measured by level of attachment). Parenting stress and a younger age at first birth had large negative impacts on effective parenting and, in turn, effective parenting and a younger age at first birth had direct effects on G3 delinquency and mediated the impact of the prior variables. For G2 mothers their adolescent antisocial behaviour only had a significant impact on parenting style which was also strongly influenced by parenting stress and a younger age at first birth. In turn, less effective parenting was the only variable that directly affected G3 delinquency and mediated the impact of the prior variables.

Overall, we have examined: (1) different sources of stress for young adults, including financial stress, parenting stress, negative life events, and depressive symptoms; (2) different aspects of parenting behaviours, including attachment, monitoring, discipline, warm/nurturing parenting, and hostile/harsh parenting, based on both interview and observational data; and (3) different aspects of the parent's adolescent antisocial behaviour and different aspects of the child's antisocial behaviour. Across these analyses it appears that parental antisocial behaviour during adolescence increases the chances that the child will also be involved in antisocial behaviour, especially for mothers and fathers who have frequent, ongoing contact with the child. It also appears that this effect is mediated, at least in part, by high levels of stress and by parenting behaviours. Both of these are major pathways included in our intergenerational theory of continuity (Thornberry 2005, 2009).

Explaining intergenerational discontinuity

Intergenerational studies have paid surprisingly little attention to *dis*continuity between parents and offspring, to different types of discontinuity (resilience versus escalation), or to measurement sensitivity which affects not only the magnitudes of observed levels of continuity and discontinuity but factors which correlate with them. Loughran et al. (2017) examined these issues focusing on substance use between ages 12 and 18. Results suggested that the degree of intergenerational continuity, resilience, and escalation, as well as correlates of each, depend heavily on how heterogeneity in substance use is taken into account. The study also highlights the importance of examining intergenerational escalation and resilience as different phenomena. We have not yet examined the issue of intergenerational escalation but, in the next section, summarize our findings about intergenerational resilience.

Intergenerational resilience

Lovegrove (2010) used trajectory models to identify G2 parents involved in adolescent delinquency and G3 children (8 to 11 years) involved in externalizing problems. He conditioned on G2 delinquency by only analysing children of G2 delinquents and compared the G3 children (32 per cent) in the trajectory group with the lowest level of externalizing behaviours indicating intergenerational resilience with all others. Several G2 characteristics were associated with discontinuity – lower levels of family poverty, older onset of parenthood, less parenting stress, and better parenting behaviours (supervision, attachment, and consistent discipline). Characteristics of the child's other caregiver were also important: less parenting stress, lower levels of violent behaviour, less financial stress, less depression, and better parenting skills.

Lizotte et al. (2015) investigated whether a G2 parent's age at first birth was a source of intergenerational resilience. They first estimated five trajectories of the prevalence of G2 violent behaviour from age 14 to 20. They then predicted the G3 children's antisocial behaviour at age 6 and at age 10 from G2 age at first birth, the five trajectory groups, and then interactions between age at first birth and each of the five groups. They reasoned that parents who wait to begin childbearing until more normative ages are more likely to buffer their children from risk. This model did not work well for 7-year-olds, probably because the children were too young to have significant social networks where antisocial behaviour could be exhibited. For 10-year-olds, however, the models worked well. G2 trajectory groups that exhibited relatively high levels of violent behaviour significantly increased G3 problem behaviour. But, delaying childrearing reduced the impact of the parent's high trajectories on children's antisocial behaviour. When parents had histories as high-level offenders, delaying childrearing appears to serve as a protective factor to reduce the G3 children's involvement in delinquency.

Dong and Krohn (2016) investigated the impact of protective factors, specifically good parenting practices, on the relationship between the parental propensity to offend over time and problem behaviour of the children during both childhood and adolescence. Trajectories of G2 offending were used as the primary risk factor for children's externalizing behaviours. Measures of parenting included attachment, involvement, and consistency of discipline.

When G3 were children, parental memberships in three delinquency trajectory groups (late bloomers, high-level chronics, and bell-shaped desistors) increased G3 externalizing scores, while parental affective ties and consistency of discipline reduced G3 externalizing scores and, for the late bloomer group, mediated the relationship between parental propensity for offending and G3 externalizing. However, the parenting measures did not interact with parental trajectory offending groups to protect children from the risk of having parents who engaged in delinquency. When G3 reached adolescence, the coefficients for the late bloomer, the bell-shaped desistors, and the high-level chronic groups were all significantly related to G3's externalizing behaviours. The parenting variables mediated the relationship between the bell-shaped desistor group and G3 externalizing behaviour. In addition, affective ties protected G3 children from the effect of their parents being in the high-level chronic group. Consistency of discipline interacted with the late bloomer group but in the opposite direction to what was predicted. These findings suggest that parenting practices (particularly affective ties between parent and child) both mediated the relationship between particular patterns of parental offending and children's externalizing behaviour and moderated (during adolescence) the effect of parental patterns of offending on the child's problematic behaviour.

Finally, Thornberry et al. (2013) examined the role of safe, stable, and nurturing relationships in accounting for intergenerational resilience for child maltreatment. During early adulthood, satisfaction with a partner, satisfaction with the parenting role, and attachment to the child were all direct protective factors, significantly reducing the likelihood the G2 engaged in maltreatment perpetration for those with a history of maltreatment victimization.

Future directions

In many ways the field of intergenerational study is in its infancy. There are still a relatively small number of multigeneration studies that follow individuals over time to understand how crime and related problem behaviours are reproduced across the generations. Continuing and expanding this line of research offers tremendous opportunity to enhance our understanding of both the origins and consequences of criminal behaviour. A few suggestions for future research follow.

Some intergenerational studies rely exclusively or primarily on official records of criminal involvement collected on multiple generations (e.g., Bijleveld and Wijkman 2009; Besemer and Farrington 2012), whereas others rely primarily on repeated interviews and self-report data (e.g., Bailey et al. 2013; Capaldi et al. 2012a; Thornberry et al. 2003a). The former studies typically have larger samples and focus on more descriptive issues about continuity and discontinuity, whereas the latter typically have smaller samples and focus on understanding the mechanisms by which continuity and discontinuity are explained. Each of these types of studies have important advantages but they can provide somewhat different answers to the same questions. An important task for future research is to begin to meld these approaches together. The larger, population studies can systematically sample subgroups to follow in greater detail over time to provide more information about explanatory processes while the smaller studies with repeated interviews can collect more comprehensive official records on the study participants. Doing so is likely to enhance the comprehensiveness of both study types and the scope of their results.

Most intergenerational studies focus on issues of continuity; that is, similarity between parents and children in crime and other problem behaviours. Much more attention needs to be given to intergenerational discontinuity to provide a fuller understanding of how criminal behavior is related across the generations. Also, as Loughran et al. (2017) have demonstrated, there are two distinct patterns of discontinuity: intergenerational resilience and intergenerational escalation. Of the two, there have been more studies of resilience and virtually nothing is known about patterns of intergenerational escalation. Each of these patterns of discontinuity need to be examined in its own right to complete our understanding of intergenerational linkages.

Similarly, most intergenerational studies focus on homotypic continuity; that is, continuity in the same problem behaviour across the generations. Less is known about patterns of heterotypic continuity from parents to children. This, too, requires systematic investigation as it is possible, indeed likely, that some patterns of parental problem behaviours will lead to multiple negative consequences for their children and involvement in a variety of problem behaviours by the offspring. Understanding these patterns is important for the design and implementation of prevention programs.

Most studies of mediating processes that try to account for intergenerational continuity in problem behaviours focus on family processes and parenting behaviours as central mediators. This is an important and fruitful area of inquiry as shown by the many studies that demonstrate that these are, indeed, important mediators. But they are not the only ones. It is important that future studies expand the investigation of mediators beyond family influences. For example, it would be fruitful to understand how such factors as educational attainment, social network characteristics, patterns of employment and unemployment, neighborhood and residential characteristics, and so forth also help explain, either directly or via family influences, intergenerational continuity and discontinuity. The current emphasis on family has been productive but it should not hinder investigations of broader mediating processes.

Clearly, there is a wide array of questions that can and should be addressed by intergenerational studies in the future. Doing so has great potential and, in the coming years, the RIGS research team plans to continue addressing these issues and to fully examining our theoretical model of intergenerational continuity and discontinuity. As the G3 sample continues to age and a larger proportion of the total sample enters and moves through adolescence, we will be able to focus specifically on adolescent substance use and on more serious forms of delinquent and criminal behaviour. Doing so will contribute more directly to the ultimate purpose of the study – to better understand adolescent problem behaviours and the role of intergenerational influences in causing them so as to provide better and more focused information to guide the development of prevention and treatment programs.

References

Achenbach, Thomas M. 1991. *Manual for the Child Behavior Checklist/4–18 and 1991 Profile.* Burlington, VT: University of Vermont, Department of Psychology.

Augustyn, Megan Bears, Terence P. Thornberry, and Marvin D. Krohn. 2014. Gang membership and pathways to maladaptive parenting. *Journal of Research on Adolescence* 24:252–267.

Bailey, Jennifer A., Karl G. Hill, Katarina Guttmannova, Sabrina Oesterle, J. David Hawkins, Richard F. Catalano, and Robert J. McMahon. 2013. The association between parent early adult drug use disorder and later observed parenting practices and child behavior problems: Testing alternate models. *Developmental Psychology* 49:887–899.

Besemer, Sytske, and David P. Farrington. 2012. Intergenerational transmission of criminal behaviour: Conviction trajectories of fathers and their children. *European Journal of Criminology* 9:120–141.

Bijleveld, Catrien J.H., and Miriam Wijkman. 2009. Intergenerational continuity in convictions: A five-generation study. *Criminal Behaviour and Mental Health* 19:142–155. doi: 10.1002/cbm.714.

Campbell, Susan B. 1990. *Behavior Problems in Preschool Children: Clinical and Developmental Issues.* New York: Guilford Press.

Capaldi, Deborah M., Katherine C. Pears, and David C. R. Kerr. 2012a. The Oregon Youth Study Three-Generational Study: Theory, design, and findings. *The International Society for the Study of Behavioural Development Bulletin* Serial No. 62:29–33.

Capaldi, Deborah M., Katherine C. Pears, David C. R. Kerr, Lee D. Owen, and Hyoun K. Kim. 2012b. Growth in externalizing and internalizing problems in childhood: A prospective study of psychopathology across three generations. *Child Development* 83:1945–1959.

Dong, Beidi, and Marvin D. Krohn. 2016. The protective effects of family support on the relationship between official intervention and general delinquency across the life course. *Journal of Developmental and Life-Course Criminology* 3:39–61.

Farnworth, Margaret, Terence P. Thornberry, Alan J. Lizotte, and Marvin D. Krohn. 1991. *Rochester Youth Development Study Technical Report: Sampling Design and Implementation.* Albany, NY: University at Albany.

Henry, Kimberly L. 2017. Fathers' alcohol and cannabis disorder and the early onset of drug use by their children. *Journal of Studies on Alcohol and Drugs* 78:458–462. PMC5440370.

Henry, Kimberly L., and Megan B. Augustyn. 2017. Intergenerational continuity in cannabis use: The role of parent's early onset and lifetime disorder on child's early onset. *Journal of Adolescent Health* 60:87–92.

Knight, Kelly E., Scott Menard, and Sara B. Simmons. 2014. Intergenerational continuity of substance use. *Substance Use & Misuse* 49:221–233.

Krohn, Marvin D., Thomas A. Loughran, Terence P. Thornberry, Daniel Wonho Jang, Adrienne Freeman-Gallant, and Erin D. Castro. 2016. Explaining adolescent drug use in adjacent generations: Testing the generality of theoretical explanations. *Journal of Drug Issues* 46:373–395.

Krohn, Marvin D., and Terence P. Thornberry. 1999. Retention of minority populations in panel studies of drug use. *Drugs & Society* 14:185–207.

Lamb, Michael E., and Catherine S. Tamis-Lemonda. 2004. The role of the father: An introduction. In *The Role of the Father in Child Development*, edited by M. E. Lamb. New York: Wiley and Sons.

Lizotte, Alan J., Matthew D. Phillips, Marvin D. Krohn, Terence P. Thornberry, Shawn D. Bushway, and Nicole M. Schmidt. 2015. Like parent like child? The role of delayed childrearing in breaking the link between parent's offending and their children's antisocial behavior. *Justice Quarterly* 32:410–444.

Loughran, Thomas A., Pilar Larroulet, and Terence P. Thornberry. 2017. Definitional elasticity in the measurement of intergenerational continuity in substance use. In *Child Development.* (published online June 22, 2017). doi: 10.1111/cdev.12849PMID28639698.

Lovegrove, Peter J. 2010. Explaining Discontinuous Cross-Generational Patterns of Delinquency, Department of Sociology, Unpublished doctoral dissertation. University of Colorado, Boulder, CO.

Melby, Janet, Rand Conger, Ruth Book, Martha Rueter, Laura Lucy, Daniel Repinski, Shauna Rogers, Barbara Rogers, and Laura Scaramella. 1998. *The Iowa Family Interaction Rating Scales.* 5th ed. Ames, IA: Iowa State University Institute for Social and Behavioral Research.

Nadel, Emily L., and Terence P. Thornberry. 2017. Intergenerational consequences of adolescent substance use: Patterns of homotypic and heterotypic continuity. *Psychology of Addictive Behaviors* 31:200–211.

Patterson, Gerald R. 1993. Orderly change in a stable world: The antisocial trait as a chimera. *Journal of Consulting and Clinical Psychology* 61:911–919.

Pogarsky, Greg, Terence P. Thornberry, and Alan J. Lizotte. 2006. Developmental outcomes for children of young mothers. *Journal of Marriage and Family* 68:332–344.

Prinzie, Peter, and Patrick Onghena. 2005. Cohort sequential design. In *Encyclopedia of Statistics in Behavioral Science*, edited by B. S. Everitt and D. C. Howell. Chichester, UK: John Wiley & Sons.

Raudenbush, Stephen W., and Anthony S. Bryk. 2002. *Hierarchical Linear Models: Applications and Data Analysis Methods.* 2nd ed. Newbury Park, CA: Sage.

Smith, Carolyn A., Timothy O. Ireland, Aely Park, Laura Elwyn, and Terence P. Thornberry. 2011. Intergenerational continuities and discontinuities in intimate partner violence: A two generational prospective study. *Journal of Interpersonal Violence* 26:3720–3752.

Thornberry, Terence P. 1987. Toward an interactional theory of delinquency. *Criminology* 25:863–891.

Thornberry, Terence P. 2005. Explaining multiple patterns of offending across the life course and across generations. *The Annals of the American Academy of Political and Social Science* 602:156–195.

Thornberry, Terence P. 2009. The apple doesn't fall far from the tree (or does it?): Intergenerational patterns of antisocial behavior. *Criminology* 47:297–325.

Thornberry, Terence P. 2016. Three generation studies: Methodological challenges and promise. In *Handbook of the Life Course*, edited by M. J. Shanahan, J. T. Mortimer and M. Kirkpatrick. Johnson: Springer International Publishing.

Thornberry, Terence P. 2017. Explaining intergenerational resilience: Why children do not necessarily follow in the delinquent footsteps of their parents. In *Liber Amicorum Gerben Bruinsma*, edited by C. Bijleveld and P. van der Laan. Den Haag: Boom Criminologie.

Thornberry, Terence P., Adrienne Freeman-Gallant, Alan J. Lizotte, Marvin D. Krohn, and Carolyn A. Smith. 2003a. Linked lives: The intergenerational transmission of antisocial behavior. *Journal of Abnormal Child Psychology* 31:171–184.

Thornberry, Terence P., Adrienne Freeman-Gallant, and Peter J. Lovegrove. 2009a. The impact of parental stressors on the intergenerational transmission of antisocial behavior. *Journal of Youth and Adolescence* 38:312–322.

Thornberry, Terence P., Adrienne Freeman-Gallant, and Peter J. Lovegrove. 2009b. Intergenerational linkages in antisocial behavior. *Criminal Behaviour and Mental Health* 19:80–93.

Thornberry, Terence P., and Kimberly L. Henry. 2013. Intergenerational continuity in maltreatment. *Journal of Abnormal Child Psychology* 41:555–569.

Thornberry, Terence P., Kimberly L. Henry, Carolyn A. Smith, Timothy O. Ireland, Sarah J. Greenman, and Rosalyn D. Lee. 2013. Breaking the cycle of maltreatment: The role of safe, stable, and nurturing relationships. *Journal of Adolescent Health* 53:S25–S31.

Thornberry, Terence P., and Marvin D. Krohn. 2005. Applying interactional theory to the explanation of continuity and change in antisocial behavior. In *Integrated Developmental and Life-Course Theories of Offending*, edited by D. P. Farrington. New Brunswick, NJ: Transaction Publishers.

Thornberry, Terence P., and Marvin D. Krohn. Forthcoming. Interactional theory: An overview. In *The Oxford Handbook on Developmental and Life-Course Criminology*, edited by D. P. Farrington, L. Kazemian and A. R. Piquero. Oxford: Oxford University Press.

Thornberry, Terence P., Marvin D. Krohn, and Adrienne Freeman-Gallant. 2006. Intergenerational roots of early onset substance use. *Journal of Drug Issues* 36:1–28.

Thornberry, Terence P., Marvin D. Krohn, Alan J. Lizotte, Carolyn A. Smith, and Kimberly Tobin. 2003b. *Gangs and Delinquency in Developmental Perspective*. New York: Cambridge University Press.

Thornberry, Terence P., Mauri Matsuda, Sarah J. Greenman, Megan Bears Augustyn, Kimberly L. Henry, Carolyn A. Smith, and Timothy O. Ireland. 2014. Adolescent risk factors for child maltreatment. *Child Abuse & Neglect* 38:706–722.

Chapter 12

First results of cross-generational (dis-)similarities between three CrimoC-generations

The relationship between experienced violent parenting practice, delinquency and own parenting style

Christina Bentrup

The Crime in the Modern City Study

Background, general design and the possibility of intergenerational research

Crime in the Modern City (CrimoC) is a prospective panel study that began in 2002, surveying 7th-grade pupils from public schools in the German city of Duisburg. It was initiated by Klaus Boers and Jost Reinecke. The self-report questionnaire study had the original goal of explaining and monitoring the emergence and development of deviant and delinquent styles of behaviour throughout the phase of adolescence (Seddig and Reinecke 2017; Reinecke et al. 2015). As possible causes of these phenomena, the study focuses not only on structural conditions and processes on the macro-level, for example, the effects of social milieus, moral orientations, lifestyle, how spare time is spent, consumer attitudes and the effects of the social surroundings (Kanz 2016), but also on individual processes which are embedded in different action theories, such as theories of planned actions and cognitive emotional theories. Furthermore, the theoretical concept of the study includes social control, which can be located on the meso-level between the structural components of the macro-level and the action theories on the micro-level. This is, on the one hand, the formal social control by the police and the judiciary which defines what should be considered as delinquent behaviour in the first place. On the other hand, it is the informal control by school (Theimann 2016), peers and parents who, at the same time, function as authorities for socialization (Bentrup 2014; Seddig 2014, 2015). This approach makes it possible to trace processes on the individual level for each survey instead of merely being able to provide details on the aggregate level (detailed information about the study can be obtained from the webpage www.crimoc.org).

Due to the satisfying re-interview rates, and the successful panel construction, the German Research Foundation (*Deutsche Forschungsgemeinschaft*, DFG) has extended its funding in three-year intervals up to now. The establishment of an intergenerational self-report study was never the original goal of the project. Rather, the possibility emerged over the last 15 years of research for the simple reason that the respondents have now reached an average age of 26 and some of them are meanwhile raising their own family. The questionnaire has been adjusted to these circumstances.

The possibilities of intergenerational analysis are restricted to the transmission of parenting styles. During the second wave, respondents were retrospectively asked to report their experienced parenting style before age 12 (G1–G2). From age 13 up to age 18, they reported their experienced parenting practices during adolescence annually (G1–G2). Since 2009, when the respondents were on average 20 years old, questions about their own family status and structure have been included. Since 2011, all respondents who report having at least one child of their own are asked about their own parenting practices (G2–G3). Currently, the study covers data from 4,076 respondents from age 13 to age 26 who have participated in at least 2 of the 11 waves of data collection (see Figure 12.1).

One important limitation of the reported results is the fact that CrimoC is a single-respondent study. The reported measures refer to a total of three generations but all information has been provided by G2 respondents. Nevertheless, CrimoC offers the rare opportunity to carry out intergenerational research completely based on self-reported (instead of official) data which has been collected annually until G2 respondents were on average 20 years old. After that, the interval was changed to a two-year period. Furthermore, the

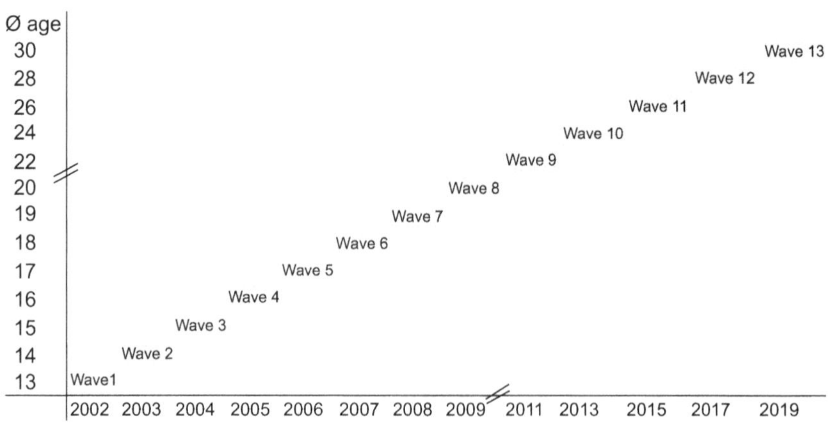

Figure 12.1 CrimoC survey design

annual re-interviewing allows the development of typical behavioural patterns over time. On the other hand, the single respondent's self-report has one main disadvantage: Conceivably, an individual is more willing to talk about one's own maltreatment victimisation than to admit conducting violence against the own children (Ball 2009; Herrenkohl et al. 1983; Heyman and Smith Slep 2002; Ney 1988; Tutty 1999).

Data collection, representativeness and challenges

The longitudinal self-report panel design evoked three major challenges: respondents' retrieval after age-related school leaving despite the assurance of anonymous answers, which includes a lot of research regarding new addresses and name changes; the necessity of different data collection modes; and the linkage of the individual data over time by simultaneous assurance of response anonymity.

At the beginning of the study the researchers attempted to collect data from all 7th graders in all schools of Duisburg, an industrial city in the Rhine-Ruhr-Area with a long tradition in coal mining. In Germany, there are five different types of schools (that follow elementary school): (1) the *Hauptschule*, a school with a lower level of education which ends after grade 9; (2) the *Realschule*, a medium-level school which ends after grade 10; (3) the *Gymnasium*, the highest educational level which ended for our cohort after grade 13;[1] (4) the *Gesamtschule*, a combination of *Realschule* and *Gymnasium* which enables more pupils to achieve a higher educational level; and (5) the *Förderschule* where pupils with learning disabilities receive special support.

The 56 schools in Duisburg include 20 Hauptschulen, 8 Realschulen, 13 Gesamtschulen, 13 Gymnasien and 2 Förderschulen. Of these schools, 16 refused to participate (5 Hauptschulen, 2 Realschulen, 4 Gesamtschulen und 5 Gymnasien). In the second data collection year in 2003, two Gymnasien and one Gesamtschule left the survey but could be replaced by two new schools (one Gymnasium and one Hauptschule). All of these schools participate in the survey at all possible points of time during school years. One school which rejected participation in the second wave could be re-activated in 2004.

The progress of data collection was adjusted to the age and life stage of the respondents. The first four waves took place in the school context while the next waves of data collection were used for a stepwise change into a postal mode. Compared to the official school statistics of Duisburg, the initial sample was, except for minor differences, representative for all 7th graders in 2002 regarding gender and school type. In the following years the representativeness compared to the grades remained. After the respondents left school, it was no longer possible to compare the sample structure with any officially registered data.

In order to be able to contact the participants after leaving their schools, all respondents were asked to share their addresses (independent of the completed questionnaire). The resulting contact database was updated within each of the following data collections. If participants changed their residence, they had the possibility to communicate the new address to the project team via the project's webpage. Respondents who did not report their new residence were searched in local registers of residence. After every postal data collection an additional face-to-face interviewing phase was carried out for all contacts in the database who did not participate in the actual wave. This can be executed despite the assurance of anonymity because all participants filled out a separate address card to receive an incentive of 25 Euro for participation.

Panel construction, attrition and datasets

Due to the serious content of the questionnaire the questioning procedure takes place under assurance of anonymity. An anonymised and over-time established code-oriented, hierarchical approach is used for classifying the questionnaires throughout the individual rounds of the survey. For this purpose, the participating youths fill out a personal code each year, which is requested in the questionnaire. This code includes time-invariant characteristics such as the first letter of the mothers' name and the last letter of the natural hair colour.

Experience has shown, however, that the reproduction of the code does not work perfectly. For this reason, a stepwise procedure of panel construction was established. Nevertheless, this complex and time-consuming procedure is not able to match all cases of an actual wave to the panel dataset and this attrition is unfortunately not random. The only alternative, however, would have been a matching procedure by using the respondents' names. Experiences in thematically comparable German studies have shown that this would result in an attrition of more than 40 per cent during the first data collection (Böttger et al. 2003: 43).

The panel dataset includes information about 4,076 respondents from age 13 to age 26 who have participated in at least 2 of the 11 waves. One-fifth have a Turkish migration background, nearly one-tenth an Eastern European background. Due to the anonymous individual codes and the typical problems of attainability over a period of 13 years, some respondents could not be re-interviewed or matched to the panel dataset. The complex study design necessitates a closer look at the different datasets. First, one has to distinguish between different terms: the cross-sectional datasets, which include all individuals who filled out a questionnaire during a data collection wave. Second, there are the complete panel datasets which contain only those respondents who have participated any time during the period of interest and which could be successfully connected to the previous individual data. Third, one can use panel data sets with missing units, which include all cases with a tolerated number of missing units.

The study started in 2002 with a survey of the initial population of 3,411 7th-grade pupils in Duisburg. In the following years, the cross-sectional re-interviewing rates ranged between 85 and 92 per cent (2003 n = 3,392; 2004 n = 3,339; 2005 n = 3,243; 2006 n = 4,548;[2] 2007 n = 3,336; 2008 n = 3,086; 2009 n = 3,090; 2011 n = 3,050; 2013 n = 2,850; 2015 n = 2,754). The proportion of males varies between 50 and 43 per cent. The complete panel dataset from 2002 to 2015 with no missing units includes 832 cases, with 33 per cent males. In contrast, the largest panel dataset from 2002 to 2015 with at least two participations includes 4,076 cases with 49.6 per cent males. Additionally, this dataset includes 497 respondents who reported having at least one child of their own.

The reported results are based on the panel data of all respondents who participated at least three times during the five waves from 2003 to 2007. This time span covers age 14 up to age 18. The dataset consists of 3,164 cases with 47.41 per cent male and a total of 445 parents; 51.20 per cent of the respondents participated in every data collection, 29.17 per cent have one missing point in time and 19.63 per cent two missing participations. Missing values are handled with the full information maximum likelihood (FIML) estimator (Enders 2001).

Compared to the total sample, the subpopulation of parents has a lower level of education. While the largest proportion of individuals in the sample have a higher education entrance qualification, the majority of parents have only a general certificate of secondary education and seldom a higher qualification. Another important difference between parents and the total sample is found for family status. While 79.90 per cent of all respondents reported to be unmarried, only 39.59 per cent of the parents belong to this category. Most of the parents are married (56.85 per cent), while the proportion of married respondents in the total sample is only 18.92 per cent. Of the unmarried respondents, 82.62 per cent reported a stable partnership. The average age of the oldest child is 2.97 years, the age range is from 0 to 12 years and the modal value is age 0.

First intergenerational results of CrimoC

Violent parenting styles: an analysis of comorbidity and heterotypic continuity

At the moment, the analysis can only refer to the transmission of parenting styles. The transmission of violence from one generation to the next is a widely discussed phenomenon. One perspective is the *cycle of maltreatment* (e.g., Conger et al. 2009; Putallaz et al. 1998) which focuses on the transmission of maltreatment in terms of victimisation experiences and later perpetration. The *cycle of violence* (Widom 1989a, 1989b) posits that experiences of maltreatment by one's parents lead to violent behavioural patterns against one's own children. The broader intergenerational hypothesis includes other behaviours which are distinct but theoretically related to child maltreatment, such as violence, violent delinquency (e.g., Heyman and Smith Slep 2002; Milaniak and Widom 2015; van der Put et al. 2015), delinquency in general (e.g., Jung et al. 2015;

Snyder and Smith 2015), partner violence (e.g., Abramovaite et al. 2015; Bevan and Higgins 2002; Pollak 2004) and/or victimisation (e.g., Weir and Kaukinen 2015; Widom et al. 2014).

In this chapter, the intergenerational transmission of violent parenting practices across generations will be analysed in view of *comorbidity* and *heterotypic continuity* in terms of delinquency. In Germany, parents are not allowed to practice any violent parenting style towards their children. Section 1631(2) of the German Federal Regulation (BGB) determines that children have a right to non-violent parenting. Physical punishments, mental injuries and other degrading measures are prohibited. Nevertheless, it is nearly impossible to compare the self-report results with official data because physicians are subject to medical confidentiality, and they can decide themselves whether they report a maltreatment suspicion. This choice leads to very low reports of suspicions.

In this first step of the analyses, the question is examined as to whether a transmission process can be observed in general. Therefore, *comorbidity* of violent parenting practices across the generations is analysed. Additionally, the relationship between experienced violent parenting and G2's involvement in delinquent behaviour is considered for the detection of *heterotypic continuity* of behavioural overlaps. The argument for the assumed relationship is not new. Widom (1989a, 1989b) notes that the cycle of violence has recently been used more broadly to represent hypotheses concerning various consequences of child maltreatment, including delinquent and criminal behaviour in general (also Smith et al. 2012; Smith and Thornberry 1995; Zingraff et al. 1993; Jung et al. 2015; Snyder and Smith 2015). The findings of these studies support the assumption.

Operationalisation, analytical strategy and applied methods

From age 13 to age 19, the CrimoC questionnaire includes items for different kinds of experienced parenting practices. From age 22 onwards, the same items are used to evaluate the parenting practices of respondents who already have children of their own. In the logic of the intergenerational perspective respondents of the initial sample cover G2, their parents G1 and the children of G2 the G3. Additionally, G2's delinquent behaviour is measured over the entire period of time.

Violent parenting practice G1 towards G2 during childhood: Six items measure the experienced violent parenting practice by G1 during the respondents' childhood (before age 12). This retrospective measurement was included in the questionnaire in wave 2. The items refer to the Conflict Tactic Scale (CTS; Straus 1979, 1983; Straus et al. 1980). The items include being punched/pushed, choked, battered, kicked, threatened with a weapon or other instruments and/or beaten. The response categories include whether the behaviour occurs (0) never, (1) seldom, (2) sometimes, (3) often or (4) very often up to age 12. According to Straus et al. (1980), one can distinguish between mild and severe modes of physical punishment. Mild forms of violent parenting experiences are being pushed or beaten. Severe maltreatment includes being choked, battered, kicked or hurt with a weapon.

Violent parenting practice G1 towards G2: The same six items measure the experienced violent parenting practice by G1 during the respondents' youth (ages 14–17). For each behaviour, respondents are asked whether their mother or father practiced the respective violent behaviour (0) never, (1) seldom, (2) sometimes, (3) often or (4) very often during the previous 12 months. An additive index is calculated for each point in time with a possible range from 0 up to 24.

Violent parenting practice G2 on G3: Since 2011 (age 22) respondents are asked about their own children and their own parenting practices towards the G3 children. The measurement of self-reported violent parenting practice includes the same items as the scale for the experienced violence by G1. The individuals with at least one child of their own are asked how often they practiced the six behaviours during the previous 12 months. An additive index is composed for all parents. This score is available for all respondents with at least one child of their own in 2015 and includes 445 individuals in the chosen dataset. In 2015, 357 of them responded to the parenting practice scale, with an additional 88 respondents in 2013 or in 2011 but not in 2015.

It is important to consider that the same scale is used for victimisation as well as for perpetration and also for different age groups. While the initial G2 sample has a homogenous age structure, G3's age structure is much more heterogeneous and many of the G3 children are still very young. Therefore, the question must be asked if all asked physical punishments are comparable, feasible and realistic at an early age. The complete scale includes items for the measurement of empathic, prohibitive, violent, empathic and contradictory parenting styles. Many studies in violent parenting practices have applied the CTS (e.g., Ball 2009; Bartlett and Easterbrooks 2012; Caliso and Milner 1992; Coohey et al. 1997).

Delinquency measurement: Delinquency is a composite measure and consists of annually self-reported prevalence rates for 15 offenses from different offense categories (property, vandalism and violent offenses). The reported prevalence rates are summed for each wave and have a range from 0 to 15. Although the mean values of reported offenses are quite low (range over time between 0.83 and 0.06), the typical age-related development of offending with its peak at age 14 and a constant decrease can be observed for the total sample.

It is analysed whether violent parenting practices of the first generation (G1) towards their offspring (G2) during childhood and/or adolescence have an impact on G2's own parenting practice towards their offspring (*comorbidity*). In a second step, *heterotypic continuity* is tested for the relationship between experienced violent parenting and delinquency during adolescence. Finally, these different pathways are linked to G2's own violent parenting style towards G3. In sum, it is assumed that intergenerational transmission processes can theoretically take place at different points in time and across different but theoretically related

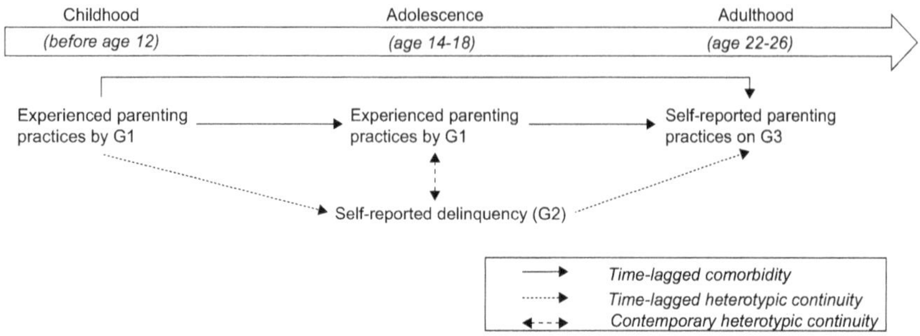

Figure 12.2 Analytical strategy

behaviours. The resulting developmental patterns for the different behaviours and different life stages are related to each other by calculating transmission rates by cross-tabs and dual trajectories (Figure 12.2).

This *dual trajectory approach* (also joint trajectory approach, Nagin and Tremblay 1999, 2001, 2005, critically Sampson and Laub 2005) offers the opportunity to detect relationships between typical behavioural patterns in the longitudinal data. Therefore, separate latent class growth analyses (LCGA; Nagin and Land 1993; Nagin 1999; Reinecke 2006, 2012; Reinecke and Weins 2013; Roeder et al. 1999; Seddig and Reinecke 2017) were evaluated for the pathways of the behaviours of interest (*here* experienced violent parenting, delinquent behaviour and own violent parenting styles).

The dual trajectory approach makes it possible to describe a relationship between time series for two different behaviours, which is tantamount to the simultaneous estimation of two LCGAs. It is based on individual developments (intra- and inter-individual changes) over time. The key outcomes of a dual trajectory approach are the likelihood of belonging to a special trajectory for one behaviour and separately for the second behaviour, as well as a table with the joint and conditional probabilities for the possible combinations between the trajectories of both behaviours. This strategy allows the estimation of individual developments and behavioural overlaps in the manifestation of similarities or dissimilarities over time.[3,4]

Results

Do violent parenting experiences beget violent parenting perpetration?

On the one hand, violent parenting practices can be deterministically classified as mild or severe violent parenting and, on the other hand, a score can be computed for each point in time which can be used for a probabilistic classification to detect typical patterns and developmental structures over time.

In our sample 21.07 per cent of the respondents reported at least one incident of physical punishment before age 12 (mild definition). The severe definition includes all cases with at least one time, sometimes, often or very often choked, battered, kicked or hurt with a weapon. These severe types of punishment were reported by 3.15 per cent of the respondents.

During adolescence, the findings show much higher victimisation rates: 65.52 per cent of the respondents reported at least one mild victimisation by their parents between ages 14 and 18, 21.05 per cent one or more severe incidents. Due to the tolerance of one missing participation, a total continuous CTS score is not feasible for the five points in time of adolescence. Instead of this, a LCGA is computed for the extent of physical punishment of G1 towards G2. The model evaluation indicates a six-class solution, which means that there are six typical developmental groups of individuals within the data.

Figure 12.3 depicts the shape of the optimal number of trajectories for the experienced parenting style during youth. Note that 34.42 per cent of the respondents have *no violent parenting experiences* during youth (n = 1,089). The second class includes 29.20 per cent of the sample (n = 924) and reflects a very *low level of violent parenting experiences* with an average lower 1 across all analysed waves. This means that the respondents belonging to this group have nearly no maltreatment experiences. The third group shows a *medium level of violent parenting* (10.15 per cent, n = 321). The fourth group, with 10.00 per cent of the respondents (n = 315), shows an increase of the violent parenting level. The fifth group shows the highest violent parenting level (8.94 per cent, n = 283) across all five dates of measurement although the extent of reported violent parenting experiences declines.

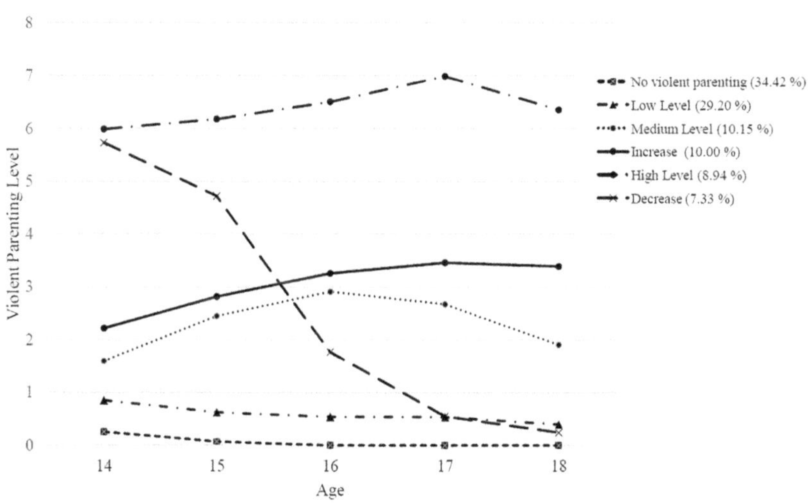

Figure 12.3 Trajectories of G1's violent parenting style towards G2

The trajectory of the sixth group includes 7.33 per cent of the respondents (n = 232) and describes a strong *decrease of violent parenting* experiences. These respondents report a comparatively high level of violence victimisation at the first point in time, followed by a steady decline. This developmental approach offers the opportunity to detect typical patterns of violent parenting practices during youth.

Regarding the behaviour of G2 towards G3, 24.19 per cent of the parents report at least one mild punishment, whereas only 2.53 per cent report a severe punishment towards their children. Even so, these rates are comparable to the self-reported experienced violent parenting practices up to age 12.

The next question to be answered now refers to the relationship between these separate findings: the intergenerational transmission.

The deterministic comparison of individuals with and without victimisation experiences by their parents and their own violent parenting style shows that neither a mild early experience nor a mild form of physical punishment during adolescence have a significant influence on mild or severe punishments towards G3 (Tables 12.1 and 12.2). For instance, 22.96 per cent of the individuals with no early violent experiences by their parents reported at least one mild maltreatment incident toward the child of their own, while those respondents with own experiences report a quite similar frequency (22.73 per cent). Only severe punishment experiences during childhood and/or adolescence have an impact on severe punishments towards G3 (χ^2 = 6.06, df1, p < .05, χ^2 = 5.43, df1, p < .05) but these results are difficult to interpret due to very low case numbers. The correlation between the sums of the CTS items for G2's experiences and the G2 perpetration is 0.07 and statistically not meaningful.

Table 12.1 G1–G2 violent parenting during childhood and G2–G3 violent parenting

G1–G2 Mild	*G2–G3 Mild*		*Total*	*G2–G3 Severe*		*Total*
	No	*Yes*		*No*	*Yes*	
No	198 (77.04%)	59 (22.96%)	257 (100.00%)	253 (98.44%)	4 (1.56%)	257 (100.00%)
Yes	51 (77.24%)	15 (22.73%)	66 (100.00%)	64 (96.97%)	2 (3.03%)	66 (100.00%)
Total	249 (77.09%)	74 (22.91%)	323 (100.00%)	317 (98.14%)	6 (1.86%)	323 (100.00%)
	χ^2 = 0.00, df1, p > .10			χ^2 = 0.63, df1, p > .10		
Severe						
No	243 (76.90%)	73 (23.10%)	316 (100.00%)	311 (98.42%)	5 (1.58%)	316 (100.00%)
Yes	6 (85.71%)	1 (14.29%)	7 (100.00%)	6 (85.71%)	1 (14.29%)	7 (100.00%)
Total	249 (77.09%)	74 (22.91%)	323 (100.00%)	317 (98.14%)	6 (1.86%)	323 (100.00%)
	χ^2 = 0.30, df1, p >.10			χ^2= 6.06, df1, p < .05		

Table 12.2 G1–G2 violent parenting during adolescence and G2–G3 violent parenting

G1–G2 Mild	*G2–G3 Mild*		*Total*	*G2–G3 Severe*		*Total*
	No	*Yes*		*No*	*Yes*	
No	110 (78.57%)	30 (21.43%)	140 (100.00%)	137 (97.86%)	3 (2.14%)	140 (100.00%)
Yes	219 (74.49%)	75 (25.51%)	294 (100.00%)	286 (97.28%)	8 (2.72%)	294 (100.00%)
Total	329 (75.81%)	105 (25.51%)	434 (100.00%)	423 (97.47%)	11 (2.53%)	434 (100.00%)
	$\chi^2 = 0.87$, df1, $p > .10$			$\chi^2 = 0.13$, df1, $p > .10$		
Severe						
No	254 (77.68%)	73 (22.32%)	327 (100.00%)	322 (98.47%)	5 (1.53%)	327 (100.00%)
Yes	75 (70.09%)	32 (29.91%)	107 (100.00%)	101 (94.39%)	6 (5.61%)	107 (100.00%)
Total	329 (75.81%)	105 (24.19%)	434 (100.00%)	423 (97.47%)	11 (2.53%)	434 (100.00%)
	$\chi^2 = 0.30$, df1, $p > .10$			$\chi^2 = 5.43$, df1, $p < .05$		

Due to the low extent of G2's reported severe punishments towards G3, the here reported transmission analysis is based on the mild parental violence definition. Therefore, every possible two-class combination of G2's violent parenting experiences during adolescence was compared to the likelihood of G3 victimisation. The chi-square test results are in line with the previously explained descriptive findings: Almost none of the class comparisons show significant differences in the risk of intergenerational continuity of maltreatment (see Table 12.3). Only individuals who belong to the *high violent parenting class* have a higher risk of practicing violent parenting styles towards their children of their own compared to the *no* and *low violent parenting* classes. In addition, respondents who belong to the *increase group* during youth are more likely to maltreat their own offspring than individuals of the *low violent parenting* group.

In sum, the results indicate that it makes sense to take a differentiated look at the phenomenon of the intergenerational transmission of parental punishments. Severe early childhood experiences seem to have an impact on this transmission. Interestingly, the impact of violent parenting experiences during youth depends on its pattern. Only the *high violent parenting class* as well as the *increase class* show a higher probability of intergenerational continuity of physical parental punishments towards their children.

Nevertheless, it is important to note that most respondents who received physical punishments by their parents do not use these practices towards their offspring. Of those individuals belonging to the *no violent parenting* class, 23.02 per cent reported at least a mild maltreatment towards G3, 18.49 per cent of the *low violent parenting* class, 22.22 per cent of the *medium violent parenting* class,

Table 12.3 G1–G2 violent parenting trajectories and G2–G3 violent parenting

G1–G2 Violent parenting class	*G2–G3 Mild*			*Significant* χ^2 *compared to class*
	No	*Yes*	*Total*	
1 No	107 (76.98%)	32 (23.02%)	139 (100.00%)	5**
2 Low level	97 (81.51%)	22 (18.49%)	119 (100.00%)	5**, 4*
3 Medium	42 (77.78%)	12 (22.22%)	54 (100.00%)	
4 Increase	31 (68.89%)	14 (31.11%)	45 (100.00%)	2*
5 High level	31 (64.58%)	17 (35.42%)	48 (100.00%)	1**, 2**
6 Decrease	21 (72.41%)	8 (27.59%)	29 (100.00%)	
Total	329 (75.80%)	105 (24.20%)	434 (100.00%)	

χ^2 = 6.98, df5, $p > .10$; * $p < .10$; ** $p < .05$.

27.59 per cent of the *decrease* class, 31.11 per cent of the *increase* class and, finally, 35.42 per cent of the *high level* class members.

Do violent parenting experiences beget other forms of antisocial behaviour?

This question is to be answered using the example of delinquency during youth. Therefore, in a first step, an LCGA is computed for the self-reported offenses between ages 14 and 18. The model evaluation suggests a five-class solution.

Figure 12.4 illustrates the shape of the five detected delinquency classes from ages 14 to 18. The largest group, with 58.34 per cent (n = 1,843), is the *low level class* which can be described by prevalence rates around zero. A *medium level* was reported by 24.72 per cent (adolescence limited, n = 782), with approximately one committed offense for each point in time. A third group shows the highest prevalence rate over time compared to the others. Nearly 7.33 per cent of the sample belong to this *high level group* (n = 232). One group with 1.58 per cent of the respondents (n = 50) started at a high delinquent level and *decreased* over time (early decliner). The fifth group, with 8.03 per cent (n = 254), started at a low level and *increased* up age 17 (late onset).

In the argumentation of heterotypic continuity, it is assumed that the extent of experienced violent parenting has an impact on the extent of delinquent involvement. In a first step, childhood victimisation of G1 towards G2 is related to the different class combinations of G2's juvenile offending. Due to the low

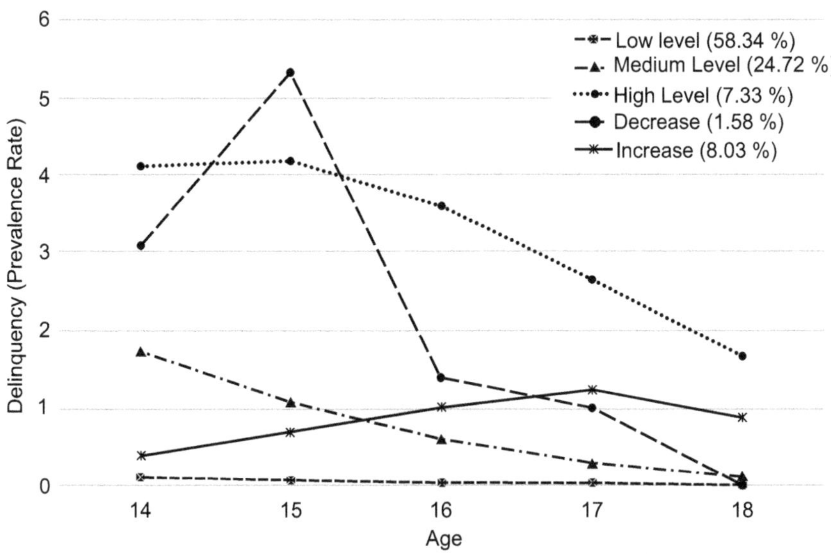

Figure 12.4 Trajectories of G2's delinquent involvement

Table 12.4 G1–G2 violent parenting during childhood and G2 delinquent trajectories

G1–G2 childhood: mild-	*Delinquency Class G2*					*Total*
	1 *Low level*	*2* *Medium*	*3* *High level*	*4* *Decrease*	*5* *Increase*	
No	1,213 (63.01%)	437 (22.70%)	106 (5.51%)	25 (1.30%)	144 (7.48%)	1,925 (100.00%)
Yes	244 (47.47%)	149 (28.99%)	57 (11.09%)	11 (2.14%)	53 (10.31%)	514 (100.00%)
Total	1,457 (59.74%)	586 (24.03%)	163 (6.68%)	36 (1.48%)	197 (8.08%)	2,439 (100.00%)
Sig. χ^2 compared to class	2**, 3**, 4**, 5**	1**, 3**	1**, 2**, 5**	1**	1**	

$\chi^2 = 47.97$, df4, $p < .05$; * $p < .10$; ** $p < .05$.

extent of severe maltreatment, the analysis focuses on every form of forbidden punishment (mild definition). Table 12.4 displays the frequencies and percentages of early childhood experience by delinquency class.

The cells of the table are highly correlated. Respondents in the *low level delinquency* class have, compared to all other delinquency classes, a lower probability of a parental maltreatment history during childhood. Individuals with a *high level delinquent* involvement have significantly more often a history of childhood maltreatment by their parents compared to all other classes except for the *decrease* class.

Finally, the previously reported G1–G2 violent parenting classes are linked to the G2 delinquency classes in a dual trajectory analyses. Table 12.5 displays the

Table 12.5 G1–G2 violent parenting trajectories and G2 delinquent trajectories during adolescence

G1–G2 Violent parenting	*G2 Delinquency*					*Total*
	1 Low	*2 Medium*	*3 High*	*4 Decrease*	*5 Increase*	
1 No	734	230	46	10	69	1,089
	67.40%	21.12%	4.22%	0.92%	6.34%	100.00%
	39.76%	29.41%	19.83%	20.00%	27.17%	34.42%
	23.20%	7.27%	1.45%	0.32%	2.18%	34.42%
2 Low level	563	222	53	11	75	924
	60.93%	24.03%	5.74%	1.19%	8.12%	100.00%
	30.50%	28.39%	22.84%	22.00%	29.53%	29.20%
	17.79%	7.02%	1.68%	0.35%	2.37%	29.20%
3 Medium	159	83	39	7	33	321
	40.53%	25.86%	12.15%	2.18%	10.28%	100.00%
	8.61%	10.61%	16.81%	14.00%	12.99%	10.15%
	5.03%	2.62%	1.23%	0.22%	1.04%	10.15%
4 Increase	175	73	31	9	27	315
	55.56%	23.17%	9.84%	2.86%	8.57%	100.00%
	9.48%	9.34%	13.36%	18.00%	10.63%	9.96%
	5.53%	2.31%	0.98%	0.28%	0.85%	9.96%
5 High level	108	88	45	5	37	283
	38.16%	31.10%	15.90%	1.77%	13.07%	100,00%
	5.85%	11.25%	19.40%	10.00%	14.57%	8.94%
	3.41%	2.78%	1.42%	0.16%	1.17%	8.94%
6 Decrease	107	86	18	8	13	232
	46.12%	37.07%	7.76%	3.45%	5.60%	100.00%
	5.80%	11.00%	7.76%	16.00%	5.12%	7.33%
	3.38%	2.72%	0.57%	0.25%	0.41%	7.33%
Total	1,846	782	232	50	254	3,164
	58.34%	24.72%	7.33%	1.58%	8.03%	100.00%
	100.00%	100.00%	100.00%	100.00%	100.00%	100.00%
	58.34%	24.72%	7.33%	1.58%	8.03%	100.00%

$\chi^2 = 160.70$, df20, $p < .05$.

results of the simultaneous estimation of the trajectories for both behavioural series. Every cell reports the *n* of the combined trajectories and the row, column and cell percentages.

The chi-square test shows a significant association between both the trajectories of both behaviours. A closer look at the frequencies supports the existence of a heterotypic behavioural overlap during adolescence between parental violence (G1–G2) and delinquent behaviour (G2). Respondents who have *not experienced violence* by their parents have a higher probability to belong to the *low level delinquency* class than all other individuals who belong to other violent parenting classes (67.40 per cent) and even a lower probability to belong to the *high level delinquency* class (4.22 per cent). On the contrary, only 38.16 per cent of the respondents of the *high level violent parenting* class belong to the *low level delinquency* class, whereas these individuals have a higher risk of belonging to the related *high level delinquency* class (15.90 per cent). A closer look at the single-class combinations makes clear that there are other relationships between the two types of behaviour for the other classes as well. Respondents who have nearly no experiences with parental violence have a decreased risk of belonging to the *high, decrease* or *increase delinquency* class, whereas nearly 85 per cent of these individuals belong to the *low* or *medium delinquency* level class. This extent decreases by belonging to the *medium violent parenting* class in which only 66 per cent belong to the *low* or *medium delinquency* class. This is a lesser proportion than for the *high level*, the *increase* and *decrease violent parenting* classes. The column percentages enhance these findings. Individuals in the *low delinquency* class are less likely to belong to the *medium, high, increase* or *decrease violent parenting* class. However, members of the *medium delinquency* class have a lower probability of *no violent parenting* experiences but an increased likelihood of belonging to the *decrease violent parenting* class. Interestingly, only 19.40 per cent of the *high level delinquency* trajectory belong to the *high level violent parenting* class. This is a quite similar likelihood as for belonging to the *no*, *low* or *medium violent parenting* class. The finding indicates a stronger influence of violent parenting on delinquency than of delinquency on violent parenting. Respondents who belong to the *decreasing delinquency* class have, compared to all other delinquency classes, the highest probability to belong to the *decrease violent parenting* class as well. The *increase delinquency* class shows no distinct relationships to the violent parenting classes.

Finally, the assumed relationship between belonging to a delinquency trajectory and an own violent parenting style differs between the identified groups (Table 12.6). Only the *low* and *medium level delinquency* class compared to the *high level* and *increase delinquent* trajectories differ significantly regarding the probability of practicing a violent parenting style. The differences are in the expected direction: a low probability of violent parenting for individuals belonging to the *low* and *medium level delinquency* classes and a higher probability for the *high level* and *increase delinquency* classes.

Table 12.6 G2 delinquent trajectories and G2–G3 violent parenting

G2 delinquency	*G2–G3 violent parenting mild*			*Sig.* χ^2 *compared to class*
	No	*Yes*	*Total*	
1 Low level	180 (77.59%)	52 (22.41%)	232 (100.00%)	3**, 5**
2 Medium level	90 (81.82%)	20 (18.18%)	110 (100.00%)	3**, 5**
3 High level	24 (60.00%)	16 (40.00%)	40 (100.00%)	1**, 2**
4 Decrease	8 (88.89%)	1 (11.11%)	9 (100.00%)[a]	
5 Increase	27 (62.79%)	16 (37.21%)	43 (100.00%)	1**, 2**
Total	329 (75.81%)	105 (24.19%)	434 (100.00%)	

χ^2 = 12.83; df4, p <.05; * p < .10; ** p < .05.
a Case numbers too small.

Discussion, theoretical integration and future plans

Discussion of the findings

The experience of violent parenting is one observed phenomenon in the large field of child maltreatment. Low case numbers, different sample selections and different operationalisations are the main issues concerning the validity and comparability of previous studies (see Dubow et al. 2003; Conger et al. 2009). A longitudinal, developmental approach for the intergenerational transmission of violent parenting (*comorbidity*) or of other related behaviours (*heterotypic continuity*) was not found in the literature. For this reason, the reported findings are discussed with regard to other intergenerational studies in which either violent parenting is not only measured for childhood but also for adolescence or which included delinquency or aggression as a behaviour related to violent parenting.

However, even if researchers have reached a relative consensus that experiences of maltreatment are a risk factor for violent conduct against one's own children, the results for the strength of the transmission rate of maltreatment experiences in general (6.7 to 70.0 per cent, Berzenski et al. 2014: 115; Schofield et al. 2013), as well as the maltreatment definitions and operationalisations, differ enormously (for a discussion: Schelbe and Geiger 2017: 2ff.; Heyman and Slep 2002). While some researchers have reported modest to moderate intergenerational transmission rates regarding the relationship between parental violence across generations (Cairns et al. 1998; Capaldi and Clark 1998; Serbin et al. 1998), other studies reported that parenting is an important factor in this transmission process (Capaldi, Pears et al. 2003; Conger et al. 2003; Hops et al. 2003; Thornberry et al. 2003). The methodological difference between these studies is the number of generations. While the first studies included two generations, the later included three generations (see Dubow et al. 2003). However, only weak support can be found in the here reported analyses for the intergenerational transmission of comorbidity for violent parenting practices. Even though the low number of cases suggests a cautious interpretation, the results indicate that G1's severe punishment during G2's childhood as well as during adolescence has an influence on G2's severe maltreatment practices towards G3. These indifferent results are in line with Thornberry and Henry (2013) who found support for different impacts of different patterns of maltreatment. Their results indicate that a childhood-limited maltreatment is no predictor for the intergenerational transmission, whereas maltreatment that occurs in adolescence or that begins in childhood and persists into adolescence does.

For testing different impacts of different developments of violent parenting during the life-course, a developmental approach detected six typical trajectories of violent parenting experiences during adolescence. The results indicate that G2's belonging to the *high violent parenting* victimisation class increases the risk of G2's own violent parenting style compared to members of the *no* or *low violent parenting* class. This approach refers to the conclusions of Doumas et al. (1994) and Dixon et al. (2009) who found different impacts on different patterns of maltreatment, although they focused on more deterministic patterns such as gender or the differentiation between cycle breakers, initiators and maintainers. The combination of two LCGAs within a dual trajectory analysis enables the consideration of individual developments during the life-course (Rivera and Fincham 2015). In contrast to nearly all recent studies, individuals are not deterministically matched to a group of maltreated individuals but probabilistically matched to long-term maltreatment patterns. This practice allows the examination of individual changes over time.

Delinquency as an example for heterotypic continuity was examined by Smith and Thornberry (1995) even if maltreatment was a binary measurement of whether an individual had an official record of maltreatment or not. The results were not distinct and differ by frequency, seriousness and type of offenses; 'the more extensively maltreated subjects, however, consistently exhibited the highest rates of delinquency' (Smith and Thornberry 1995: 469). A different influence of childhood-limited and adolescence maltreatment was found in the Rochester Youth Development Study by Thornberry et al. (2010). Childhood-limited experiences were significantly related to internalising problems while adolescence maltreatment had a broader influence on later problem behaviours such as delinquency, drug use and alcohol use. Zingraff et al. used official data for both measurements and come to the conclusion that 'maltreatment did not present significant special risks for property or violent offenses' (1993: 196).

Kruttschnitt and Dornfeld (1993) examined a clinical sample of children of abused women and a community sample with retrospectively self-report measures of delinquency. Their results are in line with the here reported findings: they suggest a larger delinquent involvement for children who experienced family violence.

In this chapter, the results of analysis of heterotypic continuity are more definite. Respondents with violent parenting experiences are more likely to be involved in delinquent behaviour independent of the point in time or extent of the maltreatment experience. The dual trajectory approach simultaneously compared patterns of violent parenting and patterns of delinquent involvement. The results indicate that violent parenting during adolescence and delinquent involvement are strongly related and that this influence is even stronger than for early childhood violent parenting experiences. These results are in line with previous findings. Brezina (1998), Capaldi, Conger et al. (2003), Thornberry et al. (2001) and Fagan (2005) demonstrate this relationship as well, but all authors emphasise the need of further research of this relationship with a special view on mediating factors (e.g., social stress, deprivation, alcohol and drugs). In a methodological discussion of intergenerational findings between parenting and child externalising behaviour, Dubow et al. (2003) focused on the direction of the causal relationships between parenting and antisocial behaviour. Their findings suggest that G2's antisocial behaviour can also influence G1's parenting practices.

Theoretical integration

No one would argue that there are no underlying explanatory processes for the transmission. In the large field of intergenerational research different theoretical argumentations have tried to understand these underlying processes which cause the intergenerational transmission.

Some researchers have used multifactorial designs to explain the transmission (Deblinger et al. 1993; DiLillo et al. 2000; Dixon et al. 2005; Frias-Armenta 2002; Pears and Capaldi 2001; Schelbe and Geiger 2017; Sidebotham and Golding 2001); others have tried to transform theoretical concepts into an intergenerational perspective (for an overview of the integration of social learning theory, social information processing theory, attachment theory and ecological models, see Schelbe and Geiger 2017: 15–24).

A developmental extension of social learning theories seems to be a promising approach. Previous findings suggest that the transmission can be seen as a result of socialization, social learning and social environment (Berlin et al. 2011; Muller et al. 1995). In a developmental social learning perspective the factor time becomes important. The influence of parents towards their offspring changes over the life-course. During childhood, the children are to large extent physically and emotionally dependent on their parents. In most families, the parents are the first socialisation institution where the learning of values and norms (*definitions*, Sutherland 1947; Burgess and Akers 1966) takes place. In the argumentation of social learning, violent parenting can function as a role model for the violence itself (*imitation*, Burgess and Akers 1966; Bandura 1969, 1977; Akers 1998) and also as a kind of reinforcement to gain acceptance (*reinforcement*, Burgess and Akers 1966; Bandura 1971). During adolescence the extent of dependency becomes weaker while other social associations such as peers and school and later partner and work become more influential for one's own attitudes. These contacts differ between individuals and contexts (*differential association*, Sutherland 1947; Burgess and Akers 1966; Akers 1998). This perspective enables the understanding of continuity and discontinuity of violent parenting and related behaviours. Additionally, according to Dubow et al. (2003), the reinforcement processes between parents and their offspring can be reciprocal. This means that the behavior of G2 can also reinforce the parenting practice of G1.

For this reason, different developments of life-courses can be observed and it should be considered that there might be different causes for transmission processes. Cicchetti and Barnett (1991: 359) state 'Not surprisingly, there is no specific single pattern exhibited by maltreated children that can be described as the profile of abuse and neglect.' A qualitative study about very young mothers and violent parenting was carried out by Bartlett and Easterbrooks. They emphasise that 'nuanced descriptions of their childhood histories are essential for understanding the cycles of maltreatment' (Bartlett and Easterbrooks 2012: 2164). Additionally, the social structure–social learning extension by Akers (1998) offers the opportunity to include the socio-economic status. Social and economic stressors have been important control variables in previous intergenerational research (see Kaufman and Zigler 1987; Smith and Thornberry 1995; Widom 1989b).

Future plans

The next step of analysis will include the developmental social learning perspective and will try to figure out the individual pathways of continuity and discontinuity across generations. Therefore, funding will be requested for surveying the G3 children within a new prospective self-reported panel-cohort. Currently, the 12th data collection has been completed. The actual 2017 questionnaire includes a Social Behavior Questionnaire (SBQ; Tremblay et al. 1992) for the evaluation of G3's antisocial behaviour. This data enables the direct comparison of G2's delinquent involvement and G3's antisocial behaviour.

Although the examination of the next generation within the CrimoC study is still at the very beginning, the large sample size, the self-report panel design, the detailed information about G2 over the last 13 years and the chance to switch to a multi-respondent study by directly surveying the G3 individuals offer great opportunities in understanding intergenerational transmission processes.

Notes

1 The Gymnasium and Gesamtschule end after grade 12.
2 The data collection in the year 2006 was the most challenging one. Due to the school leave of respondents in the lower educational level schools and the compulsory school attendance for all adolescents up to age 18, the attempt was made to retrieve these school-leavers in selected classes at vocational schools. A consequence was that the cross-sectional data includes additional cases of individuals who attended these classes but who had not participated before. These additional cases have no impact on the panel-dataset because they could not be matched to previous cases.
3 The parenting scores as well as the delinquency scores do not show a normal distribution and all scores have many zeros (no violent parenting, no delinquent behaviour). For that reason, previous analyses tested the distribution and different numbers of classes. Three different distributional assumptions were compared: the normal distribution, a Poisson model and a negative binomial distribution. Due to the large number of zeros, additional inflation parts have been estimated for the Poisson and the negative binomial models. The inflated negative binomial model gives a better representation of the data in all model variants. Therefore, further analyses will focus on LCGA assuming the inflated negative binomial distribution.
4 The optimal number of classes can be determined by the comparison of the fit indices like the Akaike Information Criterion (AIC; Akaike 1987), the Bayesian Information Criterion (BIC; Schwarz 1978), adjusted BIC (ad. BIC; Yang 1998) and the Lo, Mendell and Rubin likelihood ratio test (LMR-LRT; Lo, Mendell and Rubin 2001) between the models which are all available in the used statistics programme Mplus (Muthén and Muthén 1998–2015, for a discussion, see Nyland et al. 2007). While the AIC, BIC, and ad. BIC are more or less descriptive, and usually the model with the lowest score should be accepted, the LMR-LRT provides a test for the model variant with $k-1$ classes against the model with k-classes. The p-value from the test refers to the probability that the model is sufficient with one less class (Reinecke 2006: 105). The full information maximum likelihood estimator (FIML) was used to handle missing values (Enders 2001).

References

Abramovaite, J., Bandyopadhyay, S. and Dixon, L. (2015) 'The dynamics of intergenerational family abuse: A focus on child maltreatment and violence and abuse in intimate relationships', *Journal of Interdisciplinary Economics*, 27: 160–174.

Akaike, H. (1987) 'Factor analysis and the AIC', *Psychometrika*, 52: 317–332.

Akers, R.L. (1998) *Social learning and social structure: A general theory of crime and deviance*, Boston: Northeastern University Press.

Ball, J.D. (2009) 'Intergenerational transmission of abuse of incarcerated fathers: A study of the measurement of abuse', *Journal of Family Issues*, 30: 371–390.

Bandura, A. (1969) *Principles of behavior modification*, New York: Holt, Rinehart & Winston.

——— (1971) 'Vicarious and self-reinforcement processes', in D. Glaser (ed.) *The nature of reinforcement*, Columbus: Merril.

——— (1977) *Social learning theory*, Englewood Cliffs: Prentice Hall.

Bartlett, J.D. and Easterbrooks, M.A. (2012) 'Links between physical abuse in childhood and child neglect among adolescent mothers', *Children and Youth Services Review*, 34: 2164–2169.

Bentrup, C. (2014) *Social learning and juvenile delinquency (Lernprozesse und Jugenddelinquenz)*, Muenster: Waxmann.

Berlin, L.J., Appleyard, K. and Dodge, K.A. (2011) 'Intergenerational continuity in child maltreatment: Mediating mechanisms and implications for prevention', *Child Development*, 82: 162–176.

Berzenski, S.R., Yates, T.M. and Egeland, B. (2014) 'A Multidimensional view of continuity in intergenerational transmission of child maltreatment', in J.E. Korbin and R.D. Krugman (eds.) *Handbook of child maltreatment*, Dordrecht: Springer.

Bevan, E. and Higgins, D.J. (2002) 'Is domestic violence learned? The contribution of five forms of child maltreatment to men's violence and adjustment', *Journal of Family Violence*, 7: 223–245.

Böttger, A., Ehret, B., Othold, F., Prein, G., Schumann, K.F. and Seus, L. (2003) 'Methoden der Untersuchung', in K.F. Schumann (ed.) *Delinquenz im Lebensverlauf. Eine Längsschnittstudie zum Übergang von der Schule in den Beruf bei ehemaligen Hauptschülern*, Weinheim: Juventa.

Brezina, T. (1998) 'Adolescent maltreatment and delinquency: The question of intervening processes', *Journal of Research in Crime and Delinquency*, 35: 71–99.

Burgess, R.L. and Akers, R.L. (1966) 'A differential association-reinforcement theory of criminal behavior', *Social Problems*, 14: 128–147.

Cairns, R.B., Cairns, B.D., Xie, H., Leung, M.-C. and Hearne, S. (1998) 'Paths across generations: Academic competence and aggressive behaviors in young mothers and their children', *Developmental Psychology*, 34: 1162–1174.

Caliso, J.A. and Milner, J.S. (1992) 'Childhood history of abuse and child abuse screening', *Child Abuse and Neglect*, 16: 647–659.

Capaldi, D.M. and Clark, S. (1998) 'Prospective family predictors of aggression toward female partners for at-risk young men', *Developmental Psychology*, 34: 1175–1188.

Capaldi, D.M., Conger, R.D., Hops, H. and Thornberry, T.P. (2003) 'Introduction to special section on three-generation studies', *Journal of Abnormal Child Psychology*, 31: 123–125.

Capaldi, D.M., Pears, K.C., Patterson, G.R. and Owen, Lee D. (2003) 'Continuity of parenting practices across generations in an at-risk-sample: A prospective comparison of direct and mediated associations', *Journal of Abnormal Child Psychology*, 31: 127–142.

Cicchetti, D. and Barnett, D. (1991) 'Toward the development of a scientific nosology of child maltreatment', in W. Grover and D. Cicchetti (eds.) *Thinking clearly about psychology: Essays in honor of Paul E. Meehl, Vol.2: Personality and psychopathology*, Minneapolis: University of Minnesota Press.

Conger, R.D., Belsky, J. and Capaldi, D.M. (2009) 'The intergenerational transmission of parenting: Closing comments for the special section', *Developmental Psychology*, 45: 1276–1283.

Conger, R.D., Neppl, T., Kim, K.J. and Scaramella, L. (2003) 'Angry and aggressive behavior across three generations: A prospective, longitudinal study of parents and children', *Journal of Abnormal Child Psychology*, 31: 143–160.

Coohey, C. and Braun, N. (1997) 'Toward an integrated framework for understanding child physical abuse', *Child Abuse & Neglect*, 21: 1081–1094.

Deblinger, E., Russell Hathaway, C., Lippmann, J. and Steer, R. (1993) 'Psychosocial characteristics and correlates of symptom distress in nonoffending mothers of sexually abused children', *Journal of Interpersonal Violence*, 8: 155–168.

DiLillo, D., Tremblay, G.C. and Peterson, L. (2000) 'Linking childhood sexual abuse and abusive parenting: The mediating role of maternal anger', *Child Abuse & Neglect*, 24: 767–779.

Dixon, L., Browne, K. and Hamilton-Giachritsis, C. (2005) 'Risk factors of parents abused as children: A mediational analysis of the intergenerational continuity of child maltreatment (part I)', *Journal of Child Psychology and Psychiatry*, 46: 47–57.

——— (2009) 'Patterns of risk and protective factors in the intergenerational cycle of maltreatment', *Journal of Family Violence*, 24: 111–122.

Doumas, D., Margolin, G. and John, R.S. (1994) 'The intergenerational transmission of aggression across three generations', *Journal of Family Violence*, 9: 157–175.

Dubow, E.F., Huesmann, L.R. and Boxer, P. (2003) 'Theoretical and methodological considerations in cross-generational research on parenting and child aggressive behavior', *Journal of Abnormal Child Psychology*, 31: 185–192.

Enders, C.K. (2001) 'A primer on maximum likelihood algorithms available for use with missing data', *Structural Equation Modeling*, 8: 128–141.

Fagan, A.A. (2005) 'The relationship between adolescent physical abuse and criminal offending: Support for an enduring and generalized cycle of violence', *Journal of Family Violence*, 5: 279–290.

Frias-Armenta, M. (2002) 'Long-term effects of child punishment on Mexican women: A structural model', *Child Abuse & Neglect*, 26: 371–386.

Herrenkohl, E.C., Herrenkohl, R.C. and Toedter, L.J. (1983) 'Perspectives on the intergenerational transmission of abuse', in S. Finkelhor, R.J. Gelles, G.T. Hotaling and M.A. Straus (eds.) *The dark side of families: Current family violence research*, Beverly Hills: Sage.

Heyman, R.E. and Smith Slep, A.M. (2002) 'Do child abuse and interparental violence lead to adulthood family violence?', *Journal of Marriage and the Family*, 64: 864–870.

Hops, H., Davis, B., Leve, C. and Sheeber, L. (2003) 'Cross-generational transmission of aggressive parent behavior: A prospective, meditational examination', *Journal of Abnormal Child Psychology*, 31: 161–169.

Jung, H., Herrenkohl, T.I., Klika, J.B., Lee, J.O. and Brown, E.C. (2015) 'Does child maltreatment predict adult crime? Reexamining the question in a prospective study of gender differences, education, and marital status', *Journal of Interpersonal Violence*, 30: 2238–2257.

Kanz, K.-M. (2016) 'Mediated and moderated effects of violent media consumption on youth violence', *European Journal of Criminology*, 13: 149–168.

Kaufman, J. and Zigler, E. (1987) 'Do abused children become abusive parents?', *American Journal of Orthopsychiatry*, 57: 186–192.

Kruttschnitt, C. and Dornfeld, M. (1993) 'Exposure to family violence: A partial explanation for initial and subsequent levels of delinquency?', *Criminal Behavior and Mental Health*, 3: 61–75.

Lo, Y., Mendell, N.R. and Rubin, D.B. (2001) 'Testing the number of components in a normal mixture', *Biometrika*, 88: 767–778.

Milaniak, I. and Widom, C.S. (2015) 'Does child abuse and neglect increase risk for perpetration of violence inside and outside the home?', *Psychological Violence*, 5: 246–255.

Muller, R.T., Hunter, J.E. and Stollak, G. (1995) 'The intergenerational transmission of corporal punishment: A comparison of social learning and temperament models', *Child Abuse & Neglect*, 19: 1323–1335.

Muthén, L.K. and Muthén, B.O. (1998–2015) *Mplus user's guide*, 7th edn., Los Angeles: Muthén and Muthén.

Nagin, D.S. (1999) 'Analyzing developmental trajectories: A semi-parametric, group-based approach', *Psychological Methods*, 4: 139–157.

Nagin, D.S. and Land, K.C. (1993) 'Age, criminal careers, and population heterogeneity: Specification and estimation of a nonparametric, mixed Poisson model', *Criminology*, 31: 327–362.

Nagin, D.S. and Tremblay, R.E. (1999) 'Trajectories of boys' physical aggression, opposition, and hyperactivity on the path to physically violent and nonviolent juvenile delinquency', *Child Development*, 70: 1181–1196.

——— (2001) 'Analyzing developmental trajectories of distinct but related behaviors: A group-based method', *Psychological Methods*, 6: 18–34.

——— (2005) 'Developmental trajectory groups: Fact or a useful statistical fiction?', *Criminology*, 43: 873–904.
Ney, P.G. (1988) 'Transgenerational child abuse', *Child Psychiatry and Human Development*, 18: 151–168.
Nyland, K.L., Asparouhov, T. and Muthen, B.O. (2007) 'Deciding on the number of classes in latent class analysis and growth mixture modeling: A Monte Carlo simulation study', *Structural Equation Modeling*, 14: 535–569.
Pears, K.C. and Capaldi, D. (2001) 'Intergenerational transmission of abuse: A two-generational prospective study of an at-risk sample', *Child Abuse & Neglect*, 25: 1439–1461.
Pollak, R.A. (2004) 'An intergenerational model of domestic violence', *Journal of Population Economics*, 17: 311–329.
Putallaz, M., Costanzo, P.R., Grimes, C.L. and Sherman, D.M. (1998) 'Intergenerational continuities and their influences on children's social development', *Social Development*, 7: 389–427.
Reinecke, J. (2006) 'Longitudinal analysis of adolescents' deviant and delinquent behavior', *Methodology*, 2: 100–112.
——— (2012) 'Mixture models for longitudinal analysis: Applications of adolescents' development of delinquency', in S. Salzborn, E. Davidov and J. Reinecke (eds.) *Methods, theories, and empirical applications in the social sciences: Festschrift for Peter Schmidt*, Wiesbaden: Springer.
Reinecke, J., Meyer, M. and Boers, K. (2015) 'Stage-sequential growth mixture modeling of criminological panel data', in M. Stemmler, A. von Eye and W. Wiedermann (eds.) *Dependent data in social science research*, Wiesbaden: Springer.
Reinecke, J. and Weins, C. (2013) 'The development of delinquency during adolescence: A comparison of missing data techniques', *Quality & Quantity*, 47: 3319–3334.
Rivera, P.M. and Fincham, F.D. (2015) 'A latent class approach to understand the intergenerational transmission of violence in emerging adult relationships', in S.R. Maxwell and S.L. Blair (eds.) *Violence and crime in the family: Patterns, causes and consequences* (Contemporary Perspectives in Family Research, Volume 9), Bingley: Emerald Publishing Limited.
Roeder, K., Lynch, K.G. and Nagin, D.S. (1999) 'Modeling uncertainty in latent class membership: A case study in criminology', *Journal of the American Statistical Association*, 94: 766–776.
Sampson, R. and Laub, J.H. (2005) 'Seductions of method: Rejoinder to Nagin and Tremblay's "Developmental trajectory groups: Fact or fiction"', *Criminology*, 43: 905–914.
Schelbe, L. and Geiger, J.M. (2017) *Intergenerational transmission of child maltreatment*, Cham: Springer.
Schofield, T.J., Lee, R.D. and Merrick, M.T. (2013) 'Safe, stable, nurturing relationships as a moderator of intergenerational continuity of child maltreatment: A meta-analysis', *Journal of Adolescence Health*, 53: S32–S38.
Schwarz, G. (1978) 'Estimating the dimension of a model', *Annals of Statistics*, 6: 461–464.
Seddig, D. (2014) 'Peer group association, the acceptance of norms and violent behaviour: A longitudinal analysis of reciprocal effects', *European Journal of Criminology*, 11: 319–339.
——— (2015) 'Crime inhibiting, interactional and co-developmental patterns of school bonds and the acceptance of legal norms', *Crime and Delinquency*, 62: 1046–1071. x (ist das dann auch von Seddig?).
Seddig, D. and Reinecke, J. (2017) 'Exploration and explanation of adolescent self-reported delinquency trajectories in the Crimoc study', in A. Blokland and V. van der Geest (eds.) *The Routledge international handbook of life-course criminology*, London: Taylor & Francis.

Serbin, L.A., Cooperman, J.M., Peters, P.L. et al. (1998) 'Intergenerational transfer of psychosocial risk in women with childhood histories of aggression, withdrawal, or aggression and withdrawal', *Developmental Psychology*, 34: 1246–1262.

Sidebotham, P. and Golding, J. (2001) 'Child maltreatment in the "Children of the nineties": A longitudinal study of parental risk factors', *Child Abuse & Neglect*, 25: 1177–1200.

Smith, C.A., Park, A., Ireland, T.O., Elwyn, L. and Thornberry, T.P. (2012) 'Long-term outcomes of young adults exposed to maltreatment: The role of educational experiences in promoting resilience to crime and violence in early adulthood', *Journal of Interpersonal Violence*, 28: 121–156.

Smith, C.A. and Thornberry, T.P. (1995) 'The relationship between childhood maltreatment and adolescent involvement in delinquency', *Criminology*, 33: 451–481.

Snyder, S.M. and Smith, R.E. (2015) 'Do youth with substantiated child maltreatment investigations have distinct patterns of delinquent behaviors?', *Children and Youth Service Review*, 58: 82–89.

Straus, M.A. (1979) 'Measuring intrafamily conflict and violence: The Conflict Tactics (CT) scales', *Journal of Marriage and Family*, 41: 75–88.

——— (1983) 'Ordinary violence, child abuse and wife-beating: What do they have in common?', in D. Finkelhor, R.J. Gelles, G.T. Hotaling and M.A. Straus (eds.) *The dark side of families: Current family violence research*, Beverly Hills: Sage.

Straus, M.A., Gelles, R.J. and Steinmetz, S.K. (1980) *Behind closed doors: Violence in the American family*, New York: Anchor Books.

Sutherland, E.H. (1947) *Principles of criminology*, Philadelphia: J.B. Lippincott.

Theimann, M. (2016) 'School as a space of socialization and prevention', *European Journal of Criminology*, 13: 67–91.

Thornberry, T.P., Freeman-Gallant, A., Lizotte, A.J. et al. (2003) 'Linked lives: The intergenerational transmission of antisocial behavior', *Journal of Abnormal Child Psychology*, 31: 171–184.

Thornberry, T.P. and Henry, K.L. (2013) 'Intergenerational continuity in maltreatment', *Journal of Abnormal Child Psychology*, 41: 555–569.

Thornberry, T.P., Henry, K.L., Ireland, T.O. and Smith, C.A. (2010) 'The causal impact of childhood-limited maltreatment and adolescent maltreatment on early adult adjustment', *Journal of Adolescent Health*, 46: 359–365.

Thornberry, T.P., Ireland, T.O. and Smith, C.A. (2001) 'The importance of timing: The varying impact of childhood and adolescent maltreatment on multiple problem outcomes', *Development and Psychopathology*, 13: 957–979.

Tremblay, R.E., Vitaro, F., Gagnon, C., Piché, C. and Royer, N. (1992) 'A prosocial scale for the preschool behaviour questionnaire: Concurrent and predictive correlates', *Intergenerational Journal of Behavioural Development*, 15: 227–245.

Tutty, L.M. (1999) 'Considering emotional abuse in the link between spouse and child abuse: A review and exploratory study', *Journal of Emotional Abuse*, 1: 53–80.

van der Put, C.E., Lanctot, N., de Ruiter, C. and van Vugt, E. (2015) 'Child maltreatment among boy and girl probationers: Does type of maltreatment make a difference in offending behavior and psychosocial problems?', *Child Abuse & Neglect*, 46: 142–151.

Weir, H. and Kaukinen, C. (2015) 'Delinquent effects of childhood exposure to violent victimization: A latent longitudinal class analysis', in S.R. Maxwell and S.L. Blair (eds.) *Violence and crime in the family: Patterns, causes and consequences* (Contemporary perspectives in family research, Volume 9), Bingley: Emerald Group Publishing Limited.

Widom, C.S. (1989a) 'Child abuse, neglect, and adult behavior: Research design and findings on criminality, violence, and child abuse', *American Journal of Orthopsychiatry*, 59: 355–367.

——— (1989b) 'Does violence beget violence? A critical examination of the literature', *Psychological Bulletin*, 106: 3–28.

Widom, C.S., Czaja, S. and Dutton, M.A. (2014) 'Child abuse and neglect and intimate partner violence victimization and perpetration: A prospective investigation', *Child Abuse & Neglect*, 38: 650–663.

Yang, C.C. (1998) 'Finite mixture model selection with psychometric applications', unpublished doctoral dissertation, University of Groningen.

Zingraff, M.T., Leiter, J., Myers, K.A. and Johnsen, M.C. (1993) 'Child maltreatment and youthful problem behavior', *Criminology*, 31: 173–202.

Chapter 13

The Cambridge–Somerville Youth Study and intergenerational transmission of criminal offending

Key findings and planning for the next generation

Brandon C. Welsh, Steven N. Zane, and Andrea B. Wexler

Introduction

Started in 1939, the Cambridge–Somerville Youth Study (CSYS) is a matched-randomized controlled experiment of a delinquency prevention program embedded in a prospective longitudinal survey of offending over the life-course. The study enrolled 650 (later reduced to 506) under-privileged boys, ages 5–13 years (median = 10.5 years), from Cambridge and Somerville, Massachusetts. The boys were rated as "average" or "difficult" on externalizing behavior and placed in matched pairs, and one member of each pair was randomly assigned (by the toss of a coin) to the treatment group. Referred to as "directed friendship," the preventive intervention involved individual counseling through a range of activities and home visits for a mean average duration of 5.5 years. The control group did not receive any special services. The study was last followed-up by Joan McCord from 1975 to 1979, when participants were in their mid-to-late 40s (see below for more details), and work is underway on the age-85 follow-up of the study (see Welsh and Zimmerman 2015).

Today, the CSYS is recognized as the first randomized controlled experiment in criminology (Weisburd and Petrosino 2004), as well as one of the earliest randomized experiments of a social program (Forsetlund, Chalmers, and Bjørndal 2007). It is also known as the earliest example of a longitudinal-experimental study with criminological outcomes (Farrington 2006, 2013; Farrington and Welsh 2013). It is this novel design – an experiment embedded in a longitudinal survey – that allows for two main questions in investigating the intergenerational transmission of offending. First, based on a comparison of the treatment and control groups (matched pairs in the case of the CSYS), what is the impact of the program on offending by the children of the study participants? Second, based on the treatment group alone, is there a relationship between offending by the parents (fathers in the case of the CSYS) of the participants (G1) and the children of the participants (G3)? Building on the voluminous research and scholarship of Joan McCord, this chapter is concerned with the latter.

This chapter has two main aims. The first is to report on key findings of Joan McCord's investigations of the intergenerational transmission of offending based on the treatment group participants (G2) and their fathers (G1). The second is to describe the planning involved for extending this research to the third generation: the children of the treatment group participants (G3).

The organization of this chapter is as follows. It begins with a description of the historical context in which the study was developed and implemented, paying particular attention to its founder and first director, Richard Clarke Cabot. This is followed by a summary of the study's methodology and an overview of key findings of McCord's investigations of the intergenerational transmission of offending, respectively. The next section describes the planning for follow-up with the next generation (G3) – the important step needed to make this a developmentally appropriate intergenerational study (Thornberry 2009). The final section offers some concluding remarks.

Historical context

The CSYS was implemented at a time of tremendous innovation to prevent delinquency outside of the formal juvenile justice system, in part, to avoid the effects of labeling. It followed closely the development of the Chicago Area Project in the early 1930s (Shaw and McKay 1942) and was a predecessor to delinquency prevention programs in the 1950s and 1960s (Welsh and Pfeffer 2013).

Intriguingly, the CSYS was developed and directed by a physician and professor of clinical medicine and social ethics at Harvard University, Richard Clarke Cabot. Although his major contributions were to early studies of blood, differential diagnosis, and the etiology of heart disease (see, e.g., Cabot 1896, 1911, 1914), Cabot also made various contributions to social work, such as introducing social services to Massachusetts General Hospital (Evison 1995) and serving as president of the National Conference of Social Work (Cabot 1931).

As chair of Harvard's Department of Social Ethics, Cabot developed a relationship with criminologists Sheldon and Eleanor Glueck. This would prove instrumental to the conception of the CSYS. Sheldon Glueck participated in a social ethics seminar and credited Cabot and a guest lecturer (William Healy) with inspiring him to conduct the famous follow-up study of former inmates of the Massachusetts Reformatory (Glueck and Glueck 1930). As Glueck (1964: 319) later recalled:

> In a remarkable seminar conducted by Dr. Richard C. Cabot in the Department of Social Ethics at Harvard, the outstanding practitioners in all

> branches of social work in Boston participated . . . . At that seminar I made the point that nobody had really checked up on the human products of our reformatories and prisons . . . . Both Dr. Cabot and Dr. Healy responded enthusiastically to the idea of making a follow-up study of the graduates of the Massachusetts Reformatory.

Cabot helped secure funding for this novel study and wrote the forward to the subsequent book (Cabot 1930). Cabot later introduced the Gluecks to his cousin, Judge Frederick Cabot, who allowed them to study juvenile delinquents processed through the Boston juvenile court (Glueck and Glueck 1934).

The results of the first study (80 per cent recidivism; Cabot 1930) and second study (almost 90 per cent recidivism; Cabot 1934) were highly distressing to Cabot: "This is a damning piece of evidence – not against that Reformatory in particular, which probably stands high among institutions of its kind, but against the reformatory system in general. Here it does not work. No one knows that it works any better elsewhere" (Cabot 1930: vii). A year later, in his presidential address to the 58th annual meeting of the National Conference of Social Work, Cabot (1931: 452) concluded, "I have an idea that the treatment of juvenile delinquency is now bad, wasteful, and ineffective. This idea comes mostly from the Gluecks' studies, published and not yet published." Cabot was inspired to design a program to prevent delinquency in the *first* instance, which would be the final project of his life.

Largely owing to his medical background, Cabot used an experimental design to investigate the CSYS. Without rigorous designs, Cabot lamented, we are "forced to base our opinions of the value of any given piece of social work largely on the character, experience and expertness of those in charge of it" (1931: 445). He was critical of the lack of empirical evaluation in social work during his time, insisting that objective evidence was desperately needed:

> I appeal to you, the social workers of the country, to do far more often the thing that you have been saying you were going to do since 1923: Measure, evaluate, estimate, appraise your results, — in some form, in any terms that rest on something beyond assertion and "illustrative cases."
>
> (Cabot 1931: 450–451)

The CSYS was thus Cabot's attempt to lead by example and design the first delinquency prevention experiment. As noted by McCord (1992: 198), "The Cambridge–Somerville Youth Study grafted scientific methods onto a social action program."

Cabot's vision for delinquency prevention was character development for young boys through positive role models (deQ. Cabot 1940), and the treatment group received individual counseling and home visiting. Counselors talked to the boys, took them on trips and to recreational activities, tutored them in reading and arithmetic, encouraged them to participate in the YMCA and in summer camps, played games with them at the project's center, encouraged them to attend church, and gave advice and general support to the boys' families (McCord and McCord 1959a).

In 1942, shortly following America's entry into World War II, the program was scaled back to 253 pairs of boys due to the loss of financial resources (owing to gas shortages) as well as some of the young men who were counselors (owing to military service). Follow-ups in 1948 (Powers and Witmer 1951) and in 1956 (McCord and McCord 1959a, 1959b) indicated that the program had no measurable effect on official offending. The next follow-up, in 1975–1979, showed that the program had produced iatrogenic effects on official offending and other important life-course outcomes (McCord 1978, 1981).

Although evaluating the prevention program "to test Cabot's belief about how a child could be steered away from delinquency" may have been the primary goal of the CSYS, the study was also designed to "learn about the development of delinquent youngsters" (McCord 1992: 198). Cabot instructed counselors to keep detailed records of all encounters with the boys and their families. As P. S. deQ. Cabot[1] suggested at the program's inception, an "outstanding characteristic" of the CSYS program plan was the combination of research and casework, such that "treatment and research objectives are closely intertwined" (1940: 143, 150). As Powers (1949: 83) notes, at the time it was considered "unusual for one to carry on research with boys with whom one is at the same time attempting treatment." From its beginnings, then, the CSYS was envisioned as a *longitudinal* experimental study.

Methodology

This section summarizes key features of the methodology of the CSYS. In consideration of the planning for follow-up with the third generation of the study (see below), it pays particular attention to the samples and measures of the first and second generations. Figure 13.1 presents an overview of the study's intergenerational design. Aside from the start of the study (1939), the years along the top of the figure denote the main follow-up periods when data was collected on the two generations.

It is important to reiterate that this chapter focuses exclusively on the treatment arm of the study. It does so because the information on the control group participants and their families is limited. This was the original plan of Richard Cabot, and our focus is in line with the analytic strategy of Joan McCord (see McCord 1984). As noted above, this does not militate against extending the intergenerational design to the control group to investigate the program's impact on offending by the children of the study participants (G3 treatment vs. G3 control). This will be the subject of future research plans.

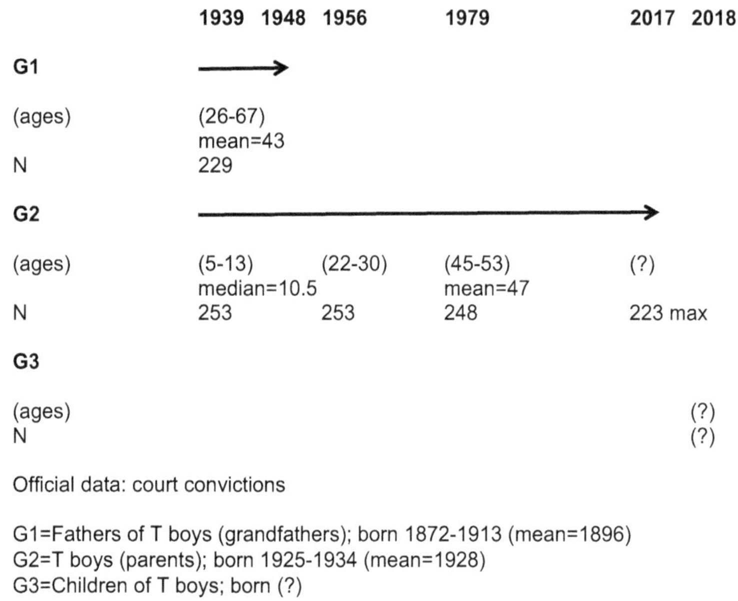

Figure 13.1 Intergenerational design of the Cambridge–Somerville Youth Study

First generation (G1)

The fathers of the treatment group boys (*N* = 229) were born between 1872 and 1913 (mean = 1896). At the start of the study, the treatment group fathers ranged in age from 26 to 67 years (mean = 43). In keeping with Richard Cabot's desire to learn about the "processes of family life and how these would be affected by the program" (McCord 1999a: 243), detailed family records were collected over the duration of the intervention (1939 to 1945).

In 1957, McCord oversaw a team of six researchers in the coding of these family case histories. Information was coded in the following four areas: (1) family's socio-economic and cultural milieu; (2) parental behavior and relationship, with a focus on aggressiveness, conflicts, drinking, and affection for one another; (3) parental interaction with the boy, with a focus on disciplinary techniques, expectations for performance, and affect toward one another; and (4) behavior and emotional state of the boy, with a focus on aggressiveness, relations with siblings, self-confidence, and dependency (McCord 1984: 524). High interrater reliability scores were achieved for the coding, and retrospective biases were eliminated because the researchers were blind to the impact of the program on the boys (McCord 1984).

Official data on offending (convictions) by the fathers was last collected in 1948 (McCord and McCord 1959b). At this time, the age range for the fathers was 35 to 76 years.

Second generation (G2)

The treatment group boys ($N = 253$) were born between 1925 and 1934 (mean = 1928) and were enrolled in the program at ages 5 to 13 years (median = 10.5 years). At the last follow-up, which took place between 1975 and 1979, McCord (1981) was successful in tracing 98.0 per cent ($N = 248$) of participants. By 1979, the mean average age of the treatment group was 47 years.

As part of this follow-up, two modes of data collection were employed. First, official records were searched for a wide range of important life-course outcomes.[2] These included offending in the juvenile and adult years (convictions), alcohol use, mental health, and death. Second, questionnaires, interviews, or both were administered. Questionnaires were sent by mail and interviews were conducted in person or by telephone. A total of 178 of the treatment group men responded to the questionnaire or completed an interview (McCord 1984), for a response rate of 79.8 per cent.[3] The questionnaire requested information on a wide range of topics, including marital status, occupation, geographic mobility, job satisfaction, and health. The interview sought information on these topics and many more, including education, children, childrearing behavior, and alcohol use (McCord 1984).

Key findings on intergenerational transmission of offending: G1 to G2

Using the follow-up data that she painstakingly collected, Joan McCord launched a prolific, decades-long program of research to investigate the relationship between parental factors (G1) and deviance and other antisocial behavior in treatment group boys (G2). Shortly after conducting the 30-year follow-up, McCord (1979) reported that a series of family variables were significantly related to future offending for the treatment group boys: parental supervision, parental conflict, parental aggressiveness, mother's self-confidence, mother's affection, father's criminality, and father's alcoholism. In looking at patterns of deviance from juvenile offending to adult criminal offending in another early study, McCord (1980) found that parental rejection, parental conflict, and parental criminality were consistently and strongly related to juvenile delinquency. As McCord (1979: 1485) reported, "parental behavior does have an important impact on subsequent behavior: predictions of adult criminality based on knowledge of home atmosphere were not only markedly more accurate than chance – they were also more accurate than predictions based on the individuals' juvenile criminal records."

Among these family risk factors, paternal deviance (i.e., criminality and alcoholism) stood out as a consistent predictor of sons' future offending (see McCord 1991b). But what causal mechanism was responsible for this transmission of offending? As McCord (2001: 223) put it, "Families contribute to criminality in at least three ways: by genetic transmission, through placement in physical and socioeconomic contexts, and by virtue of child-rearing practices." Over the next several decades, McCord investigated other family factors that may influence the relationship between a father's criminality and a sons' deviance. On the basis of this impressive body of scholarship, McCord reached the tentative conclusion that parental transmission of offending and alcoholism from G1 to G2 was largely mediated by parenting practices and other family risk factors, rather than direct social learning of deviant behavior, biological inheritance, or other causal mechanisms. As McCord (1986: 355) put it, "paternal deviance appeared to have an indirect, rather than direct, effect on criminality."

For example, McCord (1990a) examined transmission of criminal offending according to childrearing practices. Sons raised by criminal fathers were least likely to be from "good" families, while sons raised by noncriminal fathers were most likely to be exposed to "good" parenting practices.[4] Of the "worst" 38 families in the CSYS, 39 per cent of fathers had been convicted of serious crimes; of the "best" 61 families, only 11 per cent of fathers had been convicted of such crimes (statistically significant differences). McCord (1990a) suggested that transmission of offending may be an indirect process, mediated largely by childrearing practices (see also McCord 1990b).[5]

In another study, McCord (1988b) found that the best predictor of future alcoholism on G2 participants was whether the father was an alcoholic. But the study also found that maternal behavior toward the alcoholic father was important, once again suggesting a developmentally complex explanation: "results suggest that learning more about how maternal behavior influences intergenerational continuities and discontinuities could serve as a step toward understanding how genetic and environmental factors interact in the development of alcoholism" (McCord 1988b: 139). McCord (1999b) also found that both alcoholic and criminal fathers were significantly more likely to be aggressive fathers and to be married to incompetent mothers. This provided further evidence that "alcoholism and crime tend to run in families at least partially because alcoholic and criminal parents tend to provide poor socializing environments" (McCord 1999b: 114).

McCord further honed this focus on family socialization in a series of studies on the relationship between parental criminality and parental aggressiveness and physical discipline. McCord (1991a) found that criminal fathers were more likely to use physical punishment than noncriminal fathers, and that among sons with criminal fathers, physical punishment also substantially increased the likelihood of future criminality. McCord (1988a) found that exposure to general aggressiveness was more predictive of future criminality than physical discipline in otherwise nonaggressive families, and McCord (1991b) found that criminal fathers were more likely to be highly aggressive and punitive, more likely to be alcoholic, and more likely to be married to aggressive mothers. In fact, parental conflict and parental aggressiveness were the only risk factors related to future criminality for *all* G2 participants. As McCord (1986: 352) observed in an earlier study,

> criminogenic families tend to be located in a three-dimensional space that can be characterized as one in which deviant, aggressive parents show little respect for other members of the family; mothers are insecure, inconsistent, and not affectionate; and no one provides supervision or attempts to direct the children's behavior.

McCord (1991b) also extended the analysis of parental transmission of offending to a more traditional sociological question: How do family characteristics interact with neighborhood characteristics? She found that "unstable neighborhoods appeared to have a criminogenic effect only on sons who had a criminogenic heritage" (223). For G2 men with noncriminal fathers, type of neighborhood was not significantly related to future criminality. But, for sons of criminal fathers, 45 per cent of criminal sons came from the worst neighborhoods compared to only 15 per cent of noncriminal sons – a significant difference. McCord suggested that in better neighborhoods, protective factors in the community likely prevented sons of criminal fathers from following in their fathers' footsteps. These protective influences included family characteristics such as positive maternal traits (i.e., affection, self-confidence, supervision, and nonpunitive discipline). McCord (1993a: 322) likewise found that "[e]ffects of neighborhoods seem to be mediated by family socialization practices, but whether or not similar socialization practices have similar effects in different types of neighborhoods is not yet known."

McCord (1991b: 226) also explored whether parental transmission of antisocial behavior is due to "innate disposition" or "contagion from social environment." McCord (1994) concluded that the criminogenic effects of paternal criminality appeared largely due to exposure to marital discord rather than a direct (and possibly genetic) transmission that would have been observable in early childhood behavior problems. Noting that biological and social mechanisms were likely both part of the causal explanation, McCord (1994) observed that social conditions nevertheless appeared primary. McCord (1994: 248) was careful not to dismiss completely the genetic explanation, however:

> It would be a mistake . . . to conclude that this shows no genetic contribution to misbehavior. Rather, whatever genetic makeup has been passed from father to son ought to be viewed as providing susceptibilities or potentialities which require social conditioning for their expression in terms of crime.

In short, McCord's research pointed toward a "family risk factor" explanation of the transmission of offending from parents to children, where criminal parents tend to be bad parents and bad parents are more likely to produce deviant children. Early intergenerational research also suggests that "developmental risk factors" represent a dominant mechanism of transmission (see Thornberry 2005: 183). For example, Smith and Farrington (2004) found that transmission of antisocial behavior appeared to be mediated by parenting practices such as poor parental supervision – practices that continued from fathers to sons. More recently, Farrington and colleagues (2015) found further evidence in support of a risk factor mechanism. Comparing over 20 shared risk factors between G2 and G3, they found that effect sizes correlated strongly (.80) and 11 risk factors were significant predictors of criminality for both generations. Developmental risk factors would appear to be an important part of the story of intergenerational transmission, as McCord suggested.[6]

Nevertheless, McCord was well aware that the collinearity of various risk factors presents a serious challenge to any simple explanation of the causal transmission of offending from parents to children (see McCord 1993b). McCord (1994: 242) suggested that this complexity creates challenges in identifying singular causal mechanisms, observing, for example, that while parental conflict was often posited as a social cause of children's antisocial behavior, "if parental conflict were itself caused by children's misbehavior, the parental conflict might be no more than a perturbation in the linkage of aggression between generations." Her research on the relationship between G1 and G2 deviance laid the groundwork for investigating the intergenerational transmission of offending across three generations – including the complex causal mechanisms involved therein.

Planning for follow-up with the next generation

This section outlines key research questions to be investigated and plans to identify, trace, and collect data on the children of the treatment group participants (G3), the next generation of the CSYS.

Key research questions

The most important research question to be investigated concerns the transmission of offending from G2 to G3. We are also interested in investigating the most salient individual, family, and community factors in the intergenerational transmission of offending. This involves extending Joan McCord's program of research (see above). With G3 including both males and females (unlike G2), there will be the opportunity to investigate the role of gender on offending: from father to son and father to daughter. Of further interest will be to examine the findings in historical context, building on our ongoing historical research (Welsh, Dill, and Zane 2018; Welsh, Zane, and Rocque 2017; Zane, Welsh, and Zimmerman 2017).

Identifying and tracing G3

The identification of G3 begins with the wealth of personal information that Joan McCord collected on G2, including last known home address, telephone number, personal identifiers such as social security number, and next of kin. Both traditional and online search methods will be used.

Traditional search methods: The first search strategy will involve determining if the last known home telephone numbers and home addresses are still associated with the G2 participants who could provide the desired information on G3. This will be conducted by a search of paper and online telephone directories. In their age-70 follow-up of the Gluecks' longitudinal study of delinquent and nondelinquent boys from Boston, Laub and Sampson (2003) reported having some success in locating participants by using the Boston telephone directory, even though 35 years had elapsed since last contact.

Another traditional search method will involve looking for G3 information through the use of official birth records. This is made possible because the name of the father is frequently listed on the birth record. At the age-45 follow-up, 78 per cent of G2 still resided in Massachusetts (McCord 1978). It may follow that many children of G2 were born in Massachusetts, and thus will have birth records in the state.

As part of the ongoing age-85 follow-up of G2, official death records and death certificates are being searched. In many states, death certificates, which need to be purchased from the state agency, contain information on next of kin. In some instances this may be a child of the treatment group men. In other instances it may involve family members who, if tracked down, can provide information on G3.

Online search methods: The usefulness of the Internet in conducting criminological research has been noted by many researchers (Moule and Decker 2013; Giordano 2010; Laub and Sampson 2003), especially due to the labor-intensive nature of traditional search methods (Ortiz and Ballon 2007). Because these search methods draw upon public databases (e.g., home ownership records, driver's licenses, mailing addresses), they may be particularly useful in locating G3 members, some of whom may have significant community ties (Moule and Decker 2013).

Using the G2 information, the first step will be to carry out a general search of the Internet, utilizing the Google search engine. As noted by Moule and Decker (2013), Google searches are not only useful in obtaining information, but also in providing links to other sites, including web pages and Facebook profiles.

The next step will involve searching social media sites, which include various social networking platforms (e.g., Facebook, MySpace, LinkedIn, Twitter). These sites include profiles, which are frequently shared to create lists of interconnected individuals (Raacke and Bonds-Raacke 2008). Importantly, they are becoming increasingly popular with adults (Correa, Hinsley, and Gil de Zúñiga

2010). Searching these publicly available profiles will be helpful to find other people who may be links in determining the G3 sample. These potential links (individuals who are connected to G2) will undoubtedly include some of the G3 sample, since familial ties are frequently indicated on social networking sites. This will be followed by searches of more specialized websites designed to trace ancestry. Two of these sites are Intelius.com and Ancestry.com, both of which require paid subscriptions.

Collecting data on G3

Two main sources of official data will be collected on the G3 sample. The first is court convictions of serious and violent offenses covering the juvenile and adult years. Serious property offenses include larceny, auto theft, and breaking and entering. Violent or serious personal offenses include assault, attempted rape, rape, attempted murder, kidnapping, and murder. The second source of data that will be collected is official records of death. Death certificates will be subsequently obtained, and all information relevant to the project will be coded (e.g., date of death, cause of death, location of death).

Criminal records: A two-step process will be used to search for and collect criminal records of the G3 sample. It will build on the work of McCord (1978, 1981) and follow closely the procedures used by Laub and Sampson (2003). In recognition that a substantial proportion of the G3 sample will have resided in or still do reside in Massachusetts, the first step will involve searching criminal records in the state. State criminal records are held by the Department of Criminal Justice Information Services, an agency of the Executive Office of Public Safety and Security.

The second step will involve searching for criminal records of the G3 sample who either live outside of Massachusetts or who may have been convicted of a crime in another state. The Federal Bureau of Investigation, a federal government agency, maintains a national electronic database of criminal convictions.

Death records: A comprehensive and systematic set of procedures will also be used to search for and collect death records of the G3 sample. Once again, these procedures will build on the work of McCord (1978, 1981) and follow closely the procedures used by Laub and Sampson (2003). Three databases/data sources will be used: (1) the Massachusetts Registry of Vital Records and Statistics (MA Registry), (2) the National Death Index (NDI) of the Centers for Disease Control and Prevention, and (3) obituaries published in the *Boston Globe* and obituaries available through Legacy.com.

The search for and collection of death records will begin with the MA Registry. This is because it offers the most comprehensive coverage of official death records for those who have died in Massachusetts. Following the identification of records of death of G3, death certificates will be purchased from the MA Registry.

The next step will be to initiate a search of death records using the NDI. This will involve searches of the death records for all who were not located through the MA Registry. The NDI is a centralized database of death record information for all of the states. The index includes deaths from 1979 until present, and it is updated on an annual basis with a lag time of approximately 12 months. Searches of death records are performed by the NDI staff. A service called NDI Plus also provides information on cause of death, and this service will be used.

The final step will involve regular checks of the obituaries published in the *Boston Globe* and available through Legacy.com. This will commence at the beginning of the project and will continue for the full duration of the project.

Conclusion

In the words of Joan McCord (1992: 196), the Cambridge–Somerville Youth Study is a "pioneering longitudinal experimental study" in the field of criminology. With this also comes a rather unique historical perspective. Parents of the boys enrolled in the study were born in the late nineteenth century. The boys were born around the time of America's Great Depression and grew up during World War II and the country's eventual involvement in the war in 1942. Some of the older boys in the sample (in 1939, the oldest were 13 years) would go on to join the U.S. military and serve in the war. Some of these same young men and others in the sample would later serve in the Korean War.

Through the research and scholarship of Joan McCord, the CSYS has provided an important body of knowledge on the transmission of criminal offending between two generations (G1 and G2). The addition of the children of the treatment group participants (G3) will allow for a more comprehensive and developmentally appropriate investigation of intergenerational transmission of criminal offending.

The planning for this next phase of research is underway. The central challenges confronting this research have to do with identifying and locating G3. As this chapter makes clear, the good news is that these challenges can be overcome, and two key reasons stand out. First, owing to Joan McCord, we retain detailed records on G2. Importantly, as part of the age-85 follow-up, many of these records have been augmented with information provided through official death records and certificates. Second, drawing upon the lessons learned from other longitudinal researchers, we will be using a mixed methods approach of traditional and online search techniques. It is our hope that the intergenerational design of the CSYS will contribute to the growing international body of knowledge on the intergenerational transmission of offending.

Acknowledgments

We are grateful to the editors and the anonymous reviewers for insightful comments on an earlier draft.

Notes

1 Richard Clarke Cabot passed away in 1939 and a relative, P.S. deQ. Cabot, took over as the CSYS director (deQ. Cabot 1940).
2 They are referred to as outcomes because the priority of this follow-up was to evaluate the long-term impact of the program.
3 This is based on $N = 223$, with 25 treatment group men identified as deceased (based on official death records).
4 A family was rated as "good" (according to a 3-point scale) based on whether the family was above average across three dimensions: mother's competence (consistency of discipline, self-confidence, affection for son, and role in family structure); father's interaction with the family (parents' mutual esteem, parental conflict, affection for son, and aggressiveness); and family expectations for the boy (maternal restrictiveness, supervision, and demands placed on boy).
5 In a prior study, McCord (1982) had also found that boys raised in homes with parental conflict were significantly more likely to engage in crime (as adults) compared to boys raised by affectionate mothers (with absent fathers). McCord (1990b) also found that the significant relationship between father and son's criminality only held among intact families – there was no such relationship when criminal fathers were absent.
6 Direct social learning has also received early support from several intergenerational studies. For one, direct exposure appears necessary for intergenerational transmission to occur (Thornberry, Freeman-Gallant, and Lovegrove 2009; van de Weijer, Bijleveld, and Blokland 2014). Van de Rakt, Nieuwbeerta, and de Graaf (2008) also found a significant association between number of convictions of criminal fathers and criminal offspring. In addition to frequency, van de Rakt, Ruiter, de Graaf, and Nieuwbeerta (2010) found an association between criminal trajectories for specific crimes of parents and children, suggesting a direct learning process. Besemer (2014) found that parental convictions before birth of their children were less related to offspring convictions, more consistent with social learning (or shared risk factors) than a genetic explanation.

References

Besemer, S. (2014) 'The impact of timing and frequency of parental criminal behaviour and risk factors', *Psychology, Crime, & Law*, 20: 78–99.

Cabot, P.S. deQ. (1940) 'A long-term study of children: The Cambridge-Somerville Youth Study', *Child Development*, 11: 143–151.

Cabot, R.C. (1896) *A Guide to the Clinical Examination of the Blood for Diagnostic Purposes*, New York: W. Wood.

Cabot, R.C. (1911) *Differential Diagnosis*, vol. 1, Philadelphia: W.B. Sunders.

Cabot, R.C. (1914) 'The four common types of heart disease: An analysis of six-hundred cases', *Journal of the American Medical Association*, 63: 1461–1463.

Cabot, R.C. (1930) 'Foreword', in S. Glueck and E.T. Glueck (eds.) *500 Criminal Careers*, New York: Knopf.

Cabot, R.C. (1931) 'Treatment in social case work and the need of criteria and of tests of its success and failure', *Hospital Social Services*, 24: 435–453.

Cabot, R.C. (1934) '1000 delinquent boys: First findings of the Harvard Law School's survey of crime', *Survey*, 70: 38–40.

Correa, T., Hinsley, A.W. and Gil de Zúñiga, H. (2010) 'Who interacts on the Web? The intersection of users' personality and social media use', *Computers in Human Behavior*, 26: 247–253.

Evison, I.S. (1995) *Pragmatism and Idealism in the Professions: The Case of Richard Clarke Cabot, 1869–1939*, Unpublished doctoral dissertation, University of Chicago.

Farrington, D.P. (2006) 'Key longitudinal-experimental studies in criminology', *Journal of Experimental Criminology*, 2: 121–141.

Farrington, D.P. (2013) 'Longitudinal and experimental research in criminology', in M. Tonry (ed.) *Crime and Justice 1975–2025*, Chicago: University of Chicago Press.

Farrington, D.P., Ttofi, M.M., Crago, R.V., and Coid, J.W. (2015) 'Intergenerational similarities in risk factors for offending', *Journal of Developmental and Life-Course Criminology*, 1: 48–62.

Farrington, D.P. and Welsh, B.C. (2013) 'Randomized experiments in criminology: What has been learned from long-term follow-ups?', in B.C. Welsh, A.A. Braga, and G.J.N. Bruinsma (eds.) *Experimental Criminology: Prospects for Advancing Science and Public Policy*, New York: Cambridge University Press.

Forsetlund, L., Chalmers, I., and Bjørndal, A. (2007) 'When was random allocation first used to generate comparison groups in experiments to assess the effect of social interventions?', *Economics of Innovation and New Technology*, 16: 371–384.

Giordano, P.C. (2010) *Legacies of Crime: A Follow-Up of the Children of Highly Delinquent Girls and Boys*, New York: Cambridge University Press.

Glueck, S. (1964) 'Remarks in honor of William Healy, M.D.', *Mental Hygiene*, 48: 318–322.

Glueck, S. and Glueck, E.T. (1930) *500 Criminal Careers*, New York: Knopf.

Glueck, S. and Glueck, E.T. (1934) *One Thousand Juvenile Delinquents*, Cambridge, MA: Harvard University Press.

Laub, J.H. and Sampson, R.J. (2003) *Shared Beginnings, Divergent Lives: Delinquent Boys to Age 70*, Cambridge, MA: Harvard University Press.

McCord, J. (1978) 'A thirty-year follow-up of treatment effects', *American Psychologist*, 33: 284–289.

McCord, J. (1979) 'Some child-rearing antecedents of criminal behavior in adult men', *Journal of Personality and Social Psychology*, 37: 1477–1486.

McCord, J. (1980) 'Patterns of deviance', in S.B. Sells, R. Crandall, M. Roff, J. Strauss, and W. Pollin (eds.), *Human Functioning in Longitudinal Perspective: Studies of Normal and Psycopathic Populations*, Baltimore, MD: Williams & Wilkins.

McCord, J. (1981) 'Consideration of some effects of a counseling program', in S.E. Martin, L.B. Sechrest, and R. Redner (eds.), *New Directions in the Rehabilitation of Criminal Offenders*, Washington, DC: National Academy Press.

McCord, J. (1982) 'A longitudinal view of the relationship between paternal absence and crime', in J. Gunn and D.P. Farrington (eds.) *Abnormal Offenders, Delinquency, and the Criminal Justice System*, Chichester, UK: Wiley & Sons.

McCord, J. (1984) 'A longitudinal study of personality development', in S.A. Mednick, M. Harway, and K.M. Finello (eds.) *Handbook of Longitudinal Research*, vol. 2, New York: Praeger.

McCord, J. (1986) 'Instigation and insulation: How families affect antisocial aggression', in J. Block, D. Olweus, and M.R. Yarrow (eds.) *Development of Antisocial and Prosocial Behavior*, New York: Academic Press.

McCord, J. (1988a) 'Parental aggressiveness and physical punishment in long-term perspective', in G.T. Hotaling, D. Finkelhor, J.T. Kirkpatrick, and M.A. Straus (eds.) *Family Abuse and Its Consequences: New Directions in Research*, Thousand Oaks, CA: Sage.

McCord, J. (1988b) 'Alcoholism: Toward understanding genetic and social factors', *Psychiatry*, 51: 131–141.

McCord, J. (1990a) 'Crime in moral and social contexts: The American Society of Criminology, 1989 presidential address', *Criminology*, 28: 1–26.

McCord, J. (1990b) 'Long-term perspectives on parental absence', in L.N. Robins and M. Rutter (eds.) *Straight and Devious Pathways from Childhood to Adulthood*, Cambridge, UK: Cambridge University Press.

McCord, J. (1991a) 'Family relationships, juvenile delinquency, and adult criminality', *Criminology*, 82: 211–228.

McCord, J. (1991b) 'The cycle of crime and socialization practices', *Journal of Criminal Law and Criminology*, 82: 211–228.

McCord, J. (1992), 'The Cambridge-Somerville study: A pioneering longitudinal experimental study of delinquency', in J. McCord and R.E. Tremblay (eds.) *Preventing Antisocial Behavior: Interventions from Birth through Adolescence*, New York: Guilford Press.

McCord, J. (1993a) 'Conduct disorder and antisocial behavior: Some thoughts about processes', *Development and Psychopathology*, 5: 321–329.

McCord, J. (1993b) 'Descriptions and predictions: Three problems for the future of criminological research', *Journal of Research in Crime and Delinquency*, 30: 412–425.

McCord, J. (1994) 'Aggression in two generations: Current perspectives', in L.R. Huesmann (ed.) *Aggressive Behavior: Current Perspectives*, New York: Plenum.

McCord, J. (1999a) 'Understanding childhood and subsequent crime', *Aggressive Behavior*, 25: 241–253.

McCord, J. (1999b) 'Alcoholism and crime across generations', *Criminal Behaviour and Mental Health*, 9: 107–117.

McCord, J. (2001) 'Forging criminals in the family', in S. White (ed.) *Handbook of Youth and Justice*, New York: Kluwer Academic.

McCord, J. and McCord, W. (1959a) 'A follow-up report on the Cambridge-Somerville Youth Study', *Annals of the American Academy of Political and Social Science*, 32: 89–96.

McCord, W. and McCord, J. (1959b) *Origins of Crime: A New Evaluation of the Cambridge-Somerville Youth Study*, New York: Columbia University Press.

Moule, R.K. and Decker, S.H. (2013) '"Hidden in plain sight": Locating the men and women of the 1954 Boston special youth program', *Journal of Qualitative Criminal Justice and Criminology*, 1: 267–291.

Ortiz, V. and Ballon, E.G. (2007) 'Longitudinal research at the turn of the century: Searching for the Mexican American people', *Sociological Methods and Research*, 36: 112–137.

Powers, E. (1949) 'An experiment in the prevention of delinquency', *Annals of the American Academy of Political and Social Science*, 261: 77–88.

Powers, E. and Witmer, H.L. (1951) *An Experiment in the Prevention of Delinquency: The Cambridge-Somerville Youth Study*, New York: Columbia University Press.

Raacke, J. and Bonds-Raacke, J. (2008) 'MySpace and Facebook: Applying the uses and gratifications theory to exploring friend-networking sites', *Cyberpsychology & Behavior*, 11: 169–174.

Shaw, C.R. and McKay, H.D. (1942) *Juvenile Delinquency and Urban Areas*, Chicago: University of Chicago Press.

Smith, C.A. and Farrington, D.P. (2004) 'Continuities in antisocial behaviour and parenting across three generations', *Journal of Child Psychology and Psychiatry*, 45: 230–247.

Thornberry, T.P. (2005) 'Explaining multiple patterns of offending across the life course and across generations', *Annals of the American Academy of Political and Social Science*, 602: 156–195.

Thornberry, T.P. (2009) 'The apple doesn't fall far from the tree (or does it?): Intergenerational patterns of antisocial behavior', *Criminology*, 47: 297–325.

Thornberry, T.P., Freeman-Gallant, A., and Lovegrove, P.J. (2009) 'Intergenerational linkages in antisocial behaviour', *Criminal Behaviour and Mental Health*, 19: 80–93.
van de Rakt, M., Nieuwbeerta, P., and de Graaf, N.D. (2008) 'Like father, like son: The relationships between conviction trajectories of fathers and their sons and daughters', *British Journal of Criminology*, 48: 538–556.
van de Rakt, M., Ruiter, S., de Graaf, N.D., and Nieuwbeerta, P. (2010) 'When does the apple fall from the tree? Static versus dynamic theories predicting intergenerational transmission of convictions', *Journal of Quantitative Criminology*, 26: 371–389.
van de Weijer, S., Bijleveld, C.C.J.H., and Blokland, A.A.J. (2014) 'The intergenerational transmission of violent offending', *Journal of Family Violence*, 29: 109–118.
Weisburd, D. and Petrosino, A. (2004) 'Experiments, criminology', in K. Kempf-Leonard (ed.), *Encyclopedia of Social Measurement*, San Diego, CA: Academic Press.
Welsh, B.C., Dill, N.E., and Zane, S.N. (2018) 'The first delinquency prevention experiment: A socio-historical review of the origins of the Cambridge-Somerville Youth Study's research design', *Journal of Experimental Criminology*. DOI: 10.1007/s11292-018-9323-9.
Welsh, B.C. and Pfeffer, R.D. (2013) 'Reclaiming crime prevention in an age of punishment: An American history', *Punishment and Society*, 15: 534–553.
Welsh, B.C., Zane, S.N., and Rocque, M. (2017) 'Delinquency prevention for individual change: Richard Clarke Cabot and the making of the Cambridge-Somerville Youth Study', *Journal of Criminal Justice*, 52: 79–89.
Welsh, B.C. and Zimmerman, G.M. (2015) 'Who cares about a delinquency prevention experiment of Boston boys born in the 1920s and 1930s? The need for long-term follow-ups in criminology', *Criminal Behaviour and Mental Health*, 25: 331–337.
Zane, S.N., Welsh, B.C., and Zimmerman, G.M. (2017) 'Examining the historical developments and contemporary relevance of the longitudinal-experimental design of the Cambridge-Somerville Youth Study: Utility for research on intergenerational transmission of offending', *Adolescent Research Review*, 2: 99–111.

Chapter 14

The Family Transitions Project

An intergenerational study of three generations

Monica J. Martin and Katherine J. Conger

The origins of the Family Transitions Project (FTP)

In the 1980s, individuals and families living on farms across the rural Midwest and Plains experienced a historic recession in the agricultural economy that spilled over into all sectors of the economy (see K. Conger 2011; Davidson 1990). This "farm crisis" of the 1980s, as it is generally known, was the most severe economic crisis in the United States since the Great Depression and dramatically impacted the lives of families in these areas and beyond. The plummeting land values, economic decline, and dislocation that resulted from the 1980s farm crisis were particularly apparent in the rural areas and small towns of Iowa, where agriculture was the predominant feature of the economy. Rand D. Conger and other researchers at Iowa State University observed the negative impacts the farm crisis was having on the farming communities and small rural towns in Iowa and used this unique opportunity to study the influence of economic upheaval on families across a wide range of economic circumstances; those families who lost it all – including the family farm; those families who got by with taking on second and third jobs; and those who were in professions not directly connected to the agricultural economy, such as lawyers and doctors, and thus less impacted. Thus, the original goal of the study was to understand the social contexts and interpersonal processes that helped explain the linkages between macro-economic conditions and the lives of individuals and families. To that end, the Iowa Youth and Family Project (IYFP) was initiated in 1989, and a companion project, the Iowa Single Parent Project (ISPP), was begun in 1991. The IFYP studied adolescents living with both their parents in the upper Midwest during the farm crisis of the 1980s. The companion study, the ISPP, was launched 2 years later in order to study these processes in adolescents living with their mother after their parents divorced. Both projects were designed to capture the experiences of these families undergoing this dramatic change in economic circumstance in order to better understand the mechanisms and processes through which economic problems affected the health, well-being, and long-term socioeconomic opportunities of a cohort of adolescents. Descriptions of both samples are provided later in the chapter. The two projects comprise the Family Transitions Project (FTP), the focus of this chapter, which has followed these families for over 25 years. To understand the importance of placing this study in rural Iowa, we provide a summary of the historical and economic context.

In brief, this widespread economic depression was the result of a confluence of geopolitical events and related policy changes in the United States that contributed to a rapid decline in land prices, loss of overseas markets for Midwestern grain and other agricultural products, and changes in economic and bank policies that undercut the financial structure that had led to the rapid expansion of farms during the previous two decades. Due to increasing global demand for food which started in the early 1970s, many American farmers took on substantial amounts of debt to expand their operations in the 1970s and early 1980s. Encouraged by government policies, and assisted by relaxed lending practices, these farmers took out large loans based on the rapidly increasing value of land (see Lasley and Goudy 1982; Lobao 1990). Even before this expansion, much of Iowa's economy was linked to some aspect of agriculture (i.e., farming and related businesses). Farmers and businesses in the small towns and rural areas of Iowa were particularly hit hard when inflation started to rise and lending policies changed at about the same time that the export market started to collapse; across the Midwest farmers saw their land values shrink and debts skyrocket as loans were called in and income did not keep up with debts and expenses (Lasley 1994). All of these changes promoted conditions which impacted all families living in areas dependent on agriculture, regardless of whether they were engaged in farming or not. This set the stage for the FTP – a prospective, longitudinal study of how families fared as they faced economic ruin or prosperity depending on how connected they were to agriculture in small towns and rural areas across Iowa. For readers interested in more details about the origins of the agricultural crisis of the 1980s, and the ongoing challenges of rural America, see Brown and Schafft (2011), Brown and Swanson (2003), Lasley (1994), Lobao and Meyer (2001), and Smith and Tickamyer (2011). The sections that follow describe the families and individuals that make up the Family Transitions Project, information on the study design and measures, and a summary of some of the contributions the study has made to our understanding of the intergenerational transmission of problem behaviours.

The Family Transitions Project's participants

During the 25-year course of the study, the Family Transitions Project has included nearly 3,000 participants, including the second generation (G2) target (n = 559; the focal adolescents) and a closely aged sibling (n = 559); their first generation (G1) mother (n = 559) and father (n = 443), and the G2 target's child (n = 308), the third generation (G3); the sample also included the G2 target's romantic partner(s) in adulthood (n = 417). The original pool of participants for the Iowa Youth and Family Project were drawn from an eight-county area in north central Iowa which had an ethnic minority population of only about

1 per cent at that time; thus, all the participants were European Americans from primarily lower-middle and middle-class families. Interviews were first conducted in 1989 with 451 two-parent families. Eligible families included a target adolescent (G2) in seventh grade living with both of his or her biological parents (G1) and with a sibling within 4 years of his or her age. Families were recruited (by letter and a follow-up phone call) through all public and private schools in the eight rural, Iowa counties selected for the study. Of the eligible families, 78 per cent agreed to be interviewed. During the first year of the study the median education for G1 fathers and mothers was 13 years (on average, 1 year post-high school), and their median ages were 39 years (fathers) and 37 years (mothers). The average number of family members was 4.95. Median family income from all sources for the prior year (1988) was $33,700 compared to a national median income of $33,920 for two-parent, white American families in 1988. The seventh-grade G2 target adolescents ranged in age from 12 to 14 years (mean = 13.17 years) and 52.33 per cent of them were female. Selecting this cohort of seventh-grade students allowed for an examination of the strain involved in the transition from childhood to adolescence, as well as the broader impact of economic stress brought on by the farm crisis.

The Iowa Single Parent Project (ISPP) – a supplemental sample of matched ninth graders ($n = 108$), a closely aged sibling, and their single-mother parent – was added to the study in 1991. These additional participants also came from rural areas of Iowa and had lived through the economic downturn brought on by the farm crisis, and thus had similar experiences as the initial two-parent families. To be eligible for the study, the mothers in this set of families had to have been divorced within the past 2 years; thus, they had been married in 1989 when the original study began. The recruitment and assessment procedures for this supplemental sample were similar to the initial two-parent sample, and more than 90 per cent of the contacted families agreed to participate. Adding these single-parent families to the adolescent cohort increased the social and economic variability in the overall study, as indicated by their lower median household income during the past year ($21,000). Median parent education (13 years), however, was the same in the single-parent households. The median age of the single-parent mothers was 39.29 years, and there was an average of 3.94 members in the single-parent households. In 1991 (ninth grade), the target adolescents in this supplemental sample averaged 15.20 years of age and 53.3 per cent of them were female.

The combined IFYP and ISPP samples comprise the Family Transitions Project. Beginning in 1997, the oldest biological child (G3) of the G2 target was recruited for study. To be eligible for participation, the G3 child had to be at least 18 months of age and the G2 target parent must have been in regular contact with the G3 child. G3 children were added to the study when they reached the eligible age (18 months). For that reason, new children were added each year of the study (1997 and beyond). The most recent data collection occurred in 2010, when the G3 children ranged in age from 2 to 18 years of age and the G2 targets were in their mid-30s, almost as old as their parents at the beginning of the study. The average age to date (2010, the most recent assessment) at which female G2s have had their first child is 25.7 years, comparable to the U.S. average for white women at the time (25.4 years; Martin et al. 2011). The majority of the G3 children have parents who are married to one another – 75 per cent of the G2 parents of the G3 children were married to the other biological parent of the G3 child. Overall, 70 per cent of the G2 targets (with and without children) are currently married, 15 per cent have never been married, and 11 per cent were divorced or separated in 2010. In 1989, when the study began, all G2 targets lived in Iowa and most in rural areas; now 30 per cent live outside of Iowa and only 21 per cent live in rural areas.

The G2 targets have seen substantial improvements in their socioeconomic circumstance compared to their G1 parents and are comparable with other whites in their mid-30s both in Iowa and nationally. Over 90 per cent have at least a high school diploma and nearly 50 per cent have a bachelor's degree or more, which is above the national average for whites ages 35 to 39 (35.0 per cent; U.S. Census Bureau 2011). Their improved socioeconomic circumstance compared to the G1s is also reflected in income; the average per capita income for the G2s (household income divided by family size) was $31,800 in 2010–2011. Additionally, 88 per cent of the G2s were employed at least part time in 2007–2008. There is, however, variability among the G2s economic circumstance; 4 per cent of G2s lived below the poverty line and 13 per cent were near poverty (less than twice the poverty line). Additionally, nearly 26 per cent had used savings for living expenses in the past year and about 13 per cent had taken a cut in wages or salary the previous year. Yet, on the whole, the G2s appear very similar to other similarly aged white adults nationally.

The Family Transitions Project's procedures

The original study participants (G1 parents and G2 target and sibling) were interviewed annually through 1995 (the first year after high school), except in 1993 when no in-home interviews took place. After the 1995 assessment, G2 participants and their romantic partners, and beginning in 1997, G3 children aged 18 months and older, were interviewed in alternating years. The retention rate is approximately 90 per cent through 2010, currently the last assessment period.

G2 family of origin (1989–1994)

The initial years (1989–1994) of the research focused on the G2 target's family of origin. During this period, interviewers visited each family in their home for approximately 2 hours on each of two occasions per year, except for 1993 when no in-home interviews were conducted. Each participant received approximately $10 per hour for compensation for their participation. During the first home visit each year, each family member (G1 mother, G1 father, G2 target, G2 sibling) completed a set of questionnaires focusing on individual family member characteristics, family relationships, and other aspects of the broader family and community environment. Family members also completed questionnaires on non-sensitive topics (e.g., school, community, and religious activities) between the two visits. Each of the questionnaires was sealed in an envelope and given to the interviewers when they arrived for the second visit.

During the second visit, which usually occurred within 2 weeks of the first, the family members were videotaped as they engaged in several structured interaction tasks designed to stimulate family interaction and elicit information about social skills and emotional responses. A trained interviewer began the videotaping session by asking each individual to complete a short questionnaire designed to identify issues of concern that led to disagreements within the family (e.g., responsibility for chores, recreational activities, use of money, etc.). The first task (Task 1) was designed, in part, to elicit information about parenting practices and lasted approximately 30 minutes. For this task, all four family members gathered around a table and were given a set of cards that contained general questions about family life such as approaches to parenting, performance in school, household chores, and important family events. The family members were instructed to read the questions on the cards aloud and discuss their answers to the questions. During this and all other tasks, the interviewer left the room and went to another part of the house where she or he could not hear the discussion being videotaped. Task 2, which lasted approximately 15 minutes, also involved all available family members. For this task, the interviewer selected three topics based on the questionnaires completed at the beginning of the visit. The family members were asked to discuss and to try to resolve the issue that they had identified as leading to the greatest conflict in their family. If they resolved this problem, they could go on to the second or even the third issue during the task. A third task involved sibling interactions. During this 15-minute task, the G2 target and their sibling discussed their relationship and family life while parents filled out a questionnaire out of earshot of the siblings. Task 4 focused on marital interactions between the G1 mother and father. During this 30-minute romantic couple interaction, with their children out of hearing range, the G1 mother and father discussed several topics, including the history and status of their relationship, areas of agreement and disagreement, and their plans for the future.

G2 in adulthood (1995–2010)

Beginning in 1995, the year after the G2 targets had completed high school, the focus of the study changed from the family of origin to the G2 target's transition to adulthood. Trained interviewers visited the G2 targets in their homes in 1995 and in alternating years thereafter, following procedures similar to those described for G2's family of origin. Data were collected from G2 targets and their romantic partners (married or cohabiting, when applicable), and beginning in 1997, their G3 children (when applicable). The G2 target and participating romantic partner (when available) completed a series of questionnaires on parenting beliefs and behaviours, the characteristics of the G3 child, romantic and other close relationships, and family social and economic circumstances.

During these annual visits, the G2 parents and G3 child also engaged in videotaped interaction tasks. G3 children aged 10 and older participated in separate, 20-minute discussion tasks with the G2 target and with the other parent – the G2 target's romantic partner when a second parent was in the home. These discussion tasks were nearly identical to the discussion task the G2 targets participated in with their G1 parents during adolescence (Task 1, described earlier). G3 children who were 8 or 9 years old completed the same discussion task but just with the G2 target. In addition, the 8- and 9-year-olds completed a 12-minute puzzle task separately with both G2 and the other parent when one was present. In the puzzle task, parents and G3 children were presented with a puzzle that was too difficult for children to complete alone. In brief, parents were instructed that children must complete the puzzle alone, but parents could provide any assistance necessary. Puzzles varied by the child's age group so that the puzzle slightly exceeded the child's skill level. Finally, younger G3 children (ages 2 to 7) completed only the puzzle task separately with each parent. For these younger children the task lasted 5 minutes.

Measurement in the Family Transitions Project

The FTP includes a rich archive of data on the three generations of participants, which includes measures of antisocial behaviour; substance use and other problem behaviours; measures of socioeconomic status (SES; income, assets, debts, educational attainment, occupational prestige, etc.); romantic relationship quality and marital distress; employment and work conditions; measures of family members' closeness and conflict; parenting (warmth, hostility, parental monitoring, discipline strategies, etc.); social networks; community; physical and psychological health; genetic information on all three generations of participants; measures of participants' beliefs about a wide range of topics, including gender roles, marriage, parenting, politics, and religion; measures of temperament and personality; and more. Because space constraints preclude a description of the FTP's extensive archive of measures, we instead have highlighted some important aspects of the measurement strategy used in the FTP and provide brief descriptions of some key measures available in the FTP.

Multi-informant measurement approach

A great strength of the FTP is the utilization of a multi-method, multi-informant measurement strategy. Information from multiple informants was collected using self-reports from each of the family members and their reports about other family members (e.g., G1 mothers reporting on G2 targets, G2 targets reporting on G1 fathers, etc.); trained observers rated videotapes of the previously described family discussion tasks; and information was also provided by teachers' reports of the G2 targets and school records of academic performance and achievement for the G2 targets. This multi-informant measurement strategy allows for reduced biases endemic to single-informant studies (Fiske 1987; Kenny and Kashy 1992) and also allows for the opportunity to examine differences in family members' perspectives (see Lorenz and Melby 1994).

Observational measures

As described previously, families were videotaped while participating in several structured interaction tasks designed to stimulate family interaction and elicit information about social skills and emotional responses. Trained observers rated verbal and nonverbal interactions among family members from these interaction tasks using the Iowa Family Interaction Rating Scales, which have demonstrated reliability and validity (Melby and Conger 2001). Before rating any of the videotaped interactions, observers received 200 hours of training and passed extensive written and viewing reliability tests. Once reliability was established, all observers attended at least two training sessions each week to ensure continued reliability. To assess interrater reliability, approximately 20 per cent of all videotaped tasks were randomly assigned to be rated by a second, independent observer. The primary and secondary ratings were then compared, and all demonstrated adequate interrater reliability. The rating system used borrows from earlier work by Hetherington et al. (1986) and others and includes an array of categories of observed behaviours. Many of these categories capture characteristics of the individual that may reflect a general disposition (e.g., expressions of positive mood), while others reflect actions of one family toward another (e.g., G2 target's hostility toward her or his romantic partner) or the parent management styles for guiding or disciplining the adolescent or child (e.g., G2 target monitoring of the G3 child). These measures have demonstrated convergent, concurrent, and predictive validity and good reliability (Cui, Lorenz, Conger, Melby, and Bryant 2005; Lorenz et al. 2007; Melby et al. 2003). Definitions for observer ratings and descriptions of all interaction tasks are provided in Melby and Conger (2001; see also, Lorenz and Melby 1994).

Economic pressure

An important contribution of the FTP in terms of measurement was the development of a valid and reliable measure of the construct of economic pressure. Based on findings from the FTP, Conger, as had others (e.g., Conger et al. 1990, 2002; Elder, Conger, Foster, and Ardelt 1992; Kessler, Turner, and House 1988; Voydanoff and Donnelly 1988), expected that hardship conditions would influence the lives of family members primarily through the degree of economic pressure these conditions produced in everyday living; that is, they conceptualized economic pressure as the daily hassle of living with financial difficulties and associated stressful economic conditions. Economic pressure was theorized to demoralize family members and disrupt family interaction processes, thereby negatively impacting the lives of families and the individuals. Conger and colleagues operationalized this construct using three subscales. G1 mothers and fathers reported on the items making up these subscales in the initial years of the study (1989–1994), and G2 targets and romantic partners were the reporters in the subsequent years of the study (1995–2010). The first subscale, *can't make ends meet*, assesses the degree to which families had difficulty paying their bills and whether they had enough money to make ends meet. The second subscale, *material needs*, assessed the degree to which the family had enough money to meet basic material needs such as food, shelter, clothing, and medical care. For the third subscale, *financial cutbacks*, families reported the number of adjustments they had had to make in the past year due to financial need from a list of 22 cutbacks, such as taking an extra job, using savings to meet daily living expenses, reducing or eliminating medical insurance, and filing for bankruptcy. The validity and reliability of this measure has been well established (e.g., Conger and Elder 1994; Conger et al. 2002).

Antisocial behaviour and other problem behaviours

One important aspect of the FTP study is the availability of multi-informant longitudinal data on antisocial attitudes and behaviours for three generations, which provides a rare opportunity to look at change across time and across generations. The study has multiple measures on antisocial and aggressive behaviours, alcohol and substance use, and personality. Antisocial behaviour and delinquency were assessed using items adapted from Elliott, Huizinga, and Ageton (1985), such as, "How often in the past year, have you purposely damaged or destroyed property that did not belong to you?" and "How often in the past year have you beat up or fight with someone because they made you angry?" G1 mother and father antisocial behaviours were assessed using self-reports in 1990–1994, as well as reports from their spouse (e.g., G1 mothers reported on G1 fathers' antisocial behaviours). G1 mothers and fathers also provided retrospective reports of their own deviance during adolescence. G2 targets and siblings also reported on their G1 mother's and father's antisocial behaviour using the same measure in 1992 and 1993. Antisocial behaviour was assessed for the G2 targets and siblings using self-reports in 1989 through 1994; G1 mother, father, and sibling provided reports of the G2 target's delinquency. After high school, G2 targets reported on their own antisocial behaviour and that of their romantic partners using a similar measure. Romantic partners also reported on the G2 target's antisocial behaviour using the same measure. G3 conduct problems and delinquency were assessed using G2 target and romantic partner reports; child self-reports were obtained on a variety of measures depending upon the G3 child's age. Aggression was also assessed in the G1 parents, G2 targets and siblings, romantic partners and G3 children using measures such as the Minnesota Personality Questionnaire (MPQ; Harkness, Tellegen, and Waller 1995) and the Iowa Personality Questionnaire (IPQ; Donnellan, Conger, and Burzette 2005). Substance use (alcohol, tobacco, marijuana, and other substances) was assessed using self-reports of the frequency of use from participants in all years they were assessed. G2 targets, the romantic partners, and G3 children also completed structured diagnostic interviews based on the UM-CIDI assessing DSM-III-R, and later DSM-IV, criteria for a variety of disorders, including adult antisocial behaviour, alcohol abuse and dependence, antisocial personality disorder, conduct disorder, substance abuse and dependence, and conduct behaviour problems.

Contributions from the Family Transitions Project to theory and research

The FTP was designed to better understand the mechanisms and processes through which economic problems influence families and individuals, including the impact of economic hardship on the development of delinquency, aggression, and antisocial behaviour. A notable contribution of this program of research was the development of the family stress model (FSM), which was developed by Conger and his colleagues to explain how financial problems influenced the lives of rural families going through the severe downturn in the agricultural economy during the 1980s (see Conger and Conger 2002; Conger et al. 2002). The FSM is a developmental model that proposes that economic hardship increases the degree of economic pressure experienced by parents (Conger et al. 2002; Conger, Conger, and Martin 2010). Economic pressure represents the distressing realities created by economic hardship – being unable to afford essential goods and services, making significant cutbacks in daily expenditures because of limited resources, and not being able to pay monthly bills – and represents the difficult experiences that give psychological meaning to living with economic hardship (Conger et al. 2002; Conger et al. 2010). The FSM proposes that this economic pressure functions to increase parents' emotional distress (e.g., depressed mood, anxiety, anger and hostility) and that these disruptions in mothers' and fathers' emotional well-being will disturb the functioning of their interpersonal relationship, intensifying interparental conflict. That is, the increased emotional distress resulting from economic pressure will increase aggressive and angry interactions within the parental relationship (Conger and Donnellan 2007; Conger et al. 2010). Consistent with earlier research and theory, the FSM proposes that interparental conflict will, in turn, negatively affect parenting practices; that is, conflicts between caregivers will "spillover" into parent–child relationships by disrupting effective parenting behaviours (e.g., Conger et al. 2002; Conger and Donnellan 2007). For example, according to the FSM these stressful conditions will exacerbate hostility by parents toward children and will cause parents to demonstrate less care and concern toward children because of the distractions created by their stressful circumstances. Ultimately, it is through these disruptions to parenting that SES impacts adolescent development. Previous research supports predictions from the FSM across a variety of outcomes for majority (Conger et al. 1992; Conger et al. 1993; Conger et al. 2010) and minority families (Conger et al. 2002; Martin, Conger, and Robins in press; Parke et al. 2004), including outcomes of adolescent conduct problems and antisocial behaviour (e.g., Conger et al. 1992; Conger et al. 1993; Conger et al. 2002).

The FSM represents an example of the *social causation perspective*, which suggests that social conditions lead to variations in social, emotional, cognitive, and physical functioning. The antithesis to this viewpoint is the *social selection perspective*, which proposes that the traits and dispositions of parents influence their social status and the health and well-being of their children (see, e.g., Mayer 1997). Thus, social causation and social selection perspectives suggest that very different causal processes account for the associations among SES, socialization, and child and adolescent development. Thus, these perspectives suggest different causal processes in the intergenerational transmission of traits and behaviours across generations. However, although the two perspectives appear contradictory, combining the social selection and social causation perspectives may aid in our understanding of the relation between SES and developmental outcomes, and the intergenerational transmission of problematic behaviours, in particular.

The interactionist model (IM) of socioeconomic influence on development (Conger and Donnellan 2007; Conger et al. 2010; Martin et al. 2010) proposes that the association between SES and human development involves a dynamic interplay between social causation and social selection. The interactionist model was developed by Conger and his colleagues to explain continuity and discontinuity in the characteristics, traits, and behaviours observed across generations of the FTP family members. The interactionist model proposes that SES and individual differences in characteristics, traits, and behaviours interact in a transactional process over time and across generations. Specifically, the interactionist model argues that earlier parental attributes originating during childhood and adolescence affect later SES, family characteristics, and child and adolescent outcomes, as the social selection perspective suggests. However, the interactionist model also proposes that SES influences family stress processes and parental investments in children, which, in turn, affect the next generation of children. Consistent with other developmental models (e.g., Gottlieb 1996; Magnusson and Stattin 1998; Sameroff 1995), this theoretical argument hypothesizes that individual attributes and socioeconomic conditions will be reciprocally interrelated across time and generations.

Thus, the model offers a compelling explanation for intergenerational transmission of characteristics and behavioural dispositions, including problem behaviours such as antisocial behaviour and aggression. Figure 14.1 illustrates ideas from the interactionist model across three generations and includes pathways that represent ideas from both the social causation and social selection perspectives. From a social selection perspective, G1 traits, characteristics, and behaviours are expected to impact the G1 parents' SES. Positive traits and adaptive behaviours are expected to increase G1's potential SES, whereas negative traits and maladaptive behaviours are predicted to impede G1's ability to attain socioeconomic success, as represented by the path from G1 traits and characteristics to G1's SES. G1's traits and characteristics are also hypothesized to directly impact G2 traits and characteristics, depicted by the path from G1 to G2 traits. These ideas are consistent with the social selection perspective in that individual

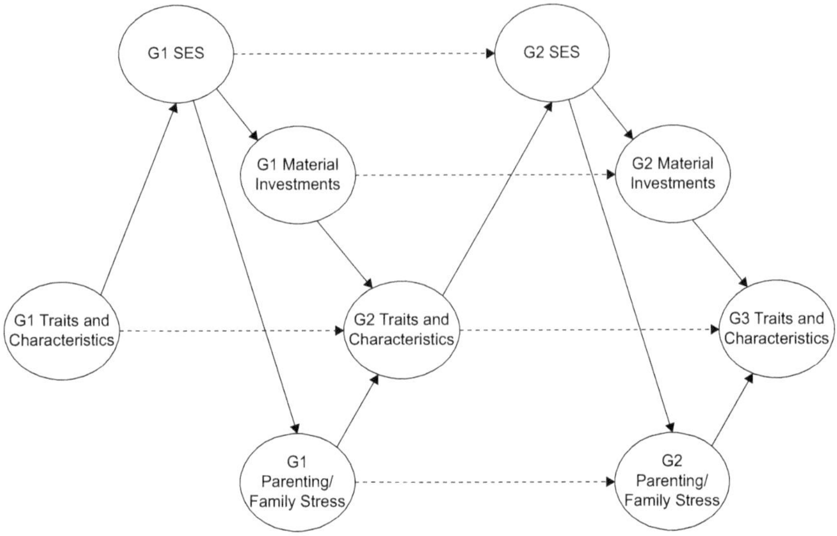

Figure 14.1 The Interactionist Model

differences in traits such as intelligence and personality are expected to facilitate the development of social advantage and are transmitted from parents to children; that is, certain parental characteristics help account for both their economic success and the adjustment of their children. The most commonly invoked mode of transmission is genetic (e.g., Rowe and Rodgers 1997), but the exact mechanisms are not essential to this argument. What is critical is the proposition that observed associations between parental SES and child and adolescent outcomes are actually caused by a third variable – parental characteristics.

Two theoretical models inform the social causation pathways of the interactionist model: the family stress model and the family investment model. As described previously, the FSM proposes that financial difficulties have an adverse influence on parents' emotions, behaviours, and relationships, which negatively impacts their parenting and socialization strategies (Conger and Conger 2002; Conger et al. 2010). These family stress processes are represented in Figure 14.1 by the pathways from G1 SES to G1 parenting and family stress, which, in turn, impact the traits and characteristics of the G2 target. The family investment model (FIM) takes a different approach to the influence of SES that is rooted in economic principles of investment and proposes that families with greater socioeconomic resources are able to make significant investments in the development of their children, whereas more disadvantaged families must invest in more immediate family needs (Becker and Thomes 1986; Bradley and Corwyn 2002; Duncan and Magnuson 2003; Haveman and Wolfe 1994; Linver, Brooks-Gunn, and Kohen 2002; Mayer 1997). These investments involve several different dimensions of family support, such as having learning materials available in the home, the family's standard of living (adequate food, housing, clothing, medical care, etc.), and residential location that fosters a child's competent development. According to the family investment model, greater SES will be positively related to parental material investments and childrearing activities expected to foster positive developmental outcomes of children and adolescents. The pathways from G1 SES to G1 material investments in the G2 adolescent represent ideas from the family investment model, as does the pathway from G1 material investments to G2 traits and characteristics.

All of these social causation and social selection processes are replicated in the second half of the model; G2 traits and characteristics are expected to impact SES in adulthood, which, in turn, impacts the material investments they make in the G3 child, as well as their parenting of the G3 child, which both have direct influence on the development of the traits and characteristics of the G3 child. The model also suggests intergenerational continuity from G1 to G2 in SES, material investments parents make in children, and parenting/family stress, but that these intergenerational paths will be mediated by the other processes included in the model. Research using data from the FTP has provided support for the interactionist model for a variety of outcomes (Conger, Schofield, Conger, and Neppl 2010; Schofield et al. 2011; Trentacosta et al. 2010), including aggression (Conger, Martin, Masarik, Widaman, and Donnellan 2015) and externalizing behaviours (Martin et al. 2010).

Particularly relevant to this chapter, Conger and colleagues (2015) demonstrated the utility of the interactionist model in explaining intergenerational continuity and discontinuity in aggressive personality across two generations of participants from the FTP. They proposed that, consistent with the interactionist model, G1 parents' aggressive personality would negatively impact G1's economic circumstance and the relationship between the G1 parents which, in turn, would reduce the material and parenting investments that the G1 parents make in the G2 adolescent, increasing aggressive personality in the G2 adolescent. In turn, G2 adolescent aggressive personality was hypothesized to have similar influences on their economic conditions and close relationships during the G2's adult years. Specifically, Conger and colleagues (2015) hypothesized that the development of the G2 aggressive traits during adolescence would impede G2's economic success, promote continuity in aggressiveness into adulthood, lead to hostility toward a romantic partner, and intensify their romantic partner's hostility toward G2 several years later during adulthood. Using data from the 279 G2 targets with romantic partners in 2005, they tested these hypotheses derived from the interactionist model using data from the FTP from 1990 to 2005, when the G2 target averaged 14.09 through 29.62 years of age.

The results were largely supportive of the hypotheses derived from the interactionist model. G1 mother and G1 father aggression in 1990 were significantly associated with lower levels of G1 economic advantage and greater G1 interparental hostility in 1990. In turn, economic advantage was associated with greater material and parental investments in the G2 child. Similarly, higher levels of G1 interparental hostility predicted lower investments in the G2 adolescent, both in terms of material and parental investments. These lower material and parental investments then predicted higher levels of G2 adolescent aggressive personality in 1994. Also consistent with the interactionist model, G2 aggressiveness during adolescence predicted significantly lower levels of G2 economic success, greater G2 aggressiveness, greater G2 hostility toward a romantic partner, and greater romantic partner's hostility 11 years later during adulthood. Thus, the results were largely consistent with the interactionist model and suggest how economic advantage, family relationships, and parenting processes interact in a transactional process to explain continuity and discontinuity in aggression across two generations of FTP families.

Similarly, research by Martin and colleagues (2010) evaluated the utility of the interactionist model in explaining intergenerational continuity in externalizing behaviour. Whereas Conger and colleagues (2015) examine the intergenerational transmission of aggression examined transmission from G1 to G2, Martin and colleagues (2010) examined intergenerational continuity in externalizing behaviours from G2 to G3. They hypothesized that, consistent with the social selection perspective, G2 externalizing behaviour during adolescence would negatively impact their later (i.e., during adulthood) socioeconomic success and predict greater family stress and fewer material and parenting investments in their G3 children. Consistent with the social causation perspective portion of the interactionist model, they also predicted that G1 parents' SES would impact G2 externalizing behaviours during adolescence, as well as G2 SES during adulthood. In turn, G2 SES during adulthood was expected to predict lower levels of family stress and greater material and parenting investments in their G3 children which, in turn, were expected to predict G3 externalizing behaviours. They tested these ideas using data from 1997 to 2005 for the 271 G2 families with G3 children in 2005. The results of their analyses were consistent with the predictions from the interactionist model. Martin and colleagues (2010) also evaluated model fit statistics for models representing only the selection perspective, only the social causation perspective, and the combined interactionist model. The results of those tests indicated that the selection-only model had the worst fit, the social causation model had significantly better fit, but the full interactionist model had significantly better fit than either the social causation or the social selection models. Thus, these results suggest the utility of combining both social causation and social selection perspectives in the interactionist model for explaining the transmission of problematic behaviours across generations.

Conclusions

The interactionist model of socioeconomic influence offers a theoretical framework to improve understanding of the ways in which SES, family processes, and individual development are interrelated over time and across generations. Thus, it provides a potentially powerful explanation for intergenerational continuity and discontinuity in behavioural dispositions such as aggression and externalizing problems. Empirical tests of the model using data from the Family Transitions Project (FTP) have provided support for the hypothesized reciprocal process between individual development and SES involving outcomes such as externalizing problems, social competence, emotional stability, and aggression (e.g., Martin et al. 2010; Schofield et al. 2011).

However, to our knowledge, thus far all tests of the interactionist model have been conducted using data from the FTP. We believe the interactionist model provides an important explanation for intergenerational continuities and discontinuities in problem behaviours and that it is likely applicable to other populations. Thus, future research should examine the utility of the interactionist model with other two- and three-generation samples and across different populations to determine whether the results, summarized here, replicate in other populations and other communities. Future research should also examine the utility of the interactionist model in explaining intergenerational transmission of additional outcomes, including more serious antisocial behaviours and crime.

Future plans for the FTP include a continued effort to seek funding to allow the study to carry on and continue to follow these three generations of participants. The oldest G3s have now entered into early adulthood, a period especially significant for research on problem behaviours, and research utilizing this third generation during this period may yield particularly fruitful findings. Another focus for future research with the FTP is using the existing data to continue to study the intergenerational transmission of problematic behaviours such as antisocial behaviour, crime and delinquency, and substance problems across these three generations of family members. For instance, Conger and colleagues (2015) demonstrated the utility of the interactionist model in explaining intergenerational continuity and discontinuity in aggressive personality across the first and second generations of participants from the FTP. Research is currently underway to extend these analyses across all three generations of study participants. Such analyses will allow for an evaluation of to what degree findings replicate across G2 to G3, as well as investigating whether the first generation's aggression has direct impacts on the G3 children. Another planned project will test a model guided by the family stress model that examines mechanisms linking aggression and maltreatment across all three generations of participants. This investigation will examine to what degree the G1 parents' emotional distress generated from economic hardship may predict greater maltreatment by the G1 of their G2 child. G1 maltreatment is then expected to predict greater G2 adolescent aggression. In turn, G2 adolescent aggression is hypothesized to be linked to lower educational attainment in adulthood, increasing the likelihood of the G2 experiencing economic hardship in adulthood. Finally, G2 economic hardship is expected to initiate the same sequence of problems in the next generation, ultimately contributing to G2 maltreatment of the G3 child. Thus, we expect G2 adolescent aggression, G2 adult educational attainment, and family stress processes (economic hardship, economic pressure, and parental distress) to mediate the association between G1 and G2 maltreatment.

We believe that the FTP has made significant contributions to research and theory on life-course development, and that the interactionist model in particular has the potential to further overall understanding of how problem behaviours in one generation lead to similar behaviours in a second generation and beyond. We hope the examples provided here encourage others to use the interactionist model and related strategies in investigating the intergenerational transmission of problematic behaviours such as antisocial behaviour, crime, and delinquency.

A great strength of the FTP is the utilization of a multi-method, multi-informant measurement strategy. Although such an approach can be costly and time consuming, this strategy has helped to make the FTP's data archive a particularly rich source of information on the study participants. We encourage researchers designing future intergenerational research to consider utilizing similar methods as this strategy allows for reduced biases endemic to single informant studies (Fiske 1987; Kenny and Kashy 1992), as well as the opportunity to examine differences in family members' perspectives (see Lorenz and Melby 1994). A particularly important aspect of the FTP data archive in this regard are the observational measures described previously. These videotaped observations of the families capture the families interacting in their own homes and offer a particularly powerful and intimate look at these families and their lives that is infrequently captured in longitudinal, intergenerational research. Future intergenerational researchers can help extend knowledge on these family processes by including similar approaches in their efforts.

References

Becker, G. S., and Thomes, N. (1986) 'Human capital and the rise and fall of families', *Journal of Labor Economics, 4*: S1–S139.

Bradley, R. H., and Corwyn, R. F. (2002) 'Socioeconomic status and child development', *Annual Review of Psychology, 53*: 371–399.

Brown, D. L., and Schafft, K. A. (2011) *Rural People and Communities in the 21st Century: Resilience and Transformation*, Cambridge, UK: Polity Press.

Brown, D. L., and Swanson, L. E. (2003) *Challenges for Rural America in the Twenty-First Century*, University Park, PA: Pennsylvania State University Press.

Conger, K. J. (2011) 'Economic hardship, parenting, and family stability in a cohort of rural adolescents', In K. E. Smith and A. R. Tickamyer (Eds.), *Economic Restructuring and Family Well-Being in Rural America* (pp. 158–174), State College, PA: Pennsylvania State University Press.

Conger, R. D., and Conger, K. J. (2002) 'Resilience in midwestern families: Selected findings from the first decade of a prospective, longitudinal study', *Journal of Marriage and Family, 64*: 361–373.

Conger, R. D., Conger, K. J., Elder, G. H., Lorenz, F. O., Simons, R. L., and Whitbeck, L. B. (1992) 'A family process model of economic hardship and adjustment of early adolescent boys', *Child Development, 63*(3): 526–541.

Conger, R. D., Conger, K. J., Elder, G. H., Lorenz, F. O., Simons, R. L., and Whitbeck, L. B. (1993) 'Family economic stress and adjustment of early adolescent girls', *Developmental Psychology, 29*(2): 206–219.

Conger, R. D., Conger, K. J., and Martin, M. J. (2010) 'Socioeconomic status, family processes, and individual development', *Journal of Marriage and Family, 72*: 685–704.

Conger, R. D., and Donnellan, M. B. (2007) 'An interactionist perspective on the socioeconomic context of human development', *Annual Review of Psychology, 58*: 175–199.

Conger, R. D., Ebert-Wallace, L., Sun, Y., Simons, R. L., McLoyd, V. C., and Brody, G. H. (2002) 'Economic pressure in African American families: A replication and extension of the family stress model', *Developmental Psychology, 38*: 179–193.

Conger, R. D., & Edler, G. H. (1994). *Families in troubled times: Adapting to change in rural America*. Hawthorne, NY: Aldine de Gruyter.

Conger, R. D., Elder Jr., G. H., Lorenz, F. O., Conger, K. J., Simons, R. L., Whitbeck, L. B., . . . Melby, J. N. (1990) 'Linking economic hardship to marital quality and instability', *Journal of Marriage and the Family*: 643–656.

Conger, R. D., Martin, M. J., Masarik, A. S., Widaman, K. F., and Donnellan, M. B. (2015) 'Social and economic antecedents and consequences of adolescent aggressive personality: Predictions from the interactionist model', *Development and Psychopathology*, *27*: 1111–1127.

Conger, R. D., Schofield, T. K., Conger, K. J., and Neppl, T. K. (2010) 'Economic pressure, parent personality and child development: An interactionist analysis', *Historical Social Research*, *35*: 169–196.

Cui, M., Lorenz, F. O., Conger, R. D., Melby, J. N., and Bryant, C. M. (2005) 'Observer, self-, and partner reports of hostile behaviors in romantic relationships', *Journal of Marriage and Family*, *67*(5): 1169–1181.

Davidson, O. G. (1990) *Broken Heartland: The Rise of America's Rural Ghetto*, New York: Free Press.

Donnellan, M. B., Conger, R. D., and Burzette, B. G. (2005). 'Criterion-related validity, self-other agreement, and longitudinal analyses for the Iowa personality questionnaire: A short alternative to the MPQ', *Journal of Research in Personality,* 39, 458–485.

Duncan, G. J., and Magnuson, K. A. (2003) 'Off with Hollingshead: Socioeconomic resources, parenting, and child development', In M. H. Bornstein and R. H. Bradley (Eds.), *Socioeconomic Status, Parenting, and Child Development* (pp. 83–106), Mahwah, NJ: Erlbaum.

Elder Jr., G. H., Conger, R. D., Foster, E. M., and Ardelt, M. (1992) 'Families under economic pressure', *Journal of Family Issues*, *13*(1): 5–37.

Elliott, D. S., Huizinga, D., and Ageton, S. S. (1985). *Explaining delinquency and drug use.* New York: Sage Publications.

Fiske, D. W. (1987). Construct invalidity comes from method effects. *Educational and Psychological Measurement*, *47*: 285–307.

Gottlieb, G. (1996) 'A systems view of psychobiological development', In D. Magnusson (Ed.), *The Lifespan Development of Individuals: Behavioral, Neurobiological, and Psychosocial Perspectives* (pp. 76–103), Cambridge: University of Cambridge Press.

Harkness, A. R., Tellegen, A., and Waller, N. (1995). 'Differential convergence of self-report and informant data for Multidimensional Personality Questionnaire traits: Implications for the construct of negative emotionality', *Journal of Personality Assessment*, *64*: 185–204.

Haveman, R., and Wolfe, B. (1994). *Succeeding generations: On the effects of investments in children.* New York: Russell Sage Foundation.

Hetherington, E. M., Clingempeel, W. G., Eisenberg, M., Hagan, M. S., Vuchinich, R., and Chase-Landsdale, L. (1986). *Manual for the family interaction coding system.* Unpublished global coding manual, Department of Psychology, University of Virginia, Charlottesville, VA.

Kenny, D. A., and Kashy, D. A. (1992) 'Analysis of the multitrait-multimethod matrix by confirmatory factor analysis', *Psychological Bulletin*, *112*(1): 165–172.

Kessler, R. C., Turner, J. B., and House, J. S. (1988) 'Effects of unemployment on health in a community survey: Main, modifying and mediating effects', *Journal of Social Issues*, *44*: 69–85.

Lasley, P. (1994) 'Rural economic and social trends', In R. D. Conger and G. H. Elder, Jr. (Eds.), *Families in Troubled Times* (pp. 57–78), Hawthorne, NY: Aldine de Gruyter.

Lasley, P., and Goudy, W. (1982) *Changes in Iowa's Agriculture: 1969–1978*, Ames: Cooperative Extension Service, Iowa State University.

Linver, M. R., Brooks-Gunn, J., and Kohen, D. (2002) 'Family processes as pathways from income to young children's development', *Developmental Psychology*, *38*: 719–734.

Lobao, L. M. (1990) *Locality and Inequality: Farm and Industry Structure and Socioeconomic Conditions*, SUNY Press.

Lobao, L., and Meyer, K. (2001) 'The great agricultural transition: Crisis, change, and social consequences of twentieth century US farming', *Annual Review of Sociology*, *27*(1): 103–124.

Lorenz, F. O., and Melby, J. N. (1994) 'Analyzing family stress and adaptation: Methods of study', In R. D. Conger and G. H. Elder, Jr. (Eds.), *Families in Troubled Times* (pp. 21–56), Hawthorne, NY: Aldine de Gruyter.

Lorenz, F. O., Melby, J. N., Conger, R. D. and Xu, X. (2007). 'The effects of context on the correspondence between observational ratings and questionnaire reports of hostile behavior: A multitrait, multimethod approach', *Journal of Family Psychology*, *21*: 498–509.

Magnusson, D., and Stattin, H. (1998) 'Person: Context interaction theories', In W. Damon and R. M. Lerner (Eds.), *Handbook of Child Psychology, Vol. 1: Theoretical Models of Human Development* (pp. 685–759), New York: Wiley.

Martin, J. A., Hamilton, B. E., Ventura, S. J., Osterman, M. J. K., Kirmeyer, S., et al. (2011) 'Births: Final data for 2009', In *National Vital Statistics Reports*, *60*, Hyattsville, MD: Department of Health and Human Services.

Martin, M. J., Conger, R. D., and Robins, R. W. (in press) 'Family stress, familism, and alcohol, tobacco and marijuana use by Mexican American adolescents', *Developmental Psychology*.

Martin, M. J., Conger, R. D., Schofield, T. J., Dogan, S. J., Widaman, K. F., Donnellan, M. B., and Neppl, T. K. (2010) 'Evaluation of the interactionist model of socioeconomic status and problem behavior: A developmental cascade across generations', *Development and Psychopathology*, *22*: 697–715.

Mayer, S. (1997) *What Money Can't Buy: Family Income and Children's Life Chances*, Cambridge, MA: Harvard University Press.

Melby, J. N., and Conger, R. D. (2001) 'The Iowa family interaction rating scales: Instrument summary', In P. K. Kerig and K. M. Lindahl (Eds.), *Family Observational Coding Systems: Resources for Systematic Research* (pp. 33–57), Mahwah, NJ: Erlbaum.

Melby, J. N., Hoyt, W. T., Bryant, C. M. (2003). 'A generalizability approach to assessing the effects of ethnicity and training on observer ratings of family interactions', *Journal of Social and Personal Relationships*, *20*: 171–191.

Parke, R. D., Coltrane, S., Duffy, S., Buriel, R., Dennis, J., Powers, J., . . . and Widaman, K. F. (2004). 'Economic stress, parenting, and child adjustment in Mexican American and European American families', *Child Development*, *75*: 1632–1656.

Rowe, D. C., and Rodgers, J. L. (1997) 'Poverty and behavior: Are environmental measures nature and nurture?', *Developmental Review*, *17*: 358–375.

Sameroff, A. J. (1995) 'General systems theory and developmental psychopathology', In D. Cicchetti and D. J. Cohen (Eds.), *Developmental Psychopathology, Vol. 1: Theory and Methods* (pp. 659–695), New York: Wiley.

Schofield, T. J., Martin, M. J., Conger, K. J., Neppl, T. M., Donnellan, M. B., and Conger, R. D. (2011) 'Intergenerational transmission of adaptive functioning: A test of the interactionist model of SES and human development', *Child Development*, *82*: 33–47.

Smith, K. E., and Tickamyer, A. R. (2011) *Economic Restructuring and Family Well-Being in Rural America*, Penn State Press.

Trentacosta, C. J., Neppl, T. K., Donnellan, M. B., Scaramella, L. V., Shaw, D. S., and Conger, R. D. (2010) 'Adolescent personality as a prospective predictor of parenting: An interactionist perspective', *Journal of Family Psychology*, *24*: 721–730.

U.S. Census Bureau. (2011) *Educational Attainment in the United States: 2011–Detailed Tables*, Washington, DC: U.S. Census Bureau.

Voydanoff, P., and Donnelly, B. W. (1988) 'Economic distress, family coping, and quality of family life', In P. Voydanoff and L. C. Majka (Eds.), *Families and Economic Distress: Coping Strategies and Social Policy* (pp. 97–117), Newbury Park, CA: Sage.

Part IV

Studies using mixed methods or qualitative data